The European Parliament's Role in

Also by Richard Corbett

THE EUROPEAN PARLIAMENT (*co-author with Francis Jacobs and Michael Shackleton*)

THE TREATY OF MAASTRICHT: From Conception to Ratification

The European Parliament's Role in Closer EU Integration

Richard Corbett, MEP

Foreword by

Klaus Hänsch
President of the European Parliament, 1994–97

First published in hardback 1998

First published in paperback 2001 by
PALGRAVE
Houndmills, Basingstoke, Hampshire RG21 6XS and
175 Fifth Avenue, New York, N. Y. 10010
Companies and representatives throughout the world

PALGRAVE is the new global academic imprint of
St. Martin's Press LLC Scholarly and Reference Division and
Palgrave Publishers Ltd (formerly Macmillan Press Ltd).

ISBN 0–333–72252–3 hardback (*outside North America*)
ISBN 0–312–21103–1 hardback (*in North America*)
ISBN 0–333–94938–2 paperback (*worldwide*)

This book is printed on paper suitable for recycling and
made from fully managed and sustained forest sources.

A catalogue record for this book is available
from the British Library.

The Library of Congress has cataloged the hardcover edition as follows:
Corbett, Richard.
    The European Parliament's role in closer EU integration /
    Richard Corbett ; foreword by Klaus Hänsch.
        p. cm.
    Includes bibliographical references (p.) and index.
    ISBN 0–312–21103–1 (cloth)
        1. European Parliament. 2. European Union. I. Title.
    JN36.C69 1998
    341.24'24—dc21
                                                    97–36089
                                                         CIP

10   9   8   7   6   5   4   3   2   1
10 09 08 07 06 05 04 03 02 01

Printed and bound in Great Britain by
Antony Rowe Ltd, Chippenham, Wiltshire

To my parents

Contents

Acknowledgements

The author would like to thank all those who have, over the years, helped him in the production of this book, either at the level of ideas and concepts or at the equally indispensable level of technical assistance. The book would never have appeared were it not for the initial idea of Dr Juliet Lodge, that I should write a doctoral thesis on the subject, which thesis produced the kernel of this book. The ideas and hypotheses explored have been greatly enriched through discussions with many others who have worked from an academic perspective on these issues, notably John Pinder, Michael Burgess, Joseph Weiler, Rita Cardozo, Rinus Van Schendelen, Wolfgang Wessels, Otto Schmuck, Jean-Paul Jacqué, Jean-Victor Louis, Martin Westlake and John Peterson, as well as colleagues in the European Parliament, notably Michael Shackleton, Francis Jacobs, Dietmar Nickel, Andrea Pierucci, Odilia Henriques, Peter Brown-Pappamikail, Chris Piening, James Spence and Kieran Bradley. Special mention must be made of the MEPs who afforded me the opportunity of working 'at the coal face', notably Altiero Spinelli, David Martin, Klaus Hänsch, Elisabeth Guigou, Jean-Pierre Cot, Pauline Green, Glyn Ford, Fernand Herman, Henry Plumb and Elmar Brok.

All this would have remained at the level of ideas were it not for assistance from Rosario Molés, Minna Piispa, Suzane Easton, Emma Mollet, Annie Dalibot, Patricia Broughan, Majella McCone, Christiane L'Olivier, Pam Stewart and Jo Tanner.

Last, but not least, thanks must go to my wife, not only for a considerable amount of typing, but also for the patience with which she endured the many hours I spent separated from her by a barrier of books and papers.

Acronyms and Abbreviations

BLG	British Labour Group (now the EPLP)
CAP	Common Agricultural Policy
CBI	Confederation of British Industry
CE	Compulsory Expenditure
CEAC	Conference of European Affairs committees (of the national parliaments and the EP)
CFI	Court of First Instance
CFSP	Common Foreign and Security Policy
CIP	See PIC
COMECON	(East European) Council for Mutual Economic Cooperation
COREPER	Committee of the Permanent Representatives of the Member States
COSAC	French acronym for CEAC
CSCE	Conference on Security and Cooperation in Europe
CSP	Confederation of Socialist Parties of the EC
DTEU	Draft Treaty establishing the European Union (EP 1984)
EAEC	European Atomic Energy Community
EBRD	European Bank for Reconstruction and Development
EC	European Community
ECB	European Central Bank
ECHR	European Convention on Human Rights (Council of Europe)
ECJ	European Court of Justice
ECOFIN	Council, meeting at the level of Economic and Finance Ministers
ECSC	European Coal and Steel Community
ECU	European Currency Unit
ED	European Democrats (largely UK Conservatives)
EDC	European Defence Community
EDF	European Development Fund (Lomé Convention)
EEA	European Economic Area
EEC	European Economic Community
EES	European Economic 'Space' (mistranslation from EEA)
EFTA	European Free Trade Association

EIB	European Investment Bank
ELD	*see* ELDR
ELDO	European Launcher Development Organization
ELDR	European Liberals, Democrats and Radicals
EMF	European Monetary Fund
EMI	European Monetary Institute
EMS	European Monetary System
EMU	Economic and Monetary Union
EP	European Parliament
EPC	European Political Cooperation (1970–93) *or* European Political Community (1951–4)
EPD	European Progressive Democrats (Gaullists and Fianna Fáil)
EPLP	European Parliamentary Labour Party
EPP	European People's Party
EPU	European Political Union
ERM	Exchange Rate Mechanism (of the EMS)
ESA	European Space Agency
ESCB	European System of Central Banks
ETUC	European Trade Union Confederation
EUI	European University Institute (Florence)
EURATOM	*see* EAEC
EUROFED	Term for Central Bank system not retained in Treaty
EUROPOL	European Criminal Investigation Office
FCO	Foreign and Commonwealth Office (UK)
GATT	General Agreement on Tariffs and Trade
GDP	Gross Domestic Product
IGC	Intergovernmental Conference
IIA	Interinstitutional Agreement
IMF	International Monetary Fund
IMPs	Integrated Mediterranean Programmes
JHA	Title VI of Treaty of Maastricht concerning cooperation in the fields of Justice and Home Affairs
MCAs	Monetary Compensatory Amounts
MEP	Member of the European Parliament
MFE	Mouvement Fédéraliste Européen
NATO	North Atlantic Treaty Organization
NCE	Non-compulsory expenditure
NGOs	Non-Governmental Organizations
OECD	Organization for Economic Cooperation and Development

OEEC	Organization for European Economic Cooperation
PES	Party of European Socialists
PESC	French acronym for CFSP
PIC	Parallel Interinstitutional Conference (more usually referred to by its French abbreviation CIP), originally, 'Preparatory' Interinstitutional Conference
PSI	Italian Socialist Party
PSDI	Italian Social Democratic Party
PU	Political Union
QMV	Qualified Majority Voting
SEA	Single European Act
SMEs	Small and Medium-sized Undertakings (Enterprises)
TEU	Treaty on European Union (Maastricht Treaty)
TREVI	Working party of the EC Member States on Terrorism, Radicalism, Extremism and Violence
UEF	Union of European Federalists
UNICE	European Employers' organization
VAT	Value Added Tax
WEU	Western European Union (defence organization of ten countries: EC minus Ireland, Denmark, Sweden and Finland)
WTO	Warsaw Treaty Organization (or 'Warsaw Pact')

Human nature does not change. But if men establish rules and institutions that govern relationships between them, and insist that these be obeyed, then that fundamentally alters relations between them. This process is the very act of civilisation.

(Jean Monnet)

It should be borne in mind that there is nothing more difficult to arrange, more doubtful of success, and more dangerous to carry through than initiating changes in a state's constitution. The innovator makes enemies of all those who prospered under the old order, and only lukewarm support is forthcoming from those who would prosper under the new. Their support is lukewarm partly from fear of their adversaries, who have the existing laws on their side, and partly because men are generally incredulous, never really trusting new things unless they have tested them by experience. In consequence, whenever those who oppose the changes can do so, they attack vigorously, and the defence made by the others is only lukewarm. So both the innovator and his friends are endangered together.

(N. Machiavelli, *The Prince*, Chapter VI)

Foreword

I welcome the appearance of this book, which provides a fascinating insight into the impact of the Parliament on the process of European integration in the years since it became a directly elected body. One of the distinguishing features of the European Parliament is that it does not regard itself as part of a finished institutional system, but as part of one requiring evolution and reform. The European Parliament has always, but especially since it became directly elected, pressed for a more effective, more open and more democratic European Union, close to its citizens. Both in the daily exercise of its responsibilities, and in putting forward proposals for reform from the Draft Treaty on European Union which it approved in 1984, to specific proposals for treaty amendments submitted to successive intergovernmental conferences, Parliament has made a significant contribution to the process of European integration. The information and analysis contained in this book show decisively how important Parliament's contribution has been.

I can think of no better person to have written this book than the author, who has been involved in Parliament's work on these issues for many years. As a member of the Secretariat of the Institutional Affairs Committee, he worked with Altiero Spinelli in the preparation of the 1984 Draft Treaty on European Union. He has worked on a number of parliamentary committees in developing Parliament's legislative and scrutiny procedures. He assisted David Martin in drafting Parliament's submissions to the Maastricht Intergovernmental Conference and worked in the Rules Committee in adapting Parliament's procedures in order to take full advantage of the possibilities offered by the Maastricht Treaty. Recently, he has combined his position as Deputy Secretary-General of the Socialist Group of the Parliament with being political adviser to Elisabeth Guigou in her work representing Parliament in the Reflection Group preparing the 1996 Intergovernmental Conference as well as in that Conference itself.

I myself have had the pleasure of benefiting from his assistance, not least in the drafting committee of the 1990 Assizes of national parliaments and the European Parliament in Rome.

Although this book dwells in particular on the period in which Parliament relaunched the process of European integration in the 1990s, it is fully up-to-date, covering events right up to the beginning of the 1996 Intergovernmental Conference. Anyone interested in the process of European integration in general, and the contribution of the Parliament in particular, will find it most interesting.

Klaus Hänsch
President of the European Parliament, 1994–7

Introduction

The process of European integration has been going on for half a century. The last 18 years have seen an elected transnational Parliament as part of that process. This book, based on the author's doctoral thesis, but shortened and updated, seeks to explore what impact the existence of an elected, full-time Parliament has had on the integration process.

Chapter 1 examines what is actually meant by European integration. It explores the various theoretical approaches in academic literature, relating them to the intentions of governments and other actors. It finds that there is wide diversity of scholarly approaches and of actors' objectives, as well as of the importance attributed to a Parliament. None the less, elements of all the main approaches give certain insights into the process and it is possible to construct an overview (or 'preliminary synthesis') taking aspects of all the theoretical approaches, but which emphasizes in particular the importance of the basic constitutional settlements laid down in the treaties and the role of the institutions, governments and other actors in using the possibilities thereby created to go further (in the right circumstances) and thereby to generate pressure for further constitutional change.

Chapter 2 examines what was expected of the elected Parliament in academic literature and in political circles prior to the first elections. Here, too, there was an enormous diversity. From this it is possible, bearing in mind the overview of integration theory developed in chapter 1, to formulate hypotheses about how an elected Parliament might effect the integration process.

The remaining chapters attempt to test the impact of the Parliament, at various levels, which overlap in time and content but remain distinct. In chapter 3, the significance of establishing a new corps of full-time politicians, with back-up support and facilities, is assessed. Independently of the powers and formal role of the institution as such, is there any evidence of a new political network developing having an influence on political classes in Member States and other European institutions?

In chapter 4, we examine what use the elected Parliament made of the existing, limited powers that it inherited from the nominated Parliament. Chapter 5 explores the attempts by Parliament to achieve incremental institutional reform within the framework of the treaties as they stood at the time of its election, notably by seeking to reach agreements with the other institutions. The bulk of the book concentrates on exploring the role of the Parliament in securing changes to the treaties themselves – that is, to find out what Parliament's contribution was to the processes leading to the Single European Act (SEA) of 1986 and the Maastricht Treaty of 1992.

Thus, chapter 6 describes how Parliament, after initial hesitation, turned to the path of Treaty revision and prepared its own draft Treaty on European Union at a time when such a path seemed to offer few prospects.

Chapter 7 briefly describes the content of Parliament's draft Treaty and analyses the main objectives it sought to achieve. Chapter 8 looks at Parliament's strategy in building up support for a reform of the Treaties and examines events leading to convening the IGC that negotiated the SEA to assess Parliament's impact. Chapter 9 takes us through that IGC with a similar eye to Parliament's role and impact. Chapter 10 assesses how all the institutions, but especially the Parliament, were affected by the SEA and were able to exploit its provisions to achieve a higher level of integration. Chapter 11 examines how Parliament remained dissatisfied and made attempts to launch a new process of Treaty reform. Chapter 12 takes us through the IGCs that produced the Maastricht Treaty, again with an eye to Parliament's role and impact.

An attempt to bring all this together is made in the concluding chapter 14, which takes up the synthesis of integration theories developed in chapter 1 and the hypotheses developed at the end of chapter 2 to see how the events explored in the intervening chapters (and the assessment made at the end of each chapter) have confirmed or invalidated them.

Clearly, this book deals with a vast process – hence its length. It involves a large amount of piecing together and describing events of the basis of primary and secondary documentary sources, and a considerable degree of participant-observation and direct contact with key actors more than surveys or statistical analysis. It is an attempt to provide an insight into one of the most complex and multifaceted ongoing political processes of our time, namely that of European integration.

1 Theoretical Approaches to European Integration

The process of European integration has generated a wealth of academic literature and analysis. What is striking, however, is the diversity of the approaches followed and the conclusions reached. Academics have, of course, been the first to recognize this diversity. The 'Jekyll and Hyde'[1] nature of the EC attracts much of the blame, the Community being described as an 'enigma' that 'furnishes hope for intergovernmentalists, confederalists and federalists alike'.[2] It is also striking that different theories have ebbed and flowed as the EC itself has gone through different phases in its history, as was evident in the neglect of neofunctionalist theories in the 20 years between the 'Luxembourg compromise' and the negotiation of the Single European Act. The recent prominence of debate about federalism also illustrates this point, but it serves too to remind us that perceptions and preoccupations can vary also according to national/cultural/political backgrounds and predispositions, and it is not only politicians who can write in a way that colours reality with their own prejudices, hopes or expectations.

Joseph Weiler[3] has drawn attention to a tendency among lawyers to focus on the EC's legal system with its several supranational features while political scientists tend to focus on the EC's decision-taking procedures with the dominant role played by national governments in the Council. Such traps can await those who specialize in a particular aspect of the EC: an analysis of competition policy with the strong role in this area of the Commission might produce a totally different impression[4] from a study of fiscal harmonization, let alone of foreign and security policy. Donald Puchala's analogy of blind men feeling an elephant and reaching different conclusions according to whether they are holding the trunk, the ears, the tail or touching the body is a telling one.[5]

It would, of course, be even worse for the blind men to persist in their respective conclusions when informed of each other's results, on the grounds that, whatever the other features of the elephant, *theirs* was the salient one. Yet that precise phenomenon is not unknown in the study of European integration, especially when one particular feature of the process lends support to a predetermined view. One is reminded

1

of the arguments among biologists when the duckbilled platypus was discovered, with competing claims that it was a mammal or a bird as it displayed features previously considered to be the defining features of each. The Community is a duckbilled platypus: it does contain at the same time features typical of federations, and features typical of intergovernmental cooperation among sovereign states. In any study of a particular feature, it is crucial not to lose sight of the whole. At the same time, it is important not to confine analysis to a superficial study of the whole. Such would be the case if Puchala's blind men were to conclude that they should, henceforth, concentrate only on the one variable that gives a consistent result, namely the texture of the skin. This is the pitfall of some empirical approaches that study only those variables capable of precise statistical measurement and approaches that concentrate exclusively on those features of the Community that can be compared to other phenomena in international relations or else in federal states, as the case may be. Scholars who put all their analytical eggs into one basket find, over time, that they have only a partial picture.

Among those who insisted on a broader approach that none the less contained considerable detail was Leon Lindberg, whose work 'Political Integration as a Multidimensional Phenomenon Requiring Multivariate Measurement'[6] was an attempt to go beyond the limitations of 'most studies of political integration [that] have concentrated on one or another aspect of what I take to be an interactive multidimensional process; that is they have described and analysed only some of these properties'.[7] Such a broad approach is necessary, provided it does not lead to our not being able to see the wood for the trees.

Approaches to integration theory also vary along a scale from description to prescription (each sometimes assorted with prediction). This is accentuated by the overlap between students *of* the process and actors *in* the process, or by the latter often consciously seeking to apply a particular model that they may even have themselves helped develop. Federalists often tend to focus more on the prescribed end-result of the integration process. Neofunctionalists have often been criticized for focusing exclusively on describing the process that starts off or continues integration while neglecting the question of its end-product.

Bearing these various considerations in mind, we shall now examine some main approaches to and theories of integration, looking especially at how they have evolved in response to events, how they have interacted and how they overlap.

CONSTITUENT FEDERALISTS

The term 'federation' has always been subject to a wide variety of definitions and in recent years has even been deliberately misconstrued by opponents of integration as meaning a 'centralized super-state'. For our purposes, the term 'federalist' can be applied to all those who favour a European federal system of government in which the Member States clearly transfer some sovereignty to a European tier of governance with real powers in limited but significant areas of policy. This end-product of the integration process might have different features, different degrees of centralization and be achieved on different time-scales, but the establishment of a more or less classical federation is the objective. In this sense, federalism is a prescriptive approach,[8] advocating the creation of a European federation on its merits as the best way to replace war with the rule of law in international affairs, or as the best way to manage common problems and to run common policies effectively and democratically. Many federalists have tended to focus on the desired result rather than the process of integration.

In much of the early literature, however, 'federalist' was given a particular meaning, which did indeed refer to the process, but related specifically to one of the possible methods for creating a European federation. The constitutional approach, and in particular the constituent assembly approach, was strongly advocated by part of the European Federalist Movement, in contrast to sectoral and step-by-step 'functionalist' (or rather, neofunctionalist) approaches to integration, and this led to the term 'federalist' being identified with those advocating that particular 'constitutional' or 'head-on' approach. In fact, many 'functionalists', not least Jean Monnet himself, were declared federalists in terms of their final objective.[9] Their method of achieving it was different.[10]

The 'constituent' approach by those committed to the federal objective seemed logical at the end of the Second World War when several major countries were about to set up constituent assemblies to redraft their own constitution and when virtually the whole continent faced political and economic reorganization. The federalist movement emerged largely from the anti-fascist resistance movements[11] which naturally thought beyond the recreation of the *status quo ante*. Documents supporting a new organization of the continent along federal lines were circulated within the resistance movements and among the various governments in exile in London,[12] and resistance leaders met as early as 1944 in Geneva to discuss postwar options and concluded in favour of a federal-style reorganization.

Probably the most influential figure in this process was Altiero Spinelli, co-author with Ernesto Rossi of the celebrated Ventotene Manifesto entitled *Towards a Free and United Europe*[13] and smuggled out of their internment camp, the island of Ventotene, as early as 1941, well before the outcome of the war was safely predictable. In this document, they argued that, at the end of the war, 'the question which must be resolved first, failing which progress is no more than mere appearance, is the definitive abolition of the division of Europe into national sovereign states'.[14] Furthermore, they argued that:

> the dividing line between progressive and reactionary parties . . . falls along a very new and substantial line: those who conceive the essential purpose and goal of struggle as being the ancient one, the conquest of national power . . . and those who see the main purpose as the creation of a solid international State, who will direct popular forces towards this goal . . .

In order to 'direct popular forces towards this goal', Spinelli, Rossi and some 20 others established, as soon as they were able to leave their internment camp, the Movimento Federalista Europeo (MFE). The founding meeting, held clandestinely in Milan on the 27–28 August 1943, adopted a 'political thesis' which, *inter alia*, stated: 'if a postwar order is established in which each State retains its complete national sovereignty, the basis for a Third World War would still exist even after the Nazi attempt to establish the domination of the German race in Europe has been frustrated'.[15]

These arguments are, of course, part of a long tradition of federalism as 'a theory of international pacification'[16] stretching back as far as the leagues of the ancient Greek city-states. Numerous plans and schemes were drafted over the centuries,[17] becoming more precise once they could draw upon concrete federal experiences, notably that of the USA. The 'Federalist Papers' of Hamilton and Madison provided a major source and inspiration for European writers for the next two centuries. By 1897, a British prime minister could say that a federalist Europe 'is our sole hope of escaping from the constant terror and calamity of war, the constant pressure of the burdens of an armed peace. . . . The Federation of Europe is the only hope we have.'[18] The experience of the First World War and the subsequent failure of the League of Nations to maintain international order and peace stimulated the first governmental initiative for a federation of European states, that of French Foreign Minister Briand (1929) and the first movements such as Coudenhove-Kalergi's Pan-European Movement (Vienna, 1926). Intellectual contributions flourished. A group in the UK known as Federal Union flourished on the eve of the Second World War[19] and is acknowledged by Spinelli as the intellectual source of his federalism,[20] still frequently quoted by the MFE.

In drawing upon these traditions, Spinelli and his supporters in 1941 hoped that the circumstances were about to arrive in which a European federation could be established:

> At the end of this war, in the midst of a short period of national and international crisis, when the structure of the national States will either partly or completely collapse we must seek to lay the foundations of real peace. This time there must be no repetition of 1919; the peace settlement must not be the outcome of diplomatic intrigue and the ambitions of ministers as though it were no concern of the people how the peace is organized. It will therefore be necessary to give firm support to that country or those countries which favour the creation of a federal organization and to mobilize within every nation all popular forces behind this demand for a federal solution. For only during such a revolutionary period, and so long as the memories of the horrors of wars are still alive, will the European Federation be able to withstand pettiness, treason and nationalist interests and become a reality. If we allow this decisive moment to go by, the progressive forces will have fought in vain . . .[21]

The aim was thus to draw up a federal constitutional framework for the whole of Europe at the end of the war. These ideas were taken up in the meeting of the resistance movements of eight countries in May 1944 in Geneva, winning supporters in several countries.

As we know, the course of history was different. The old nations and state structures re-emerged as countries were liberated one after the other, as traditional political parties resurfaced, as the resistance movements began to divide along communist/non-communist lines and, as Spinelli later saw it:

> the federalist idea was completely eclipsed in the last year of the war and the first two years of the postwar period, because Europe was not brought to a position where it was forced to raise the question of its new international status. Europe was entirely conquered by the Soviet and Anglo-American forces who restored the old national states as a matter of course, which were formally sovereign but in actual fact controlled by the conquering forces.[22]

Why then, did the 'constituent' approach continue after the failure to create a new European order in 1945? How has such a strategy continued to the present day to have a body of support in less propitious circumstances?

The answer lies in that, despite the failure to create a new European order in one go at the end of the war, several states did embark on a gradual and partial integration process, but one which was, to many federalists, insufficient and unsatisfactory. Successive compromises among governments led to a conviction in the MFE that governments were incapable of delivering the desired result. It was affirmed by the MFE that 'it is indispensable to . . . call a constituent federal assembly made up of representations of the people and not the governments.'[23] Rejecting the

> illusion that economic integration might lead sooner or later to political integration, . . . federalists faithful to the constituent method, which is the only democratic method because it makes it possible for the people to participate in the process of European unification, denounced the functionalist approach.[24]

Thus, both reasons of principle ('more democratic' and, indeed, the traditional way in several countries of preparing new constitutions) and of strategy (to bypass governments) led many federalists to continue to press for a constituent assembly to draft a European constitution. These federalists were convinced that what we now call the neo-functionalist dynamic was in itself not sufficient to produce the desired result. Not all of them were dismissive about the achievements of the EC, which were generally recognized, not least by Spinelli himself, but these were felt to be too limited and incapable of developing beyond certain limits.

Of course, some supported this approach as a tactic, believing that a small organized group such as the MFE/UEF should argue strongly for an ambitious but clear objective on its merits, knowing perfectly well that the governments would do no more than muddle through with half-baked compromises – but even this required some 'maximalist' pressure.

The constituent assembly approach therefore continued to have a body of support. This has lasted right up to the present decade, with the Italian government accepting a resolution from its own Chamber of Deputies on 20 November 1990 'stressing the urgent need to transform the relations between the Member States of the Community into a Union on a federal basis . . . on the basis of a draft constitution drawn up by the European Parliament.'[25] The constituent objective has, of course, never been achieved. Nevertheless, the impact of its supporters has been significant, not only in terms of constantly expounding and advocating federalism (in which they were not alone), but in particular in the emphasis they have always given to the role of an assembly or Parliament, preferably directly elected.

As we have seen, this emphasis arose from their belief that such an assembly could play a constituent role, or at the very least, provide a source of democratic legitimacy that was independent of national governments. Other schools of thought regarding the process of integration have, as we shall see, tended to give far less importance to the role of a Parliament in the process (whatever their views on the role of a Parliament in the resultant institutional system).

On several occasions, the contribution brought by the supporters of the constituent approach has been of significant importance to events and developments in Europe.

The first of these occasions was during the discussions and negotiations of 1947–9 which led to the creation of the Council of Europe. The arguments of the federalist movement began to receive wider backing. Even in Britain, which had not gone through the experience of occupation and resistance, motions were tabled in the House of Commons in January 1947 and signed by over 70 (largely Labour) MPs asking the government 'to affirm Britain's readiness to federate with any other nation willing to do so on the basis of a federal Constitution to be agreed by a representative constituent assembly', and again in March 1948, signed by 179 MPs (over 100 Labour) calling for a democratic federation of Europe and for the governments of Western Europe to convene a constituent assembly so that it might frame the federal constitution.[26]

In the Hague Congress of Europe in May 1948,[27] the federalists' advocacy of the need for a representative assembly ensured that such an assembly was called for in the resolution of that Congress, even if they remained in a minority in calling for such an assembly to have constituent powers, or indeed, for it to be immediately elected by universal suffrage.[28] French Foreign Minister Bidault proposed on 20 July to the Brussels Treaty powers 'an immediate practical study' of both a European Assembly and an economic and customs union, and the second Congress of the European Parliamentary Union, meeting in Interlaken and, unlike the Hague Congress, composed entirely of parliamentarians, called for the various governments to convene an official parliamentary assembly to deliberate and vote on a draft constitution, which it had prepared.[29]

An assembly of parliamentary character was duly established in the Council of Europe framework when this was set up in 1949, despite difficulties in the intergovernmental negotiations between those supporting an autonomous assembly elected by national parliaments and those who wanted the national governments to appoint its members, national delegations to sit and vote as a bloc and its powers to be minimized.[30]

It is important to assess the significance of this in the context of its time. The creation of the Council of Europe was a first attempt to establish a political structure for European integration. A structure for functional-type cooperation – the Organization for European Economic Cooperation (OEEC) – had, after all, been set up only the previous year but was not generally considered to be a potential vehicle for integration.[31] The Council of Europe was the first organization specifically set up for furthering European unity – and only four years after the war. Its remit was potentially large. The inclusion of a parliamentary assembly – the first international organization to have one – meant that its deliberations were not confined to ministers and diplomats but involved a wider political circle.[32]

Certainly, these achievements fell far short of what many had hoped. The results of the intergovernmental negotiations were a compromise that tended to the position of the most cautious and restrictive governments (notably the UK and the Scandinavian countries) – a characteristic of negotiations requiring consensus that was to be repeated many times over. The power to take decisions in the Council of Europe was given to the Committee of Ministers, acting unanimously. No Member State could be bound against its will. International conventions needing ratification by those Member States accepting them would be the usual normative instrument. Little, then, to comfort federalists. Yet one 'federal' feature, albeit in muted form, was the existence of the Assembly. This formed a precedent: all subsequent European organizations would have one too. It also created further precedents in winning some of its early battles – members to vote as individuals and not in national blocs, the right to fix its own agenda and a degree of operational autonomy. Such features were subsequently of crucial importance to the European Parliament. Finally, the Assembly provided a forum which for the first two years of its existence was of great significance in debating further moves towards European unity. Leading political figures other than government ministers participated. In particular, these debates made it clear that a strengthening of the Council of Europe itself was not possible, and that those countries wishing to go further would have to do so by themselves. This paved the way for the Schuman Plan of 1950.

A second episode when the approach of the 'constituent assembly federalists' was important was that of the '*ad hoc* Assembly' of 1952–3. It was Spinelli who persuaded De Gasperi to insist in the EDC negotiation on provision in the treaty for the Assembly to draw up plans for placing the EDC, the ECSC and any other development within a global constitutional framework. As a result, Article 38 of the EDC Treaty provided for the Assembly to prepare proposals to 'replace the present provisional organization' and referred to 'a subsequent federal or confederal structure based on the principle of the separation of powers and having, in particular, a two-chamber system of representation'. The Assembly was invited to submit its proposals within six months of its constitutive meeting following the entry into force of the EDC Treaty. In fact, the Foreign Ministers, meeting three months after the signature of the EDC Treaty,[33] invited the ECSC Assembly immediately to draft a 'treaty constituting a European Political Authority' without waiting for ratification of the EDC Treaty. In so doing, the Ministers acknowledged that they were responding to a resolution[34] of the Parliamentary assembly of the wider Council of Europe calling upon the EDC states

> to choose, by whichever procedure is the speedier, the Assembly which will be responsible for drafting the Statute of a supra-national Political Community open to all Member States of the Council of Europe and offering opportunities of association to such of these States as do not become full members of the Political Community.

In asking the ECSC Assembly (now the European Parliament) to prepare the draft, the Ministers asked it to coopt extra members from among the members of the Council of Europe Assembly in order to bring the number of members up to what was envisaged for the EDC Treaty – hence the designation '*ad hoc* Assembly' as it was not, strictly speaking, the ECSC 'Common Assembly' that alone performed this task, but with nine extra members.

This was the closest Europe ever came to following the 'constituent assembly' path to a federal Europe. Even then, the procedure provided for the Assembly's proposal to be submitted to the national governments who would consider it in an intergovernmental conference. This latter process had, indeed, already begun (the Assembly having completed its draft within six months) before the vote in the French National Assembly of 30 August 1954 brought the whole EDC-EPC scaffolding tumbling down.

None the less, the political significance of the procedure should not be underestimated. Within a month of the first supra-national Community (the ECSC) coming into operation, its Assembly at its very first session was being asked by the governments of the Member States to prepare a draft treaty or constitution with a bicameral Parliament. The ECSC in terms of its powers and decision-taking procedures had already gone well beyond the level of traditional international organizations, as we shall see. Yet it had been in existence for scarcely a month before plans were made to go much further and to do so by a procedure that broke with all traditional forms of treaty negotiation. No functionalist gradualism here! The 'constituent assembly' branch of the federalists seemed, for a few months, to have signposted the right direction.

This episode was important despite its failure. The draft produced by the Assembly sowed seeds that grew later. The initial work on the problems of creating a customs union and a common market helped prepare the ground for the EEC treaty negotiations. The exploration of the institutional issues involved helped to clarify some of the options.[35] It generated much academic literature.[36] In terms of examining different schools of integration theory, it serves to show that before partial 'functional' integration processes became dominant, there was a significant attempt to proceed through the drafting of a global constitution by a representative assembly. The political capital invested in this attempt was considerable, and its failure may well have dampened any idea of repeating the attempt, but at the same time meant that the more modest, partial proposals (for a common market and Euratom) simply could not fail without major political fallout.

The failure of the EDC–EPC proposals was a major setback for the constituent assembly approach. The federalist movement actually split in 1956, with only the smaller branch continuing to press for the establishment of a constituent assembly, and organizing campaigns to that end. These were largely ineffectual at a time at which European integration, through the 'relaunch' and the negotiation of the EEC and EAEC treaties seemed to be progressing. Following the 1965 'empty chair' crisis, when France boycotted the Council until the Member States agreed on the 'Luxembourg compromise', the MFE found wider support, especially as it began to concentrate on securing direct elections to the European Parliament. The treaty provision for direct elections had remained a dead letter and there seemed little prospect of them being agreed. Yet, for this approach to federalism in particular, an elected Parliament remained an important strategic objective:

Europe is no longer, unlike when we began our struggle, a mere historical forecast. It is an economic reality with a complex community administration, as well as an increasingly obvious political necessity. But besides this imposing European reality, there is a European Parliament which still has no political basis. If we ask that it be elected we are asking for something which everybody, except for Europe's enemies, finds right. We need to make the most of this feeling. . . . We need only recall that the first European elections will force the parties to form European alliances and to fight for European consensus, to realise that the positions they take up and the struggle they carry out are nothing more than the concrete transfer of power from the national arena to the European one. Once the political struggle has shifted from the national to the European arena, the substantial barriers cutting us off from European democracy will have been overcome. All other objectives, including the constitution and the constituent are merely what in military strategy, are called exploiting the advantage.[37]

This was the third major contribution of the supporters of the constituent assembly approach. Direct elections were finally agreed in 1976 and first held in 1979. Of course, the federalists were far from being alone in advocating them and campaigning for them, but given their particular focus on the potential role of the Assembly, they were correspondingly committed and active, forcing attention to be paid to this issue by other organizations in the European Movement, causing a Bill to be submitted to the Italian parliament in 1969 in favour of unilateral direct elections of the Italian MEPs (followed by similar action in other Member States), organizing demonstrations at 'summit' meetings,[38] and so on.

A fourth contribution was the drafting by the elected Parliament in 1982–4 of a 'Draft Treaty Establishing the European Union', in which Spinelli himself played an important role. This will be looked at in more detail later.

In recent times, Italy actually held a national referendum in 1989 on the same day as the European elections in which 88.1 per cent of the Italian electorate voted (on a 74 per cent turnout) in favour of

proceeding to the transformation of the European Community into an effective European Union endowed with a government responsible to the Parliament, and entrusting the European Parliament with the mandate to prepare a draft constitution to submit directly to the competent organs of the Member States for ratification.[39]

The EP responded to this by producing an interim report on the constitutional basis of European Union (Colombo Report, 1990) laying down the guidelines for a constitution for the European Union which it proposed to draft after the conclusion of the 1991 IGCs, the results of which would be taken into account.[40] Similarly, the Conference of the national parliaments of the EC and the EP held in Rome in November 1990, in its concluding Declaration[41] adopted by 150 votes to 13, stated that:

> the time is right to transform the entire complex of relations between the Member States into a European Union on the basis of a proposal for a constitution drawn up with the aid of procedures in which the European Parliament and national parliaments will take part.

Some national parties, such as the German SPD, incorporated this objective into their manifestos or programmes.[42]

Thus, those federalists who advocate the drafting of a federal constitution by the European Parliament as the most appropriate (or only) way to achieve a federal union have continued throughout the last half-century to play an active part on the European scene and one that has not been without effect on events and, in certain countries and institutions, has undoubtedly played a role in shaping attitudes, opinions and strategies.

GRADUALIST FEDERALISTS

Not all federalists or advocates of a constitution, however, support the constituent assembly approach. Many federalists have remained unconvinced of the need or the feasibility of such a method. Whether or not they believe in the inevitability of neofunctionalist integration, they might envisage the drafting of a constitution as a key step in the integration process, but such a constitution is seen by them as more likely to emerge by negotiations among governments. For many,[43] it would be a step that would crown the integration process, consolidating years of achievement, rather than the crucial first step to enable integration to take place, as perceived by many 'constituent assembly federalists', at least in the early years.

The division between these two views was among the reasons that led to the split in the Federalist Movement from the 1950s to 1972, with the AEF organization representing those who did not believe in the constituent assembly approach, but including many who nevertheless recognized the importance of a constitution. The two views are still visible. While Italy, through the referendum referred to above, restated its commitment to the constituent method, Germany and the Netherlands, according to a Joint Statement of their Foreign Ministers,[44] envisaged the 1991 IGCs resulting in a 'qualitative leap towards European Union, with the goal being a constitution with a federal structure' – no mention of a constituent assembly, but a clear constitutional perspective.

Many gradualist federalists see the Community treaties themselves as constitutional in that they establish, and legally entrench, institutions and rules that prefigure federal organs, albeit initially with limited competences and procedures that safeguard national prerogatives. These institutions could gain new competences and stronger powers over time both in practical terms within the possibilities afforded by the treaties and through constitutional (i.e. treaty) revision. The treaties would *in practice* take on more and more the characteristics of a constitution, whether or not they were actually given that name.

Certainly, the ECSC Treaty gave the Community from the very beginning a character that went well beyond traditional international organizations, and clearly intended to do so. Traditionally, international organizations were

> based on three principles. In the first place, decisions of the organizations are taken by organs composed of government representatives. Secondly, participating states are not legally bound by these decisions against their will. . . . Thirdly, the implementation of decisions is reserved to the participating states themselves. There are, of course, exceptions to each of these three principles, but it is the abandonment of these principles as a starting-point for the association of states in an international organization which [was a] breakthrough from the classical pattern of international organization which in itself was revolutionary.[45]

This reflected the intention of the Schuman Declaration to 'lead to the realization of the first concrete foundation of a European *Federation*',[46] recalled in Schuman's speech to the opening session of he ECSC negotiations: 'never before have States undertaken or even envisaged the joint delegation of part of their national *sovereignty* to an independent, suprational body' (my emphasis).

As pointed out by Brugmans, 'Schuman, Monnet, De Gasperi, Spaak, Adenauer and the like were not, when they created the ECSC, aiming to improve the management of the production of [coal and steel]. Their basic objective was to create a "new" Europe'.[47] In any case, coal and steel were not the marginal, declining industries that they are now: coal was by far the principal energy source, and steel was perceived as being the foundation of war-making capacity. They were both central to powerful economies. This was no small step in a minor field that might lead on to progress in significant ones: it was from the outset a revolution in a sector of fundamental importance, inspired by security considerations far more than by economic ones. Coal and steel are not mentioned in the first two paragraphs of the Schuman Declaration, which instead refers to peace and the need to organize and unite Europe. Coal and steel come in later as a 'limited but decisive point' on which to take immediate action.

It was also perceived at the time as a *constitutional* revolution, laying the basis for future development. As Konrad Adenauer pointed out, speaking as President of the Council to the first session of the European Parliament (Common Assembly), this Community included 'the first sovereign Parliament established on a supranational basis' whose position together with the Council was 'comparable, in certain respects, to the relations between two chambers in the constitutional life of a state'.[48] Jean Monnet, speaking as President of the Commission (High Authority) in the same debate, stated that the Community was sovereign in the areas of its responsibility (notably in that it had certain powers of direct taxation and its law was directly applicable to legal persons), that it was based on the principle of separation of powers among the institutions and that 'the great European revolution of our era ... begins these very days with the constitution of the first supranational institutions of Europe'.[49] Nothing of the sort had, after all, ever been seen before in Europe. From the outset, the perception of the principal actors was a revolutionary constitutional step, laying down the first institutional structures capable of prefiguring a federal structure with an executive High Authority, bicameral Council-Assembly and independent Court. These 'extensive institutional provisions were thus primarily justified by the political perspective stated in the preamble of the treaty ... to lay the foundation for institutions which will give direction to a destiny henceforward shared'.[50] As we saw earlier, it had not yet begun to function before negotiations began to move ahead in the area of defence, no less.

The failure of the EDC did not sound the death-knell of European integration. It was relaunched on economic lines within three years via the Messina Conference and the Spaak Committee leading to the negotiation of the EEC and Euratom treaties. These again laid down procedures, distributed powers and established institutions. They thus provided again a constitutional basis for gradual development of European policies. The institutions were essentially the same as those of the ECSC (and were indeed merged in 1965), but slightly less supranational[51] in flavour (a precaution to ensure ratification by the French Assemblée Nationale, avoiding repetition of the EDC débâcle).[52] This was balanced by widening the scope of policy areas and competences to embrace practically the whole economy.

Thus, the EEC Treaty too came to be seen by many as a constitution, if not initially then as a result of a process of 'constitutionalization' of the treaties, the most notable aspects of which were the rulings of the European Court of Justice (ECJ) in 1963–4, which established the direct effect and the supremacy of Community law, and the ECJ's general tendency to defend the prerogatives that the treaties give to the Community institutions. It is worth, indeed, citing part of the 1963 ruling on direct effect:

> The objective of the EEC Treaty, which is to establish a common market, the functioning of which is of direct concern to interested parties in the Community, implies that this Treaty is more than an agreement which merely creates mutual obligations between the Contracting States. This view is confirmed by the preamble to the Treaty which refers not only to governments but to peoples. It is also confirmed more specifically by the establishment of institutions endowed with sovereign rights, the exercise of which affects Member States and also their citizens. Furthermore, it must be noted that the nationals of the States brought together in the Community are called upon to cooperate in the functioning of this Community through the intermediary of the European Parliament and the Economic and Social Committee ... This confirms that the States have acknowledged that Community law has an authority which can be invoked by their nationals before those courts and tribunals ... The conclusion to be drawn from this is that the Community constitutes a new legal order of international law for the benefit of which the States have limited their sovereign rights, albeit within limited fields, and the subjects of which comprise not only Member States but also their nationals.[53]

Similarly, the ruling on the supremacy of Community law states that:

> 'By contrast with ordinary international treaties, the EEC treaty has created its own legal system which, on the entry into force of the

Treaty, became an integral part of the legal system of the Member States and which their courts are bound to apply. By creating a Community of unlimited duration, having its own institutions, its own personality, its own legal capacity and capacity of representation on the international plane and, more particularly, real powers stemming from a limitation of sovereignty or a transfer of powers from the States to the Community, the Member States have limited their sovereign rights, albeit within limited fields, and have thus created a body of law which binds both their nationals and themselves. The integration into the laws of each Member State of provisions which derive from the Community, and more generally, the terms and the spirit of the Treaty, make it impossible for the States, as a corollary, to accord precedence to a unilateral and subsequent measure over a legal system accepted by them on a basis of reciprocity. Such a measure cannot therefore be inconsistent with that legal system. The executive force of the Community law cannot vary from one State to another in deference to subsequent domestic laws without jeopardizing the attainment of the objectives of the treaty'.[54]

Interestingly, the Court relied, *inter alia*, on the existence of the EP to justify the involvement of and direct effect on citizens. These rulings were, in legal terms, a landmark in the 'constitutionalization of the Treaty of Rome'[55] by which the Treaty was 'interpreted by techniques associated with constitutional documents rather than multipartite treaties [and it] assumed the 'higher law' attributes of a constitution'.[56] Similarly, the German Federal Constitutional Court recognized in 1967, that the EEC Treaty 'is, as it were, the constitution of the Community'.[57]

Subsequently, other rulings of the ECJ consolidated and extended the doctrines of direct effect and supremacy of Community law, to the extent that even directives – the legislative instrument intended to leave maximum leeway to Member States to adopt their national provisions and which at first sight would not suggest the possibility of directly granting rights or duties on individuals without action by national authorities – are now held to have, at least in certain circumstances, direct effect.[58]

The ECJ is sometimes accused of bias and of giving political judgements not fully based on the Treaties.[59] This is, of course, denied by the Court itself. 'The Court never takes political decisions, but from time to time it reminds politicians of what they have agreed'.[60] In these matters, however, the judges had to settle an issue that was not clear in the treaties, and did so against the express views of the governments of a number of Member States.[61] The fact that, over subsequent years, the supreme national jurisdictions of all the Member States have come around to accepting direct effect and supremacy,

> amounts in effect to a quiet revolution in the legal orders of the Member States. For, in respect of any matter coming within the competence of the Community, the legal 'Grundnorm' will have been effectively shifted, placing Community norms at the top of the legal pyramid.[62]

This reinforcement of the Community's 'normative supranationalism' to the extent of creating what resembles a federal legal system was balanced in the 1960s and 1970s by a decline in 'decisional supranationalism'.[63] Indeed, these two trends may have been linked.[64] Yet in setting up four institutions, each formally independent and with specific prerogatives, having general competence after the 1965 Merger Treaty for the full range of Community policies (rather than, for instance, having separate agencies or maintaining separate Commissions for different sectors), the treaties established a basic structure that went well beyond traditional international organizations. For federalists, it was easy to see the prefiguration of future federal institutions with the Commission developing into a government and the Council and Parliament into a bicameral legislature. As Hallstein, the first President of the EEC Commission said, 'the pattern of the Rome treaties, in so far as they supply one, is federal not confederal'.[65]

Although the trend in decision-making, at least between 1965 and 1985, was towards an intergovernmental Council, working by consensus, dominating the whole system, there were crumbs of comfort for federalists. First, as Community policies developed, Member States were correspondingly obliged to act jointly; even if this was through Council and even if unanimity had to be reached, policy had to be made (or, increasingly, changed) through the Council: Member States could not act unilaterally. Second, Council, although composed of members of national governments, was a Community institution subject to treaty provisions and rules, including the need for a Commission proposal for it to act on. Third, the practice of avoiding majority voting was based on the 'Luxembourg compromise', which was subject to divergent interpretations and had no legal standing; it might therefore be eroded or overcome as it was not part of the constitutional 'bottom line' – the treaties which provided the legal fallback in the case of a dispute. As we shall see, such a trend began to emerge in the 1980s. Fourth, the ECJ could step in at least to oblige Council to respect the prerogatives of the other institutions, as it did in a number of cases, such as the Isoglucose Ruling of 1980 which upheld Parliament's rights in the legislative procedure and in which the Court stated that the provisions in the Treaty requiring consultation of Parliament[66] 'reflects at Community level the fundamental principle that the peoples should take part in the exercise of power through the intermediary of a representative assembly'. Fifth, new institutional developments foreseen in the treaties, such as direct elections to the EP, or not foreseen, might reverse the trend.

These elements were enough to keep alive 'decisional supranationalism', or at least hopes for its development which, alongside the considerable development of normative supranationalism, gave sustenance to the view that the treaties were unique in character and capable of development into a federal constitution.

Some even felt that the treaties were sufficient in this respect as they stood. By 1984, Sir Christopher Prout MEP, later chairman of the EP's Legal Affairs Committee and leader of the Conservative Group, argued that 'Federalism involves the transfer of power by states to a common authority. Each time the Council of Ministers adopts a Regulation, its terms become legally binding on the ten Member States without the intervention of their national parliaments.'[67] He added: 'the most successful constitutions develop gradually.' By 1991, a *Financial Times* leader felt able to refer to the Community as 'this federation of which Britain is a part'.[68] Most, however, felt that, although the Treaties provided a base, treaty revision or development would be required, and this strategy has been pursued by most of those seeking steps forward in a federal direction and not without some success: financial autonomy and virtually bicameral decision-taking procedures for the budget (1970 and 1975), direct elections for the EP (1976), increased majority voting provisions, a greater role for the EP in the legislative procedure, broadening of Community competence, and closer links to the EC of the parallel intergovernmental EPC structure (1986 and 1992). By the mid-1990s, 'Europeans make federalism what Mr Jourdain made prose' (Croisat Quermoune, 1996).

Burgess considered the SEA to be 'yet another, albeit small, step in an overall process of federalization' and Pinder felt that 'it may well be legitimate to see the development of the Community up to now as a process of incremental federalism'.[69] At the same time, he criticized the tendency of 'classical' (i.e. constituent assembly) federalists for not giving 'enough thought to the idea of the Community experience as a series of steps towards federation', although he credited them for having acted in support of the Community's step-by-step development. On the institutional front (as opposed to the competence side) he felt that the Community had by 1986 come so far that it needed only 'majority voting [in Council] and legislative co-decision [EP Council] to convert the Community institutions into federal form'.[70] Indeed, this would bring the Community close to the model of the Federal Republic of Germany in which most legislation requires the approval of both the directly elected Bundestag and the Bundesrat, composed of Ministers from the *Länder* governments who cast weighted bloc votes on behalf of their *Land*. Operationally, the Bundesrat displays remarkable similarities to the Council (preparation of meetings by permanent representatives, 'A' points and 'B' points on the agenda according to whether agreement has already been reached at that level, the inter-ministerial character of the meetings, the weighted bloc vote, the *Vermittlungsauβschuss* or conciliation procedure, etc.),[71] but with a wider requirement for majority voting, a wider area of shared power (co-decision) with the elected chamber and facing a strong executive appointed only by the elected chamber.

Thus, the Community would require only a few key changes to bring it close to an existing and functioning federal system as regards its decision-taking structures (complementing, as we have seen, its existing federal legal system). In terms of competences, however, it lacked responsibilities in key areas traditionally considered as being appropriate for the central government in a federal system, notably money, taxation and armed forces. Even non-military aspects of foreign policy have been kept in a separate largely intergovernmental framework. In all these areas, notably money, the Maastricht Treaty envisages significant developments, thus potentially lending further credence to the incremental federalist interpretation, but up to now these areas of 'high politics' have proved difficult. In general economic matters, by contrast, President Delors estimated that up to '80 per cent of our economic legislation and perhaps even our fiscal and social legislation as well, will be of Community origin'.[72] Even if the figure is only half as high, it would still represent a considerable proportion of public policy-making. The EEC Treaty of course already 'provided for many of the other common policies to be expected in a federal system',[73] such as free movement, no internal tariffs, common policies in agriculture, transport and competition.

Furthermore, the treaty framework has been used as a vehicle for developing policies in areas that were not explicitly foreseen in the treaties and where it would have been quite feasible to use or to establish other frameworks. The EMS, for example, could easily have been set up to include certain EFTA countries. The EC's research capacity, cultural and youth exchanges, and others did not begin in the EC as a result of functional spillover – deliberate political decisions to complete the EC's fields of competence to give it a wider range were taken.

Thus, the incremental federalist approach based on seeing the Treaties as a constitutional basis, already possessing important federal characteristics, and capable of evolving through the addition of new competences and a strengthening of the powers of the institutions and their procedures into a federal system, is not without credibility and has also played a crucial role in shaping attitudes, opinions and strategies.

This approach has some considerable overlap with the academic school of neofunctionalism which we shall now consider. The differences are to be found in the degree of importance attached by federalists to constitutional steps forward – usually of a highly political character – as the key factor; their clearer concept of an 'end-product' of the integration process; the resultant emphasis given to *all* the aspects of a balanced federal constitutional system including the need for democratic control and the rule of law rather than concentrating on technocratic aspects; a recognition of the role of political leadership, both in enabling and blocking the process; a greater emphasis on the political commitment needed to start the process off in the first place and a greater attention to Parliament, at least as a crucial element in the emerging constitution and for many as a prime mover in its emergence.

NEOFUNCTIONALISTS

The failure in the postwar years to establish a European federation in one go, but to follow instead a path of sectoral and step-by-step integration (albeit as we have seen in areas perceived as of fundamental political importance and with an emphasis on the constitutional and supranational features thereof), generated interest in how functional integration might develop and eventually lead to full political integration. Further interest was generated by the Messina 'relaunch' of Europe via economic integration and setting up the EEC.

Politicians spoke of functional integration, but to academic minds 'functionalism' in its traditional form, expounded notably by David Mitrany,[74] was not the appropriate term to apply here. Mitrany's functionalism envisaged the gradual establishment of functionally specific international organizations, geared to problem-solving in a technocratic fashion, relying on expertise and *avoiding* political or ideological confrontations. [Only when the habit of cooperation in such frameworks was well established, and citizens were well aware of the advantages of such cooperation, could it be envisaged that more political matters be tackled jointly or that the loyalties of citizens towards national governments might be refocused.] It was dangerous if not impossible to challenge sovereignty directly.

This, however, is precisely what the federalist functionalism of Monnet hoped to do. In envisaging functional integration in an unmistakably political context, with a single organizational system and including, as we have seen, a number of federal-type features, the new functionalism was clearly different from that of Mitrany. The term 'neofunctionalism' was coined to describe it.

In part, the differences between the two hinged on the nature of community and loyalty, of identity and society. Functionalists, like intergovernmentalists, believed that the gut loyalty of citizens was linked to what has been called the 'socio-psychological community',[75] in the sense of a community of beliefs, values and attitudes (typically coinciding with the nation-state). Neofunctionalists placed emphasis on the pluralism of interests within modern states and societies and on the function of institutions as providing the framework for accommodation, compromise and conflict resolution. Their capacity to do so was what would attract loyalty or, at least, acceptance. The

> fundamental feature of the pluralistic, industrialized societies in Western Europe was the interplay of group interests in the political system. The staking of claims and demands in return for political loyalties reinforced the authority of the system as a whole. Neofunctionalism regarded this pattern of political activity as directly transferable to an international setting.[76]

As has often been pointed out, the distinction is similar to that made by Tönnies[77] between [*Gemeinschaft* and *Gesellschaft*,] the former being a community with a sense of belonging together, sharing values and loyalties, a sense of duty and perhaps kinship; the latter being a society based on a framework and rules for competing interests.

The key issue dividing neofunctionalists from traditional functionalists, and indeed from opponents of European integration or protagonists of intergovernmental cooperation, was whether political integration could proceed on the basis of integrating *Gesellschaft* rather than (or, at least before) *Gemeinschaft*, though some would argue that Europe already had a degree of *Gemeinschaft* comparable to that of some of its Member States and sufficient for it to function.

Recent events have shown how complex such relationships can be. Three federations that functioned for most of a century in a highly integrated way – Yugoslavia, Czechoslovakia and the USSR – fell apart because of a lack of *Gemeinschaft*. The *Gesellschaft*, however, was orchestrated by a totalitarian system and there was also a perceived domination by one of the units in each federation. We can also witness how unity based almost entirely on *Gemeinschaft* with little initial *Gesellschaft* can run into difficulties (as in reunited Germany) or even fail to occur as anticipated (as between Romania and Moldova). Clearly, the distinction between *Gesellschaft* and *Gemeinschaft* is a complex one and both may be necessary, to a degree, for political integration to be achieved without coercion. Suffice to say for our present purposes, that neofunctionalists tended to the view that the key process in the initial stages of European integration was the interpenetration of *Gesellschaft*.

Federalists (especially constituent Assembly federalists) tended to the view that integration of *Gesellschaft* and *Gemeinschaft* would follow the crucial integration of the political framework, or else that integration of *Gemeinschaft* was not indispensable – federation being a method of allowing different *Gemeinschafts* to work together constructively without losing their own identity needing only a willingness to do so and some reassurance that the system would work fairly and without threat to their identity.[78] Intergovernmentalists tended to argue that a sense of *Gemeinschaft* is essential and that unless and until this was established over a lengthy period of functional cooperation, it was futile or dangerous to proceed down the path of political integration.

Neofunctionalist academics developed models of considerably greater detail and complexity than the politicians who set out on the step-by-step road to integration had spelled out. Politicians spoke of concrete steps 'creating a sense of common purpose' (Schuman), of creating, by establishing an economic community, 'the basis for a broader and deeper Community' (ECSC Treaty preamble), of going 'a step further towards the construction of Europe ... first of all in the economic field' (Messina Resolution of the Foreign Ministers, June 1955); of 'laying the foundations for an ever closer union' (EEC Treaty preamble), of economic federation producing 'a considerable degree of political federation' (1948 US Congress Report on aid to Europe), of 'implementation of common policies [requiring] corresponding developments in the specifically political sphere' (1970 Report of the Foreign Ministers on political unification), of 'advances towards integration [resulting in] disequilibria if economic policy cannot be harmonized effectively'

(Werner Report, 1970), of 'the development of the Union's external relations [not occurring] without the development of common policies internally, [and neither] being achieved without consolidating the authority and effectiveness of common institutions' (Tindemans Report, 1975), or simply of 'the European Union to be created step by step' (Genscher–Colombo draft Act, 1981). More recently, Jacques Delors put it this way:

> Historically, the EC has advanced through a process of dynamic disequilibrium. For example, the internal market led to the Single European Act which prompted the implementation of common policies in related fields. Similarly, monetary union will promote economic union with the same spillover effect.[79]

Politicians envisaged a step-by-step approach, each step helping to create the conditions for the next one. Neofunctionalist academics took this up and developed models and theories of considerable complexity, often audacious in claiming predictive properties.

The central argument of neofunctionalism is that integration in one sector will automatically spill over into integration in other sectors and that as this process continues, political actors will incrementally shift the focus of their activities, their expectations and even their loyalties to the new integrated institutions and procedures.[80] These two aspects – functional spillover and political spillover – were interlinked, as the tensions created in another sector by the integration of one sector could be resolved in one of two ways: integration of the new sector or disintegration of the integrated sector. The latter would be prevented by the political support of those benefiting from the integrated sector who would not only resist any dismantling but would also actively support further integration and persuade other sectors of the benefits thereof. Competing interests in society could achieve more beneficial compromises at this higher level of integration. At the same time the new central authority – the Commission – would build up its own direct links to interest groups, politicians and bureaucracies bypassing or putting pressure on national governments.

Similarly, periodic crises, caused by failures or insufficiencies of the supranational agency, would lead to reassessments of its level (power) or scope of authority. This normally would lead to an increase in one or both, as the alternative of retrenchment is resisted by beneficiaries. Thus the supranational agency 'slowly extends its authority so as to progressively undermine the independence of the nation state'.[81] To illustrate this point, neofunctionalists explored the dynamics of negotiation, bargaining, package-dealing, side-payments and log rolling. Haas notably distinguished modes that would rise from initial 'lowest common denominator' bargaining to 'splitting the difference' to 'upgrading the common interest' where partners agree to focus on common interests and deliberately delay divergences until more propitious circumstances arise. Progress would be enhanced by the networks and habits developed by working together, (*engrenage*). All this was focused on the 'élites' of national and supranational bureaucrats, ministers and interest groups, (and in the EC, on the Commission, not the EP):

> Converging economic goals, embedded in the bureaucratic, pluralistic and industrial life of modern Europe provided the crucial impetus. The economic technician, the planner, the innovating industrialist and trade unionist advanced the movement, not the politician, the scholar, the poet or the writer.[82]

The emphasis on bargaining among pluralistic interests is a different emphasis from the incremental federalist approach. Indeed, Monnet dismissively said: 'We don't negotiate, we find common solutions to common problems'.[83] On the other hand, neofunctionalists were often dismissive of arguments of a general ideological, political or abstract character in favour of European Union. Haas stated:

> perhaps the most salient conclusion we can draw from the community-building experience is the fact that major interest groups as well as politicians determine their support of, or opposition to, new central institutions on the basis of a calculation of advantage. The 'good Europeans' are not the main creators.[84]

He went on to say:

> rather than relying on a scheme of integration which posits 'altruistic' or 'idealistic' motives as the conditioners of conduct, it seems more reasonable to focus – assuming the pluralistic nature of politics – on the interests and values defended by the major groups involved in the process, experience showing that these are far too complex to be described in such simple terms as 'the desire for Franco-German peace' or 'the will to a United Europe'.[85]

Yet, such aspirations were, as we have seen, among the main motivations for the postwar integration effort, and Haas himself recognized that '"United Europe" seems to be a remarkably resilient and adaptable symbol ... and the heterogeneity of movements specifically devoted to the realization of the symbol in fact is equally impressive'.[86] He even quotes Hallstein exhorting support for the ECSC in Germany, 'not because it may be profitable in terms of dividends but only because it is one of those efforts through which mankind can progress'.[87] The commitment to the principle of unity, emphasized by the federalists, was crucial in getting underway the process of establishing the first supranational authorities around which the interest groups could act. Only at that stage is the analysis of Haas and other neofunctionalists relevant, and Haas is less forthcoming on the reasons for – and dynamic of – the original motivation. He did, however, refer to the ability of the ECSC Council to overcome differences that appeared insurmountable in intergovernmental contexts such as the OEEC, and this thanks to the 'atmosphere of cooperation' and the 'engagement'[88] present in the ECSC. It would appear, then, that the political/ constitutional dimension created the space for the interest group/ sectoral bargaining dimension rather than the other way around. Haas only hints at this and neofunctionalist literature generally ignores or downplays the constitutional (or 'federal bargain') elements of starting the process.

After the creation of the Communities, scholars in the 1950s and early 1960s focused on pressure to integrate other market sectors arising out of the integration of coal and steel, how a common market would require harmonization of competition rules which would lead on to pressure for a common system of regional aids, and so on. They could witness how sectoral interests began to work directly with the High Authority through the ECSC consultative committee, and how farmers' organizations, trade unions and others began to organize at European level. Many such interests were indeed supporters of the integration process once it took off in their sector. Similarly as regards external relations, Schmitter argued that 'once agreement is reached and made operative on a policy pertaining to intermember or intraregional relations, participants will find themselves compelled . . . to hammer out a collective external position'.[89] Thus, the common market required a common external tariff, which required a common position in trade negotiations and a common strategy thereto, including its foreign policy aspects.

Early neofunctionalism saw this double process of spillover extending smoothly from purely economic to political fields, and doing so rapidly. Haas claimed in 1958 that 'the spillover may make a political community out of Europe in fact before the end of the transition period' (i.e. 1969).[90]

It was perhaps because of this optimistic assessment of the speed and inevitability of the integration process that neofunctionalist theorists were so taken aback by de Gaulle and the 1965 'empty chair' crisis. It immediately provoked an agonizing reassessment of the theory by its leading exponents. There was also, not unnaturally, criticism of neofunctionalism from other perspectives. Intergovernmentalists pointed to the resilience of nationalism and the ease with which it could put a spanner in the works.[91] They cast serious doubt on the political spillover notion, pointing out that it was governments and the Council rather than the Commission which had become the centre of power in the Community. Federalists criticized neofunctionalism for its reliance on élite *engrenage*, and giving too little 'weight to constitutional values such as democracy and the rule of law',[92] and for avoiding the issue of sovereignty.[93]

But it was the neofunctionalists' own self-criticisms that were the most spectacular, first in reassessing and then in abandoning their theory. Haas and Lindberg's first reflections after the 1965 crisis were that they had underestimated both nationalism and the role of 'dramatic-political actors' and political leadership generally, and that spillover should not be considered automatic. Haas now considered neofunctionalism (and other approaches) to be merely a 'pre-theory'. Furthermore, the integration process might go in one of three directions: towards a 'regional state', a loose 'regional commune' or an 'asymmetrical overlap' with various levels of authority distributed among several centres.[94] Haas abandoned the idea of transfers of élite *loyalties* (always somewhat curious in the context of neofunctionalist emphasis on interests) in favour of a 'master-concept' of 'authority-legitimacy' transfers. Lindberg took refuge in emphasizing the need to measure a larger number of variables including 'leadership' and 'resources for collective decision-taking' (such as a sense of mutual political identification, legitimacy and prior agreement on what can be decided collectively).[95]

Perhaps more impressive was Schmitter's 'Revised Theory of Regional Integration'[96] which, relying on traditional neofunctionalist foci, challenged the automaticity of partial integration causing problems that can best be solved by further integration. He argued that problems cause crises which can, in fact, be solved in a number of ways: spillover (increased authority and scope for the institution); build-up (increased authority, same scope); spill-around (increased scope, same authority); muddle-about (lower authority, increased scope); spill-back (lower scope, lower authority) or retrenchment (lower scope, higher authority). The precise solution of each crisis would depend on the nature of the issue and the strength of variables at the time.[97] An integration process would evolve in cycles from crisis to crisis, each one resolved in one way or the other. He considered it unlikely that many processes would move upwards beyond the 'integrative showdown' – the point at which there is 'resistance to activism on the part of regional bureaucrats unaccountable to popular masses [and a] reaction of governmental decision makers to the erosion of their monopolistic control'. Significantly, he considered that the most likely integration processes to move beyond this were those where the *initial* scope and level of authority was high. This he called the 'functionalist paradox'. Usually, however, he considered the most likely long-term outcome to be 'encapsulation': the reaching of 'a state of stable selfmaintenance'.

If indeed 'encapsulation' at one level or another – but normally falling short of a fundamental challenge to national sovereignty – was the most likely outcome of integration processes, then it is only a short step to conclude that the phenomenon being considered is not integration in a far-reaching sense, but the creation and maintenance (or otherwise) of 'regimes' for the management of 'interdependence'. This was the field which many former integration theorists moved on to (and which we shall examine below) encouraged by Haas's further revisions of his views where he went so far as to suggest that regional integration theory was 'obsolete',[98] and by the apparent inability of the EC to make much progress in terms of its scope or authority for many years following the Luxembourg 'compromise'.

But were the neofunctionalists too hasty in abandoning an approach that had produced many insights, fleeing at the first whiff of grapeshot? Was this again a case of academic approaches to the Community reacting to the current state-of-play rather than the long term? Certainly some theorists, writing at a later time when integration was again more visible, seemed to think so. Taylor, for instance, had by 1989 come around to the view that 'the student of the EC . . . needs to return to the writings of a group of scholars – the neofunctionalists – whose writings have for many years been unfashionable'.[99]

A nuanced retrospective look at some central aspects of neofunctionalist predictions shows that some of them have at least partially occurred, albeit over a longer timescale than originally conceived. Let us examine in detail the process of spillover. It can be broken down into two aspects: spillover of scope (Schmitter's 'spill-around') and spillover of level ('build-up'). In each case, functional spillover and political spillover[100] must be considered.

Spillovers of scope have occurred most clearly in the key central area of creating a common or single market. Many of these were, of course, functional spillovers foreseen in the EEC Treaty itself, which provided for Community competence in areas such as competition policy, external trade and areas which no government left entirely to market forces and where separate regulations could cause large distortions (agriculture and transport) – a wide package and difficult to unravel. Other consequences of the single market were not explicitly foreseen in the Treaty. Examples of this include regional policy and consumer protection. It is important to note, however, that development of these policy areas was facilitated by the deliberate open-ended formulation of certain treaty articles, notably Articles 100 and 235, i.e. spillover within certain limits, even for areas that were not initially foreseen, was provided for from the beginning in the constitutional package of the Treaty. In areas where such articles could not be used, such as foreign policy or monetary union, spillover pressures have been present, but could not produce results in the same way or on the same timescale (but could help build up pressure to revise the treaties).[101] Thus, the actual operation of functional 'spillover' depends partly on the constitutional possibilities offered by the treaties.

But above all, it is the key importance of the field chosen – the common market – that is important. In merging the market it would ultimately be necessary to merge or at least coordinate closely all the areas in which public authorities intervene to organize, regulate, correct, shape, limit or control the market and where separate national efforts would increasingly be either less effective or distorting. Over time, with greater interpenetration causing still greater interdependence in this respect, pressures would inevitably increase and reach such critical fields as the need for a single currency in a single market. Integration beginning in other fields could not have the same impact. Space research in ELDO and later the ESA did not spill over into technological research generally nor into military research. Military frameworks (NATO and WEU) did not spill over very far into non-military fields. The Rhine Commission did not spill over into regulating river transport generally. Cooperation in the fields of civil law, education, culture and labour market together, in the Nordic Council, failed to produce a more broad-sense approach. Even with the EC framework, the integration of coal in the ECSC did not spill over into energy generally (the single market eventually forced that). Does Schmitter's 'functionalist paradox' apply? Certainly, the wide initial scope in an area which of its nature had implications for many policy areas and crucially set in the context of a constitutional system allowing flexibility and extensions was important.

What then of *political* spillover of scope? Here, the results seem mixed. Interest groups, government departments and political parties did not automatically defend integrated areas in time of crisis or rush to press for further areas of integration. Reactions were dependent in each case and in each country (or sometimes region) on the balance of perceived advantage or disadvantage, sometimes coloured by more general attitudes.[102]

Nor was there a learning process or value of example in the way that some had seen it, with the success of one step inspiring similar steps in other areas. After all, the ECSC was not set up because of the inspiring success of the Council of Europe, but because of its per-ceived inadequacies. The EDC negotiations started before the ECSC had a chance to succeed or fail. The EEC was considered to be a relaunch after a period of failure. Its successes did not inspire similar solutions for foreign policy integration. No doubt the value of exam-ple has played a role in encouraging policy development *within* the Community frameworks, with some policies being tested initially in a limited way before being extended. But it has equally been deliber-ately avoided as a model for EPC. Thus, in terms of wider functional spillovers, the value of example has not been as significant as predicted.

We can thus see that at least the *pressure* for spillover in the *scope* of Community activity predicted by the neofunctionalists has been present, though more as functional spillover than political spillover. But what about spillover in the *level* of integration ('build-up')? Here both the functional and the political aspects seem to apply.

Political spillover in the level of integration can occur in a number of ways. For instance, when actors begin to deal with the Community authorities directly and, in so doing, increase the possibilities for these authorities to build political support bypassing national governments. Another example would be in working *with* national authorities, if the Community develops respect or habits of cooperation or new proce-dures which enhance the authority of the system as a whole. Let us look at both these cases.

Most sectoral interest groups are primarily organized at national level and have a more intimate relationship with their national government than with the European institutions, for reasons of proximity, habit, culture and finance. But this is not always so – British trade unions under the Thatcher government are an obvious example, enjoying a better relationship with the Commission than with the UK government. And even if an interest is supported by 'its' government, it will still find advantage in securing support for its position across the Community,

particularly if the matter might be settled by a majority vote in Council
or by the Commission or, typically in budgetary matters, by Parliament
(again, we see a constitutional aspect affecting the way neofunctionalist
pressures work in practice). This tends to draw such groups into
transnational bargaining, compromise formulation and even a small stake
in the system.[103] And there has indeed been a spectacular build-up of
direct interest group representation in Brussels and of transnational
organizations. The Commission has estimated that around 3000 interest
groups employing 10,000 people are lobbying in some way or another
around Brussels.[104]

The Community institutions cannot always use such groups to bypass or put pressure on national governments, but it has certainly been
possible in a number of cases, such as the support given to the Commission by some UK local authorities in its dispute with the UK government over 'additionality' in the Regional Fund; backing given to
Commission proposals by environmental and consumer protection organizations; the support of industrialists for the single market programme
and of trade unions for the social charter; or of youth and student
organizations for establishing and extending the various EC exchange
schemes.

The Community institutions themselves have been involved in setting up channels that bypass national governments. This has been done
in a variety of ways ranging from formal acts, such as the 1988 Commission decision[105] setting up a Consultative Council of Regional and
Local Authorities, to informal encouragement combined with financial
assistance, as with the creation of the EC Youth Forum.[106] Budgetary
support voted by the EP and administered by the Commission has indeed been a frequently used mechanism helping, *inter alia*, European
consumer organizations, the trade unions, the European Movement and
various educational establishments. Within the EP, some of the informal 'intergroups', such as the Industry Council, the Trade Union
Intergroup or the Kangaroo Group, provide a channel of communication between MEPs and a variety of interests or citizen's organizations.

Also significant are the direct links growing up between local authorities and European institutions. Most German *Länder* and other regional governments now have offices in Brussels, providing a direct
link and channel of communication. Even without Brussels offices, local
authorities have established European departments for the same reason. It has been estimated that within the UK, there are about 400
professional European offices in 290 local authorities and that these
'European offices now tend to have senior rank, run their own small

departments and become involved with managing large-scale programmes'.[107]

This gradual but constant build-up of networks of contact, dialogue and influence that link the supranational institutions directly to non-governmental actors is an aspect of political spillover in the level of integration that was correctly predicted by neofunctionalists, even if some of them might have overestimated its consequences. Again, though, we can see that its development was crucially encouraged by the constitutional set-up of the Community. The existence of an executive body with a degree of independence and, as we shall examine more closely later, the impact of a Parliament functioning on a non-national basis, provided scope for non-governmental actors to influence at least some decisions directly at European level.

As regards working *with* governments and national administrations, the development of the role of Council and of 'comitology'[108] can be seen in two ways. On the one hand, it has been seen as a reassertion of national influence on the Community. On the other hand, it can be seen as increasing *engrenage* of national administrations into the Community system, with more time and energy devoted by national actors to *collective* policy-making in Brussels as opposed to separate, national policy-making in an exclusively national context. It means that habits of cooperation, transnational linkages and coalitions and increased understanding of common problems all have greater scope to develop.

Judged by volume of activity, neofunctionalist political spillover has materialized, especially if seen less as a transfer of power from national administrations to the Commission (as many neofunctionalists initially focused on) and more as a transfer from individual national decision-taking to collective decision-taking through the Community system as a whole, including the Council as a Community institution.

As to *functional* spillover in the level of integration, this occurs when an existing Community policy requires an increase in the authority of Community institutions to survive or to function more effectively. This has been seen on a number of occasions. Increases in Community finance to pay for the CAP is an example (irrespective of the merits of the case), as indeed many other increases in the EC budget. Similarly, stronger powers for the Commission to manage the CAP (e.g. authority to introduce stabilizers introduced in 1988), or in its competition policy powers (e.g. the 1989 Merger Control Regulation),[109] and changing from unanimity to majority voting in Council can also be seen as examples. They may be limited, they may not have occurred at all in some areas, they sometimes required legislation and sometimes treaty revision. Nevertheless, as an observable feature, they have taken place.

In this regard, the issue of majority voting is worth exploring further as it illustrates well the sort of pressures that can contribute to incremental charge in the system. We saw earlier how the Luxembourg compromise was an agreement to disagree. Whereas all Member States accepted that, where important national interests were at stake, an attempt should be made to find a solution acceptable to all, they did not agree as to what should happen if no such solution was found within a reasonable period of time. France considered that the discussions should continue indefinitely. *All* other Member States took the view that a vote should be taken in accordance with the treaties.

In practice, in the years following the 'Luxembourg compromise', very little voting took place in Council. This was partly due to a reluctance to force a new crisis with France, but the tendency was reinforced in 1973 by the accession of new Member States which essentially shared the French view on these matters. Together, France, the UK and Denmark constituted a large enough minority to prevent decisions even by a qualified majority. In other words, if a matter were put to the vote against the express national interests of *any* Member State, it would not get through as these countries would not vote for a proposal in such circumstances. It therefore became habitual to negotiate on all texts, virtually line by line, until all Member States agreed, before taking a decision in Council.

By the 1980s, this working method was coming under increasing strain. A number of negative consequences were becoming increasingly apparent:

- such a decision-making procedure was grossly inefficient (it took 17 years, for instance, to agree on a directive on the mutual recognition of the qualifications for architects);
- virtually any Community policy or action could only be the lowest common denominator acceptable to all Member States;
- such detailed and time-consuming negotiations could only be carried out by national civil servants, which led to a bureaucratization of the whole Community system, undermining the Commission's right of initiative, the role of the EP and even the role of ministers in the Council;
- above all, it became apparent that, while unanimity when agreeing on *new* Community policies was one thing, unanimity for the management or revision of *existing* policies was another. In these cases,

the Community as a whole had a vital interest in ensuring that it could take decisions, and the blocking power given to individual States was a threat to the viability of Community policies.

It was clear that national ministers were capable of deeming almost anything to be an 'important national interest' when their state had an advantage in the status quo. CAP reforms, for instance, were all too easy to block by any Member State gaining from the system, even when this was at huge expense to the Community as a whole. This applied in varying degrees to all Community policies and to all Member States. The right of veto proved to be the dictatorship of the minority, used for selfish national interests.

The first major crack in the practice of unanimity came in 1982 when the UK attempted to block the annual package of farm prices (details of which it had already agreed) in order to exact concessions in separate negotiations on the Community's budget. This was perceived by other Member States to be tantamount to blackmail. The Community had to decide urgently on the agricultural prices for that year, and Britain was not objecting to the contents of that decision but merely using its supposed right of veto to extract concessions on another matter. This attitude provoked a sufficient majority of Member States – including France – to adopt the package by a vote, putting Britain in a minority. This was possible because the 'bottom line', constitutionally, was the treaty provision for majority voting in this area, rather than the political understanding (and a disputed one at that) of the 'Luxembourg compromise'.

A shift in the attitude of some Member States was confirmed in 1983, on the occasion of the adoption of the Solemn Declaration on European Union. The Declaration itself referred to a need to improve the Community's capacity to act by applying the decision-making procedures laid down in the treaties. In statements appended, however, each Member State laid down its interpretation of when a vote should take place. Only Britain and Denmark supported the original French position of 1965. France and Ireland now spelt out that the national interest in question must relate directly to the subject under discussion and they, like Greece, took the view that the vote should only be postponed if a Member State invokes an '*essential* national interest' *in writing*. Belgium, Germany, Luxembourg, Italy and the Netherlands took the view that a vote should be held *whenever* the treaties provide for it.

In 1984, the EP put forward a proposal for a new treaty on European Union, which envisaged the introduction, over a ten-year period, of majority voting without the right of veto for *all* existing Community policies (not foreign policy cooperation), but retained unanimity for the introduction of new policies. As we shall see later, this, and a growing realization that key objectives such as a completed single market would not be achieved without more efficient decision-taking, led the Member States to agree in the Single European Act, to extend by ten the number of articles in the treaties which required majority voting.

A change in the treaties could not in itself affect the Luxembourg compromise, as a political agreement with no legal basis, let alone a treaty one. Indeed, Thatcher declared in the House of Commons that it remained in force. However, such a change to the treaties, duly ratified by all national parliaments, changed the constitutional framework within which the decisions concerned would be taken, and signified at least an intention to take majority votes more frequently. There would, after all, be little point in modifying the treaties if this were not the case. Furthermore, Council followed this up with an amendment to its internal Rules of Procedure, whereby its President is obliged to move to a vote upon the request of the Commission or the representative of any Member State, provided that the request is supported by a simple majority of Member States. The context was also changed by the accession of Spain and Portugal. It was no longer clear that states seeking to invoke the Luxembourg compromise would have sufficient support in Council to constitute a blocking minority.

Following these developments, voting began to take place in the Council in the areas where this was allowed by the treaties. There were even cases in which Member States in the minority, rather than invoke the Luxembourg compromise appealed to the Court of Justice on grounds of an incorrect legal basis – arguing that an article requiring unanimity should have been used.[110] Nor have votes been confined to non-controversial areas. They have been taken on subjects as varied as emission standards for car pollution, a ban on hormones in meat (leading to a 'trade war' with the USA), permitted radioactivity levels in foodstuffs, rules for transfrontier television broadcasts, several fishing controversies, foreign aid and some of the crucial CAP reforms.

Thus, it can be seen that, within certain constraints (crucially those embodied in the constitutional structure of the EC) several of the processes predicted by neofunctionalists have taken place. In particular, functional spillover, both in the scope and in the level of integration, and political spillover in the level of integration have been a feature of the past decades, even if neither proceeded as smoothly nor as rapidly as some writers initially suggested. The vast literature of the neofunctionalists generally provides numerous insights into the mechanisms of integration but without addressing sufficiently the question of where the process will lead to, at what point key political/constitutional watersheds will be reached or, indeed, what constitutional prerequisites are necessary for a process of gradual integration to take off. Furthermore, in placing so much emphasis on the interaction of the Commission with national officials and with interest groups, neofunctionalists tended to ignore the role or potential role of the European Parliament, of political parties and of the media, although many of their hypotheses might well be tested in such contexts too.

INTERDEPENDENCE THEORIES

Although not strictly a theory of integration (or one of only limited integration) the notion of *interdependence* is of interest here as it held sway over many academic analyses of the Community, including many who had abandoned neofunctionalism. Yet again, however, we can observe that a particular approach had its apotheosis at a time at which events in the Community seemed to correspond to it. The period from 1965 to 1984 was one of apparent stagnation in the Community, and many considered that it had reached what Taylor called the 'limits of integration' where 'the development of further common or centralized regimes [was] unlikely' and 'the goal of unification [should be] consciously abandoned'.[111] Busch and Puchala claimed that 'the EC system has not changed for quite some time and we hazard to speculate that it will probably not change in the foreseeable future'.[112] Webb considered that 'it is clear from previous theoretical critiques and empirical studies of the EC that anything resembling a European Union . . . is very unlikely to result from present and foreseeable trends'.[113]

Indeed, the EC continued, without great change, through several crises (1965 empty chair, 1967 second rebuff to UK application, 1972 monetary crisis, 1974 oil crisis, 1975 UK renegotiations, 1979 oil crisis, 1980–4 budgetary disputes, 1983 EMS crisis), enlargements (1973, 1981) and attempts at reform (1975–6 Tindemans Report, 1977 'Three Wise Men', 1981–3 Genscher–Colombo initiative). Although some feared disintegration rather than mere encapsulation',[114] most scholars concluded that it would remain a rather messy 'institutional regime',[115] 'concordance system'[116] 'system of managed interdependence'[117] or 'partial political system',[118] occasionally subject to small changes and adjustments but, in essence, stable.

This approach is generally known as the interdependence model, and seemed to some to 'offer the best way forward for academic research'[119] in the 1980s. It was an approach concerned with a far wider range of international systems than the EC. The EC was seen as merely 'one example (albeit a particularly intense one) of trends that affect all governments and societies in the advanced industrialized part of the world'.[120] This may facilitate comparisons but tends to deflect attention from some of the institutional features that are particular to the EC.[121] Interdependence analysts tend to focus on policy formulation and how governments use the regional framework jointly to retrieve a degree of control in policy areas where the subject or the interests concerned extend beyond the domestic arena.

Interdependence analysts must nevertheless be distinguished from intergovernmentalists or 'realists'. The latter emphasize the continuing *primary* role of national governments and attach continued importance to sovereignty in its legal and formal sense. Interdependence analysts are close to neofunctionalists in pointing to the 'cobweb' of transnational networks and interests that governments have to contend with (though not sharing the neofunctionalist analysis that such networks could eventually bypass or marginalize governments) and even look at 'transgovernmental' coalitions (such as Agriculture Ministers versus Budget Ministers).

The interdependence model can be seen as a halfway house. Unlike the 'realists', interdependence theorists recognized that integration has gone beyond intergovernmentalism but unlike neofunctionalists they considered that it would probably not go much further. Like intergovernmentalists they recognized that national governments are and will be of key importance, but like neofunctionalists they placed them among a plurality of diverse and often transnational interests.

The interdependence approach is therefore flexible and provides descriptive insights. However, as a model in its own right it fails to explain why there are so many challenges to the status quo, and it is of limited value in understanding the integration process, as it does not consider that there is necessarily such a process. In short, it is 'for scholars and politicians who wish, for different reasons, to keep their options open on the evolution of the EC'.[122]

INTERGOVERNMENTALISTS

Intergovernmentalists have a 'billiard ball' view of international relations, with governments clearly in control, negotiating on behalf of their country within which interests have been aggregated and the 'national interest' determined, with other governments in a similar position. In their view, the EC may have some unusual features, but it does not go 'very far beyond' intergovernmental relationships as governments, through the dominance of the Council, the 'Luxembourg compromise', the establishment of the European Council, and the work of COREPER and comitology committees have established control and kept 'high politics' out of EC terms of reference.[123] Under this view, the EP plays only an insignificant role. The Commission is viewed mainly as a secretariat. Policy is thrashed out in 'gladiatorial' negotiations among governments. National sovereignty is intact.

There were and are some who share that view from a prescriptive standpoint. De Gaulle's view was that 'there is and can be no Europe other than a Europe of the States – except, of course, for myths, fictions and pageants.'[124] Thatcher fulminated against those who wished to 'suppress nationhood' and called for 'cooperation between independent sovereign states',[125] a view that has been echoed in the last few years by the Conservative Eurosceptics. The Danish government and parliament have consistently taken an intergovernmental view and refer to European 'cooperation', never 'integration'. Resistance to majority voting in Council, to the introduction of direct elections to the EP and even to direct contacts between subnational authorities and the Commission were all battles fought (and largely lost) by prescriptive intergovernmentalists over the years.

Kirchner is probably right to say that the intergovernmentalist/realist perspective 'never became a central focus among scholars for studying the EC, and its credentials seemed to wane further once the Single European Act was signed and ratified',[126] but it would be foolish to dismiss intergovernmentalism entirely. The marked preference for that view on the part of some actors makes it part of the equation of Community developments, and the work of intergovernmentalist scholars has the important merit of reminding us of the resilience of national governments, whose role has not waned in the way predicted by the neofunctionalists.

Furthermore, certain intergovernmental characteristics of the EC, perceived as safeguards of national sovereignty, became important benchmarks in some national debates on European integration. The 'Yes' side in the referendums of 1972 in Denmark, and of 1975 in the UK, used the argument that the 'veto' safeguarded the national interest to persuade floating voters, with the result that it became part of the national consensus on which membership of the EC was based.

Intergovernmentalism also serves as a reminder of the fragility of the system. Member States are subjects of international law and can undo by treaty all that they have done by treaty. The break-up of existing federations in Eastern Europe shows that that can even be done without agreement and by units that are (or were) not subjects of international law and that were in situations of considerable interdependence and longstanding integration. The EC is made up of peoples recently at war, speaking different languages and with little 'we feeling'. The argument that the gut loyalties of the public does not reside with European institutions is a telling one, although in some Member States they might not lie entirely with the state either, but with smaller component units, be they Flanders, Catalonia or Scotland.

But is loyalty necessary? The discussion above on *Gemeinschaft* and *Gesellschaft* is relevant here. And federalists claim that federation is about unity in diversity, allowing the component units of the federation to remain intact, to keep their identity and to participate as such in federal decision-taking. A federal loyalty might develop, but as an *addition* to national loyalty (man being pluri-dimensional) or in a different sense, that of recognizing the benefits of the federal system without it carrying the emotional links of national loyalty.[127] (This too is, perhaps, not unknown in some states.) In this sense, it is possible to establish federal structure provided there is a shared perception of the need to do so, and no fears of loss of identity as would be the case for instance if one unit or group were perceived to be dominant. The EC at least fulfils this latter prerequisite: it has at all stages[128] had a reasonable balance of large countries (themselves of similar size) and small, of North and South, of Latin and Germanic. Fears of hegemony have been minimalized.

Intergovernmentalists remind us too of the importance of military, strategic and geopolitical considerations. These have certainly played a role at the time of the creation of the EC, and the latter would not have survived certain geopolitical scenarios. It is indeed crucial that the Member States, despite divergences, were in a *geopolitically compatible* situation, permitting integration to reach even the fringes of security policy. By way of illustration, such factors probably go some way in explaining why integration never took off in the same way in the Nordic Council, whose members were in geopolitically incompatible situations throughout the Cold War, and where the relatively recent independence of Finland, Iceland and Norway may also have meant that there were residual fears of domination (in Finland's case by a cultural grouping which it was alone in not belonging to).

Intergovernmentalists remind us of the often deep roots of national loyalties and attitudes. The divergent attitudes to integration of the Member States are rooted in the differences of historic experience and culture. After all, in the long run, interdependence and the interplay of interests as described by neofunctionalists should affect states in similar positions to a similar degree. Yet the consistently more favourable attitude of certain countries and hostile attitudes of others must give food for thought to all integrationists.

Britain's attitude to European integration is not just a result of the peculiarities of its two-party political system in which both parties have been divided on Europe but is often explained in terms of its island location, its worldwide links to its former empire, its cultural links to the superpower with which it shares a common language and its experience in the Second World War where it was the only European state involved to emerge without having experienced occupation and with its state institutions intact and perceived to be successful.

But it is not just *recent* historical experience that leaves traces. It has been suggested[129] that attitudes to integration can vary in function of:

- participation of a country or region in past European systems notably the Roman, Carolingian, Holy Roman or Habsburg empires;
- Catholicism, which fosters the notion of allegiance to an authority beyond the state, whereas several Protestant churches are state churches;
- being part of 'city-belt' Europe (most of Germany, northern Italy, Benelux, Alsace-Lorraine and Burgundy) – a concept developed by Rokkan in examining the emergence of trading cities from the end of the feudal period;
- having had an extensive empire turning attention and trade and cultural links away from Europe.

These deep-rooted differences in cultural attitudes, combined with different experiences connected to military conflicts in the past few centuries, (including war, independence struggles, occupation and resistance), and also combined with differences in how current problems affect each country mean that Member States' underlying attitudes to European integration are unlikely to even themselves out in a foreseeable future. Even if cultural differences were not so varied, there is no certainty that there would be greater convergence of national attitudes, as the example of the Central American integration process demonstrates. Here, countries speaking the same language and sharing a similar culture and history, display quite different attitudes to integration. Even when these factors converge, the divergence arising from separate political systems, conflicting legal developments and different electoral timetables cannot be ignored. Nor can the vested interests of national bureaucracies.

Thus, any particular stage in the integration process is unlikely to find Member States equally disposed to moving forward. If unanimity is required, then reluctant states will need to be persuaded, cajoled, compensated or bypassed. Intergovernmental bargaining will be crucial at such junctures.

A PRELIMINARY SYNTHESIS?

With the benefit of half a century of hindsight, we have seen how the various theoretical approaches to European integration have all risen and fallen in credibility in various periods, how they all seem to capture some aspects of reality or of what some substantial actors would like reality to be. Yet they cover an enormous spectrum:

Intergovernmentalism:	National governments are/should be the key actors. They remain in control and all significant decisions are taken by them.
Interdependence theory:	Governments have lost their dominant position to a system of diffuse interdependence where they share power with a variety of other actors.
Neofunctionalism:	This will lead to a new government-type power at European level.
Federalists:	Not without a constitutional framework and deliberate legal transfers of sovereignty.
Constituent federalists:	This would best be done by creating democratically a clear framework in one go, with a constitution allowing flexibility but avoiding the blockages and half-measures characterized by gradual integration.

The pace and the nature of European integration has depended crucially on the attitude of the various Member States to the process. Just as the various academic theories of European integration cover a wide spectrum, so do the perceptions of the Member States as to what the process is about. It is arguable that the history of European integration since the creation of the ECSC can best be seen as a process of virtually uninterrupted negotiation[130] among the Member States on the fun-

damental structure of the Community in which successive compromises
have been reached between proponents of federalism, supporters of
intergovernmentalism and those who are simply content to find ways
of managing economic, ecological and, increasingly, political interdependence. The outcomes have been compromises between states but
also in effect, between the different theoretical schools, reflecting –
and affecting – the relative strength of each, though with the need for
unanimity providing an in-built minimalist bias.

Initially, there can be no doubt that the ECSC was set up by a determined federalist push. Neither interdependence models nor
neofunctionalism can explain why, in a context of intense discussions
about the future organization of the continent following the Second
World War, the Six broke away from the new Council of Europe framework and set up, in an area of high political sensitivity, the ECSC as
a 'first step toward a European federation'. There is no doubt as to the
deliberate, political and constitutional nature of this act, and that an
institutional system with unprecedented federal-type features was being set up for the first time in Europe.

But if they were willing to go so far, why did the Six not immediately go further? The move had to be capable of being ratified in France,
where there was no guarantee that a proposal for a fully-fledged federation, covering all main sectors, would be ratified. Unlike the other
five original Member States, where more far-reaching proposals would
probably have obtained a majority, this was not the case in France.
Monnet's proposal to proceed on a step-by-step and sectoral basis offered better prospects.

None the less, the initial step was, as we have seen, ambitious. It
was also envisaged that the steps would follow each other relatively
quickly. Negotiations on the Defence Community began before the ink
was dry on the ECSC Treaty. The Political Community was not far
behind. The ratification of the Defence Community treaty by most of
the Six states shows how far and how fast they were willing to move
in a federal direction. But its rejection by the French National Assembly showed how justified the fears of French reluctance had been, and
how a single state could hold back the process.

Once the Community framework had been set up, and broadened by
the EEC Treaty, its further constitutional development depended on
how far the more reticent Member States could be persuaded by the
more integrationist majority to move forward. Among the original Six,
it was France which, for internal reasons, was the most reticent. It was
France, accordingly, which governed the pace of integration. Had France

been more forthcoming, the constitutional system would have developed more quickly.

Post-1973, in the enlarged Community, Britain and Denmark and, on occasion (or at least on some issues) Greece and Ireland reinforced and later overtook France as leaders of the minimalist approach. The accession of Spain and Portugal helped strengthen the integrationist camp, though with each additional Member State there is an increase in the number of sectoral issues which may cause difficulties, and an increase in the number of actors whose agreement is needed for decisions requiring unanimity.

Neofunctionalist theories of spillover, linkage and *engrenage* go some way to explain how the Community continued to develop despite having opponents of far-reaching integration in crucial positions in its Member States. It is, after all, remarkable that in the first 32 years of the EEC, 11 saw de Gaulle in power in France and another 11 saw Thatcher in power in Britain. The 10 years in between these two 'dramatic-political actors' were dominated by the oil and monetary crises and the first enlargement of the Community. Yet the integration process moved on, partly because the framework had a number of particular features that enabled neofunctionalist-type processes to take place. These features were the particular legal and institutional system, and the central objective of a common market. The legal system, with the particular role of the Court, meant that entrenchment was greater and there was scope for judicial interpretation of the treaties. The institutional system, containing a Commission (and later an elected Parliament), meant that there were supranational actors, interplaying with national and subnational ones, and reinforcing the processes of integration. The feature of the common market meant that the central policy area was a large one, spilling over into many others. It would not encapsulate quickly, but would generate further pressure for integration.

A process of functional and political spillover therefore took place even if it took longer than many had initially predicted. It took place, however, within the limits of the constitutional space provided. Policies developed and expanded, the institutions did likewise, Community spending increased, until the limits of what was possible within the treaties was reached. Even with generous interpretation, the treaties were a constitutional limit, beyond which development became more difficult. But reaching these limits helped generate the pressure for a new constitutional revision, and a new negotiation, starting at a higher level than the previous one, with new pressures for reforms. Such reforms might include extensions of scope, but would increasingly move on to questions of level – as common policies became more significant, the capacity of the EC to manage them effectively needed to increase. This in turn raised further constitutional questions concerning accountability and democratic control.

It is possible to construct a simplified model of this pattern:

Initial structure and common policies established → increased objective interdependence → an increase in common decision-taking → new problems requiring more integration → more powers being exercised jointly through the central institutions → involvement of a greater number of actors and interests → growing perception of suboptimal solutions caused by the need for unanimity (lowest common denominator or the need to 'pay off' individual states) → pressure for more effective decision-taking (e.g. majority voting, stronger Commission) → constitutional negotiations (IGC) → greater capacity for decision-taking → pressures to democratize decision-taking → further constitutional negotiations.

Thus, after the initial establishment of the ECSC, the first IGCs dealt largely with extension of scope, the ECSC already having stretched the interpretation of its own scope to the limit (e.g. spilling over to transport of coal and steel, but not able to spill over into atomic energy). The EEC and EAEC Treaties expanded the area of Community activity considerably. The Fouchet Plan negotiations sought to introduce the areas of foreign policy and culture into the field of activity albeit at a lower level. With the 1965 Merger Treaty, the 1970 and 1975 Budget Treaties, the EC turned to constitutional aspects of how to manage its existing scope of activities, achieving improvements in its institutional capacity. The SEA and the TEU dealt with both scope and level, with questions of the Community's capacity to act effectively (majority voting in Council, powers of the Commission) featuring prominently in the negotiations. These four treaties also had to address the issue of democratic accountability of the by now large scope of budgetary and legislative activity – an issue kept to the fore both by the federalists (not least in the EP) and by opponents of European integration.

This description might seem to imply that there is a 'conveyor-belt to federalism' but this conveyor-belt can easily be stopped by any one of the Member States. The Community's history is full of instances where a single national actor has caused the process to come to a halt, or slowed it down for many years (rejection of the EDC treaty, de Gaulle's empty chair crisis, etc.) and others where a similar situation very nearly arose. This can be done for a variety of motives, from temporary internal political difficulties to principled defence of national sovereignty. This fact has caused some theorists to describe national governments as 'gatekeepers', deciding what goes into the Community arena and what does not. However, neofunctionalist pressures have ensured that the gatekeepers have faced a whole crowd of issues seeking to get past them. Furthermore, the gate is kept collectively by several gatekeepers who disagree on what should be let through. Even though the requirements for unanimity impose a high threshold for getting past the gate, the combination of the large numbers seeking to pass and the disagreements among the gatekeepers ensures that the gate is, from time to time, ajar.

Crucially, the need for unanimity is no absolute guarantee for a minority opposed to further integrative development. On the one hand, the need for give-and-take in the life of the Community generally and in IGCs too makes some flexibility likely. On the other hand, if an unduly rigid position were taken, it remains conceivable that the majority might decide to proceed without the minority. This is what laid the basis for the ECSC vis-à-vis the Council of Europe and, as we shall see, other situations making this a potential option were to arise again. In such cases, the minority might prefer to compromise rather than to be left behind. Although bias in an IGC is towards the lowest common denominator, and most IGCs would have produced a far more integrative result had they been able to decide by a majority, the degree of cohesion of the integrative majority when faced with a recalcitrant minority is crucial to the dynamics of negotiation. Such an integrative group continues to exist. French Foreign Minister de Charrette stated on 26 June 1996: 'There exists a circle of countries subscribing fully to the objective of the Preamble of the Treaty of Rome of creating an ever-close union of its members. This is the group of countries which can identify a federative European project. . . . These countries do not define themselves by size or wealth or by their economical budgetary performances or their seniority in the Community. . . . The only criterion is . . . the deepening of their common commitment to the European project . . .'[131]

Already at the beginning when the ECSC was established, the fact that a group of states went ahead without the others proved crucial. As François Duchêne has pointed out: 'Without that, nothing would have happened. The decisiveness of the minority soon proved the locomotive for the rest. Most countries joined later for fear of being marginalized and loosing influence.'[132] If it could be done once, it could be done again.

Thus, an initial federalist-type constitutional settlement provided the space in which neofunctionalist-type processes could develop. Those processes can themselves take the Community further down the road to integration, but not much beyond the limits set by the previous constitutional settlement. They can, however, help generate the pressures that will lead to a revision of such settlements. In such revisions, the bottom line is always the compromise emerging from the need for unanimity in intergovernmental conferences. At such junctures, other pressures – strategic, domestic – are crucial. The intergovernmentalists are at their strongest at this point, but until now, most IGCs or similar negotiations have produced results, as even the most reticent governments have not wanted to pay the political and diplomatic price of total isolation, which might also have internal political repercussions.

Having examined the main theoretical approaches to European integration and established a preliminary synthesis which draws on the gradual constitutional-federalist and the neofunctionalist approaches in particular, it is now time to turn to the European Parliament, and to examine how this body affects both the on-going neofunctional type of day-to-day development of the EC and the more fundamental constitutional development.

2 What to Expect of the European Parliament?

Relatively little attention was paid to the European Parliament in large swathes of integration literature prior to, or even in the years following, direct elections. Webb, for instance, makes only one reference to the Parliament in her review of integration theories (and then only to say that no change is expected).[1] George ignores it in his 'European Integration in Theory and Practice',[2] as does Taylor in his own review of European integration theory.[3]

Committed intergovernmentalists tended to oppose the introduction of direct elections. Debré, de Gaulle's first prime minister, argued even after his election to the EP in the first elections that 'intergovernmental cooperation must lie at the base of the European idea' and 'the dreamers' should recognize that only sovereign national institutions 'built on a foundation of thorough, sincere and repeatedly affirmed consent [can] govern men'.[4] Less dogmatic intergovernmentalists and many interdependence theorists might simply have 'comforted themselves by the belief that without a substantial further extension of parliamentary powers, the decision [to hold direct elections] carries merely symbolic weight'.[5]

Neofunctionalist writers tended to concentrate more on the Commission as the focus of supranational development, or else subsumed the Parliament and the MEPs into their general analysis of how actors and interest groups adapt their behaviour and attitudes. Haas did address some of the issues in his classic *The Uniting of Europe*,[6] in a chapter entitled 'Supranational Political Parties', by which he meant the Political Groups in the ECSC Assembly. Although Haas was sceptical as regards the usefulness of early direct elections, as 'voter ignorance' would magnify 'the voices of local pressure groups hostile to integration', he did highlight two reasons why MEPs would be 'crucial actors on the stage of integration'. First, they would 'deliberately and self-consciously seek to create a federal Europe by prescribing appropriate policies' and 'stimulating the conclusion of new treaties looking towards further integration'. Second, they would further 'the growth of practices and codes of behaviour typical of federations'.

As regards the first role, he felt that the ECSC Assembly already, was a 'supranational parliamentary lobby putting pressure for more integration on the six governments'. Although much of its routine work took 'place in a vacuum' its 'long-range role' was in establishing 'supranational communications channels'.[7] As regards the second role, he felt that

> the truly vital development is the growth of a code of conduct considered appropriate to supranational legislations: the right to be continually consulted by executive agencies, to put forward programmes not clearly previously declared to be national policy and to organize . . . on the basis of opinions and convictions developed . . . with ideologically kindred but nationally different colleagues.

Thus, he attached importance to the development of the Assembly's powers of control[8] (developing the perception and habit of typical executive-legislative relations at the European level), to the 'mere fact that [MEPs] develop into the European parliamentary élite' (developing policies themselves, which might be taken up nationally, rather than vice versa) and to the development of the Political Groups (replacing national divisions with ideological ones). Indeed, he considered the Groups/parties to be 'far more crucial carriers of political integration than even supranationally organized interest groups', and the behaviour of the EP's Groups to be 'a more cogent source of materials for the analysis of community formation processes than the immediate decisions of "the other institution or national governments"'.[9]

Haas alluded (in a footnote) to the development of European party structures *outside* Parliament, as opposed to the Groups *inside*. He reported on the creation of an organization of ECSC Socialist Parties as an intended means 'to reassert national control over their deputies' when national parties 'began to be concerned over the freedom enjoyed by their respective delegations'. However,

> so dependent is this organization on the expertise of supranational officials that it made the Secretary of the ECSC Socialist Group its chief administrative official. While the initial purpose of the step was to increase national party control, its implications may well be the overcoming of the schism between the Common Assembly and the national parliaments'.[10]

Such an analysis could apply with greater pertinence in the context of the elected EP. In these early reflections of Haas we see the essence of what remains the thrust of the neofunctionalist expectations of the

EP. To neofunctionalists, the importance of the EP – elected or nominated – was in developing habits of behaviour at the supranational level, enabling political parties to organize and focus activities at that level, substituting national divisions with transnational ideological ones, providing a channel of communication and developing a body with an interest in further integration. However, neofunctionalists did not attach great importance to direct elections as such. Their focus on élite bargaining and gradual shifting of interest group expectations and actions did not predispose them to seeing a legitimizing role in direct elections, and they even saw potential dangers in them.

Federalists, on the other hand, tended to support direct elections. As we saw in chapter 1, federalists gave considerable importance to the elected Parliament. Nevertheless, opinion varied enormously among the federalists about the timing of direct elections and their effect on the integration process. Although there was consensus that the institutional structure of the federation must include an elected chamber, opinion diverged as to whether this should be instituted only once a federal system was achieved, or whether it could be a part of the process of getting there.

The constituent federalists were especially keen on an elected Parliament being given the task of drawing up a European constitution. But some of them were reticent about the desirability of electing a Parliament unless it was given that task from the outset. Spinelli, in the early 1960s, felt that the Dehousse proposals of the Parliament, which envisaged direct elections without linking them to any change in Parliament's powers, were positively dangerous in 'putting in motion a gigantic European electoral machine to elect an assembly endowed merely with consultative powers'.[11] For Chiti-Batelli, a Parliament without a strong interlocutor in the form of an executive from which it could take power was unlikely to progress or to achieve anything. Direct elections would therefore only make sense if the Parliament were given the role of a constituent assembly to design a European system of government.[12]

Some gradualist federalists were equally reticent, arguing that it was pointless and indeed dangerous to ask the electorate to turn out to elect a largely consultative body. Direct elections should take place only if they were preceded by or linked to an increase in the EP's powers. For Morand, in the period in which the Member States 'are permanently reinforcing their position in the structure of the Communities', it would be an 'aberration to implant a parliamentary institution'. There would 'be a radical incompatibility between a parliament and a classic international structure'. Predicting a turnout of under 25 per cent, he felt that 'the European voter would soon discover that real power remains in the hands of the States and not of the body he has been invited to choose'.[13] For Goriely, direct elections represented the 'illusion that a representative parliamentary assembly with a certain popular legitimacy could in itself develop the energy, the authority and the power that its creators denied it'.[14] He pointed to the long list of parliaments which collapsed in front of more powerful authorities in the nineteenth and early twentieth centuries.

Mansholt, former President of the Commission, asked whether 'it is really desirable to organize elections to a parliament without powers?' He predicted that the second direct elections would be a disaster once the electorate realized that they were electing a body powerless to achieve anything.[15] Even Brugmans,[16] whilst arguing that direct elections offered certain opportunities, admitted that 'he had not always been favourable to direct elections, in the current circumstances'. He argued that the first need was to create a strong European executive, and then to establish a parliament to control it. For Goossens, parliaments were generally held in low esteem by the public, and the election of a parliament at European level was not the best way of relaunching the European idea.[17]

This reticence had a long pedigree. As far back as the Hague Congress in 1948 where the federalists obtained majority support for the creation of an Assembly at European level, only a small minority supported directly electing that body in the immediate. When the ECSC was created, the authors of the Treaty, although responding to pressure from the Parliamentary Assembly of the Council of Europe and the French National Assembly in favour of envisaging the eventual election of that body, none the less gave it a minimal role fearing that 'its members would be merely the spokesmen of national interests towards the independent and supranational higher authority'.[18]

For other federalists, however, the election of the Parliament would be the *starting point* for an increase in its powers. For Vedel,

> The birth act of Europe will be signed only the day when European elections by direct universal suffrage take place, the rest can follow: the extension of the powers of the Parliament and the constitution of an executive . . . but we must start with elections'.[19]

For Teitgen,

> as soon as it is elected, the Assembly will have the means and the procedures to relaunch (European integration). It will be able to insist

from the Commission and the Council that they debate with it the major problems of the Community. . . . Harassed by an Assembly, which, in its resolutions, will be expressing itself in the name of universal suffrage, the Council will not be able to avoid responding'.[20]

Thus, direct elections would in themselves confer a new 'democratic legitimacy' on the Parliament and *ipso facto* increase its role and authority. Rifflet went so far as to say that he 'would like to see what any national authority replies to a parliamentarian who paraphrases Mirabeau and says "I am here through the will of the people"'. For Spénale, President of the Parliament from 1976 to 1977, 'a Parliament elected by universal suffrage, because it would have a greater political weight, would obtain greater powers in the interinstitutional dialogue than those of the current Assembly'.[21] For Sasse, it was necess-ary for the Community, in order to develop, to be based on 'the same institutional characteristics as dominate the exercise of public authority in the States'.[22] It would, according to him, 'be impossible to refuse to the Community what goes without saying in the States' and that, once directly elected, the 'Assembly could more easily pressure the governments'. For Willy Brandt, it would be a 'permanent constituent'.[23]

The legitimacy of an elected Parliament was also perceived to be in the political interests of the Commission. As Schwed, Director in the Commission responsible for relations with the Parliament, pointed out: 'It is through its relations with the European Parliament that the Commission gives a political dimension to its actions' and that it is through its political responsibility to Parliament that 'the Commission can be considered as a political institution'.[24] This was likely to be reinforced with a directly elected Parliament. Clearly, the Commission saw Parliament as an ally, and would be likely to support increased Parliament powers *vis-à-vis* the Council, but more reticent to accept increased Parliament powers *vis-à-vis* itself.

When it came to describing precisely how Parliament would achieve or use this greater authority, most writers remained imprecise. Was it simply that the Council and the Commission could be expected to bow before the will of the Parliament now that it represented the will of the people? Some appeared to think so, but others were sceptical.

Of those holding a more optimistic view, some felt that the election process itself would overcome the 'publicity gap' and provide a basis for popular support for European unification. For Rey, former Commission President, the elections would be the 'motor' of European unification. The mobilization of the electorate would bring European integration out of the domain of a few specialists, involve public debate and support, and make it impossible for governments to ignore the Parliament.[25] Thus, the elections would be a 'driving force' for constitutional transformation.[26] Some felt they would force political parties to organize[27] and develop medium- to long-term policies and strategies at European level. For Rifflet, the elections in themselves would provoke debates *within* every political party between those more and less supportive of Europe, and presumably the future MEPs would be in a stronger position within their parties.

Helen Wallace pointed to the elections marking a 'watershed' in the 'political development' of the Community, as

> the mere fact of the election being held at all is an event of considerable significance, precisely because the member governments have accepted that the EC are qualitatively different from any other international organization to which they belong.[28]

She pointed to direct elections being one of a number of factors politicizing the EC in a way that contradicted those who thought EC cooperation 'would consist of joint positions on a limited range of those issues that lay far from the core of politics'.

However, she felt that 'a new constitutional settlement for the EC is unlikely in the near future',[29] pointing out that 'there is enormous resistance . . . to any explicit extension of the Parliament's powers'.

She was not alone in expressing this pessimism. Nord and Taylor, both senior Parliament officials, felt that the new Parliament would remain 'much the same'.[30] Given the difficulties in increasing Parliament's powers, they felt able to 'forecast with some confidence that it will be using its existing powers more fully, rather than seeking new ones'. They pointed to the fact that two national parliaments – France and UK – had enacted legislation expressly prohibiting increases in the powers of the EP without their specific approval,[31] Writing in the mid-1970s, Steed warned that in countries where the electorate is used to elections producing tangible results as regards the government, the absence of such a link in European elections would make the electoral stake unclear. Especially if conducted through separate national electoral procedures and with national media arrangements, they could easily degenerate into series of mid-term tests of the national governments with large anti-government swings and low turnouts. This would not enhance the EP's position, and especially not with national governments.[32]

A few commentators pointed to the key aspect of professionalization. For Mary Robinson, a crucial new element was that MEPs would be 'full-time, with good documentation services, in a word, real professionals, which would allow the Parliament to gain real powers'.[33] She also felt that the Commission would use a strong and directly elected Parliament to pressure the Council in the numerous cases where the latter lacked the political will to take decisions, a point developed further by Louis:

> a Parliament of professionals whose primary allegiance will be European. In other words, political activity within the European Parliament will no longer be based on travellers essentially preoccupied with national tasks, but people who will, above all else be Members of the new Assembly,[34]

Similarly, Helen Wallace pointed out that 'the new European parliamentarians will have a vested interest in making the Parliament relevant',[35] a view shared by the then Secretary General of the Parliament, Nord, who said that 'the new Parliament will have one supremely important asset, namely that for the first time, Members will depend exclusively on making a success of the Parliament'.[36] Reif *et al.*, in their study of attitudes of 'middle level party élites' (i.e. delegates to party conferences of 39 national parties from 1978 to 1980), concluded that the new 'Eurospecialists' within parties (MEPs, staff, delegates to European party federation congresses) would be likely to have a 'pivotal role' in interacting with these middle-élites. They found a high degree of passive support for European integration among these élites, e.g. 'at least 75 per cent support the election of the Commission President by the Parliament', but a far smaller number consider this to be important – it had never been a 'hot political issue'.[37] The creation of a body of active politicians with a strong interest in pushing such an issue could make a crucial difference.

The opposite view was expressed by retiring MEP, Lord Bruce, who argued that the nominated Parliament had power and influence because its members were also members of national parliaments where they exercised some leverage over their governments. Without this asset the elected Parliament would be ignored by the Council.[38]

The prospect of professionalization and the creation of a European political class led the Danish government to request that all MEPs should be holders of a dual mandate, i.e. that candidates in the European elections would have to be members of their national parliament. In the absence of support for this, it requested a derogation for Denmark allowing it to impose such a requirement nationally, but this too was not accepted by its partners.

For Rey, it was not so much the specialist professionalism, but the prospect of prominent national leaders sitting in the EP (Brandt and Mitterrand had already announced their intention to stand) that would lend it an authority which could not be ignored.

Most felt it would be up to the new elected MEPs to fight for more powers – but for which ones? The Tindemans Report had been cautious in this regard, but had pointed the way towards involving Parliament in the choice of the President of the Commission and in giving Parliament a right of legislative initiative. Such caution was widespread in the years prior to direct elections, lest the prospect of increased powers jeopardize the ratification of the European Elections Act in Denmark, the UK and France (where the Gaullists opposed it from within the government). The EP itself had shelved a report it was drafting on the subject.[39] Nevertheless, most of the literature at the time, and most of Parliament's own thoughts, envisaged mainly a development of its existing powers, notably:

- making use of its new budgetary powers by redefining the categories of expenditure over which it had the final say and by using its right to create new items in the budget;
- developing its role in the legislative procedure by applying the conciliation procedure wherever Council and Parliament diverge and by obliging the Commission to withdraw any proposals specifically rejected by Parliament;
- recognizing a right of initiative by Parliament;
- subjecting the appointment of the President of the Commission to its approval and reinforcing his role in the choice of the rest of the Commission;
- enlarging its right to appeal to the Court of Justice;
- giving it equal rights with Council for the approval of international agreements.

Significantly, at least the first four items on this 'shopping list' could conceivably be achieved without Treaty amendment.

Despite the wide range of views, the prevailing mood in the 1970s is best summed up by Vedel:

> One might perhaps question the value of the Parliament's playing a major role in promoting integration. ... but in the present circumstances it happens that the other paths to European integration have been blocked. ... When all the paths so far explored are blocked, one is compelled to try new, hitherto unexplored ways.[40]

Thus, a broad body of European opinion favoured direct elections without knowing where it would lead them. It was truly a 'journey to an unknown destination'.

PARTY ATTITUDES PRIOR TO THE FIRST DIRECT ELECTIONS

How did the political parties envisage the development of the EP? The involvement of national parties in European-wide cooperative structures was still in an embryonic stage prior to the first European elections, but those elections themselves forced them to intensify their cooperation within these frameworks and to attempt to draw up common manifestos. Here again, we can see an enormous divergence.

The Christian Democrats established a federal party structure at EC level in 1978 in view of direct elections, replacing their previous, looser form of cooperation. Called the European People's Party (EPP), it portrayed itself as *the* party of European unity both for reasons of principle and for electoral appeal. Its literature frequently referred to Adenauer, Schuman and de Gasperi as the founding fathers of Europe (conveniently forgetting non-Christian Democrats, such as Monnet and Spaak). It sought either to initiate or be closely involved with all integration proposals.

In the political programme adopted at the EPP's first Congress in March 1978,[41] it envisaged that 'in the transitional period leading up to political union and economic and monetary union' it was 'crucially important for the Community to move towards the establishment of a single Community decision-making centre' (a euphemism for government/executive, taken from the Tindemans Report). The directly elected Parliament was expected 'to provide a new constitutional and institutional impetus for the achievement of European Union and progress towards a European federation, the ultimate political aim of unification'. Besides a fuller exploitation of the existing treaties, the EPP advocated more powers for the EC institutions so that they could cope with present responsibilities and prepare 'for the transition to the next phase of the process of European integration, the achievement of European Union as described in the Tindemans Report'. Such new powers were a 'central aim' to be achieved in the EP's first term of office. They were to be sought 'on the basis of proposals submitted by the Commission in agreement with the European Parliament'. The EPP called for the European Council to 'stimulate and encourage European unification by defining the various stages involved'. For its part the Commission was called to be 'the motive force behind European unification' and to 'become much less technocratic'.[42]

It would appear that the Christian Democrats expected initiatives for more radical proposals to be left to the European Council and the Commission, the European Parliament merely providing an 'impetus'. Despite their federalist aims for a final political union, they appeared to aim in the immediate at a fuller exploitation of the existing treaties.

The Liberals were also committed to a European Union. Their 'Programme for Europe', adopted by the ELD Congress in November 1977, provided a detailed account of their vision. European Union was not to be a 'reincarnation of the nation state at European level' but an 'original' institutional structure. The directly elected EP was to be one element of that structure and had five main tasks to accomplish during its first mandate: (1) devising a proportional European electoral system; (2) continuing its efforts to improve the distribution of powers between the EC institutions; (3) insisting on rational decisions concerning their location; (4) drawing up a declaration of human and civil rights of the European citizen, and (5) 'the drawing up of a draft treaty setting up a European Union'.[43] Their proposals were thus more specific than those of the EPP but not incompatible.

None of the other party groupings was able to adopt agreed programmes on these issues. The cohesion of the Confederation of Socialist Parties of the EC (CSP) was at that time weakened by diverging attitudes to integration. National parties failed to approve a draft common election manifesto prepared by the CSP and the 1979 campaign was conducted on the basis of national manifestos. They did approve a common 'Appeal to the Electorate',[44] in which they stated that 'the directly elected European Parliament must initially develop within the framework of the existing treaties. We recognize that any further transfer of powers from national governments to the Community institutions or from national parliaments to the European Parliament can take place only with the clear and direct assent of the national governments and parliaments'.[45] An examination of national party programmes reveals the divisions which existed.

In Belgium, the PS manifesto stated that the European Parliament elections 'will open the way to an extension of its powers and competences ... by a revision of the treaties ... culminating in the transformation of this Assembly into a genuine legislative body ...' The Flemish SP took a similar line, arguing that 'no important decision should be taken without the agreement of Parliament'.[46]

The German SPD had a long history of support for direct elections, which it had sought to initiate unilaterally in Germany, in a Bundestag Bill in 1962–3. It had confirmed its commitment to a 'federal European Union, with a democratic constitution' at its 1977 Hamburg Congress.[47] Its Manifesto for the European elections repeated this objective and called for the EP's powers to be increased to allow it to amend any part of the EC budget, to pass Bills, to require its approval for any treaty changes and to appoint the Members of the Commission on a proposal of the Council.[48]

The Italian Socialist parties' manifestos reflected their strong support – traditional in the case of the PSDI, more recent in the case of the PSI – for integration, heralding direct elections as a crucial step forward. The PSDI used the CSP 'Appeal to the Electorate' as its national manifesto, as did the Luxembourg socialists, the latter appending a short statement of their own reconfirming their view of a 'federal Europe of the future' but cautious about the effect of direct elections, calling them an 'advance', but considering that the EP could not 'speed up the process of unification'.[49] The Dutch PvdA's 'European Policy Programme' criticized the EP's lack of powers and called for it to have full budgetary powers and to 'have the decisive vote in the appointment of Members of the Commission'. However, the party's Youth Section called for abstentions in the elections on the grounds that the EP lacked any powers to fulfil voters' aspirations.[50]

In the French PS, the situation was complex. They had been in opposition for nearly 20 years, were in an electoral alliance with the Communists, and attitudes to Europe had cooled. The left-wing CERES faction developed an anti-integration line not dissimilar to that of the 'anti-marketeers' in the British Labour Party. The party as a whole tended to criticize the EC as capitalist, even if the need for European integration was recognized. The party's Comité Directeur voted 97:34 in favour of direct elections. Mitterrand spoke of the elections giving the EP 'the authority and prestige of which it is now deprived and will clearly establish in public opinion the European idea which up to now has been fuzzy'.[51] A manifesto for the European elections was published in October 1978 which spoke of the need for democratic control and for the EP to exert control over directives that now escape national parliaments.[52] Yet this support for developing the Parliament was put into question on the eve of the first elections at the party's Metz Congress in April 1979. Rivalry between Rocard and Mitterrand in view of the presidential nomination for 1981 had led to a situation in which Mitterrand was able to maintain his majority in the party only by allying with the CERES faction. As a result, the tone of the party's resolution was far more reticent:

> Although favourable . . . to the reinforcement of the powers of control of the European Assembly, the Socialist Party does not intend to see the competence of this Assembly expanded at the expense of national parliaments. There is no way that the present Common Market – the market of big capital interests – can be acceptable to us'.[53]

In Denmark, the Social Democrats split in the Folketing vote on the direct elections legislation. The party congress of 1977 stated they did not believe in 'changes of the institutions or relocation of competence between the institutions'. The 1979 European election manifesto stated that the party 'rejects a supranational development of the EC in the direction of a real political union'.[54]

The British Labour Party was badly split over European elections. Two days after the Labour government signed the EC Act on direct elections, the party conference rejected the principle by 4 million to 2.2 million votes, not enough to make it automatically a policy for the party manifesto, but a clear indication of the trend. The manifesto drawn up for the 1979 European elections specified that Labour was 'firmly opposed to any extension of [Parliament's] powers' and that it would seek to amend the treaties to recognize the right of the national parliaments to have the final say on EC legislation in their countries.

The Irish Labour Party was the only Socialist Party of the three new Member States to support direct elections and their manifesto suggested increasing the EP's budgetary powers, and granting it a right of legislative initiative and a say in the appointment of the Commission.[55]

Thus, the bulk of Socialist Parties in Europe favoured further integration, saw direct elections as a step forward, and supported an increase in the powers of the European Parliament. In the nine Member States at the time, only the British Labour Party, the Danish Social Democrats and a proportion of the French socialists did not share this view.

Apart from these three political families organized as such at European level, the positions of some other parties not so organized is worth noting. The British Conservatives, in their manifesto, considered that no case presently existed 'for any major increase in the powers of the Parliament'. A strong case nevertheless existed for 'a number of practical improvements in the way Parliament's existing powers were exercised'.[56]

The Communists were split. The Italian Communist Party argued in favour of treaty revision to provide an effective framework for dealing with the problems facing the EC. In the interest of a democratic rather than a 'bureaucratic or technocratic' Community, they supported an increase in the EP's powers.[57] In the words of their Group Chairman, Amendola,

> if the majority in the Assembly wants to extend its powers, if influential members of national parties take up seats in it, capable of bringing strong influence to bear on the transformation of the Community, the process of active integration will proceed with greater chances of success.[58]

By contrast, the French Communists had always defended national sovereignty and opposed any increases in the EP's powers or moves towards supranationality.[59]

The French Gaullists (RPR) and the Irish Fianna Fáil Party, who sat in the same EP Group, took a less supranational view of Europe than the Christian Democrats, echoing de Gaulle's intergovernmental concept of 'l'Europe des patries'. They opposed increasing Parliament's powers.

Thus, party attitudes to further integration, to the principle of direct elections, and to the future development of the EP were diverse. Support for Community reform was potentially large, but disparate. The EPP, the ELD and most Socialists were committed to take initiatives within the elected Parliament, but the question remained whether they could work together, agree a strategy or rally wider support.

HYPOTHESIS FOR TESTING

We saw in chapter 1 the tremendous variety in the approaches to European integration itself and in this chapter the diversity in expectations regarding the elected Parliament. It is also notable that the spectrum of views on the Parliament did not fit neatly into that on integration, either in terms of the desirability of introducing direct elections in the circumstances of the late 1970s or in terms of the likely development of the Parliament itself.

Let us re-examine the range of expectations that we have encountered, but express them in terms of hypothesis, starting from the most 'pessimistic' from an integration point of view and finishing with more 'optimistic' ones, though the progression cannot be strictly linear.

1. That the directly elected Parliament cannot achieve anything as only national authorities have the necessary legitimacy and power. It will remain purely symbolic (view held by many intergovernmentalists).

2. The elections therefore will produce nationalist whiplash (view held by many intergovernmentalists and some neofunctionalists).

3. The elections will achieve little public interest with a low turnout and national issues dominating (view held by some writers of all schools of thought, in particular if EP not given more powers first to choose executive/to act as a constituent/to adopt legislation).

4. The elected MEPs will have less influence than the nominated ones who were members of their national parliaments (various).

5. The elected Parliament will be much the same as before (various).

6. The elected Parliament will carry greater weight, authority and legitimacy simply by virtue of being directly elected and this will in itself lead to Council and Commission following its recommendations (some gradual federalists).

7. The elected Parliament will be more effective simply by virtue of being full-time and professional (some federalists and neo-functionalists). This in particular will lead to:

   (a) the EP being an important 'lobby' for integration and institutional reform (gradual federalists and some neofunctionalists).
   (b) the development of European parliamentary practices, habits and networks (neofunctionalists).

8. The elections and the activities of the elected Parliament will stimulate the development of transnational political parties, which will in turn be a factor for integration by influencing their national components and by substituting national divisions with ideological ones (some neofunctionalists).

9. The elections themselves will stimulate public debate and interest and will mobilize public support for European unification, putting pressure on governments (some federalists).

10. The elected Parliament will force a readjustment of the balance of power among the European institutions, but without being able to obtain changes to the treaties (various neofunctionalist and interdependence theorists).

11. The elected Parliament will be able to obtain significant changes to the treaties, advancing European integration and also increasing its own powers (gradual federalists, some tactical constituent federalists and some neofunctionalists).

12. The elected Parliament will be able (or should be given powers) to act as a constituent assembly, preparing a constitution for a (federal) European Union (constituent federalists).

Clearly, many of the above hypotheses are not incompatible and some are even complementary. Some concern the dynamic of the elections themselves, whereas others address the issue of how the elected Parliament will act and what impact it will have. Furthermore, there may be interactions between the various hypotheses – MEPs might well change attitudes in function of their experience and this might lead the EP to explore avenues that it initially eschewed.

Bearing this in mind, we shall now examine the actions and the effects of the elected Parliament in order to enable us to assess the validity of the various hypotheses. However, for reasons of space, and because this has been covered by numerous other publications, we shall *not* dwell on the specific effects of the elections themselves, about which only a few brief words will be said in the next section.

Having regard to our 'preliminary synthesis' of integration theories developed at the end of chapter 1, we shall pay most attention to those hypotheses which pertain to developments at constitutional level (i.e. changes to the treaties or complementary documents), the full exploitation of the treaties and the building up of networks supportive of the integration process. We shall attempt to see whether the effect of the elected Parliament gives enhancement to the credibility of our 'preliminary synthesis'.

A FEW WORDS ABOUT THE ELECTIONS

The four elections held so far have all had some features that might give succour to the more pessimistic hypotheses mentioned above, and to the views of some intergovernmentalists, but not conclusively. *Turnout* (63 per cent in 1979, 61. per cent in 1984, 58.5 per cent in 1989 and 56.4 per cent in 1994)[60] has been relatively low compared to national elections, but not so much if compared to local elections and certainly remains higher than for federal elections (both Presidential and Congressional) in the USA. Morand's dire predictions of 25 per cent have certainly not been met, even at the lower end of the quite large spread from one Member State to another (with the UK lowest at 32.3 per cent, 32.6 per cent and 36.2 per cent in the first three elections). A European average of over 50 per cent is, perhaps, the minimum level necessary to avoid major questions of legitimacy. But MEPs cannot claim, on the basis of turnout, a legitimacy equal to that of national parliaments – to do so they must rely on the specificity of the European mandate.

As to the *character* of the campaign, there is no doubt that national issues have normally played a greater role than European ones, with Steed's prediction of them becoming a mid-term test of national governments' popularity being largely borne out. None the less, European issues have featured as well – certainly to a greater extent than in most national elections – and parties and the media, at least, have had to address European questions. To this extent, the European elections resemble local elections and the treatment of local issues in most Member States. The 'legitimacy' – always a difficult concept to measure – conferred by virtue of election is perhaps of a similar order of magnitude.

Has there been a nationalist or anti-integration whiplash on the occasion of European elections (hypothesis no. 2)? A specific anti-European movement put up candidates in Denmark, winning four (out of 16) seats in each of the European elections so far and in the 1994 elections in France an anti-Maastricht and anti-GATT list called 'Alternative Europe' gained 13 of the 87 French seats. In no other Member State has a specific anti-European movement gained seats,[61] but there have been traditional parties who have taken an anti-EC or anti-further integration positions. For instance, the Socialist People's Party in Denmark, the extreme right in a number of countries, ultra-Protestant parties in the Netherlands and in Northern Ireland, some Communist Parties and, in 1984, the British Labour Party have taken anti-EC positions, seeking the withdrawal of their country or the watering-down of the EC. While broadly accepting the EC as it stands, the French Gaullists, some Green Parties and others have stood on a platform opposing further losses of national sovereignty. Table 2.1 seeks to give an approximate idea of the number of seats gained by such parties in the nine Member States that were in the EC from the first European elections, except for the UK which is analysed separately because of its electoral system and because of the major divisions running *within* each of the main parties.

The UK requires particular treatment. In terms of political parties, it is arguable that Labour should be classified in column 3 in 1984 and possibly 1979, column 2 or even 1 in 1989 and 1996. The Conservatives were probably perceived by the electorate as supporting further integration in 1979 and opposing it in 1989 and 1994. In both cases, however, individual candidates had their own positions and even, in

Table 2.1   *Basic attitudes to European integration, according to parties, of MEPs from eight Member States*

		1 Pro-integration	2 Pro-EC, but no further integration	3 Anti-Europe
B	1979	23	1	0
	1984	22	2	0
	1989	22	1	1
	1994	21	1	3
DK	1979	6	4	6
	1984	7	3	6
	1989	7	4	5
	1994	7	5	4
F	1979	47	15	19
	1984	40	21	20
	1989	51	13	17
	1994	42	14	31
D	1979	81	0	0
	1984	74	7	0
	1989	67	8	6
	1994	87	12	0
IRL	1979	5	10	0
	1984	7	8	0
	1989	6	8	1
	1994	5	10	0
I	1979	76	0	5
	1984	75	0	6
	1989	76	0	5
	1994	71	0	16
LUX	1979	6	0	0
	1984	6	0	0
	1989	6	0	0
	1994	5	1	0
NL	1979	25	0	0
	1984	22	2	1
	1989	22	2	1
	1994	28	1	2
TOTAL	1979	269 (82%)	30 (9%)	30 (9%)
	1984	253 (77%)	43 (13%)	33 (10%)
	1989	257 (78%)	36 (11%)	36 (11%)
	1994	266 (73%)	44 (12%)	56 (15%)

Belgium: Volksunie classified in column 2, but they support 'Europe of Regions' concept. Extreme Right is in col. 3

Denmark: Socialist People's Party (until 1994); Greenland member and People's movement in column 3. Social Democrats and Progress Party in column 2, masking a range of views in these parties.

France: Socialists counted as pro-integration, although in 1979 their platform was cautious, and at each election until 1989, 2 or 3 members of anti-integration CERES faction were elected. Communists and National Front counted as anti-Europe even though they did not advocate French withdrawal from EC. Joint Gaullist-UDF lists in 1984, 1989 and 1994 are divided equally between column 1 and 2. Greens count in column 1 for rejecting Maastricht on ultra-federalists grounds, but some of their rhetoric appeals to anti-Europeans.

Germany & Luxembourg: Greens counted in column 2, masking a range of views.

Ireland: Fine Gael counted in column 1. Fianna Fáil and Greens in column 2. Labour also in 2, masking a range of views that have evolved in a pro-integration direction. Two independents (Blaney and Maher) split one each to 1 and 2. Workers's Party counted as anti-integration, PD as pro.

Italy: Extreme Right and Proletarian Democracy + Rifondazione counted as anti-European although not advocating Italian withdrawal from EC. All other parties consistently pro-integration.

Netherlands: Ultra-Calvinists in column 3. Green-Progressive alliance in column 2, masking a range of views.

many cases, campaigned on that basis in their constituency. An educated guess, erring on the side of caution in an anti-integration direction, would give the following figures for the 81 (87 in 1994) UK MEPs *as individuals* (counting SNP in column 2 and Ulster MEPs one in each column), at the time of the election (many evolved subsequently after each election):

	Pro-integration	Pro-EC, but no further integration	Anti-Europe
1979	46	23	12
1984	48	11	22
1989	58	9	14
1994	58	17	12

Even including the UK, pro-integrationists won well over 70 per cent of the seats in the first four European elections in the nine states. Concerning the three Member States which joined between 1979 and 1994, it is arguable that in the case of Greece, a large majority of MEPs were elected on an anti-EC platform in the initial election in 1981, when PASOK still opposed Greek membership of the EC. By 1989, all but five could be classified in column 1. In the case of Spain, anti-EC (column 3) MEPs numbered no more than three (on a generous definition) in either 1987 or 1989. In Portugal, the Communists won three seats in 1987 and 1994 and four in 1989 on an anti-EC platform.

Even allowing for the approximative nature of such a table, it is clear that there was no breakthrough with direct elections for anti-integration parties, except in Denmark (and France in 1994). The Danish European elections engendered a new political movement contesting only European elections. Its success entrenched it, with the four seats it won motivating its supporters and providing, through the EP itself (as we shall see) facilities and financial support that established and maintained a permanent network of activists, willing and able to seize on any European issue that would stir up anti-integration sentiment. It remained, however, a unique phenomenon, at least until 1994. As to *traditional* parties taking anti-European positions, *none* of them did conspicuously better in the European elections than they would have expected in national elections.[62]

Thus, hypothesis no. 3 would appear not to have general application at least as regards the emergence of new movements or swings in support towards established anti-integration parties. But could there have been a shift in the position of established pro-integration parties towards more cautious positions or of parties accepting the EC but opposed to further integration towards a more anti-EC position? This appears not to have been the case in Germany, Italy, the Benelux countries or Ireland. In Denmark, the UK and France, however, this effect may well have featured.

In Denmark, perhaps especially because of the anti-EC People's Movement, parties which felt that a proportion of their electoral support was vulnerable, or which were internally divided, took cautious or anti-European positions in the electoral campaigns. This was especially true of the Social Democrats (who had been divided), the Socialist People's Party (which had already been opposed to further integration) and the Progress Party (whose electorate was hostile). All became encamped on positions that may well have otherwise (without the publicity of the elections and the higher profile given to the European issue) evolved into a more European position. Similarly, in France, the Gaullists' traditional position became publicly entrenched, the Communists saw no reason to change, and the Socialists, as we have seen, became more cautious. In the UK the main parties were divided, but the salience and bitterness of the division was enhanced by virtue of the elections. To this extent, hypothesis no. 3 has an element of proof – in some parties and in some Member States, but remaining, in overall terms, a distinct minority.

What of the opposite phenomenon expressed in hypothesis no. 9? Could it be that pro-European parties, especially in government, would be obliged to take more vigorous action to live up to their professed beliefs in those countries where the electorate was generally pro-integration and might ask what was delaying European integration? Given the level of turnout and the trend towards opposition parties in many Member States, it cannot be claimed that there was an electoral stampede towards pro-integration parties. None the less, parties supporting further integration won over 80 per cent of the seats outside the UK. They were clearly not handicapped in the election. As we saw earlier, most of them had developed specific policy commitments for the election supporting further integration. They had to face the question of the slow pace of integration, the realism of their proposals and what they would do to achieve them. In this general sense, there was moderate pressure on pro-integration parties in pro-integration countries to deliver. What and how they could deliver would, inevitably, be a major preoccupation for their elected MEPs.

3 A New Political Network

The creation of a directly elected European Parliament in 1979 was not just a change in status for the MEPs. It meant that a new corps of full-time politicians was created. Unlike the nominated members in the old Parliament, these elected members were, for the most part, not simultaneously holding time-consuming national mandates. They were able to devote far more time to pursuing their European responsibilities. Their position was in most cases no longer a mere adjunct or accessory to a domestic position, but was a political position – and even a potential career – in its own right. In short, this new corps, equipped and backed up by the Parliament, appeared on the political landscape and became part and parcel of the life of Europe's political networks.

Before looking at the issue of the Parliament's powers, we shall use this chapter to examine some characteristics of the MEPs, how they fit into the political landscape, and the possibilities they have to take part in national and European level networks, at the intersection of which they are placed.

THE NATURE AND LIKELY COMMITMENT OF THE NEW MEPs

Did the fact that a new class of political creature had been brought into existence mean that its members would have a vested interest in strengthening the European Parliament, in developing European integration and in constitutional reform? As we saw in chapter 2, this was the expectation of a number of writers before direct elections, and is expressed in our hypothesis no. 7(a). After direct elections, this was also the view of, notably, Cotta, who felt that 'a political élite that is not based in national political institutions but in a supra-national institution ... has therefore a vested interest in the strengthening of the European Parliament and more broadly in the promotion of European integration.[1] Such a view is intuitively correct, in the absence of notable electoral victories for opponents of European integration, as we saw in chapter 2.

But Cotta based his theory on two conditions, both of which appear to be in doubt in the case of the EP: a degree of stability of membership over time and a degree of distinctiveness and autonomy. Would his theory remain true if the EP were to contain a large number of 'ageing party war-horses put out to grass'?[2] If there were a constantly high turnover of MEPs? Or if a large number regarded the EP merely as a stepping stone to national careers?

The elected Parliament was characterized by a high level of all three features. One sixth of the MEPs elected in 1979 had former *governmental* experience, declining slightly to 13 per cent after the 1984 elections[3] (14 per cent in 1989, 11 per cent in 1994). Of those elected in 1979 146 members (45 per cent) had national *parliamentary* experience (35 per cent in the 1984 elections, 26 per cent in the 1989 elections and 30 per cent in 1994).[4] A decline was to be expected, given that some 78 (almost 20 per cent) of the members elected in 1979 had previously been members of the nominated Parliament. Nevertheless, the proportion has remained quite high. Furthermore, Kirchner[5] found a 'strong relationship between a high level of domestic political experience and leadership role in the European Parliament', implying that former national ministers, many of whom were in the twilight of their political career, played a more important role in the EP than the average member. If so, this was not striking in terms of leadership of the main political groups from 1979 to 1984, most of whom were not former ministers, (but all of whom were former national parliamentarians), but more in terms of the Bureau and committee chairs. Kirchner found that 65 per cent of 'leadership positions' were held by former ministers in 1980.

At the opposite end of the spectrum, some (particularly younger) MEPs clearly saw the EP as a stepping stone to national politics. The danger here was that 'if MEPs had to choose between remaining in the EP and fighting for constitutional reform, or nothing, there is little doubt that they would remain and fight. But . . . they can choose to go elsewhere and membership of the Parliament can even help them to get elsewhere.'[6] How common was this? Westlake's study, although confined to the UK MEPs (initially the least experienced national delegation in the Parliament), found that 'departure for Westminster was the second most important factor for electoral turnover after electoral defeat', involving 15 of the 81 elected in 1979 – and this in a constituency-based system where moving from one Parliament to another is more problematic than in a list-based system. Furthermore, he found another 12 who tried unsuccessfully to win a Westminster seat. Even before they came to the EP, 30–40 per cent of the UK MEPs first elected in 1979, 1984 and again in 1989 had previously contested a Westminster seat.[7]

It is therefore not surprising that there is a high turnover in membership of the elected Parliament. In 1984, over 40 per cent of the members elected were new members (including more than half the French, Italian, Irish and Dutch members). In 1989, half the seats were won by new members (including more than 60 per cent of the Italian, French and Luxembourg members). Of those elected in 1989, 'with the exception of the memberships of the Federal Republic, Ireland, the Netherlands and the UK, less than 50 per cent in any Member State contingent had more than 5 years experience of the European Parliament'.[8] In 1994, the same phenomenon, combined with an increase in the size of the EP, resulted in 57 per cent of members being new. Even between elections, there was a high turnover in the early years, in particular with countries operating list systems for election where departure would not cause a by-election but merely by succession of the next member on the party's list or list of substitutes. Thus, over 5.5 per cent of members changed *every year* during the first four years of the elected Parliament,[9] though this was partly because the French Gaullist Party had promised that its first candidates elected would stand down after one year to be replaced by the following names on the list, and that the same process would be undertaken each year throughout the five-year period. Although not fully adhered to, this caused a steady turnover in membership which, in this case, was deliberately aimed at weakening the Parliament's corporate identity.

Did these three factors (of a proportion of elder statesmen virtually retired from their domestic political career, younger members more interested in moving on to national parliaments and a generally high level of turnover) weaken the Parliament's identity, its ability to function effectively and, above all, the commitment of its members to strengthening the Parliament? The evidence appears to show that, despite these weaknesses, Cotta's theory still holds. Despite the high turnover there has, of course, remained a hard core of members remaining in the Parliament for many years who, together with the secretariat and the officials, constitute the 'memory' of the Parliament and ensure that lack of experience of new MEPs does not imply that Parliament's work is constantly starting from scratch. Even if some members only remain for a short period, in terms of the Parliament as an institution it is still realistic to speak of a distinct identity.

Certainly, there is evidence of a general 'European' attitude. Van Schendelen found that only two years after direct elections, 92 per cent of Dutch MEPs considered themselves to be more 'a European parliamentarian' than a 'Dutch parliamentarian in Europe'.[10] More concretely, as we shall see in subsequent chapters, the commitment of the Parliament to institutional reform was strong and grew further. Westlake concluded his study, in which he specifically tested Cotta's theory on the British MEPs, with the conclusion that 'the figures show some, albeit very weak, behavioral evidence of Cotta's theory at work'.[11] Studying the voting records on 14 integrationist resolutions, he concluded that 'the most remarkable feature in this analysis from the point of view of Cotta's theory has been the steady decline of active opposition, accompanied by, in the first instance, a rise in abstention or absenteeism and then, in the longer term, a gentle rise in active support [for integrationist resolutions]'.

A 1996 survey by Sheffield and Nottingham Trent Universities showed a significantly more integrationist attitude displayed by Labour MEPs as compared to MPs on a range of issues.

That Cotta's theory applies despite the above handicaps is also illustrated by instances where MEPs voted in ways that demonstrate considerable independence from their national party line. This was, as we shall see in subsequent chapters, largely a matter of interpreting the party line creatively or remaining ahead of perhaps not very well defined national party positions. However, in some cases, it involved a difficult public break with the party line. The UK Conservatives, for instance, publicly disassociated themselves from the UK government's attempt to veto the 1982 farm price package, where the other Member States ultimately overrode UK opposition and adopted the package by a majority vote. The UK Conservative MEPs had urged that such a vote should take place.[12] Similarly, leading CDU MEPs recently wrote an open letter supporting the Commission against CDU ministers in Germany in a dispute over subsidies to Volkswagen,[13] and SDP MEPs criticized the anti-EMU stance taken by Lafontaine in 1995.

Conversion of MEPs from hostility or indifference to support for European integration certainly seems to have featured. Involvement in the Parliament, either because of a process of socialization or because of better acquaintance with European realities or because of career interest, appears to have helped convince a number of MEPs of the merits of European integration. Evidence can be found among the largest initial intake of Eurosceptic members, the UK Labour members: Castle,[14] Clwyd, Boyes, Adam and Rogers[15] from the 1979 intake; Martin,[16] Hoon,[17] Ford[18] and others from the 1984 intake (and preceding the party's own change in policy). A recent survey found Labour MEPs to hold more integrationist views than Labour MPs on a whole range of subjects and that, particulary since 1983, both groups were becoming more pro-European.[19]

A similar process took place among Greek PASOK members with 'the experiences of our MEPs in the Socialist Group being among the factors which led to the Party revising its position on Europe'.[20] Ove Fich, Danish Social Democrat, admits to a similar conversion.[21]

One can even consider whether the three features mentioned not only fail to undermine Cotta's theory but also constitute, in fact, *strengths* for the European Parliament. In terms of creating a political network, it is certainly no disadvantage to MEPs to have a number of former colleagues in national parliaments. Interestingly, of the eight MEPs first elected to Westminster in 1983/4 and the five elected in 1987, every single one of them has since been promoted to positions in government or on the opposition frontbench.[22] Furthermore, they have played a prominent part in European affairs: six have served on the Commons Select Committee on European legislation, several played an important role in major European debates (Clwyd in the SEA ratification debate in 1987, and Hoon in the Maastricht ratification procedure)[23] and Quinn became Labour's European affairs spokesman (and shadow minister). Some have become ministers where their European experience would be likely to have been relevant.[24] Thus, 'Strasbourg was certainly well represented in Westminster.'[25] In the words of an MEP who became a Minister: 'in senior positions in national governments, increasingly the new men are people who have served their apprenticeship in Europe and are formed by a European dimension.'[26]

The above comments (and Westlake's study) have been confined to the UK where seepage back to national politics is complicated by the constituency system and by the fact that both major British parties now frown on MEPs standing for selection as Westminster candidates. In other Member States, the osmosis between European and national politics is easier, thanks notably to the list system and, in some Member States, to the fact that ministers do not have to be MPs. Thus, in some Member States, a stint as an MEP is not infrequently a part of a political career. In France, for instance, eight of the 14 prime ministers who have held office in the Fifth Republic have, at one stage or another in their careers, been directly elected MEPs[27] (and four out of the six presidents).[28] Five out of 14 post-war Belgian prime ministers have similarly been MEPs (though only two after direct elections) and ten Italian prime ministers (six after direct elections). Indeed, by 1994, the only Member States never to have had a prime minister who has spent part of his/her political career in the EP were the UK, Ireland and Greece.

Several of these prime ministers only subsequently became MEPs. But the role of elder statesmen in the EP can also be advantageous to the Parliament. They bring with them not only considerable political experience but also a network of contacts, an ability to attract more than the average share of media attention and are household names. The former heads of government and heads of state that have sat in the European Parliament, whether or not at the end of their political careers,[29] have made major contributions to the European debate, usually in an integrative direction.

All these factors imply that MEPs are not simply an isolated political group with no links or interconnections with the rest of the political class. The osmosis with national politics has not eroded its identity, nor the commitment of the majority of MEPs to strengthening the Parliament in its own right, but has given the Parliament the added advantage of being an integral part of Europe's political network. Indeed, it is the part *par excellence* where politicians from different Member States are in regular contact. No other group of politicians in Europe is in such constant contact with colleagues from other Member States. Inevitably, exchanges of ideas between political parties of similar views, between members interested in the same issues and between the political élites generally, pass through the EP.

MEPs AND NATIONAL POLITICAL PARTIES

The bulk of members elected in 1979 were middle-ranking politicians in terms of the 'pecking order' within national political parties (though as we saw about 15 per cent were former prime ministers or ministers). None the less, it did mean that almost every main political party in Europe now contained a number of full-time politicians whose primary interest and activity concerned European affairs.

The way in which these new political creatures were integrated into the formal structure of each political party varied enormously according to the characteristics of each one and sometimes according to the party's attitude to Europe. None the less, over a period of years, virtually every political party adapted its structure to give a role to MEPs in its organs.

In the case of the two main British parties, for instance, this was achieved over a period of time, albeit in different ways, reflecting the very different structures that they have. By 1993, Conservatives MEPs were represented by three seats (out of 20) in the National Union of Conservative Associations which runs the party and party conference. They had one seat on the Board of Management (out of about ten), which handles party finances. Conservative MEPs have a right to attend and speak at backbench committees of House of Commons Conservative MPs, including the 1922 Committee and all sectoral committees. They are frequently invited specifically to speak on certain subjects. When it comes to the drafting of the party manifesto for European elections, the MEPs played 'virtually no role in 1984, a better one in 1989 and better still in 1994'[30] (with four out of the 15 seats on the manifesto committee). This insertion into the structure of the Conservative Party has been *ad hoc* and benefits from no statutory protection – it could easily be reversed.[31] A well-placed observer said that it has served 'at least to counter the attacks of the Euro-sceptics'.[32]

As regards the Labour Party, MEPs were given initially only a marginal role, with the right to attend and speak at party conference (like MPs) and with the leader of the Labour MEPs attending, without the right to vote, meetings of the National Executive Committee of the party. Apart from this, they were kept at arm's length for many years, notably because of the party's attitude to Europe at that time.[33] Gradually, the attitude to MEPs began to change and, after considerable discussion, a packet of changes to the party constitution agreed in the 1991 Labour conference in Brighton brought in dramatic improvements for the role of the Labour MEPs. This gave them the same rights as Westminster MPs to vote in the elections of party leader and deputy leader; the EPLP has five places on the Labour Party's policy forum and input into its policy commissions; the European manifesto drafted by the NEC must now be done in consultation with the EPLP; a regular national conference for European constituency Labour Parties was instituted (similar to the local government conference), enabling the party to hold more detailed debates on European affairs; and MEPs in each region can now elect one of their members to the regional executives, with voting rights.[34] These changes 'both assimilate the EPLP into the formal policy-making structure of the British Labour Party and increase our influence which I contend has not been inconsiderable in the past'.[35] In the following years, each front bench team appointed one of its members to be a liaison officer with MEPs. By 1995, Labour's European policy was drafted by a working group of 4 shadow ministers and 4 MEPs, chaired by party leader Tony Blair.

In order to obtain an idea as to the degree of integration of MEPs into the structures of their national parties, a case study was made comparing the main socialist parties of the five largest Member States and of four of the smaller states.[36] The results show:

- in eight of the ten parties examined, MEPs participate *ex-officio* with speaking rights in the party congress. In four cases this includes an *ex-officio* voting right whereas in other parties voting rights are reserved for delegates from local or regional party structures;
- in seven out of ten cases MEPs are represented *ex-officio* (normally by their leader) in the party Executive/Bureau (itself a body that varies in size from six or seven up to 50 members). In two cases there is no *ex-officio* position, but an MEP is 'normally' elected to the Executive;
- five of the parties allow MEPs to attend and speak as of right in meetings of the parliamentary group in the national parliament (and its working parties);
- the staff employed by the delegation of MEPs collectively in the national capital varies from one (Italy) to ten (several countries);
- four parties have a structure comprising a liaison committee of the leaders of their group in the two chambers of the national parliament and the European Parliament (and, in Germany, the leaders of the party groups in the Landtags);
- in some parties MEPs sit *ex-officio* on regional executives (France, UK, Germany).

The extent to which MEPs actually influence the European policies of their national parties varies, of course, from party to party. It is also practically impossible to measure empirically. We have seen how MEPs are present both through formal structures and through general debate and dialogue within their national parties. Intuitively one can assume that such presence and input into discussions must imply some influence.

This could be especially true for those parties who consider the European Parliament to be more important than their national parliament. Such might be the case, for instance, for smaller regionalist parties seeking to build bridges with Brussels that by-pass their national government. Thus, Westlake found that

> the most an SNP MP could have hoped for, in career terms, at Westminster, would have been a distinguished career as a backbencher; the party was, and remains too small to have much power

of patronage and it certainly had no possibility of access to government. Moreover, since the Highlands and Islands region of Scotland was a major recipient of Community regional aid and houses other major interest groups (above all the fishing industry) more affected by policy emanating from Brussels than from Westminster, Strasbourg may clearly have appeared more, or at least as, attractive to the SNP as Westminster.[37]

But even in major national parties, MEPs can exert an influence on their party's European policy. Labour's conversion to Europe was, in the view of at least some, partly thanks to Labour MEPs. Barbara Castle, in her memoirs, argues that her own conversion to Europe, and the newly emerging pro-European majority within the Labour MEPs, helped to change the points of view of both Michael Foot and Neil Kinnock.[38] Although the gradual conversion of the original intake of Labour MEPs to Europe was partly undermined by a new intake of anti-marketeers in 1984, leaving the delegation balanced on a knife-edge and prone to internal struggles,[39] the pro-European and vocally federalist majority after the 1989 elections certainly helped build up Labour's support for the Maastricht Treaty. David Martin MEP argued that

> our informal individual influence is greater than [we are given] credit for. This informal influence has much to do with the detailed knowledge many Euro-MPs have of the EC and the speed at which the Community is evolving. As the leader of the British Labour MEPs, I served on the Labour Party's influential Policy Review Group, Britain and the World, where substantial changes were made in Labour's policy towards the EC. I do not think it is possible to over-emphasise how important the Policy Review process has been in re-structuring the Labour Party nor how important Labour's change on the EC was within that review.[40]

He also went on to describe the dynamics of his work in the Institutional Committee of Parliament, saying that his reports on Parliament's strategy for European Union in the 1989–92 period 'were not against Labour Party policy so much as ahead of, or in anticipation of, Labour Party policy. In fact, the British Labour Party has [now] adopted, almost entirely, the agenda put forward in the Martin Reports'.

Corroborative evidence can be found in the *Times Guide to 1992*, which stated that:

> the key event in the emergence of Labour's new policy was the decision at the beginning of 1988 by Neil Kinnock, the Party Leader,

to abandon Labour's previous commitment to withdrawing Britain from the EC if it won power. The intellectual ground for that change was prepared in a Fabian pamphlet written by David Martin MEP, then the leader of the Labour Group at Strasbourg, and published in February 1988.[41]

Kinnock wrote a preface to that pamphlet, the full title of which was *Bringing Common Sense To the Common Market: A Left Agenda For Europe*. Much of the detailed agenda set out therein later became official Labour Party policy.

Similarly, Tribune has argued that the insertion of the Labour Party into the 'growing web of Community-wide bodies' was one of the major factors in Labour's conversion to Europe.[42] A comparable process took place in the 1979–84 Parliament with the members from the Northern League of Italy.[43]

Quite apart from formal structures, MEPs play a part in the wider political debate in their parties. They write articles in party newspapers, speak at party meetings, brief party spokesmen, publish leaflets, socialize with party members, give interviews and take part in debates. Intuitively, one can assume that this must have an impact and, given the general pro-integrationist viewpoint of the majority of MEPs, that this impact is in a pro-integration direction.

In order to illustrate the increase of MEPs' *informal* impact in this way, a case study can be made of the fringe meetings of Labour Party conferences. The Labour Party is perhaps unique in Europe in the number and variety of meetings that take place on the occasion of its week-long annual conference. These are not a formal part of its proceedings, but take place at lunch-time or in the evening and are organized by a whole variety of groups not necessarily formally part of the Labour Party, but involving ordinary Labour Party members. The subject, venue and list of speakers of each meeting are published in the conference guide. Some 200 or more meetings are listed every year and constitute a unique insight into the subjects and themes being discussed in the party, and who is addressing them.[44] Other than studying party publications, where the choice of the editor would in any case affect the content, this is probably the best way to have an insight into the informal and non-official discussions going on in a political party. The free access, 'open forum' nature makes it quite representative.

The number of meetings explicitly listing a European subject, and the number of MEPs listed as speaking to meetings on any subject in the years 1987, 1990, 1993 and 1995 have been examined (see Table 3.1).

Table 3.1   *Labour Party Conference Fringe Meetings*

	1987	1990	1993	1995
Meetings with a European subject*	3	9	14	10
MEPs listed as speakers at meetings (on any subject)*	13	24	32	62

* After subtracting the three annual institutionalized meetings on Europe organized by the Labour Movement in Europe, the Common Market Safeguards Campaign and the EPLP/BLG.

None of these years were Euro-elections years nor years of IGCs (of the SEA and Maastricht), in which the level of Euro-debate may well have been abnormally high.[45]

These figures do not, of course, include meetings where Europe came up in the discussions without being mentioned in the title of the meeting, nor meetings in which MEPs (or their staff) participated in the discussions which invariably follow the initial speeches.

What is striking about these figures is that there has been a marked increase in meetings with a European theme and that the increase in the number of advertised speaking engagements of MEPs is far greater than the increase in the number of Labour MEPs during that period. It would appear that Europe, and MEPs, are featuring more frequently in the informal party discussions, as well as gaining in prominence in formal structures as we saw above. Thus, quite apart from formal structures, MEPs inevitably played a role in the general political debate in their parties. They were able to bring a European perspective to discussions on a variety of subjects and, of course, played a prominent role in discussions on Europe as such and the attitude of their party to European integration.[46]

TRANSNATIONAL PARTY FEDERATIONS

Another way in which MEPs have helped develop a network for contacts and policy-making is in the development of transnational political parties. These remained embryonic until the eve of the first European elections, when the challenge of those elections encouraged them to improve their organization and to elaborate common policies. The Liberal and Christian Democrat federations managed to adopt common manifestos for these first elections, but the Confederation of Socialist Parties of the EC failed to do so, agreeing only on a common 'Appeal to the European electorate'. By the second elections in 1984, all three agreed on common manifestos, although individual national parties were allowed to express reservations in footnotes to individual items in the socialist manifesto. By 1994, even the footnotes had disappeared and the European federations were joined by another, that of the Green parties.

What was the role of the elected MEPs in this development? The answer is to be found in the resources that the EP political groups provide. Not only are they by far the largest provider of financial resources to the party federations, without which they could hardly exist, but they also provide the staff for the secretariats thereof. These secretariats organize the meetings and the network of contacts bringing the national parties together. They also provide the basic documentation for meetings, often including the first drafts of policy documents which they prepare in close cooperation with their colleagues in the EP group secretariats. Although such documents are always reworked by the national party representatives, and must ultimately be accepted by them, the starting point is the text that emerges from the European secretariat, strongly influenced by attitudes in the corresponding political group in the EP.

Furthermore, national parties began to use their MEPs as their representatives in such bodies. The International Secretaries of the French, Greek and Dutch Socialist Parties, for instance, were MEPs in 1993–4. For drafting the 1994 PES manifesto, no fewer than six parties were represented by one of their MEPs.[47] Parties no doubt wish to take advantage of the expertise among their MEPs, but it also implies a degree of acceptance of the predispositions and attitudes that MEPs are likely to display.

The EP Groups and their MEPs can play a vanguard role within their European parties. In the case of the Socialists, a high-profile campaign in 1991 by the parliamentary group in favour of replacing the 'Confederation of Socialist Parties' by a 'European Socialist Party' with a stronger structure (including majority voting) overcame initial reticence by some of the member parties and led to the creation of the 'Party of European Socialists' (PES) in 1992.

The development of the activities of the party federations has been significant, and has gone far beyond the adoption of a manifesto every five years, significant as that was for starting the process of encouraging member parties to embark on joint policy formation. Working parties have been set up in key areas, developing common policies in a growing number of fields. By 1993, for instance, the PES presented its own policy initiative on employment to the Commission and the Council just as the Commission was working on its 'White Book' on the same subject for the European Council meeting in Brussels. The PES document was drawn up with the assistance of the economic policy advisers of the Socialist Prime Ministers and Party Leaders in cooperation with the EP Socialist Group and in contact with the Socialist Commissioners.

From the mid-1980s, the EPP and later the PES began to hold 'pre-summits' of the prime ministers, party leaders, commissioners and foreign secretaries of their political family, together with the leader of their EP Group, prior to each European Council meeting. By the mid-1990s, these were prepared by 'sherpa' meetings.

These meetings were significant for two reasons: they began to introduce a party-political element into the European Council, and they provided a vehicle in which the EP political groups and the Commissioners could have another input into discussions at the level of heads of government, and a further opportunity to initiate new developments. Furthermore, they gave representatives from opposition parties not represented directly at the European Council a chance to participate in the debate. Frequently, the dynamic at such meetings (which usually adopt joint statements) is one of putting pressure on the more reticent parties to adopt a more forthcoming position.

MEPs AND NATIONAL PARLIAMENTS

With direct elections, the EP did suffer from a weakening of its links with national parliaments. These were previously automatic in that every MEP was also a member of his/her national parliament. Each national parliament therefore contained a number of MPs who, by virtue of being MEPs, were relatively well briefed on European issues. As President Dankert remarked, loss of contact with national parliaments led to a lack of information on Community matters at the national level, and fewer opportunities for MEPs to influence their ministers through the national assembly.[48] Although some MEPs retained a dual mandate, the impossibility of doing what were now two full-time jobs simultaneously[49] led to the number of such MEPs declining rapidly (about 10 per cent after the first European election to about 2 per cent in 1994). To compensate, a number of structures were developed over the years to provide links to national parliaments. These include:

- an annual meeting of the presidents of national parliaments with the president of the EP. This is able to decide on administrative links, cooperation among parliamentary libraries and research departments, and procedures for cooperation among parliamentary committees. It cannot, however, debate substantive issues as the status of the Speaker in some national parliaments precludes this.
- Cooperation among parliamentary committees with the same field of responsibilities. This is where the detailed cooperation takes place using tools such as joint meetings, exchange of documents and hearings with each other's rapporteurs. They have continued to grow in number.
- Cooperation at the level of equivalent political groups (which we have examined).
- The 'Conference of European Affairs Committees' (CEAC, more commonly known by its French acronym, COSAC). This was established only in 1989 and brings together six members from each national parliament (drawn from the members of its specialist European Committee) and six MEPs. It meets biannually in the country holding the presidency of the Council. It hears statements from the Commission and the Council presidency and holds general discussions on current European issues. It is the main channel for bringing into direct contact the members of each national parliament who are the most involved in European affairs.

In all such fora, MEPs tend to be better informed and up-to-date with their European information than the national MPs. Despite the petty jealousies that this can sometimes give rise to, 'MEPs are frequently in the situation of explaining and justifying European policies to their national colleagues, or enlisting their support for proposals for change'.[50]

MEPs AND THEIR CONSTITUENCIES

Only two Member States have a formal constituency-based system, though in a number of others the political parties compose their lists in such a way as to ensure each area is represented by 'a constituency' MEP. In such countries, MEPs act as a link person with local interests. Typically, MEPs will maintain contact with the local government in their area (indeed, 21 per cent of MEPs were elected local or regional representatives prior to their election in the 1979 intake).[51] They will be in frequent contact with local business interests and trade unions and a host of other organizations in their area. The exact mix of a member's contacts will vary according to his/her preferences, working methods and political viewpoint.

Quantitative analysis of this is difficult to come by. None the less, it can be gauged by studying the frequency of contact through local surgeries, the circulation of members' local newsletters, the size of their mailbag and the number of constituency engagements. To get an idea of this, a case study of a number of UK MEPs was carried out. Eighteen MEPs including at least one from each region (Scotland, Wales and the English planning regions) and from both main parties were interviewed,[52] producing the following results:

- all but four held no regular surgeries but meet constituents by appointment, meeting between 6 and 90 people a week, averaging 20;
- all but one circulate a local newsletter on a monthly, quarterly or biannual basis. Circulations varied from 1200 to 40,000 (averaging 5400) targeted at party members, business/trade unions, local authorities, voluntary organizations, libraries, church groups, schools and universities (with only marginal variation in target groups from one member to another);
- their mailbag varied from 200 letters per month to 4000 (excluding junk mail and circulars) (averaging 1090) with the proportion estimated as local ranging from one third (in the case of a committee chairman) to 80 per cent (averaging 54 per cent);
- the members averaged 24.6 constituency speaking engagements per month typically with small companies, voluntary organizations, schools and colleges, church groups, etc.

This degree of activity is evidence of a local profile for MEPs at least among organized groups. However, the size of the Euro constituencies precludes direct contact with a large proportion of their electorate.

INTEREST GROUPS

Interest groups and lobbyists are another part of MEPs' political environment. The tendency of pressure groups to influence parliamentary assemblies is not exclusive to the European Parliament and, indeed, given its small powers in the early years following direct elections, it attracted relatively little interest from lobbyists and interest groups. None the less, lobbying activities featured spectacularly in one of the early legislative consultation procedures after direct elections, namely on the Vredeling proposals on employee information and consultation in multinational companies. The latter lobbied massively against the proposals.[53] Counter-lobbying by trade union organizations also featured. This was the start of a steady increase in lobbying activities, with some 3000 lobbyists based in Brussels devoting a growing proportion of their time to dealing with the EP.

Lobbying can be carried out directly by particular organizations or by consultants acting on behalf of clients. It takes many forms 'from briefings in Strasbourg hotels for 100 or more members down to lobbying of individual MEPs in their constituencies'.[54] It is estimated that some 150 lobbyists per day attend Parliament's sessions.[55]

By 1988, Hrbek was able to conclude that the

> steadily growing network of informal contact between MEPs and organisations defending and promoting special interests do contribute to integrate the EP deeper into the complex decision-making system of the EC and to make it an acknowledged co-player in the arena where EC issues are dealt with.[56]

He felt that the fact that interest groups themselves take the initiative of establishing contact with the EP 'can be taken as an indicator for the role and reputation the EP has achieved since 1979'. He pointed to the benefit for MEPs:

> interest associations can provide MEPs with detailed information on specific fields where they have expert knowledge but where they can bring at the same time their particular perspective and interest. Parliamentarians in search of extending their influence and power might be ready and open to receive and use such information. And they will understandably try to establish and maintain such links in line with their representative function.[57]

Some interest groups use the Parliament to lobby against the position of their national government when they find (or fear) that their views will not be those defended by the national minister in the Council. Such was the case, for example, of the many UK groups lobbying MEPs to oppose the draft directive on data processing as it would curtail their direct-mailing activities.[58] This included both commercial organizations and voluntary groups such as the Terence Higgins Trust. Such evidence contradicts the intergovernmentalist view that interests are aggregated by national governments.

The interface between MEPs and interest groups sometimes takes place in what are known as *intergroups*. These consist of members from different political groups with common interests in a particular political theme. They are enormously diverse in aims, subject and size, and they have no official status within the EP. They permit members to specialize, make contacts with outside interest groups on a more informal basis than in committee meetings and to develop a network of contacts outside their own political groups, including with like-minded members from other groups. They therefore help to form cross-group networks and even coalitions on specific issues as well as to forge wider political friendships which can be used in other circumstances. There are more than 50 such intergroups.[59] Those that most obviously link up with outside interest groups include the trade union intergroup, a mining regions intergroup, a SME intergroup and a social economy (cooperatives) intergroup. Some intergroups focus on a third country, such as the 'Friends of Israel' and 'Friends of Poland' intergroups. Many promote public interest causes such as the disability intergroup, or the animal welfare intergroup.

Collectively, they contribute to MEPs' networks of contacts and methods of interacting with third parties, developing neofunctionalist style linkages between the supranational institutions and civil society, bypassing national governments. Of all the EC institutions, the EP is the most open to the 'meso-level'.[60]

PARLIAMENT AND THE COMMISSION

The executive in any political system is the natural focus of much of the political work of parliamentarians. The European Community is no exception. Besides the interactions between MEPs and the Commission in the legislative, budgetary and scrutiny fields, which we shall examine in subsequent chapters, MEPs' direct links to the Commission were and are an important element of their work. Direct elections brought significant developments in this respect.

The Commission had always supported direct elections to the EP, not least because it hoped for popular legitimation of its policy proposals and administrative actions. Where the Commission could claim that it had the support of Parliament, it was likely to feel itself to be in a stronger position when arguing with the Council. As soon as direct elections took place in 1979, the Commission held a seminar at the Val Duchesse conference centre in Brussels to examine its relations with the Parliament. According to President Jenkins, the Commission welcomed the elected Parliament but 'also regarded [it] with suitable apprehension'.[61] The outcome of this meeting 'was a general agreement on the need for each member of the Commission to accept a greater personal responsibility for, and devote more time to, parliamentary affairs'.[62]

A number of practical measures were decided, the most notable being an administrative reorganization whereby each member of the Commission would appoint a parliamentary attaché among the members of his/her cabinet and that these would meet weekly as the 'parliamentary affairs group' chaired by the President's cabinet. It would prepare the Commission meetings with regard to parliamentary matters and coordinate relations with the Parliament generally, notably by examining the agenda of each parliamentary sitting in order to ensure that a Commission position was prepared wherever necessary, examine Parliament's resolutions to prepare the Commission's follow-up and keep an eye on draft answers to parliamentary questions.[63] Representatives of the Legal Service and the Secretariat General of the Commission also take part in meetings of the parliamentary affairs group, the latter providing administrative back-up to relations with the Parliament through a directorate specifically responsible. This has some ten administrators, who monitor the work of the Parliament both in plenary and in committee on a permanent basis, ensuring that the specialized colleagues and relevant members of the Commission attend at appropriate junctures.

The Commission at the same time decided on new arrangements for handling parliamentary questions (faster answers and the attribution of authorship to responsible Commissioners, which had not been the case in the past), and to step up the attendance of the Commissioners at EP committee meetings. New internal rules provided for earlier transmission of documents to the Parliament, and the prioritization of correspondence with MEPs. Given the volume of correspondence (the Commission President alone receives up to 13,000 letters per year)[64] prioritization for MEPs correspondence is indispensable.

These arrangements were reviewed and confirmed by the Commission in April 1980. At that point the Commission took a new series of administrative measures to ensure that an inventory be made of all Commission undertakings made in EP debates each month to be discussed by the parliamentary affairs group the following week to ensure follow-up. Commission staff were told that they were authorized to talk to MEPs, but should inform their Director-General or the responsible cabinet in writing if policy or the work of the Commission was involved. It was agreed that the Commissioner responsible for any given dossier (rather than the Commissioner responsible for coordinating relations with the Parliament)[65] should participate in all EP debates wherever possible, except some of those taking place on Fridays, when the Commissioner coordinating relations with the Parliament would handle the debate.

Indeed, the Commission's presence in Parliament is a striking aspect of the relationship between the two institutions. The Commission is present at all parliamentary debates (except those on purely internal EP affairs, such as the waiver of parliamentary immunity of an MEP) and Commission officials or the Commissioners themselves are similarly present at all EP committee meetings. Indeed, between 10 and 20 Commission officials will actually speak at a meeting of a typical parliamentary committee, though others will be present at well.[66]

From the above it can be seen that MEPs are in constant dialogue with the Commission, both at the level of the Commissioners themselves and at the level of their civil servants. Access is free and open and, indeed, privileged. This means that MEPs are well placed to act as go-betweens or contacts, as the 'man or woman in Brussels' to whom national political parties, local government and other interests can turn.

The mutual understanding of the Commission and the Parliament has been enhanced since direct elections by an increasing trend to appoint former MEPs to the Commission. Prior to direct elections, only one member each of the three preceding Commissions was a former MEP. Since then, the number has risen to between 30 per cent and 35 per cent in the last four Commissions (see Table 3.2). Indeed, Portugal and the UK (and the three new states which could not have) are now

Table 3.2   *Former MEPs in the Commission*

Commission	Year	No. of members	No. of MEPs
Mansholt	1972	9	1 (Scarascia Mugnozza)
Ortoli	1973–7	13	1 (Scarascia Mugnozza)
Jenkins	1977–81	13	1 (Vredeling)
Thorn	1981–5	13	3 (Thorn, Dalsager, Pisani)
Delors I	1985–9	14	3 (Delors, Ripa di Meana, Varfis)
Delors II	1989–93	17	6 (Delors, Bangemann, Ripa di Meana, Scrivener, McSharry, Van Miert)
Delors III	1993–5	17	5 (Delors, Bangemann, Van Miert, Scrivener, Orjea)
Santer	1995–	20	7 (Santer, Bangemann, Van Miert, Oreja, Cresson, Bonino, Papoutsis)

the only Member States never to have nominated a former MEP to the Commission. The reverse phenomenon – of former Commissioners becoming MEPs – is a phenomenon that was rather unusual before direct elections.[67] From the point of view of networking and contacts, such members must be regarded as assets to the Parliament.

INTERNATIONAL CONTACTS

The elected Parliament developed a substantial network of international contacts through its interparliamentary delegations. These are established with third countries or groups of countries either as a result of the provisions of treaties and international agreements signed by the Council or by joint agreement with the parliament concerned. Such delegations tend to meet once a year (twice in the case of joint parliamentary committees with associated or applicant states and the US delegation), but the members concerned serve as a conduit for contacts between meetings. Discussions at meetings normally concentrate on mutual briefings on recent developments, discussion of bilateral issues and on common problems. Any follow-up must be made in the respective parliaments.[68] Between meetings, Parliament's delegation members keep abreast of developments and are frequently briefed by the ambassador to the Union of the country concerned and/or the Commissioner responsible. On occasion, delegations may meet to hear a visiting VIP from the country concerned. The number of such interparliamentary delegations has increased considerably since direct elections. Prior to direct elections in 1978, there were only seven such delegations. This number rose to 18 in 1982, 23 from 1985 to 1989 and to 30 following the fall of the communist regimes in Eastern Europe.[69]

The elected Parliament has also become a favourite platform for foreign heads of state to address the European Union. It has received, in formal sittings, some 20 foreign heads of state, beginning with Anwar El-Sadat in 1981. President Reagan, the Pope, Vaclav Havel, King Hussein, President Herzog are among those to have addressed the Parliament in this way. The heads of state of the EU's Member States have also done so. Such visits are a media occasion, but they are also an important channel of communication with the visiting head of state and the accompanying delegation of officials and ministers.

These international contacts are a channel of communication that is not usually available to MPs in the national parliaments of the smaller Member States. Just as the EU's foreign policy activities are proportionately of greater significance for the smaller states, the same is true for their parliamentarians as regards the parliamentary aspect of international relations.

THE INFORMATION MARKET

Much of the above illustrates how the EP is at the centre of a large network of contacts – both formal and informal – and channels of communication. MEPs can, at the very least, be reasonably well-informed and up-to-date as regards developments in the EU. This in turn makes them a valuable asset to their national political parties. They tend to become party 'experts' on Europe. 'Whenever we wanted to know what was going on in the EC we called an MEP,'[70] said one Labour official. They can similarly become valuable assets to local governments, interest groups and others.

To a certain extent, MEPs' networks of contacts tend to cluster around what Petersen has called 'policy networks' at the 'meso-level'. The three political institutions organize their internal work on a subject basis (Commission DGs, Council formations and parliamentary committees) and this means that those specializing on any given subject within the institutions tend to know each other. Those outside the institutions dealing with the same subject will similarly have a degree of familiarity with them. This applies whether the subject is transport, agriculture, regional policy, consumer protection or whatever. For van Schendelen,[71] the participation of MEPs in such networks is as important a means of influence as their formal powers. It means they know who to see, when and about what. Indeed, van Schendelen went on to assess the degree of contacts of the Dutch MEPs in 1981, finding that:

- 48 per cent of them have monthly and 8 per cent weekly contacts with Dutch Ministers in the Council;
- 52 per cent have monthly and 12 per cent weekly meetings with the Dutch Permanent Representation;
- 60 per cent have monthly and 20 per cent weekly contacts with a member of the Commission;
- 36 per cent have monthly and 28 per cent weekly contacts with high-level Commission officials;
- 64 per cent have monthly and 20 per cent weekly contacts with MPs in their national Parliament.

It is likely that all such contacts would have become more frequent since 1981.

The information market is most spectacularly illustrated on the occasion of the plenary sessions in Strasbourg. It has been commented on in two recent publications. For Westlake, 'the hothouse atmosphere of plenary sessions at Strasbourg, where almost without exception everybody is away from home and family [and] the Commission's Strasbourg offices and meeting rooms adjoin those of the Parliament (they actually belong to the Parliament), . . . much informal business and bridge-building is transacted in the corridors between the Commission's offices and the Parliament's chamber.'[72] For Jacobs et al., Strasbourg is 'an opportunity for an intense round of contacts as MEPs are joined by the entire Commission, ministers of the Council, and so on. This relatively open week-long "conclave" enables MEPs to 'collar' Commissioners away from their civil servants. All concerned are also virtually obliged to socialize, being 'away from home' in a congress atmosphere.'[73] One can only add that others too have stalls in this market: journalists, lobbyists, visitors from national parliaments, the Parliament's staff, members' assistants, officials from the Permanent Representations of the Member States and others.

MEPs AND THE WIDER PUBLIC

We have seen in the preceding sections considerable evidence of MEPs having the possibility to network with other interested parties, be they national or supranational élites or interest groups. The same cannot be said of the MEPs' abilities to relate to the mass of their electorates. Even in Member States with a constituency system, the size of the constituencies is prohibitive when it comes to direct contact with the electorate. In terms of national media attention, MEPs received little coverage. The media was not interested in a relatively powerless Parliament, with the distance and language compounding the problem and for the first three years after direct elections, media coverage of the Parliament declined. It has since more than recovered (see Table 3.3), but few MEPs are household names. Yet, this is not very different from most national MPs. It is usual for only those in government or leading the opposition to obtain a large amount of media attention. Few backbenchers (other than those formerly occupying frontbench positions or leading 'revolts') are household names. Media coverage of MEPs, none of whom can be 'ministers' in the EC system while

Table 3.3 *Media Coverage of the European Parliament*

	1979	1980	1981	1982	1983	1984	1985[a]	1986	1987	1988	1989	1990	1991	1992	1993	1994
Average number of journalists attending sessions[b]	130	116	109	106	117	156	134	146	137	172	192	187	160	195	220	245
Number of TV reports of sessions	n.a.	347	216	182	392	394	413	488	576	676	792	742	868	868	872	1847
Number of hours of TV reports of sessions	57.10	52.30	28	25.34	46.15	58.15	39.41	58.24	58.34	79.15	96.50	93	93	114	129	325

Source: DG III.

Notes: All these figures represent only those journalists/stations accredited during Strasbourg sessions of Parliament or using its facilities. They do not include productions in Member States nor coverage of EP activities between sessions (committees, hearings, etc.).

a. All figures for 1985 exclude the month of May (President Reagan's visit) which had an exceptional high media coverage.

b. Excluding journalists coming as a group (e.g. of specialized press for a particular debate).

Trend: All figures were in decline until 1982, since when they have more than recovered, especially for TV coverage which is higher than ever. Figures tend to sag following each election (1979, 1984, 1989).

they are MEPs, is more appropriately compared to backbenchers. Westlake detects 'a general build-up in media interest in the Parliament' and looking at the situation in the UK, he states that 'they are beginning to enjoy similar levels of national public exposure to those enjoyed by the average backbench MP'.[74] None the less, the impact is small.

Parliament has taken a number of steps to try to make itself accessible:

- Established information offices in each of the national capitals with up to a dozen members of staff. These provide documentation, speakers and maintain contacts with national authorities.
- Published a monthly 'newspaper' (the English language version of which is called *EP News* and has a print-run of 45,000). These are circulated to parliamentarians, libraries, universities, interest groups and representative bodies in each Member State. It mainly describes recent EP debates and resolutions.[75]
- Made a particular effort to help visitors. Visitors' groups may apply for a special subsidy and a programme of meetings with members and staff is arranged. Such groups are typically constituency party sections, universities, professional associations, trade unions, etc. The number of visitors coming to Parliament sessions increased from 36,000 in 1979 to 150,000 in 1991.[76]
- Established procedures allowing members of the public to petition it (now formalized in the Maastricht Treaty). The number of petitions has grown from fewer than 30 per annum prior to direct elections to over 1000 by the mid-1990s. Some have been mass petitions receiving over a million signatures (e.g. on the import of baby seal skins, on cruelty to animals and on the testing of cosmetic products on animals). Petitions are handled by a parliamentary committee (since 1987 a special committee) which works in close liaison with a unit in the Commission. Petitions have also become one of the important sources of information on failures to apply Community law, leading to Commission proceedings against the Member State(s) concerned.

OWN INFRASTRUCTURE

One thing that the elected Parliament immediately embarked on was the development of its *own infrastructure* in terms of facilities and back-up support for its own members. It not only ensured that each MEP would have his/her own office and telephone (something that might seem obvious, but which is not immediately available in every national parliament, nor was it available in the pre-1979 EP), but it also developed staff back-up.

Analyses of the EP staffing levels usually quote the increase in overall size following the first direct elections (from 1821 in 1979 to 2593 in 1982 – an increase of 42 per cent, which stabilized thereafter, rising only a further 0.5 per cent in the next two years). It is, however, more significant to take the figures for certain categories of staff, given the large number of technical and linguistic staff which are also included in the global figures. The number of A grades (executives) also rose by a similar magnitude between 1979 and 1982 (rising from 207 to 291 – 41 per cent – stabilizing at that level for the next few years), but, interestingly the A grade staff of the political groups – working directly with members on their political work – rose from 66 in 1979 to 123 in 1982 (over 86 per cent), continuing to rise gradually thereafter. This faster increase in the size of the political Group staff is an indication of the politicization of the Parliament after direct elections. It has continued more gradually since then.[77]

Most striking of all, however, is the assistance provided by Parliament to enable MEPs to recruit their own personal assistants or researchers, working in their constituency office or their Brussels office. This did not exist at all in the pre-1979 EP. By the end of the 1980s, MEPs would typically have three or four such assistants helping with research, or constituency work and general organization.

An increase in staff level is a mixed blessing. It sometimes leads to accusations of rampant bureaucracy and profligacy with public expenditure. The overall levels are, however, small compared to certain national parliaments or, especially, the US Congress. In any case staff back-up is important in terms of allowing MEPs to receive independent advice, to act as the 'memory' of the institution, to have their own research capacity and general back-up. Without it, the position of the MEPs in arguments and discussions with the Commission and the Council would be severely handicapped. The development of Parliament staffing levels in the years following the first direct election was therefore crucial.

ASSESSMENT

This chapter has provided evidence and arguments to show how, despite the absence of a significant public profile, the very existence of a full-time elected Parliament generated the establishment of new political networks through a number of channels, bringing a European dimension more systematically into national politics and into political parties in particular. However, the establishment of the network was one thing – increasing the political weight of MEPs to give them more clout in internal party discussions was another. Of course, formal competences are only one aspect of political influence: access to information, capacity to respond rapidly, access to and even friendship with key political actors, ability to attract media attention and so on are all major political assets and MEPs dispose of these to at least some degree. However, they are all more powerful assets if they are combined with real power. In the absence of perceptible powers for the Parliament, MEPs lacked weight. In terms of the importance attributed by national parties to Europe, and in terms of the development of European political parties, the EP's importance was not sufficient to engender major structural changes. As pointed out by Sweeney, an increase in Parliament's powers was required. 'A comparison with American political parties is illustrative . . . fifty independent state parties do not compromise out of an altruistic wish to integrate the nation, but out of a pragmatic desire to reap the spoils of victory.'[78]

Thus, the networking itself was only of limited significance. It helped in the transmission of information and in general debate. It might help in arguing to gain more powers for the Parliament. But it would only have greater impact once Parliament had gained powers. Powers which would excite the interest of national political parties and which would be visible to the electorate would help the most: those that brought the 'spoils of victory' such as a say in the appointment of the Commission or a decisive voice in the adoption of legislation or the budget.

4 Exploiting its Existing Powers

As we saw in chapter 2, although a majority of the political parties represented in the EP felt that direct elections were a major step forward in European integration, not all of them agreed on the need for immediate institutional reforms and, of those that did, there was a diversity of views as to what they should be, how they were to be formulated and by whom. Moreover, the sharpened competition caused by direct elections meant that the political Groups were becoming less willing to support initiatives launched under a rival Group's banner.

As regards treaty revision, the procedures assigned to Parliament only a consultative role on the decision to convene an intergovernmental conference.[1] Revision required approval by common accord of the Member States. Under such a procedure, any EP proposals would have to elicit support from the Commission or member governments, and would be entirely in the hands of the intergovernmental negotiations, not at first sight an attractive prospect for the EP. Initially, Parliament preferred to concentrate on (1) exploiting the Parliament's powers as they stood at that time, and (2) seeking improvements to Parliament's position through agreements with the other institutions which did not require treaty amendment.

This chapter examines how Parliament attempted to make use of its existing powers and chapter 5 examines its approach to institutional reform within the treaties. In both cases we shall analyse what Parliament did and assess its achievements and their consequences.

As we saw in chapter 2, these approaches had been anticipated in the literature and are formulated in our hypotheses no. 6 and 10 respectively (with 7b and 7a also relevant). In this chapter we are therefore examining material that sheds light on the validity of hypotheses 6 and 10, but if it were shown that the Parliament were to have little impact, then hypothesis 4 or 5 could be confirmed as more appropriate.

The chapter is divided into the different types of power exercised or sought by the Parliament: budgetary, legislative and scrutiny/control powers.

THE PARLIAMENT'S BUDGETARY POWERS.

The Setting: Parliament's Budgetary Powers at the Time of the First Direct Elections

At the time of the first direct elections, Parliament's legislative powers were merely consultative, but it had recently acquired significant budgetary powers.

The *1970 Treaty of Luxembourg*, amending certain budgetary provisions of the original treaties, which came into effect in 1972 increased Parliament's budgetary powers in two phases. A first phase, which applied to the 1973/1974/1975 budgets, gave Parliament the right to propose modifications to Council's draft, which Council could overrule only by a qualified majority where the modification did not have the effect of increasing the total amount of expenditure, but which required the approval of a qualified majority in Council where it did increase total expenditure. A second phase, used as of the 1976 budget, dropped the distinction between modifications increasing or not increasing expenditure, and introduced a new distinction between 'expenditure necessarily resulting from the treaties or from acts adopted in accordance therewith' and other expenditure (henceforth Compulsory Expenditure (CE), or Non-Compulsory Expenditure (NCE)). For CE, Council could accept Parliament's modifications by a qualified majority. For NCE, Council could modify Parliament's amendments by a qualified majority, such modifications being referred back to a second reading in Parliament which could, by a three-fifths majority, amend them again, provided that total NCE did not rise beyond the 'maximum rate' of increase of this expenditure calculated by the Commission on the basis of certain economic indicators (GNP growth, inflation and average variation in the budgets of the Member States) unless both Council and Parliament agreed to raise the maximum rate. However, if Council itself used up more than half of the maximum rate in its own draft, Parliament could raise expenditure by a further half without the need to set a new maximum rate (often referred to as Parliament's 'margin of manoeuvre'). The second phase also transferred the right to sign the budget into law upon completion of the procedure from the President of the Council to the President of Parliament. The 1970 Treaty also gave Parliament and Council jointly the right to vote discharge on the Commission.

The second phase of the 1970 Treaty was used for three budgets only (1976, 1977 and 1978), when it was superseded by the entry into force of the *1975 Treaty of Brussels*, amending the financial provisions of the Community treaties. This introduced the budgetary provisions that still apply in the treaties and have not, as such, been modified since, although as we shall see, there have been other significant developments. The 1975 Treaty also introduced an independent Court of Auditors to monitor *post facto* Community expenditure patterns and to assist in the discharge procedure. It also gave Parliament alone the right to take the final decision on the discharge. As regards the procedure for adopting the budget, it modified only slightly the second phase of the 1970 Treaty, notably to reintroduce for CE the distinction between EP modifications increasing or decreasing expenditure, the latter requiring a qualified majority for Council to overrule the EP,[2] and to give the EP the explicit right to reject the budget as a whole. It thus established the following 'rules of the game'.[3]

The Budget: Rules of the Game

The budget procedure begins with the Commission preparing its estimates for Community policies (and adding each institution's estimates for its own administrative expenditure) in the form of a preliminary draft budget which it forwards to Council. Council, acting by a qualified majority, then prepares a draft budget which it must forward to Parliament by 5 October. Parliament then:

- adopts 'modifications' to 'compulsory expenditure' (essentially agriculture, administrative refunds to Member States and expenditure arising out of agreements with third countries) by a simple majority;
- adopts 'amendments' to 'non-compulsory expenditure' (including the Regional and Social Funds, energy and research, transport, development aid, the environment, education and culture) by a majority.

The Budget is then referred back to Council for a second reading. Concerning Parliament's 'modifications' to compulsory expenditure, Council has 15 days to take a final decision, needing:

- a qualified majority to approve any modification that increases expenditure;
- a qualified majority to overrule any modification that does not increase expenditure (cuts or transfers).

Concerning Parliament's 'amendments' to non-compulsory expenditure, Council may modify them, but only by a qualified majority, and such modifications are referred back to Parliament for its second reading.

In this second reading, Parliament has 15 days to amend these latter modifications, which require three-fifths of the vote cast and at least a majority of members. Parliament may also by a similar majority reject the draft budget as a whole, in which case the whole procedure must start again, Community expenditure in the meantime being frozen at the previous year's level (or, if it is lower, the level of the preliminary draft) on a month-by-month basis for every item ('provisional twelfths').

Council and Parliament may not increase non-compulsory expenditure beyond a 'maximum rate' worked out (by the Commission) from economic indicators (GDP, inflation, government spending). However, they may jointly (by qualified majority in Council and majority of members and three-fifths of votes cast in Parliament) agree on a higher rate and Parliament anyway may allocate an amount equal to half the maximum rate, even if Council has used more than half or all. Finally, it is up to the President of Parliament to sign the budget into law when all the procedures have been completed.

To this it should be added that there are, in effect, two sets of figures adopted each year: appropriations for payment to be paid, in principle, during that year, and appropriations for commitment to legal obligations entered into that year but which will be paid over a number of years. Some items, such as CAP guarantee payments, are not differentiated (commitment and payment should, in principle, be completed in a single budget year). Most areas of NCE, where Parliament's powers are stronger, include both sorts of appropriations with commitments, by definition, being a higher level (an average of one third higher from 1979 to 1987 and about 10 per cent higher in the 1990s).

This budget procedure thus had the trappings of a bicameral system for the adoption of the budget, with two readings in each body and the final say in some areas for one branch, provided it had the necessary majority to overrule the other, and in other areas for the other branch. Joint agreement was necessary for major increases. However, the significance of this system was limited, from Parliament's perspective, by a number of factors. First, although large by the standards of international organizations, the Community budget was small as a 'federal budget', representing in 1978 merely 1.7 per cent of total public expenditure in Member States (and 2.7 per cent of national government budgets) or 0.78 per cent of GDP.[5] Second, it was not easy to change this as increases were subject to a double limitation: the ceiling of own resources – at the time capped at 1 per cent of VAT – which could be modified only with the unanimous approval of every Member State following national ratification procedures and, within that, each year's spending could in any case only be raised, as far as NCE was concerned, by no more than the maximum rate unless Council agreed. Third, Parliament's powers were not nearly as strong as regards CE as they were concerning NCE. Granted, any parliamentary amendment reducing CE could be overruled only by a qualified majority in Council, but in the areas concerned – mainly agriculture and expenditure arising from agreements with third countries, the collegiate attitude of Council – often pursuant to previous compromises within Council achieved only with difficulty – was such that such a qualified majority was easily forthcoming. As to Parliament's modifications increasing CE, they needed the approval of Council.

As regards NCE, however, Parliament was in a far stronger position, provided it could muster a three-fifths majority to overrule Council. Within the ceilings and the limit of the maximum rate of increase, Parliament had the final say on the allocation of spending between competing budget lines. But NCE represented, in 1979, only 16.95 per cent of total payment appropriations.

How had this development in the treaties come about? It was linked to one of the 'constitutional' developments of the Union, namely the introduction of the Community's 'own resources' replacing national budgetary contributions 'with tax revenue allocated once and for all to the Community and accruing to it automatically without the need for any subsequent decision by national authorities'.[6] This followed logically from the introduction of the common external tariff and the setting up of the CAP, including a number of agricultural levies. Both these forms of revenue could hardly accrue to the state collecting them, when they were a result of common policies and, indeed, might be levied on products in transit. They would therefore go into the Community pot. None the less, the introduction of 'own resources' to be managed under the authority of the common institutions was resisted by de Gaulle, and was one of the elements that gave rise to the 1965 'empty chair' crisis, precisely because he recognized – and opposed – the federal characteristic of such a development. However, the secure funding of the CAP was also a major French objective, and France was unable to resist the introduction of such a system, which was clinched after de Gaulle's resignation in 1969. The decision of 21 April 1970 replaced national contributions with own resources comprising agricultural levies, customs duties and a budget-balancing resource of up to 1 per cent of VAT.

The Dutch parliament had made it clear that it would ratify the own resources system only if the decision-taking on sums that would now escape the control of national parliaments be brought under the control of the EP.[7] It was this that led to the introduction of some powers for the Parliament in the 1970 Treaty. These limited powers were a compromise between those states wanting more and those wanting less power for the EP. Part of the compromise was a promise by the Commission to introduce new proposals for a further treaty modification. The Commission eventually did so after having been threatened by the EP in 1972 with a motion of censure. Its new proposals led to the negotiation of the 1975 Treaty.

The Battles

The unelected Parliament had gained budgetary powers, but it would fall to the elected Parliament to make use of them. Only once, for the adoption of the *1979 budget* in the autumn of 1978, did the nominated Parliament have available to it the full procedure of the 1975 Treaty. That year's procedure already illustrated how Parliament could take advantage of the procedures in order to develop Community policies somewhat beyond the intention of most Member States. It voted substantial increases to the embryonic Regional Fund, bringing sums in question to a figure well beyond that agreed in the December 1977 European Council. In its second reading, however, Council was unable to muster the qualified majority necessary to reject Parliament's amendment to this item of non-compulsory expenditure, though Council did argue that, in its second reading, Parliament remained under the obligation to bring the budget below the maximum rate, which its amendments had exceeded. In the event, Parliament did not amend Council's second reading draft at all which resulted, under the Treaty, in Council's version of the draft becoming law when signed by Parliament's President. If Council wished to challenge this, it would virtually be taking itself to Court. In winning this victory, Parliament not only gave a boost to fledgling new policies (almost doubling the regional fund appropriations), it also affirmed the principle that 'for any regulation to include specific resource allocation may not prejudice the final decision of the budgetary authority'.[8]

These clashes had highlighted Parliament's budgetary powers on the eve of direct elections. As we saw in chapter 2, much of the academic literature and the political discourse prior to these elections had highlighted Parliament's budgetary powers as the vehicle which Parliament could initially use to develop its role. In the circumstances, it is not surprising that the *1980 budgetary procedure*, taking place in the autumn of 1979 only a few months after the first direct elections, and with predominately new and enthusiastic MEPs, should give rise to an attempt by Parliament to assert itself and to seek major changes in the pattern of Community spending. In doing so, however, Parliament was entering into conflict with the combined power of the finance ministries of the Member States (as regards the areas where it wished to increase expenditure) and with the agriculture ministers (where it wished to decrease expenditure). As can be seen in national contexts, conflicts with the Treasury are not easily won.

In its first reading, Parliament increased the total volume of appropriations by 311 m ECU.[9] However, it reduced farm spending to the dairy sector by 280 m ECUs, entering 250 m of them into the Reserve (Chapter 100). In its second reading, Council reduced Parliament's increases to 85 m ECUs and rejected entirely the cuts in farm spending. In its second reading, Parliament therefore used for the first time its power to reject the budget, by 288 votes to 64. In its accompanying resolution it emphasized its intention to 'restructure' the budget and ensure that it was better balanced, and, without challenging the principles of the CAP, 'to control its cost in an equitable manner so that its constant increase does not, in the long run, endanger the very basis of that policy'.

What happened next was a severe blow to Parliament's aspirations. Although the Commission submitted a new preliminary draft budget in February 1980, Council simply did not act upon it for several months, hoping to wear Parliament down through the 'provisional twelfths system' whereby expenditure was, in the interim, frozen each month at one-twelfth of the previous year's level. For Parliament's internal operations, this was a major problem in that the previous year's budget had been largely for the smaller nominated Parliament, and so was totally insufficient for the new Parliament. With severe difficulties for everything from staff recruitment, the payment of travel expenses, the hiring of freelance interpreters to basic material needs, the new Parliament – already facing a difficult task of finding its way – faced a long list of petty irritations. Above all, however, Council showed that, if Parliament pushed it over the brink, the consequences could be dire for all Community policies, putting the pressure as much on Parliament as on the Council.

The budget was finally adopted only in July 1980, after the agricultural prices for that year had been fixed in May. Parliament's face was saved by the fact that these price decisions were more moderate than might have been expected, and by Council agreeing to increases in the

Regional Fund. Thus, Parliament had obtained some small incremental changes, but its aspirations to provoke a wholesale reassessment of budgetary priorities came to nought.

The events surrounding the 1980 budget had a dual effect on MEPs' perceptions. The attitude of the Council in holding together and refusing to make any significant concessions to the views of the freshly elected Parliament had a radicalizing effect on many MEPs. There is little doubt that this episode helped convince many of the need for fundamental reform in the Community system, as it appeared that Parliament, even in the one area where it already had significant powers, would in practice have little scope to use them. We shall examine the results of this more radical approach in chapter 6.

The second effect was within the budgetary sphere itself, where Parliament prepared itself for a war of attrition, seeking to reshape the Community budget not in one go, but over a period of years.

Indeed, subsequent years were to see spectacular battles with Parliament each time probing Council in different ways, and achieving some notable successes. In 1980, for *the 1981 budget*, Parliament again sought to limit agricultural spending, proposing a reduction of 70 m ECU in EAGGF guarantee appropriations and a transfer of 254 m ECU to an *ad hoc* reserve (an across-the-board reduction of 2 per cent). It further pressed to develop other Community policies by adding 834 m ECU of NCE, notably to items concerning energy policy, development co-operation, social and regional expenditure. Council could not muster a qualified majority to overrule the 2 per cent reduction of agricultural expenditure, but opposed the proposed increases in NCE, agreeing to accept only 183 m ECU of the 834 m proposed by Parliament. At its second reading, Parliament also happened to be voting on a supplementary budget for the previous year to cover claims for previous commitments. Parliament could not add more than 24 m ECU to the draft 1981 budget, given the maximum rate of increase, but added 266 m ECU to the supplementary budget for 1980. Although this money could not possibly be spent by the end of the year (two weeks later), it would be carried over to 1981. Council was outmanoeuvred.

The 1982 budget had Spinelli as Parliament's rapporteur. In its first reading, Parliament again proposed to cut agricultural spending (this time by reducing 300 m ECUs from the appropriations intended for monetary compensatory amounts – the mechanism for offsetting the effect on agricultural prices of currency realignments), whilst increasing other appropriations by 366 m ECU. Council accepted most of the reductions for the MCAs, but accepted only half the increases proposed by Parliament for social and regional expenditure. In its second reading, Parliament reinstated a further 204 m ECU from its first reading amendments, which Council considered went beyond the maximum rate of increase for non-compulsory expenditure, which could only be raised with Council's consent. Parliament's view was that it had not exceeded the maximum rate, but this depended on how certain items were classified – CE or NCE. The situation gave rise to a difficult situation within Council, with a majority accepting a Belgian Presidency compromise whereby Council brought an appeal to the Court of Justice against Parliament but at the same time agreed to open talks with it on the classification of expenditure. Council thereby acknowledged for the first time that the classification of items as CE or NCE could not be determined unilaterally by Council, but required negotiation and agreement. An interinstitutional agreement was signed by the Presidents of the Parliament, Council and Commission on 30 June 1982 (ratified by Parliament in July) on 'various measures to improve the budgetary procedure'. It included a classification of all existing items in the budget. Council then withdrew appeal to the ECJ.

The 1983 budget was considered in parallel to a supplementary and amending budget for 1982 brought in to provide for compensatory payments to the UK as part of the Council's package to settle (temporarily) the longstanding dispute over the UK's net budgetary contribution. For the 1983 budget Parliament yet again put forward cuts in CAP spending and increases in other areas. Council, in its second reading, rejected the CAP reductions but agreed to an increase of 324.7 m ECU (out of just over 600 m ECU proposed by Parliament) in the other areas. In its second reading, Parliament reinstated some 138 m ECU, arguing that it still had some margin of manoeuvre remaining at its second reading because the volume of NCE for the previous year, to which the maximum rate applied, had been increased in the course of the year by budget transfers from one item to another. Council argued that such transfers – allowed under the Financial Regulation under certain conditions – did not count towards establishing the volume of NCE in the budget – only an amending budget could do that. Parliament nevertheless proceeded and Council did not challenge Parliament in the Court as the whole dispute was overshadowed by Parliament's rejection of the supplementary budget containing the UK refund. On this, Parliament had argued for conditions: that it should be the last *ad hoc* compensatory measure (i.e. that a permanent system should be agreed), that they should be allocated under existing Community policies (and that Parliament should be able to monitor the use to which the funds were put) and that payments should be made in two stages with the second instalment paid only once a permanent system had been agreed. Council had been unwilling to meet these conditions and Parliament rejected the supplementary budget by 259 votes to 78. Supplementary budgets can be rejected without any effect on the annual budget already adopted, i.e. there is no reversion to 'provisional twelfths' and Parliament's bargaining position was therefore stronger. As a result, the Commission submitted a new supplementary budget for the same level of funding, but with half the expenditure classified as non-compulsory and with 10 per cent of the funds to be paid *ex-post facto* to allow monitoring by Parliament. This satisfied Parliament, although Council was unwilling to give any formal undertaking not to resort to *ad hoc* solutions in the future.

The 1984 budget was considered in circumstances in which the Community had reached the ceiling of own resources, and Parliament's amendments could be constrained, not by the maximum rate, but by that ceiling. In its first reading, Parliament added 546 m ECU to Council's draft, calling on the European Council in Athens to agree on raising the ceiling on own resources. Athens was only the latest in a series of attempts by Member States to reach agreement on this issue, so to add punch to its requests Parliament froze (in the reserve – see below) the British rebate and 5 per cent of CAP spending. Parliament's second reading took place after the European Council failed to reach agreement. Although the budget Council had accepted 377 m ECU out of the 546 m ECU increase proposed by Parliament, there were many in Parliament who supported outright rejection of the budget, as the Member States had failed to take the necessary decisions to guarantee its operation. In the event, Parliament refrained from compounding the sense of crisis, simply adding 132 m ECU to the Council's second reading and maintaining the freeze on compensatory payments to the UK. Although Council felt that Parliament had yet again exceeded its powers, the general relief that Parliament had not rejected the budget, and the need to concentrate on negotiating a new ceiling for own resources, led Council to let the matter rest.

The Fontainebleau European Council in June 1984 solved the twin problems of the UK budgetary contribution and the need to raise the ceiling on own resources. It agreed on a system to compensate the UK on the revenue side of the budget and to raise the ceiling on the VAT component of the Community's own resources from 1 per cent to 1.4 per cent. The UK's agreement was conditional upon Parliament releasing the funds that it had frozen, and Parliament agreed to do this.

A supplementary budget for 1984 was put forward, supplementing the Community's own resources with 'advances' from the Member States to be refunded in subsequent years. This would enable the Community to meet its 1984 obligations, including the British rebate. Parliament accepted that it could not amend such an item of revenue, but it did vote amendments to the estimates of revenue from customs duties, thereby underlining that its budgetary powers include the revenue side, within the parameters of the own resources decision.

For *the 1985 budget*, a similar problem of exhaustion of own resources remained, as the raising of the ceiling of own resources would only take effect after national ratification in 1986. A 'topping up' by national contributions was again necessary. The simplest solution would have been for Member States to agree to cover the level of expenditure resulting from the budgetary procedure. However, a number of Member States were clearly reluctant to do so. Council therefore put forward a draft budget which, for agriculture, covered only 10 months of the year. Council recognized that an additional budget would be needed by 1 October. This would violate the Financial Regulation which specified that an extra budget is permitted only to finance expenditure not anticipated when the original budget is drawn up. Parliament sought to rectify this in its first reading, but Council's response was to put the extra amounts in the budget in brackets – a hitherto unknown budgetary device – explaining that these sums could be used only when the necessary revenue had been made available to the Community. Parliament could not accept this procedure, the legality of which it doubted, and it rejected the draft budget as a whole for the second time in its history by 321 votes to 3. A new budget was eventually agreed in June 1985 once Member States had agreed on a new system of advances (this time non-refundable) to top up the budget. It covered the whole year and incorporated Parliament's amendments on food aid and the structural funds, financed partly by a Parliament amendment to the revenue side.

The 1986 budget was the first budget for the enlarged Community including Spain and Portugal. Parliament felt that Council's draft had not made the adaptations necessary. 'Last year we had a budget for ten months out of twelve, this year for ten Member States out of twelve,' exclaimed the chairman of the Budget Committee, Jean-Pierre Cot. Furthermore, the Commission had set the 'maximum rate' at 7.1 per cent, which clearly did not take account of enlargement. Nor had account been taken of the need to meet commitments entered into in previous years which were now becoming due for payment (referred to as 'the weight of the past'). In its first reading, Parliament therefore voted to rectify this situation, raising the total budget to 34.06 bn ECU (as compared to 31.8 bn in Council's draft). In its second reading, Council accepted only 32.7 bn ECU. Even this implied raising the maximum rate for NCE to 20.5 per cent and Council was thereby admitting that its first draft was incomplete. In its second reading, Parliament persevered, adopting a budget of 33.3 bn ECU, despite the absence of an agreement with Council on raising the maximum rate to this level. The President of Parliament none the less signed the budget into law, immediately provoking a Court case.[10] On 2 July 1986, the Court ruled that the act of the President of Parliament whereby he declared the budget for 1986 finally adopted was illegal, as it had 'occurred at a time when the budgetary procedure had not yet been completed for want of an agreement between the two institutions concerned on . . . the new maximum rate of increase'. The Court spelt out that agreement may not 'be inferred on the basis of the presumed intention of one or another of those institutions'. Although technically a ruling against Parliament, the effect of the judgment was that whenever expenditure was projected to rise beyond the maximum rate, an *explicit* agreement between the two branches was necessary. Thus, when Council had voted sums beyond the maximum rate in its second reading, it was in a similar position to that of Parliament when the latter had done the same in its second reading. In both cases, an explicit agreement on a new maximum rate was required between the two institutions, and Council could not infer that the rate resulting from *its* amendments was implicitly agreed when Parliament wanted a higher rate. For the future, this underlined equality of the two branches in deciding expenditure levels beyond the maximum rate. For the 1986 budgetary procedure, it implied that negotiations must continue between the institutions. A new budget was eventually agreed on 10 July, by which time the Commission and the Council had recognized the strength of Parliament's arguments on the substance of the matter: a budget of 35.2 bn ECU was adopted, with the rate of increase in NCE fixed at 39.18 per cent.

The 1987 budget was characterized by the Community again coming up against the ceiling of own resources, in this case the new 1.4 per cent VAT ceiling.[11] Council's solution was to cut expenditure on development aid and research policy, whilst maintaining the level foreseen for agricultural guarantee. Parliament adopted a series of amendments to speed up the disposal of agricultural stocks and to reduce milk production on the agricultural side, and to reinstate the sums for research policy and development cooperation. Council refused to accept either aspect of Parliament's wishes. It wanted to keep below the maximum rate, whereas Parliament was keen to protect other policies from being raided to preserve agricultural spending. In its second reading, Parliament did this by exceeding the maximum rate, thereby making it impossible for the President of Parliament to sign the budget, in view of the Court ruling earlier that year. Parliament then pursued negotiations with Council on this basis, and agreement was reached the following February, involving some movement on the vexed question of agricultural expenditure in the Council, and a raise in the maximum rate from 8.1 per cent to 8.149 per cent – a remarkable compromise allowing Council to argue that the rate applied only to the first decimal point, and therefore had not been increased at all!

In 1988, the debate on budgets took an entirely different turn. The discussions among Member States on raising the ceiling on the Community's own resources (having reached the new ceiling of 1.4 per cent of VAT) had been linked to the commitments made in the context of the single market (the 1992 project) for a substantial increase in the structural funds helping the weakest economies to adapt. The 'Delors package' agreed by the European Council envisaged, as proposed by the Commission and the Parliament, a doubling of the Structural Funds by 1993. Such doubling could not take place without the normal maximum rates being substantially exceeded in the intervening years. Theoretically, once a higher maximum rate had been agreed, there was nothing to prevent Parliament spending it on something entirely different – research programmes, development aid, transport, education or whatever. This fact was a powerful incentive for Council to agree to negotiate an Interinstitutional Agreement with Parliament as proposed by the latter spelling out an orderly development over a period of five years in which the Structural Funds would be gradually doubled. It also provided for 'financial perspectives' in five categories of expenditure, limiting increases in agricultural spending (from Parliament's viewpoint, the main feature of the 'budgetary discipline' that was part of the agreement) but allowing increases in areas of new Community policies. In effect, Parliament was agreeing to use the possibilities given to it (by the need to raise the maximum rate) in the way that Council wanted as far as the structural funds were concerned, and in exchange received guarantees that other policy areas would not be crowded out, but would have the chance to develop as well. As a substantial increase in structural funds was in any case a longstanding Parliament objective, it proved relatively easy to agree to the 'interinstitutional agreement on budgetary discipline and the improvement of the budgetary procedure'.[12]

Thus, the institutions entered a period often described as 'budgetary peace' yet the 'peace treaty' contained longstanding Parliament objectives, such as the limitation on the growth of agricultural spending and the considerable development of the structural funds. After four years in which the Community had begun the year without an agreed budget, the following years saw relatively smooth budgetary procedures with agreements reached on time.

This does not mean to say that all scope for argument was removed. For *the 1990 budget*, Parliament was anxious to provide assistance for Eastern European countries embarking on a process of reform, arguing for the provision of such assistance on a multilateral basis through the EC rather than just by Member States separately. Parliament managed to persuade Council to include such an item in the budget, and to agree to a corresponding revision of the financial perspective, adding 500 m ECUs to category four (external policy).

For 1991, Parliament managed to ensure that the integration of the former GDR into the Community, and thereby into EC spending policies, should not take place at the expense of existing policies but should be in the form of additional expenditure, as a mark of Community solidarity. Parliament also created a new financial instrument for environment policy (LIFE) and revised the financial perspective to provide for aid to countries affected by the Gulf crisis and to enlarge the eastern European programme (PHARE).

For the *1992 budget*, Council produced a draft well below the ceiling of the financial perspectives, notably by financing extended support for the Soviet Union by means of cutting internal policies. Parliament responded by reinstating the sums for internal policies and placing over 1000 m ECU, including the sums for the Soviet Union, in reserve, to be released only when Council agreed to finance it through a revision of the perspectives. However by December 1991, no agreement had been reached and the 1992 budget was adopted without a revision. The issue was only settled by a supplementary budget in February 1992.

The *1993 budget* was debated in the context of new negotiations on the ceilings of own resources and the financial perspectives for 1993–99, described in chapter 13.

Altogether, apart from the technical adjustments to cater for movements in GNP and prices and conditions of implementation, Parliament obtained seven revisions of the financial perspectives between

1990 and 1992, totalling some 6641 m ECU – all to non-agricultural policy areas (and mostly external policy). The Inter-Institutional Agreement was not a straitjacket.

Assessing the Results

These often spectacular conflicts resulted in changes to the budget that were initially resisted by many of the Member States represented in Council. In that sense, it went well beyond simple intergovernmental decision-taking. But in the long run, what real impact can we attribute to the EP? Is it significant in terms of the process of European integration? At first sight, Parliament's impact appears to be small. First, it is in the context of a budget which is itself small as a proportion of GDP when compared to Member States' budgets. Second, Parliament's amendments rarely resulted in increases of more than a couple of percentage points over what Council had adopted in its first reading, with the exception of 1985 and 1986 for reasons described above. Third, in terms of Parliament's constant objectives of reining in agricultural expenditure on the one hand, and using the budget to develop other Community programmes and policy areas on the other hand, the first impression is that Parliament did not have an enormous success in that EAGGF guarantee spending, which comprised some 70 per cent of the budget in 1979, still represented some 56 per cent in 1991. Closer analysis, however, gives a more nuanced picture.

On the overall size of the budget, it is indeed a small percentage of Member States budgets (rising from 1.8 per cent of Member States' budgets in 1979 to some 2.4 per cent in 1993),[13] but such a percentage of half a continent's public expenditure is, in absolute terms, larger than the budgets of a number of the smaller Member States. Furthermore, in its areas of responsibility, which do not comprise the big spending areas of national budgets such as defence, education or social security, the Community's budget is not without significance especially as it is overwhelmingly operational, not administrative expenditure. Agricultural support is an obvious example, but the funding under the structural funds is also highly significant in the regions which are most dependent on it: approximately half of infrastructure spending in Ireland, Greece and Portugal is funded through Community programmes. Some of the smaller items in the budget, including those developed by Parliament, such as educational exchanges, are of tremendous significance in the areas concerned. Let us take the example of Parliament's amendment to the Erasmus programme in the 1989 budget. Parliament voted to increase appropriations for this exchange programme designed to encourage university students to spend part of their study time in another Community country, raising the amount to some 9.5 m ECU more than Council wanted and, indeed, 7.5 m ECU more than the Commission had asked for. Although a small amount as a proportion of the whole budget, for that item it was a 20 per cent increase over the previous year, enabling a substantial development of the programme affecting many thousands of students.

As regards the failure substantially to reduce the percentage of agricultural spending, we have already noted that in this area, classified as compulsory expenditure, the final word lies with Council if it can achieve a qualified majority to overrule parliamentary modifications cutting expenditure. Furthermore, the spending levels are, in practice, shaped by the legislation adopted by the Council, notably when fixing agricultural prices, and Council was generally unwilling to revise the packages negotiated at length by its agricultural ministers. During the period in question, agricultural spending rose sharply – what is remarkable is that it did not become an even higher proportion of Community spending. This is in no small measure thanks to Parliament achieving some success in its objective of developing other areas of spending.[14]

As to Parliament's amendments only comprising a small percentage of the budget every year, it is worth recalling the words of Aaron Wyldavsky: 'Budgets are almost never actively reviewed as a whole, in the sense of considering at one time the value of all existing programmes compared to all possible alternatives. Instead, this year's budget is based on last year's budget, with special attention given to a narrow range of increases or decreases. The greatest part of any budget is a product of previous decisions.'[15] This is all the more true for the Community budget. Furthermore, Parliament is only part of the budgetary authority together with Council. None the less, the *cumulative* effect of its amendments over the years was of great significance.

Let us examine more carefully what Parliament has achieved with its own amendments. We noted earlier that Parliament (like Council) is restricted to a maximum rate of increase for NCE – the area in which Parliament's budgetary powers are potentially the greatest. Although this leaves Parliament with considerable powers of *allocation* within the maximum rate, it would leave Parliament with only limited scope for increasing expenditure overall in these areas and developing new policies. For the years 1979–88, the maximum rate never exceeded by more than 5 per cent the rate of inflation (and on average exceeded it by 2.6 per cent in this period).[16] Yet Parliament managed, in successive years, to go beyond this, either by persuading Council to accept a higher maximum rate or, when Council had itself used up more than half the maximum rate, by using its right to go a further half of the rate beyond Council's draft. Thus, the increase exceeded the maximum rate by over 13 per cent in 1980, 7 per cent in 1981, 10 per cent in 1982, 19 per cent in 1983, 32 per cent in 1986 as regards appropriations for payments. As regards appropriations for commitments, the increases were sometimes higher.

Furthermore, Parliament managed to play on the distinction between payments and commitments. We referred earlier to the two sets of figures in the budget, with the latter necessarily higher. In some years, particularly in the years immediately after direct elections, budgetary disputes between Parliament and Council were sometimes settled with the agreement to raise commitments rather than payments. For instance, in the 1980 budget, commitments for NCE were 70 per cent higher than payments. In 1981 the figure was 52 per cent. The maximum rate applies to both sets of figures. As it is in terms of a percentage, the same rate will produce a greater increase in absolute terms for commitments, once the level of commitments has been raised beyond that for payments. The effect over time of this was called the 'weight of the past': outstanding commitments that had to be covered by new payments. The weight of the past rose from 2231 m ECU in 1979 to 10,510 m ECU in 1987,[17] and therefore became one of the elements forcing a major increase that year in payment appropriations to catch up with the level of commitments.

Through these various means, expenditure on policies falling under NCE developed faster than on policies falling under CE, despite the enormous growth in CAP spending under CE. NCE rose from only 16.95 per cent of the total for payment appropriations in 1979 to 37.1 per cent in 1992.[18] Thus, the sums over which Parliament had the final say were a growing proportion of a growing budget. In absolute terms, they rose from 2.3 m ECU in 1979 to 25.6 m ECU in 1992 – a 1121 per cent increase in nominal terms and a 440 per cent increase after allowing for inflation.

In terms of policies, the most notable development is that of the structural funds. The regional development fund was a mere 400 m ECU in 1977. By 1992 some 8559 m ECU were spent on it. On the social fund, 173 m ECU were spent in 1977, compared to 4303 m ECU in 1992. Research policy was a mere 181 m ECU in 1977, reaching 1945 m ECU in 1992. Yet it is especially on some of the smaller items that Parliament was able to use its powers to a greater proportional effect, helping to develop a wide range of new Community policies.

One way for Parliament to do this was to create new items in the Community budget and to allocate funds to them. This practice soon gave rise to a major conflict with the Council, which held that Parliament could not do so unless there was already a legal basis provided through appropriate Community legislation to allow action in the area concerned. Parliament held that, as Article 205 of the EC Treaty requires the Commission to execute the budget, the inclusion of an item in the budget is itself a sufficient legal basis. In 1982, in the context of the interinstitutional agreement on the budget mentioned earlier, a compromise was reached on the subject, the basis of which had been the Commission's half-way house position. It was agreed that legislation would be required where such a budget line created 'significant' new Community action. When this was the case, the Commission would put forward the necessary proposal by the end of January, and Council and Parliament would use their best endeavours to adopt the necessary regulation before the end of May (failing which the Commission would propose transfers to other budget items, thus ensuring that the appropriations were not lost entirely). As to amounts not deemed to be 'significant' – and there was still much scope for debate as to the definition of this word – the adoption of an item in the budget by Parliament was deemed to be sufficient.

Parliament has made use of the possibility to create new budget lines every year. Table 4.1 gives an idea of the number of items and the total volume of expenditure in question. Sometimes, Parliament enters a new item in the budget but does not allocate any sums of money to it, merely entering a token item (PM-pro memoriam). Such an approach allows money to be transferred in the course of the year from other items, or may be the precursor for allocating sums of money in subsequent years, or may be a recognition that, for the case in question, a legal base is necessary.

Among the items initiated in this way by Parliament over the years, have been the 'European City of Culture' programme (item 6707 of 1985), Community assistance for the private agricultural sector in Poland (2 m ECU in item 991 of 1985), the foundation of the Euro-Arab University (item 9451 of 1986), help to NGOs in Chile during the military dictatorship (item 992 of 1986), Community assistance to environmental protection NGOs (item 6617 in 1986), the special programme for the development of Portuguese industry – PEDIP (item 760 of 1987), Community funding for research against AIDS (item

Table 4.1   *Budget Items Created by the European Parliament*

Year	Number of items created by EP amendment	Of which with money on line or in reserve (i.e. not P.M.)	Total appropriation for payments (ECU m)	Total appropriation for committments (ECU m)
1985	10	3	3	3
1986	30	12	21.38	37.38
1987	12	4	14.5	14.5
1988	15	5	5.25	6.25
1989	13	7	7.6	10
1990	12	3	4.7	4.7
1991	29	20	50.3	132.8
1992	36	20	65.884	95.084

Source: Compiled on basis of information listed in briefing note 92/09/084 of EP Research & Studies D.G. *Haushaltplan der EG: Haushaltzeilen die vom EP initiiert wurden.*

6486 of 1987), a research programme for safer heavy goods vehicles (item 7353 of 1988), the SPRINT programme (item 7521 of 1989), the LIFE financial instruments for environmental policy (item B4-320 of 1991), the establishment of the European Law Academy (item A 3290 of 1991) and the establishment of the PERIFRA programme (item B2-610 of 1991).[19]

The counterpart to creating new items in the budget is the deletion of items. Rather than delete entirely, Parliament has usually used a more subtle instrument namely that of 'freezing' items in the budget, releasing them only when it has received satisfactory assurances from the Commission. It can do this by placing individual items in the reserve (chapter 100 or BO-40), from which they can be released only by a decision of the budgetary authority – in the case of NCE, the Parliament.

One of the most spectacular uses of this power was in 1982/3 when Parliament used it to provide for refunds to the UK amounting to 850 m ECUs to be used on specific infrastructure programmes of European interest in the UK instead of a direct reimbursement to the UK Treasury. Usually, however, the entry of appropriations in chapter 100 is used as a discreet way of bargaining with the Commission, in order to get assurances on the use of a particular line and the implementation of programmes. In 1989, for example, Parliament entered sums covering an increase in the Commission's staff into chapter 100, releasing them only in the course of the year when it received satisfactory information as to how the staff would be deployed.

Parliament's amendments to the budget are not restricted to revenue and expenditure. Next to every line of the budget there are remarks which specify the use to which appropriations are to be put. Many amendments are concerned to modify these remarks, something that Council initially saw with reluctance. Parliament has frequently adopted amendments changing or adding to these remarks. For example, in the 1990 procedure, Parliament modified the remarks next to certain aid provisions of the budget in such a way as to exclude the possibility of payments to China, following the events at Tienanmin square in the summer of 1989.

The procedure is also open to pressure from outside. In 1989, for example, there was an amendment to the 1990 draft budget to add 1.26 m ECUs to the Community action programme to assist the handicapped. This amendment was the focal point of a 'fair deal' campaign launched by the European coordinating body of disability organizations. This gained the support of the political groups, the Budgetary Committee and finally the Plenary.

Thus, it can be seen that Parliament used the budgetary powers provided to it in the Treaties of 1970 and 1975 to develop its role in the adoption and implementation of the Community budget and even beyond that in using the budget to initiate new policies or to influence the implementation of existing policies. In terms of the impact of this assertive role by the elected Parliament, there is considerable material to provide comfort to intergovernmentalists and federalists alike. Intergovernmentalists will point to the top limit on revenues available being fixed by the Member States with any change requiring unanimous agreement and ratification at a national level (but even this ties Member States into a legal system of common concern, which is a far cry from voluntary contributions that can be withheld). Federalists will point to the character of the resources given to the Community and to the fact that the budgetary procedures display a genuine bicameralism with the Council and the Parliament as almost equal chambers. There can be no doubt that much of the detail in the budget and even the development of some major items have been quite different from what would have resulted from classic intergovernmental structures. In the words of a UK Treasury minister, 'I think we have to face up to the fact that when [the Commons] passed the EC Finance Bills, it did hand over a stream of revenue to the European institutions without annual legislation and our ability to influence and check that is correspondingly diminished' (Heathcoat-Amory, 1996).

Neofunctionalists too can find considerable material in the interaction that takes place during the budgetary procedure among various interests involved. The whole process is an interaction between Community and national authorities, frequently displaying a pattern of national authorities being drawn into bargaining which 'upgrades the common interest': to obtain particular objectives, it is necessary to accommodate the objectives of others. Within the ceilings available, this is more easily done in an upwards rather than a downwards direction. When a ceiling is reached, vested interests that have been developed make it easier to raise the ceiling rather than to prune existing policies.

Perhaps we can again see here how the different integration theories each form part of the picture and each contain an element of truth as part of the whole. Clearly, an initial 'constitutional' development took place which had a federal character in that it transferred certain resources to the Community and laid down, in the Treaties, a constitutional text governing the powers of the Community institutions and the decision-taking procedures to exercise the powers so transferred. Clearly, the federal characteristics were limited in that Member States were to keep a 'gatekeeper' role, setting in particular a ceiling on the own resources available to the Community and providing a major role for themselves in the decision-taking through their representatives in the Council. Clearly, within the regime thereby created, neofunctionalist type interactions have taken place, enabling a development in the scope and level of Community action, the drawing in of other actors, and interaction of government and supranational élites – all within the parameters (of the Community's own resources) laid down by the governments. But the results have also built up the pressure to go beyond those parameters – as happened when the ceiling of own resources was raised in 1984, 1987 and 1992 – a decision firmly in the hands of the governments with their diverse approaches to European integration and their various interests, but which they have felt constrained to take not least as a result of these pressures.

From whatever perspective it is looked at, the existence of the elected Parliament with its activist policy on the budget played a major role in developing the pace and direction of European integration in the budgetary sphere. In terms of the hypotheses developed in chapter 2, it would appear that the evidence on the budgetary front is sufficient to refute nos 4 and 5: the elected Parliament exploited the budgetary powers more systematically and to greater effect than the nominated Parliament. Hypothesis 7b would appear to be applicable in view of the growth in techniques and practices developed by the Parliament,[20] the procedural developments agreed with the other institutions and the interaction developed with external actors affected by budget decisions. However, in terms of the main hypothesis likely to be confirmed or otherwise in this chapter, namely no. 6, there is a mixed picture. There is little evidence to assert that the Commission and the Council followed Parliament's guidance simply because it carried more weight by virtue of direct elections. Much of what Parliament achieved was obtained after initial resistance by the Council and after considerable conflict and even litigation. The legitimacy of direct elections would appear to be less important than the activism and commitment resulting from full-time MEPs.

THE PARLIAMENT'S LEGISLATIVE POWERS

The Setting: Parliament's Legislative Powers at the Time of the First Direct Elections

Under the 1951 ECSC Treaty, Parliament merely exercised powers of control over the High Authority (Commission), and did not participate in the adoption of legislation. The 1957 EEC and Euratom Treaties gave the Community a more wide-ranging power to adopt legislation and correspondingly provided for EP participation in legislative procedures. This was done by laying down in 22 articles in the EEC Treaty and 11 articles in the Euratom Treaty provisions obliging Council to consult Parliament on Commission proposals before their adoption. The Treaties sometimes provided for Council to consult the Economic and Social Committee as well in certain cases, but in the case of this body, Council could stipulate a deadline within which it must adopt its opinion. No such deadline was provided for in the case of the Parliament, and as we shall see, this difference was to prove important.

Over the years, through agreements with the other institutions and through interpretation of the Treaties, Parliament sought to maximize the significance of this consultation procedure. Even before direct elections a number of concessions were obtained, both in the scope and in the content of the procedure.

In March 1960, Council undertook to extend the scope of the procedure to all important problems, whether or not the Treaties specifically required the consultation of Parliament (voluntary consultations or *consultations facultatives*). In February 1964, it agreed to extend these beyond 'important problems' to all legislative texts except those of a purely technical or temporary nature. In November 1968, it undertook to consult Parliament on non-legislative texts as well. These include Commission memoranda and Council resolutions which, whilst not legally binding, nevertheless lay down guidelines, timetables and commitments which provide the framework for forthcoming legislative measures. At the same time, the Commission undertook to send to Parliament all memoranda and communications that it sends to Council. Parliament has the option of debating them, or even drafting its own report and adopting a resolution.

In successive letters in November 1969, March 1970 and July 1970, Council committed itself to informing Parliament of the reasons for departing from Parliament's opinion when adopting Community legislation, initially for legislation with financial consequences and subsequently for all important questions. This information would be provided upon request either orally or in writing.

The Paris Summit of Heads of Government following the enlargement of the Community in 1973 invited the Council and the Commission 'to put into effect without delay practical measures designed to achieve the reinforcement of the powers of control of the European Parliament and to improve the relations both of Council and of the Commission with the Assembly'. As a result of this Declaration, Council agreed in October 1973:

- that it would consult Parliament on Commission proposals, in principle, within one week of receiving the proposal;
- that 'except in cases of urgency when it will enter into contact with the Parliament, and subject to the fulfilment of its obligations, not to examine a proposal of the Commission on which the Parliament has been consulted until the opinion of the Parliament has been received, provided that such opinions are given by an appropriate date which may, in certain cases, be fixed by common agreement';
- to provide better information to Parliament as to the action taken by Council on its opinions and to this end, in addition to existing procedures, to have quarterly meetings of the Presidents of Parliament and Council.

Also pursuant to the 1973 Summit, the Commission agreed on 30 May 1973:

- to propose consulting Parliament on all proposals of any kind other than those of minor importance, or confidential matters;

- to express its opinion in Parliament's plenary on all amendments and to justify its opposition to any amendments in writing or orally in plenary;
- to amend its proposals to Council on the basis of Article 149(2) of the EEC Treaty in order to incorporate Parliament's amendments, even when these were only technical (it should be recalled that Council can only amend the Commission's text unanimously whereas a qualified majority is often sufficient to adopt it);
- to send directly to Parliament the proposals it sends to Council.

Also in 1973, the Commission and Council agreed that Parliament should be *re*consulted whenever significant changes were made to the text on which Parliament initially delivered its opinion.

The result of all these developments was that MEPs could at least be involved in all discussions on Community legislation and policy-making. The development of Parliament's committee system was, at least in part, an attempt to maximize these possibilities and in particular to provide for dialogue both with Commissioners and with their officials at all levels. However, until direct elections and full-time MEPs as of 1979, the practical use made of these possibilities was limited, by the part-time nature of the job, with national parliamentarians' attendance necessarily constrained (and even subject to frequent last-minute changes) due to domestic parliamentary duties. Nevertheless, the establishment of these procedures laid down a basis on which the elected Parliament could build.

However, no matter how extensive the possibilities for parliamentary involvement in the discussion of Community legislation, the bottom line of being able to block proposals or impose its will on the other institutions was lacking. Most national parliaments have such powers, even if they rarely make use of them. The EP could make its opinion known at all stages, but prior to direct elections, it had little leverage if the other institutions failed to respond to its views. It 'remained largely marginal in the Community's legislative process.'[21]

One area that seemed to offer hope of going further was in the field of legislation with consequences for the EC budget, where a 'conciliation procedure' (in French '*procédure de concertation*' not to be confused with the '*procédure de conciliation*' set up later by the Maastricht Treaty) was instituted by a Joint Declaration of Parliament, Council and Commission on 4 March 1975. Such a Joint Declaration can be considered to be a sort of constitutional convention between Council and Parliament, laying down procedures which they both undertake to follow. Whether such provisions are legally binding has still not been tested, though the Court of Justice has referred to their existence. The conciliation procedure resulted from a realization that the EP might be in a position to use its new budgetary powers (see above) to prevent the implementation of legislation with budgetary consequences. Council was therefore willing to negotiate and agree on a procedure aimed at reducing the risk of such conflicts by first seeking agreement with Parliament on the legislation. The 1975 Declaration is as follows[22] (my emphasis):

(i) A conciliation procedure between the European Parliament and the Council with the active assistance of the Commission is hereby instituted.

(ii) This procedure may be followed for Community acts of general application which have appreciable financial implications, and of which the adoption is not required by virtue of acts already in existence.

(iii) When submitting its proposal the Commission shall indicate whether the act in question is, in its opinion, capable of being the subject of the conciliation procedure. The European Parliament, when giving its opinion, and the Council may request that this procedure be initiated.

(iv) The procedure shall be initiated if the criteria laid down in paragraph (ii) are met and if the Council intends to depart from the opinion adopted by the European Parliament.

(v) The conciliation procedure shall take place in a 'Conciliation Committee' consisting of the Council and representatives of the European Parliament. The Commission shall participate in the work of the Conciliation Committee.

(vi) *The aim of the procedure shall be to seek an agreement between the European Parliament and the Council.*

The procedure should normally take place during a period not exceeding three months, unless the act in question has to be adopted before a specific date or if the matter is urgent, in which case the Council may fix an appropriate time limit.

(vii) *When the positions of the two institutions are sufficiently close,* the European Parliament may give a new opinion, after which the Council shall take definitive action.

The Declaration thus used terms that imply a certain number of obligations for Council, and its formal aim was to 'seek agreement between the European Parliament and the Council'. However, as the ultimate power to legislate was almost entirely in the hands of the

Council, the procedure amounted in practice merely to an attempt by MEPs to beg Members of Council to think again. The parliamentary delegation had no bargaining position *vis-à-vis* Council other than, possibly, threatening not to vote the necessary credits when it came to the following year's budget. Unless Parliament was totally opposed to the proposal, such a stance lacked credibility. Council had therefore little incentive to make major concessions to Parliament in the conciliation negotiations, especially when this would reopen negotiations within Council itself, and quite possibly endanger a compromise which Council may have reached only with the greatest difficulty.

In practice, prior to direct elections, the conciliation procedure did not achieve the breakthrough that some had hoped for. Apart from the conciliation in 1977 on the Financial Regulation, an area intimately intertwined with the very operation of Parliament's budgetary powers, no spectacular successes were achieved. Most damning of all, however, is the fact that the procedure itself was used only five times prior to direct elections. The unelected Parliament was unable to make the most of this limited breakthrough.

One final aspect of Parliament's legislative powers as they stood at that time concerns the *right to initiate* legislation. This right is traditionally associated with parliaments. But in practice, in most countries, this role has been taken over by governments. In the UK, for example, MPs have to rely on a lottery system (the ballot for 'Private Members' Bills') to introduce a limited category of legislative proposals themselves. In France, the government is given a virtual monopoly in this respect by the Constitution. Even in countries where there are no constitutional or regulatory limitations on Parliament in this respect, the detailed and technical nature of much modern legislation means that, in practice, most legislation is initiated by the Executive.

Correspondingly, the treaties gave the Commission a virtual monopoly of legislative initiative. The EP had no formal right to initiate legislation, except for the purpose of adopting a uniform electoral procedure for European elections. Similarly, the Council cannot normally initiate Community legislation. Nevertheless, as in national situations, the formal provisions do not grant the Executive a monopoly on ideas nor the right to exercise these powers without due regard to the wishes of Council and Parliament. Council, indeed, was given the right under the original treaties (Article 152 EEC) to request the Commission to undertake studies and to submit to it the appropriate proposals, but no equivalent right was given to Parliament. None the less, the nominated Parliament had developed the practice of adopting reports and resolutions at its own initiative, frequently calling upon the Commission to bring forward proposals or to take other action. The Commission responded to such initiatives in the debates thereon, but whether it would use its power of initiating legislation to take the matter further was entirely a matter for the Commission's discretion. Parliament had little leverage over the Commission, other than the motion of censure which was not plausible in most such cases.[23]

The Battles: The New Parliament Attempts to Make the Most of the Procedures

One of the first acts of the elected Parliament was to intervene in a case before the Court of Justice in which a Council directive was being challenged on the ground that Parliament had not given its opinion on the proposal. Prior to direct elections, Parliament had never intervened nor brought a case itself to the Court, and had only once even participated in proceedings in a case which turned on the duration of Parliament's session. The elected Parliament was not such a reluctant litigant.

The consequent ruling of the Court of Justice[24] made it clear that Council could not adopt Community legislation before receiving Parliament's opinion, where this was required under the Treaties. In this ruling, the Court stated as we saw in chapter 1 that the provisions in the Treaty requiring the consultation of Parliament were:

> the means which allows the Parliament to play an actual part in the legislative process of the Community. Such a power represents an essential factor in the institutional balance intended by the Treaty. Although limited, it reflects at Community level the fundamental principle that the peoples should take part in the exercise of power through the intermediary of a representative assembly. Due consultation of the Parliament in the cases provided for by the Treaty therefore constitutes an essential formality disregard of which means that the measure concerned is void.

It is important to note that this ruling was favourable to Parliament despite the fact that:

- Parliament had actually had a debate in plenary on the issue on the basis of the report from its committee, and had finished its consideration of its position on the proposal, but had not taken a final vote on the resolution as a whole, referring the text back to the relevant parliamentary committee.

- There was an objectively justifiable deadline for taking a quick decision in order to avoid a legal lacuna.
- Council maintained that, in the circumstances, it did try to get Parliament's opinion but that 'Parliament, by its own conduct, made the observance of that requirement impossible'.
- The Commission intervened on the side of Council.

Parliament included in the arguments on its side of the case the fact that Council had not exhausted all the possibilities of obtaining the opinion of Parliament in that it did not request the application of the urgent procedure provided for by the internal rules of Parliament nor did it make use of the possibility it had under Article 139 of the Treaty to ask for an extraordinary session of Parliament. In its judgment, the Court expressly avoided taking a position on what the situation would have been had Council availed of these procedures and had Parliament still not delivered its opinion. If Council were to exhaust its procedural possibilities to obtain Parliament's opinion, or if Parliament were to state openly that it was withholding its opinion in order deliberately to block decision-taking in the Community, the Court might not rule the same way. The Court had often referred to the duty of loyal cooperation among the institutions, and it was possible that if Parliament were to block indefinitely, the Court might rule against it. However, this was not tested until 1995 (by which time Parliament had gained other powers) when the Court ruled against Parliament in a case (C-69/95) turning on the unusual circumstances of Parliament accepting an urgency request from Council, but then postponing its decision. Council had then adopted the regulation in question in order to avoid an impending legal lacunae. The Court ruled that, in the particular circumstances, Council was entitled to take such action.

Parliament was thus able to take advantage of the 'Isoglucose' Ruling which coincided with the major overhaul of Parliament's internal Rules of Procedure which it was carrying out following the first direct elections. Parliament put in its new rules provisions whereby it could decide to postpone the final vote on the Commission's proposal until the Commission had taken a position on its amendments. Where the Commission refused to accept these, it could refer the matter back to committee for reconsideration, thereby delaying its 'opinion' and holding up the procedure. When it gained a sufficient assurance from the Commission or when a compromise was reached, it could move to a final vote in plenary. The significance of the Commission's acceptance of Parliament's amendments lay in the fact that they would be incorporated into a revised proposal and could then only be removed by a unanimous Council.

The procedure of referral back to committee was, however, used rather infrequently in the early 1980s. Referral back was not automatic, but only if requested by the Chairman or rapporteur. This was corrected in a revision of Parliament's Rules of Procedure in 1987.

Council sometimes responded by taking a decision 'in principle' or 'subject to Parliament's opinion' before this opinion had been delivered. This happened, for instance, 11 times in 1986, 8 in 1987, 12 in 1988, 7 in 1989) This broke Council's 1973 undertaking, as well as the spirit and probably the letter of the Isoglucose principle: in such circumstances Council clearly intended to ignore Parliament's opinion. A combination of Parliament and Commission opposition to this practice, however, led to it falling into disuse: in the next five years, Council tried this on only nine occasions, and in most of the cases where Parliament anyway sought to amend the text, Council in the end accepted amendments.

In any case, the 'Isoglucose' Ruling gave Parliament a potentially important device to fall back on when it was not satisfied with the response to its emerging position. Clearly, the device was more significant for urgent matters where any delay could cause problems that the Commission and even the Council would wish to avoid. In such cases Parliament then had a strong bargaining position to fall back on.[25]

The elected Parliament also sought to make more of *the 1975 conciliation procedure*. After initial hesitation (there were no such procedures in the first three years of the elected Parliament) the number of conciliations rose to about five a year from 1982. Some were notably successful in that Parliament was able to secure significant changes to Council's position and reach agreement with it. Examples include the Food Aid Regulation adopted in 1986; the New Community Instrument Regulation (NIC IV) of March 1987 extending the Community's borrowing and lending capacity to assist small and medium-sized undertakings; the new regulation on agricultural structures of June 1987; the budgetary discipline provision of 1988; the reform of the Regional and Social Funds in 1989; and the regulation on the collection of own resources of 1989 which strengthened the Commission's rights of inspection in Member States.

The procedure had some merits: it allowed a direct confrontation between Parliament and Council as a whole. Ministers were faced by the physical presence of MEPs, giving them a direct input to Council not previously filtered by the Commission. It was difficult for Council systematically to refuse all Parliament requests. Council is not monolithic and it was sometimes possible to reopen discussions within Council. Last but not least, it helped Council get accustomed to negotiating with Parliament and to developing closer working relations with it. In this respect, it was a precedent for future reforms to build on.

Finally, as regards Parliament's attempts to *initiate* legislation, the elected Parliament made far greater use of 'own initiative' reports, adopting a large number in the first few years after 1979. In many ways, it gave greater priority to this than to the legislative consultation procedure,[26] apparently hoping that major setpiece debates and proposals for the future orientation of EC policy would carry the authority and legitimacy of the elected Parliament and would therefore automatically elicit a response from the other institutions. This was not to be. The Commission would not agree automatically to subjugate its right of initiative to Parliament's wishes, and the Council would not and could not make general promises as to future legislation.

Despite this, examples of Parliament initiating legislation are not hard to find. Parliament took the initiative in 1982 of pressing for a ban on the import of baby seal skins to the Community. In this, it was supported by public campaigning including a petition with over one million signatures. These efforts resulted in Commission proposals, then backed by Parliament in the legislative procedure, and the adoption of a Council regulation, despite initial reluctance by both the Commission and Council. Another example was the directive on transfrontier TV broadcasts, laying down rules for such broadcasts, which also originated with an EP own-initiative report, as did the proposal to ban tobacco advertising, and the directives banning ozone-depleting substances and limiting leaded petrol. In the field of external relations too, parliamentary initiatives can lead to results. Thus the STABEX fund in the Lomé Convention, which helps stabilize the export earnings for certain products of the ACP countries, as well as the human rights clauses in that same Convention, owe their origin to EP initiatives. As we saw in the previous section, Parliament has also used its budgetary powers as a means to initiate new Community policies by creating new items in the budget and endowing them with funds. It can also initiate policy changes by cutting certain items of non-compulsory expenditure, or to propose cuts in compulsory expenditure which Council can only overrule by a qualified majority. This technique has been used to press for the revision of legislation governing the use of such expenditures, notably regarding the CAP.

Parliament also initiates policy in a wider sense than specific items of legislation by addressing major issues concerning the development of the European Union. This was done most notably in the 1980s in the case of pressing for the completion of the Common Market – one of the original objectives of the EEC Treaty which remained unfulfilled. The work of several parliamentary committees seemed to indicate that its completion would be a key element of European economic recovery from the recession of the early 1980s. The Parliament commissioned a report from two leading economists (M. Michel Albert and Pr. J. Ball), who reported to a coordinating group of chairmen of the relevant committees. This report, submitted in 1983, pioneered the concept of the 'cost of non-Europe', highlighting the economic cost of insufficient economic integration. Albert subsequently published a paperback version of the report which topped the book sales chart in France. The 'European Round Table' of leading industralists also took up and developed this theme.

This report was followed up by a special committee which produced a 'programme for European economic recovery' just before the 1984 European elections. It highlighted the volume of outstanding draft legislation necessary for completing the single market that remained blocked in the Council. Parallel to the formal work by the Parliament, one of the intergroups, known as the 'Kangaroo Group', was extraordinarily active on the issue of removing internal barriers to trade. Composed of members of all political groups, it produced a regular newspaper and held conferences across the Union. These initiatives together did much to create the drive for completing the single market and, ultimately, the 1992 programme.

Assessing the Results

The elected Parliament was able to 'give teeth'[27] to the legislative consultation procedure by taking advantage of the 'Isoglucose' court case – in which it itself intervened – in 1979/80 and it was able to develop a little the conciliation procedure that involved it in direct talks with Council. However, the significance of these developments, at least prior to 1987 as we shall see in later chapters, was limited. The 'delaying tactic' could be deployed only with difficulty, it did not *formally* exist (and to assert that it did might jeopardize its *de facto* existence) and was not easily explicable to the public. The conciliation procedure was applicable only to a small category of legislation and Parliament's leverage in the negotiations was usually highly limited.

In terms of public visibility, Parliament remained stranded in a perceived secondary role. Even where its influence may have been great, it was Council that adopted the legislation and it was within Council (or the European Council) that the major political deals were made. Not surprisingly, media coverage of the Parliament declined (whether measured by the number of journalists attending sessions, the number of TV reports, the hours of television coverage or the use of the EPs radio studios) in 1980, again in 1981 and further still in 1982.[28]

Similarly, as regards Parliament's attempts to initiate legislation, although there were a number of successes, only a few were spectacular enough to be noticeable to public opinion. Within EC circles and within interest groups affected or potentially affected, as with Parliament's powers under the consultation procedure, there were those who would notice and who would try to exploit the possibilities, be they environmental organizations, commercial interests or professional lobbyists. In this respect, Parliament's 'legislative' functions did begin, in the period 1979–87, to involve interaction with other interested parties who thereby found a non-government and non-Commission input into EC decision-taking. This therefore contributed to developing a more complete political system in the EC. Furthermore, Parliament did have a perceptible influence on the outcome in at least some cases. However, the overall result can only have been disappointing in light of the aspirations and expectations outlined in chapter 2. The net effect is, therefore, likely to have been a radicalizing one on MEPs and on their determination to fight for institutional change, to overcome what they began to call a 'democratic deficit' in the Community.

If we examine this situation from the point of view of the various integration theories, as with Parliament's budgetary powers, we can see that the legislative powers that it inherited in 1979 illuminate aspects of all approaches, but to different degrees. The original 'constitution'/treaties gave the EC certain federal-type legislative powers, but exercised, to a greater degree than for the budget, by the representatives of the national governments in the Council. Some space was available, within the system created, for the scope and level of Community legislation to develop beyond what at least some governments had intended on some issues, and this partly through the actions of the Parliament and its interactions with other actors. Yet the impact in the first years after direct elections was not enough to change the character of the system, which remained in this respect encapsulated in a regime that did not give a strong role to the Parliament.

In terms of the hypotheses developed in chapter 2, we can reach largely the same conclusions as on the budgetary powers, despite the possibly lower level of impact. Hypotheses 4 and 5 can be largely refuted, and 7b cautiously (and within limits) confirmed, for the same reasons as those we outlined above for the budget.

Hypothesis no. 6 requires a more nuanced approach. The Commission was in a better position to respond to the Parliament than in the budget procedure, and the Commission at least was more susceptible to arguments of democratic legitimacy than was the Council. Nevertheless, the Parliament's influence on legislation, like the budget, did not noticeably increase as a result of having greater legitimacy, as illustrated by the Commission's failure to respond automatically to 'own-initiative' proposals of the EP. The progress made by Parliament to improve its position in the legislation procedure was based largely on its delaying capacity and its ability to publicize issues, and to that extent was conflictual rather than based on deference to the EP.

THE PARLIAMENT'S POWERS OF SCRUTINY AND CONTROL

The Trends after 1979

The elected Parliament was also more vigorous than the nominated Parliament in making use of the various instruments of scrutiny and control (or, in American terminology, 'oversight') available to it.

Parliament had a number of powers described as 'supervisory' in the Treaty consisting of the right to question the Commission (orally or in writing), to debate its activities and, ultimately, to adopt a motion of censure on it.[29] The budget treaties added the right to give or withold a discharge to the Commission in respect of the implementation of the budget.[30] The elected Parliament sought to make the most of these, and also to develop other tools of parliamentary scrutiny.

Let us first illustrate the quantitative increase with two examples: questions and hearings.

Parliamentary questions, notably to the Commission, rose substantially after direct elections. In the 1970s the unelected Parliament averaged under 1000 written questions a year and fewer than 500 oral questions at Question Time. In the 1980s, the average in the elected Parliament had more than doubled to about 2250 written questions a year and just under 1000 oral questions at Question Time.[31]

The number of *public hearings* held by standing committees of the Parliament rose from scarcely two a year from 1974 to 1979, to an average of about 20 a year from 1980 to 1989.[32] Hearings enable committees to discuss directly with experts or interested parties, but also provide an opportunity for representative groups and interests to have a direct input at European level to the deliberations of the institutions.

Moving beyond quantitative analysis, let us examine how the elected Parliament made use of various powers. The right to grant *discharge* on the stewardship of the budget is more than a mere endorsement of the accounts. Article 90 of the Financial Regulation requires all institutions to 'take all appropriate steps to act on the comments appearing in the decisions giving discharge'. The same article also requires them to report on the measures taken in the light of these comments if requested by the Parliament. Neither the treaties nor the Financial Regulation specify what should happen should the Parliament refuse to grant discharge. It would clearly represent a major political reprimand for the Commission, representing a public statement by Parliament that either the Commission's management has been irregular or uneconomic, or that the Commission has failed to respect the objectives set when the budget was adopted. The likely political consequences were spelt out by the Budget Commissioner Tugendhat who stated to Parliament[33] that 'refusal to grant discharge ... is a political sanction ... which would be extremely serious; the Commission thus censored would, I think, have to be replaced'. This has never been put to the test, as the one time Parliament did refuse discharge (for the 1982 financial year) by a vote in November 1984, the then Commission was anyway at the end of its term and due to leave office a few weeks later.

Rather than going that far, Parliament has generally sought to use the procedure to exact information or concessions from the Commission, notably by resorting to the possibility of postponing the discharge until satisfaction is achieved in these respects. It has also sought to follow up the implementation of the recommendations contained in the discharge decision to ensure that they are being respected, in accordance with the financial regulation.

As an example, let us examine Parliament's report on the 1992 discharge for the 1990 financial year. Here, the EP committee recommended to postpone discharge until the Commission:

- annulled a decision waiving the recovery of certain revenues concerning Italian milk;
- made available the terms of reference and a full report of its internal inquiries concerning allegations of fraud in its tobacco division; and

- gave Parliament a commitment to transfer 50 staff posts to the anti-fraud unit.

Following the first direct elections in 1979, Parliament set up a new standing committee on Budgetary Control responsible for these matters. Prior to direct elections, the matter was dealt with in the Budgets Committee, most of whose time is devoted to the procedures for adopting the following year's budget. Having a separate committee, together with its back-up in terms of secretariat, procedural privileges and its own membership concentrating on these issues, was a way of reinforcing Parliament's role in these matters. We again see the elected, full-time Parliament developing its potential in a way that the nominated Parliament did not.

The effectiveness of Parliament's budgetary control is limited by the time gaps involved and by the fact that many discharge decisions concern preceding Commissions. The Budgetary Control Committee attempted to enhance continuity and consistency of its monitoring by allocating specific sectors to each of its members for them to specialize in for a number of years. This is also something which the nominated Parliament, with constantly shifting membership, could only do with difficulty.

Litigation was also an area left virtually unexplored by the nominated Parliament,[34] but which the elected Parliament took up in a big way. Reference has already been made to the 'Isoglucose' Ruling, with the important consequences this had for Parliament's position in the consultation procedure. Three years later, Parliament made legal history by taking the first interinstitutional action under Article 175 EEC against the Council for its failure to adopt a common transport policy.[35] Parliament's very right to bring such a case was challenged by Council, but the Court ruled in Parliament's favour both on the admissibility and on the substance. The Court ruled that in delaying decisions on matters where it was required to take action under the treaties, Council had failed in its responsibilities. The Court ruling was undoubtedly a major factor in reactivating Community policy-making in this area.

The early years after direct elections were also notable for cases being brought, for the first time, against Parliament. The first two actions, brought by Luxembourg, concerned issues related to the seat and working place of Parliament, seeking to declare void parliamentary decisions transferring staff or activities to Brussels. These were based on Article 38 of the ECSC Treaty which expressly provides that the Commission or a member state can proceed against Parliament in this way, and therefore did not deal with the question of whether proceedings could be brought against Parliament under the more broadly based Article 173 EEC, which only expressly identifies the Council and Commission as defendants. In its judgment of 23 April 1986, however, the Court answered this question in the affirmative in an action taken by the French Green Party contesting Parliament's decisions on the distribution of funding to parties for the second direct elections in 1984. Six weeks later, an action against Parliament by the Council, also based on 173 EEC, was admitted when the Court overturned the declaration by the President of the Parliament that the 1986 budget had been adopted.

These precedents led Parliament to take the view, in a resolution of 9 October 1986, that, as the Treaty had established a complete system of legal remedies and procedures to enable the Court to review the legality of measures of the institutions, Article 173 should be interpreted so as to permit Parliament to take proceedings for *annulment* under this provision. A first such action was commenced on 2 October 1987 when Parliament attacked the validity of a Council decision,[36] another was on the adoption of a directive based on what Parliament considered to be an incorrect legal base that avoided Parliament's prerogatives.

In the first of these cases, the Court ruled that Parliament did not have the right to bring cases for annulment as it is not specifically mentioned in Article 173. In view of the Court's previous ruling that Parliament could be proceeded *against* under the same article, the ruling caused much surprise in legal circles. It was partly reversed in the second of the above-mentioned cases in which the Court allowed Parliament to proceed for annulment in those cases where its own rights had not been fully respected in the Community's decision-taking procedures – a crucial right for defending Parliament's own prerogatives.

Litigation proceedings by the Parliament have since become a regular feature. Although Parliament has not always met with success, it has extended the scope and range of actions that come before the ECJ and thereby enhanced the latter's role as a 'Supreme Court', ruling on constitutional conflicts among the institutions.

Parliament started to make systematic use of the parliamentary instrument of a *committee of inquiry* after the first direct elections in 1979. Prior to this they were unknown. In the first three legislatures (1969–94), the elected Parliament established committees on:

- the situation of women in Europe (1980);
- the treatment of toxic and dangerous substances, notably on transfrontier shipment of dangerous waste following the Seveso accident (1983–4);
- on the rise of fascism and racism in Europe (following the winning of seats in the EP in 1984 by the Front National in France);
- drugs;
- agricultural stocks;
- the handling of nuclear materials, following the Mol/Transnuclear scandal;
- hormones in meat;
- application of the joint declaration against racism and fascism;
- transfrontier crime linked to drug trafficking.

As we saw above, another way the elected Parliament has found of exerting pressure on the Commission is that of using its budgetary powers to *'freeze' certain items in the Commission's budget*, releasing them only when it has received satisfactory assurances from the Commission.

The 1975 Budget Treaty also gave Parliament the right to be consulted on *appointments to the Court of Auditors*. Although this is only a consultative vote, Parliament made the most of this by providing for a thorough procedure involving a hearing of the candidate in front of the Budgetary Control Committee. This enabled Parliament to scrutinize the candidates, and obliged the Member States to take care when choosing their nominees. The test of what would happen should Parliament give a negative opinion on a proposed candidate first occurred in November 1989, when Parliament was consulted on the appointment or reappointment of six candidates. Parliament approved four of them, but felt 'unable to give a favourable opinion' in respect of the French and Greek candidates. The French government immediately responded by withdrawing the nominated candidate and putting forward a new candidate who, after he appeared before Parliament's Budgetary Control Committee, was approved by Parliament and duly appointed. The Greek government, which was in the middle of a government crisis and between two general elections in succession, claimed to be unable to find a more suitable candidate. Thus, the elected Parliament, with its specialist committee, carried enough weight to be able to ensure that 'consultation' involved the appearance of a candidate at a public hearing and a chance to question and probe the candidates. Rejection by Parliament, however, would not guarantee the withdrawal of the candidacy (further rejection in 1993 of a candidate seeking a second term did not lead to his withdrawal), but was clearly a significant enough act to make such an eventuality possible.

Scrutiny within the parliamentary committees, with regular questioning both of Commissioners and of their civil servants, developed considerably in the elected Parliament. Whereas before direct elections, appearances of Commissioners before a parliamentary committee such as the Economic and Monetary Affairs Committee would take place two or three times a year, since direct elections it is virtually a monthly occurrence.[37] Committees thus monitor the Commission and its departments, cross-examining both Commissioners and their civil servants on their implementation of Community policies and their new proposals. In some committees, a more formalized 'Question Time' to the Commission has been introduced.

There has also been an increased presence of ministers from the country holding the Council Presidency. During a six-month Council Presidency, there are now normally between some 20 and 30 ministerial appearances before parliamentary committees, with the main ministers appearing both at the beginning and the end of their Presidency. Prior to direct elections, this was restricted typically to three or four ministerial appearances per Presidency.

Assessing the Results

The area of Parliamentary scrutiny and control is one which displays the effect of a full-time professional Parliament exploiting more fully the possibilities available. From parliamentary questions, to public hearings; from exploiting the discharge procedure in order to put pressure on the Commission, to cross-examination of Commissioners and their officials in committee; from litigation in the Court of Justice, to appointments to the Court of Auditors; from committees of inquiry, to freezing funds – the elected Parliament was more vigourous, more systematic and more forceful than the nominated one.

In terms of the main integration theories, we can see again that the basic possibilities were created by the institutional features of the treaties, that they left some space for incremental development, that Parliament was able to exploit this space, but that there were limits to what could be achieved. In this area, Parliament's use of the existing treaties developed some traditional parliamentary functions at European level. Whatever the intended effect on policy, this added to perceptions of a functioning political system at EC level in which the Parliament played a role. The MEPs indeed fulfilled the role that Haas attributed to them of 'furthering the growth of practices and codes of behaviour typical of federations'.[38] This could not, however, substitute for the lack of other traditional parliamentary powers over legislation and over the constitution of the executive on which the Parliament's credibility depended – ultimately even to exercise effective scrutiny.

Returning to the hypotheses developed in chapter 2, it would appear from the above that nos 4 and 5 do not apply, the elected Parliament being both more active and more effective than its predecessor. There is certainly considerable evidence in this field to sustain hypothesis 7b. As to hypothesis 6, there is some evidence of greater respect being paid to the elected Parliament through more frequent appearances of Commissioners and Ministers at EP Committees, the voluntary cooperation with committees of inquiry, new arrangements within the Commission to respond to the EP and its Members, and the withdrawal of a candidate for the Court of Auditors to whom Parliament objected when consulted. The evidence is not conclusive (and the last one cannot be compared with the nominated Parliament where the situation never arose). The more significant steps forward by the EP in this area appear to have been on its own initiative (e.g. its use of the discharge provisions of the Treaty) or through litigation or by using its budgetary powers.

In all three areas surveyed in this chapter – budgetary powers, legislation and scrutiny/control – the conclusions we have reached have been broadly identical. In all cases, the treaty gave Parliament certain constitutional rights, which the elected Parliament sought to exploit and interpret to a greater extent than did the nominated Parliament. In all cases, the Parliament could not go (far) beyond the constitutional provisions of the treaties. In the words of President Dankert at the end of its first term of office, 'We have used our existing powers to the full. We have stretched them like a piece of elastic and in doing so, we have strengthened our role and status in interinstitutional relations. However, even elasticity has its limits.'[39] Support among MEPs for reforms enhancing the role of the EP is likely to have grown as a result of experience. In terms of the hypotheses developed in chapter 2, nos 4 and 5 do not find sustenance and can be refuted. No. 6 is not refuted, but the evidence in its favour is not substantial. Considerable evidence, however, has been found in favour of hypothesis no. 7 (in particular 7b), and modest evidence in favour of no. 10.

It is now time to turn to the attempts by Parliament not merely to exploit its existing powers, but to change the parameters of these powers.

5 Reform within the Treaties

The second strand of the elected Parliament's initial approach was to press for institutional reform within the existing treaties. As we saw at the beginning of the previous chapter, treaty revision was not initially seen as a realistic or attractive option. On the other hand, the prospect for institutional reform *within* the treaties, notably by means of inter-institutional agreements, was held to be possible, with MEPs looking to the precedents of the Joint Declaration with the Council and the Commission on the Conciliation Procedure (see chapter 4) and the 'Luns-Westerterp procedures' whereby Council had agreed to involve Parliament more closely in discussions on international agreements with third countries.[1] As explained by Klaus Hänsch:

> 'It is a realistic [approach] confined to what can be done up to 1984, the year of the second direct elections. . . . We must be able to show that we have actually achieved something. . . . The Treaty could not be amended by 1984, even if that was what was wanted, because the time is too short.[2]

On 12 October 1979 a subcommittee of the Political Affairs Committee was set up to deal with institutional problems. It was given the specific task of investigating relations between the EP and other institutions. Work was to proceed in two stages: a first stage was to lead to the adoption by the EP of a series of proposals, whilst the second stage was intended 'to ensure their implementation as a result of a continuous dialogue with the institutions to which those proposals were addressed'.[3] Eight rapporteurs were appointed and their reports concerned:

(a) the right of legislative initiative and the role of the EP in the legislative process of the Community: Van Miert (B/Soc);

(b) relations between the EP and the Council of the Community: Hänsch (D/Soc);

(c) relations between the EP and the Commission with a view to the appointment of a new Commission: Rey (B/Lib);

(d) relations between the EP and national parliaments: Nothomb (B/EPP) then (when he left the EP to become Foreign Affairs Minister in Belgium) Diligent (F/EPP);

(e) European political cooperation and the role of the EP: Lady Elles (UK/EDG);

(f) relations between the EP and the Economic and Social Commit-
     tee: Baduel Glorioso (I/Com);
(g) relations between the EP and the European Council: Antoniozzi
     (I/EPP);
(h) the role of Parliament in the negotiation and ratification of treaties
     of accession and of other treaties and agreements between the EC
     and third countries: Blumenfeld (D/EPP).

The political experience of several rapporteurs matched the subject
of their report. It was hoped that this would be a valuable asset throughout
both stages of work. For instance, Jean Rey was a former President of
the Commission, Nothomb a former President of the Belgian Chamber
of Deputies and Baduel Glorioso a former President of the ESC.

The Rey Report was the first to be debated and adopted in April
1980, brought forward to ensure that it preceded the beginning of the
procedure to appoint the new Commission due to take office in 1981.
The other reports were discussed and approved in a major institutional
debate in July 1981, except the Antoniozzi and Blumenfeld Reports,
which were dealt with later. These resolutions aimed mainly to involve Parliament more closely, according to defined procedures, in the
exercise of powers attributed by the treaties to the other institutions,
by means of joint agreements with them.

What precisely did Parliament seek to obtain through these reports?
An examination of the resolutions[4] adopted allows 12 main demands
to be distilled:

1. to be able to debate and vote on the candidate proposed by the
   Member States to become President of the Commission;
2. to hold 'a vote ratifying and expressing confidence' in the appointment of the Commission as a whole following a debate on its
   programme;
3. that the Commission should consult the Parliament on preliminary
   draft legislative proposals before making a formal proposal to the
   Council;
4. that the Commission should agree to introduce the formal legislative initiatives needed to give form to EP own initiative resolutions (or to explain its reasons to Parliament should it have
   substantive reasons for not being able or not wishing to introduce
   such proposals – in which case Parliament would still have the
   right to insist);
5. that the Commission should change its proposals in accordance
   with amendments adopted to them by the Parliament;

6. that the Commission should 'withdraw as a matter of course any proposal which is rejected *in toto* by the Parliament';
7. that Council return to majority decision-making, where provided for in the treaties;
8. that Council formalize and respect its previous undertakings to Parliament concerning the operation of the legislative consultation procedure, notably as regards the information it provides to Parliament and re-consultation of Parliament when Council wishes to amend the text;
9. that the conciliation procedure be improved and extended to cover all proposals 'to which Parliament attaches a special importance';
10. that committees of national civil servants involved in assisting the Commission in its executive duties should be purely advisory;
11. that Council should submit a third report on European Political Cooperation (foreign policy) in order to introduce improvements to the procedure, to set up a permanent secretariat for EPC, to submit an annual report in writing to the Parliament prior to a debate thereon, to establish an emergency procedure under which the foreign ministers would meet within 48 hours at the request of three Member States, to discuss security questions, to admit the Commission to all parts of EPC, to hold regular colloquies with the relevant EP committee.
12. that the European Council be formalized, that it act as the Council in conformity with the treaties and that its President report to the EP after each meeting.

The Commission reacted to Parliament's institutional resolutions in a communication sent to the other institutions on 14 October 1981.[5] Although it stated that it supported a strengthening of Parliament's role, both from the legislative point of view and from the point of view of the negotiation and conclusion of international agreements, it nevertheless stressed its special responsibilities under the Treaties, 'which prevented it from adopting Parliament's legislative proposals as they stood':[6] in other words, the Commission would not accept automatically to withdraw proposals Parliament rejected nor automatically to accept parliamentary amendments. It did, however, promise that it would explain its reasons in detail to Parliament if it had major objections to Parliament's position. The Commission joined with Parliament in calling for Council to revert to majority voting more often and agreed also with Parliament's criticisms concerning the restrictions (in the form of committees of national civil servants) placed by Council on the

Commission's executive powers. The Commission agreed to submit a proposal for a new interinstitutional agreement to improve and extend the conciliation procedure, which indeed it did on 17 December 1981.

As to the Council, it agreed that the President of the European Council should report to the EP after each meeting[7] and to hold a meeting on 17 November at the level of its Foreign Ministers with the EP Enlarged Bureau.[8] This meeting – the first of its kind – discussed the general need for a new impetus for the EC, majority voting in Council (Council President Carrington stated[9] on behalf of Council merely that he 'hoped that more decisions could be reached by majority vote'), attendance by Ministers at EP meetings, the treatment of parliamentary questions addressed to Council, the extension and improvement of the conciliation procedure and reconsultation of the EP when proposals are amended. It eventually gave rise to a letter from the Council to Parliament[10] containing a response from Council to some of the less important of Parliament's institutional demands. It stated that incoming Council Presidencies 'will endeavour to supply' their programme in writing (memorandum or text of speech) in advance of the EP debate on it; that it would reply 'exhaustively' to parliamentary questions; that Council Presidents of sectoral Councils would continue to meet once per Presidency with the relevant parliamentary committees 'depending on the time available'; that optional consultations of Parliament (where not required by the treaty) would continue on a 'flexible' basis; that reconsultation of Parliament would take place, as in the past, where appropriate; that all EP resolutions would be entered on the agenda of the Council (General Affairs); and that it would inform Parliament, upon request, in writing or orally (as already agreed in 1970) of its reasons for not complying with parliamentary opinions. It stated that Council 'did not intend to give an opinion' on the Procedural Rules in Parliament (taking advantage of the 'Isoglucose' judgment), but drew Parliament's attention to the danger of lengthening the legislative procedure.

This response, after almost a year, concerned only minor elements of Parliament's demands and was, even then, extraordinarily minimalist. But, discussions on the main issues within Council had already been overtaken by discussions on the 'Genscher–Colombo Initiative', officially launched in November 1981 by a letter to all Member States and the Commission and a formal presentation by Genscher and Colombo (respectively the German and Italian foreign ministers) to the EP. This initiative took over a large number of the proposals contained in Parliament's resolutions based on the reports of its Political Affairs Committee. Colombo had chaired that committee when it began its work on these issues, resigning from the EP to become foreign minister in April 1980. He spelt out in this presentation that 'we have taken heed of what Parliament wants'.

The Genscher–Colombo proposal, although presented as a draft 'Act', was, like Parliament's proposals, an attempt to make progress within the existing treaties by interpreting and supplementing them. It was to be 'a declaration of major political importance',[11] rather than a treaty which the authors thought would be 'little short of unrealistic'. It was not a new architectural design, but a set of improvements to the efficiency and scope of the existing Communities.

Genscher–Colombo was discussed at the London European Council meeting on 26–27 November 1981, which invited the Foreign Ministers to examine the proposal and report back to a future meeting. The Foreign Ministers established an *ad hoc* working party consisting of senior officials under the chairmanship of Belgium's ambassador to the EC, De Schoutheete, which met for the first time on 19 January 1982. Although it produced an interim document as early as February 1982, the Foreign Ministers, meeting on 24 May and again on 20 June 1982, were unable to reach agreement. Discussions continued under the Danish and German Presidencies in the working party, with disagreements centring notably on the issues of majority voting in the Council, parliamentary investiture of the Commission, the extension of the conciliation procedure and the rights of the Parliament in relation to the conclusion of international treaties – all key points in Parliament's institutional resolutions.

A new meeting of Parliament's Enlarged Bureau with the Foreign Ministers on 24 January 1983 discussed the Genscher–Colombo proposals, with Council refusing to accept a Parliament suggestion that a 'contact group' be set up between Parliament and the permanent representatives to involve Parliament in the ongoing discussions. Parliament debated the Genscher–Colombo proposals again in March 1983,[12] adopting a resolution calling on the Act to take full account of Parliament's previous institutional proposals. It suggested that some issues could be settled by means of an interinstitutional agreement and it again proposed setting up a 'contact group'.

It was eventually only in the Stuttgart European Council in June 1983 that the Member States agreed on a 'Solemn Declaration on European Union' – almost two years after Parliament's main institutional proposals and after the submission of the draft Act by Genscher and Colombo. Furthermore, its contents were considerably watered down, as we shall see.

Meanwhile, some progress was achieved on the front of European Political Cooperation, with the adoption of the 'London Report' by the Foreign Ministers on 13 October 1981, subsequently endorsed by the European Council on 26–27 November. This report was the successor to the so-called Luxembourg and Copenhagen Reports (or Davignon I and Davignon II Reports), which, on the basis of political declarations signed by the Member States, laid down the basis for foreign policy cooperation without providing for any legal or treaty base. This third report followed in the same tradition, but brought in a number of innovations into existing practices, some of which corresponded to EP requests.

If we are to examine the 12 key demands we identified earlier as the essence of Parliament's proposals for incremental change within the treaties, what was the outcome in the form of the Solemn Declaration, the London Report and undertakings by the Commission and the Council?

1. On the request to be able to debate and vote on the candidate proposed by Member States to become *President of the Commission*, the Solemn Declaration provided that the 'President of the representatives of the governments of the Member States seeks the opinion of the Enlarged Bureau of the European Parliament'. The Genscher–Colombo draft had proposed that only the President of the Parliament be consulted. Either way, it is a more limited formulation than the consultation of Parliament as a whole – involving a vote in plenary – that Parliament had sought. Reporting on the agreement to the Parliament, Genscher stated[13] that 'the essentials . . . were accepted. Yet some partners found they could not agree to the European Parliament's request that the opinion of the plenary session instead of that of the Enlarged Bureau of Parliament should be obtained.' The procedure was applied for the first time with the first appointment of Delors in July 1984 when Irish PM Garett Fitzgerald, as President of the European Council, met the Enlarged Bureau of the Parliament beforehand to discuss the proposal. Whether or not such a procedure could, at least in certain circumstances, give Parliament a real influence, it certainly lacked the visibility, weight and public impact of a vote in plenary.

2. The second main demand, namely to hold a vote ratifying and expressing confidence in the *appointment of the Commission*, had been carried out unilaterally by Parliament in February 1981. Parliament held a debate and a vote of confidence on the incoming Thorn Commission in February 1981. Parliament was effec-

tively counting on its own legitimacy as an elected Assembly to imply that it was unthinkable that a Commission could take office if rejected by Parliament. It was to repeat this for subsequent Commissions, and as of the Delors I Commission in 1985, the Commissioners delayed their oath-taking ceremony at the Court of Justice until after obtaining the Parliament's confidence. The Solemn Declaration gave some recognition to the practice developed by Parliament by providing that 'after the appointment of the members of the Commission by the governments of the Member States, the Commission presents its programme to the European Parliament to debate and vote on the programme'. This formulation fell short of Parliament 'ratifying and expressing confidence' in the Commission, but it at least recognized the principle of a debate and a vote.

3. The third request was that the Commission should consult it on *preliminary draft legislative proposals* before making a formal proposal to the Council. The Commission responded in its communication of 14 October in which it stated that it 'intends to consult the House and committees in advance more frequently on important issues, such as decisions affecting the future of the Community, before it makes formal proposals. In the case of major ongoing initiatives with political implications the Commission normally sends Parliament and the Council communications setting out the main issues involved. It intends to step up this practice and to draw on the views expressed by Parliament in the ensuing parliamentary political debate when the time comes to shape its proposals.'[14] This can be considered as some progress, though the Commission's undertaking was far from representing a systematic commitment always to discuss draft proposals with Parliament.

4. As to *legislative initiative*, the Commission's response[15] again gave only partial satisfaction. It stated that:

> the Commission's right to initiate Community legislation is one of the original and cardinal features of the Community structure. The Commission recognises and supports Parliament's aspirations but it is also anxious to discharge the function assigned to it by the treaties [though] it is politically accountable to Parliament for the way in which it performs this task.

It went on to say that:

it is quite legitimate for a directly elected Parliament to discuss initiatives to develop the Community and press for implementation of its findings. After debates in the House, the Commission takes a careful look at the suggestions put by Parliament with a view to seeing if and how it can act on them. It attaches the utmost importance to the ideas adopted by Parliament and incorporated into formal proposals and it is more than willing to draw on them provided that there are no objections of substance. If there are, it will give Parliament a detailed and timely explanation of the reasons for its reservations.

It was subsequently agreed that the Commission would produce written reports every six months on how it has responded to EP own initiative resolutions. Thus, the Commission was willing to make public signals of its goodwill towards Parliament, but not to guarantee that all parliamentary initiatives would be taken up. With the decline of parliamentary initiative generally – most national legislation is in practice initiated by the executive – such goodwill might be considered to be a positive asset and an achievement. However, without the *formal* right to initiate legislative proposals, the Parliament was in an unfavourable position when compared to most[16] national parliaments, and MEPs could not, in discussions or in election campaigns, undertake to introduce legislation.

5/6. As regards the fifth and sixth demands, namely that the Commission should *automatically take up parliamentary amendments* to its proposals and *withdraw proposals rejected by Parliament*, we have already seen that the Commission refused to accept any automaticity in its response to Parliament's positions. It felt that this would be incompatible with its monopoly of the right of initiative under the treaty, and would also limit its margin of manoeuvre *vis-à-vis* Council. None the less, the Commission[17] did state that it 'understands the real significance of the recent changes to Parliament's rules of procedure' (namely those seeking to take advantage of the 'Isoglucose' Ruling of the Court of Justice). It went on to say that 'it is aware that they make provision for conciliation between the Commission and Parliament and is ready to act accordingly without, however, jeopardizing its own institutional responsibilities or needlessly blocking the decisions which are needed for the development of the Community'. As regards 'Isoglucose', this was as far as the Commission could reasonably be expected to go. However, the failure to agree to withdraw proposals rejected by the elected Parliament was clearly likely to be perceived by MEPs as a clear case of democratic deficit.

7. The demand, that Council return to *majority decision-making*, was crucial for the efficiency and the capacity of the Community system. It gave rise to lengthy discussions in the negotiations on the Solemn Declaration. Eventually, the latter simply stated that 'the application of the decision-making procedures laid down in the treaties of Paris and Rome is of vital importance in order to improve the European Community's capacity to act'. However, in declarations appended to the minutes, each Member State laid down its interpretation of when a vote should take place. As we saw in chapter 1, only Britain and Denmark supported the original French position of 1965 which gave rise to the 'Luxembourg Compromise'. Belgium, West Germany, Luxembourg, Italy and the Netherlands took the view that votes should be held whenever the treaties provide for it. France and Ireland spelt out that, if a vote is to be postponed pursuant to an important national interest, that interest must relate directly to the subject and they, like Greece, took the view that the vote should be postponed only if a Member State invoke an *essential* national interest *in writing*. As we saw in chapter 1, a number of factors had contributed to this evolution of attitudes. The EP was adding its voice to many others. In that it was such a central issue, the persistence of the argument by Parliament and by MEPs through their various channels of communication including through national parties may well have helped produce the shift that took place. But the progress made was relatively minor, concerning shifts in attitudes of Member States about a failure fully to apply the existing treaties. The prospects for achieving a real change in practice were far from certain.

8. As regards the proper *application of the consultation procedure* Council simply reiterated, in its letter of 6 April 1982, that it respects its existing commitments in this field. It was not willing to admit that such commitments had, perhaps, not been fully applied in the past, nor that there was scope for improving aspects such as re-consultation, the provision of information, or timetabling.

9. The extension of the *conciliation procedure* was another key demand of the Parliament. As we saw, the Commission responded positively with a new draft second joint declaration,[18] the main points of which Parliament accepted.[19] Council, however, was

unable to reach agreement because of a reservation on the part of the Danish government. In the Solemn Declaration, the European Council undertook to 'enter into talks with the European Parliament and the Commission with the aim, within the framework of a new agreement, of improving and extending the scope of the conciliation procedure'. Despite this, Denmark alone continued to block the matter within Council. Although theoretically a matter on which Council could take a decision by a simple majority vote, the other Member States were unwilling to proceed on this constitutional issue without unanimity. No extension or improvement to the 1975 conciliation procedure was agreed, though Council did interpret the concept of legislation 'with appreciable financial implications' more flexibly, allowing conciliations, in some cases, on proposals which did not obviously fall into this category. None the less, the great hope of the Parliament to develop its legislative powers by the extension and improvement of the conciliation procedure was dashed.

10. The tenth demand concerning *the Commission's executive powers* was not taken up at all by Council in the Solemn Declaration, or elsewhere. Parliament's views were supported by the Commission, but to no avail. Council continued to establish committees of national civil servants to vet Commission implementing decisions, endowed with the power, in many cases, to refer the matter to the Council.

11. Parliament's demands concerning *European Political Cooperation* were partly taken up in the London Report and in the Solemn Declaration. The London Report agreed on a new emergency procedure, that the Foreign Ministers could meet within 48 hours at the request of three Member States. The Solemn Declaration agreed that EPC should ensure 'coordination of positions of Member States on the political and economic aspects of security'. The London Report stated that the Member States 'attach importance to the Commission . . . being fully associated with political cooperation at all levels', and the Stuttgart Declaration simply stated that 'the Commission *is* fully associated' with EPC. The London Report stated that there would be four annual colloquies with the Political Affairs Committee of the Parliament and that Presidency reports to Parliament would include EPC matters. All these aspects met Parliament's requests contained in the Elles Report.[20]

12. Finally concerning the *European Council*, the Solemn Declaration did state that 'when the European Council acts in matters

within the scope of the European Communities, it does so in its capacity as the Council within the meaning of the treaties'. The Declaration confirmed that the European Council 'will address a report to the EP after each of its meetings' to be presented 'at least once during each Presidency' by the President of the European Council. It will also address an annual written report to Parliament on progress towards European Union. This was an important symbol with potential significance for the media, but none the less, a largely symbolic concession.

Attempts to achieve interinstitutional reform within the context of the existing treaties show that the elected Parliament was activist in the sense of hypothesis 7(a) of chapter 2. But in terms of forcing 'a readjustment of the balance of power among the European institutions' (hypothesis no. 10), the initial achievements were limited. Two years of discussions had obtained relatively meagre results. As we shall see in the next chapter, Parliament was beginning work on a more ambitious project. The disappointments of the gradualist interinstitutional approach were to provide further motivation for taking a more radical and bold approach to try to set in motion a political dynamic of a higher order.

6 Parliament Turns to Treaty Revision[1]

Already by the time of the July 1981 debates on reform within the treaties, many MEPs had come to believe that more radical proposals for amending the treaties were also necessary. The reports of the Political Affairs Committee were somewhat overshadowed by the decision, the same day, to create a new committee to deal with treaty amendments and the construction of European Union.[2]

By that time, MEPs had had two years' experience of the EP. We saw in chapters 4 and 5 how some of the early experiences might well have produced changes of attitude and incited MEPs to take a more vigorous position on institutional reform. This assessment is corroborated by Spinelli, who said in the sixth Jean Monnet lecture, which he gave in 1983 at the European University Institute (EUI) in Florence:

> Initially, Parliament had not been driven by any great incentive for reform. It was scarcely a hot-bed of revolutionaries and dogmatists. Most of its members were ... on European questions moderates ... prepared to fulfil their mandates with caution, abiding by the responsibilities conferred upon them by the Treaties.

But he felt that the experience of the rejection of the 1980 budget, the ignoring of EP 'own initiative' resolutions, inadequate response to EP legislative amendments and the lack of a Community authority to execute a common foreign policy had changed Members' attitudes. A growing perception of how inadequate Community instruments, powers and resources were, how little influence Parliament had, led to a radicalization of attitudes. In his words:

> The obvious impossibility of overcoming the glaring contradiction between the needs of Europe, and the policy of Europe run by the Council to respond to these needs, was the bitter experience which led the Parliament, composed as it was of moderates, to take [a more radical approach].[3]

This did not mean abandoning the 'small steps' strategy: MEPs simply thought it would not be sufficient. The fact that the decision to set up the new committee was taken the same day as the adoption of resolu-

tions advocating incremental changes showed that the EP saw no contradiction in pursuing both approaches. But in advocating treaty amendment, the EP was proposing to follow a route which had been shied
away from for many years, not only by Parliament itself, which had
carefully tailored its proposals (e.g. its submission in 1975 for the
Tindemans Report)[4] to avoid the need for treaty revision, but also by
the Member States (e.g. in not taking up Tindemans' modest proposals
in this regard), and by proposals and studies such as that of the 'Three
Wise Men' requested by the European Council in 1978 and who reported in October 1979.

Earlier attempts to follow this route had foundered. In September
1979, the EPP Group had tabled a motion 'on the extension of the
legal bases of the Community',[5] proposing to supplement the existing
treaties with a new treaty which would, *inter alia*, entrench human
rights, provide a framework for EPC, strengthen the EP's position with
respect to appointment of the Commission, the ratification of treaties
and the conciliation procedure; and provide for the functions of the
Community to be modified according to the principle of subsidiarity
(no definition was provided). This proposal failed to get past the committee stage, not even attracting support from the EPP chairman of the
Political Affairs Committee, the former Italian prime minister, Mariano
Rumor, who favoured postponing the examination of 'the basic principles' and structures of Community institutions 'until such time as Parliament was familiar with the tasks allocated to it and had established
itself sufficiently to ensure the success of such a vast undertaking'.[6]
These conflicting views within the EPP Group were to continue. Some
discussion papers at the Group meeting in May 1980 counselled an
approach limited to what was currently possible and without a major
initiatory role for the Parliament,[7] while others urged the bolder approach of putting forward treaty amendment.[8] There was certainly no
shortage of discussion papers by Christian Democrats on the Community's further integration. As we saw in chapter 2, what appeared to be
missing was agreement on a strategy and an intention to widen the
debate beyond Christian Democratic circles.

The Liberal Group (ELD) also tabled a number of motions for resolution seeking to set in train a procedure for amending the treaties.[9]
These proposals were also shelved while Parliament concentrated on
the approaches outlined in chapters 3 and 4.

To undertake the task of revising the treaties required a broad degree of support from integrationists who might otherwise be political
opponents. To form an alliance on a high profile initiative that would

be bound to attract considerable public attention went against the competitive nature of the political Groups. Thus, Christian Democrats wished to maintain their own image of being the most *avant-garde* integrationists. The Socialists were not particularly interested in broad-based coalitions when they were attempting to highlight their differences from the bourgeois parties and their commitment to an alternative, social Europe. Furthermore, Groups that were divided on European integration, such as the Socialists at that time, were unlikely to embrace with enthusiasm initiatives which would highlight their own divisions, preferring the lower profile approaches described in the previous chapters.

For all these reasons, Parliament initially avoided the high-profile approach of Treaty revision. But, as we have seen, pressure was growing. It took a non-party 'catalyst' who could involve Members from all the Groups in a project not identified with any single one, and who would arbitrate as necessary, to start the process and to make it impossible for Groups to resist the momentum by making it more expedient for them to join in. The 'catalyst' was Altiero Spinelli. As one MEP said: 'If Spinelli hadn't existed, Parliament would have had to invent him.'[10]

THE CROCODILE INITIATIVE

Spinelli was elected to the EP as an independent on the list of the Italian Communist Party, a party which he had left in the 1930s. We saw in chapter 1 how, towards the end of his 17 years' imprisonment under Mussolini, he and fellow prisoner Rossi had written the 1941 'Manifesto di Ventotene' which was widely circulated in the resistance movements and led to the creation of the European Federalist Movement (MFE). As a leader of the MFE from 1946 to 1962, Spinelli was a prominent lobbyist during the creation of the Communities and during the *ad hoc* Assembly episode. From 1970 to 1976 he was a member of the Commission. His experience, contacts, political independence and clarity of purpose were the assets that made him a suitable 'catalyst'.[11]

Spinelli had consistently argued that the Community needed a new constitution prepared by a directly elected EP, which would thus assume the 'constituent' role advocated by a large part of the federalist movement. As the main political parties would be represented, a proposal for greater integration would 'gather momentum in the debates of the Assembly, whereas it would lose it in a conference of national diplomats'. In his view: 'if the final draft is accepted by a massive majority in the Assembly, it will arrive at the national Parliaments for the final ratification with a political force behind it which no diplomatic intergovernmental conference could provide. The chances for both a worthwhile reform and its acceptance by the Member States are therefore high.'[12] Thus we can see a strategy close to that of the constituent federalists described in chapter 1, aiming at a federal constitution.[13]

Spinelli began by circulating a letter to all MEPs, in June 1980, setting out his idea for an EP initiative. With eight MEPs of various nationalities and political persuasions who responded, he organized a dinner at the Crocodile restaurant in Strasbourg on 9 July 1980. The nine agreed that the elected Parliament had a duty to assume responsibility for debating and voting reforms which would be submitted for approval to the appropriate constitutional bodies of the Member States in order to avoid immediate burial in a Council working party. It was decided to form a club named after its place of origin. Meetings of the new Crocodile Club took place monthly during parliamentary sessions and the first Crocodile newsletter was circulated in October 1980.

Gradually, and especially after the experience of rejecting the 1980 budget described in chapter 4 had been digested, more and more MEPs came to sympathize with the more radical approach advocated by Spinelli. By December 1980 nearly 80 MEPs had expressed interest in the club's aims and 'The Crocodile draft resolution' was drawn up for MEPs to sign, on the understanding that the signatures would be listed alphabetically to avoid suspicions of partisanship, and that it would be submitted only when the number of signatures was high enough to demonstrate considerable strength of support.[14]

The text put forward both the strategy agreed at the original dinner and a procedure to overcome the impasse that had blocked other initiatives. It proposed the creation of an *ad hoc* organ – a working party representing all the Groups and currents of thought in the EP – devoted exclusively to this task. By 26 June 1981 it had attracted 179 signatures.[15] Predictably, in view of their opposition to EC institutions gaining more powers, no Gaullists or French Communists signed. More surprisingly, there were only 17 Christian Democrats.

The Christian Democrats felt upstaged. In their words: 'the EPP Group did not rise to the Crocodile initiative, considering that in matters of federalist initiative and orthodoxy, it had greater seniority and continuity of thought than any other political Group.'[16] Only when it became clear that the Crocodile motion would be carried without their support did they rally to it after a Group meeting in Aachen on 1–4 June 1981.[17] Spinelli, who had directed a series of arguments specifically at the EPP Group in the Crocodile Newsletter,[18] struck a deal with them, accepting some EPP amendments to the 'Crocodile' text to set up a full parliamentary committee rather than an *ad hoc* working party as had been proposed. The other pro-European forces in Parliament (Liberals, most Socialists, Italian Communists, most British Conservatives and some smaller parties) thus demonstrated that the EPP was not indispensable to launch an initiative and forced the EPP to embark on a joint effort.

The amended 'Crocodile Resolution' was adopted on 9 July 1981 by 164 votes to 24.[19] Spinelli had succeeded in welding a majority to launch this initiative. His task was now to keep it together. As he reminded Parliament: 'I beg you to remember that a project like this one demands the participation of all the great political families of our countries and that each one must contribute its legitimate claims to the final agreement.'[20]

THE WORK OF THE COMMITTEE ON INSTITUTIONAL AFFAIRS

The Setting-up of the Committee

The Committee started work in January 1982, the half-way point in Parliament's term of office when the committee memberships are renewed and officers re-elected. Membership of each committee broadly reflects the size of each political Group in the EP as a whole: once the shares are worked out, it is up to each Group to nominate its members. Like any other committee, membership therefore reflected the overall political balance, including the proportion of opponents or critics of the Community. However, its size was larger than average: 37 full members (and, therefore, 37 'substitutes' entitled to participate in the work of the committee but able to vote only in the absence of a full member), and there was deliberate overlap with membership of the Legal Affairs and the Political Affairs Committees,[21] including four of the latter's rapporteurs on institutional matters.[22] The Committee attracted the membership of three political Group leaders and four chairmen of other committees.[23]

For committee chairmen and vice-chairmen, the Groups agree on a proportional distribution of posts; for this committee, they had agreed that Ferri (Soc.) would chair the committee and that Jonker (EPP), Pannella (TCD Radical) and Nord (Lib) would be vice-chairmen. Their election at the constituent meeting of the Committee was a formality. Less of a formality was the appointment of Spinelli as rapporteur. An informal understanding had been reached during the Group negotiations that the Communist Group would give up a committee vice-chairmanship in exchange for an assurance that Spinelli would be made General Rapporteur of the new Committee. This understanding was not formalized as there was a certain reluctance to start involving rapporteurships in the already complicated negotiations over chairmanships. At the first meeting of the Committee, the EPP Members, apparently unaware of this understanding, expressed some opposition to Spinelli's appointment. Having been elected courtesy of the Italian Communists, he was politically unsound for some (notably German) Christian Democrats, and the EPP was again trying to assert its own role in the project. The matter was resolved by stressing the nature of the appointment as *primus inter pares* and Spinelli was called 'Coordinating Rapporteur' instead of the normal 'General Rapporteur', and it was agreed that co-rapporteurs would later be nominated for specific sections. As the work progressed, resentment at Spinelli's role appeared to lessen as Members gained experience of working with him and the realization grew that he did not wish to have the project identified too much with himself, but to emphasize its character as a broad agreement thrashed out by the main political parties. He was clearly going to 'play it straight' and increasingly came to be relied upon as an honest broker between the main political groups.[24]

The Parliament secretariat set up a team of four administrators for this new committee. Each political group also designated a member of their own staff to follow the Committee. Unlike any other committee, they would all be working on a single project, the success of which was the whole *raison d'être* of the Committee.

The Committee approved Spinelli's proposal for a procedure and timetable at its second meeting. It was intended that proposals for reform would emerge from a broad consensus negotiated among the political forces, that the debate would spread beyond the confines of Parliament, and that political Groups would involve their national parties. The proposals would eventually need to be ratified by the appropriate constitutional authorities of the Member States and would therefore be sent to national authorities (governments and parliaments). They would become an issue confronting actors in all Member States, starting with the 1984 elections. The work of the Committee would proceed in three phases, each culminating in a debate and vote in plenary session, thus ensuring maximum involvement of Parliament as a whole in all stages;

the first phase would establish *guidelines* for the reform; the second and longest phase would draw up detailed proposals on the *contents* of a new treaty; and the final phase would *translate* this into the legal language of treaty articles in a *Draft Treaty*.

Phase I: Establishing Guidelines

The Committee first published a selection of texts containing the main official proposals for reform made by national and Community bodies from 1950 to 1982.[25] This served two purposes: it was a useful reference during the work of the Committee; it also showed, as Ferri put it in his introduction, that all reports by governments, experts and institutions had concluded that stronger institutions were necessary, but that few proposals were implemented, partly because the negotiations were 'entrusted to intergovernmental committees' in which national views predominated over the common interest. The Committee also organized a series of hearings with presidents of other institutions, the social partners, academics and others.[26] The Committee avoided debates about federalism, confederalism and intergovernmentalism on the grounds that this would cloud the issue and give ample opportunity for opponents of the proposal to seize on controversial language, recognizing that such vocabulary stimulated varying reactions in Member States. Nor did the Committee specify whether it aimed at amending the existing treaties or replacing them with a new one. Spinelli certainly referred to a new treaty in all his speeches and in the documents he put forward, and although the majority of the Committee was prepared to follow him, a significant proportion still had doubts. In order to accommodate the largest number, the guidelines referred to 'a draft of modification of the treaties',[27] to keep all options open at that stage and to ensure maximum support.

Several motions for resolution concerning European Union were tabled by Political Groups and referred to the Committee in accordance with Parliament's Rules of Procedure. These included a fully-fledged draft treaty 'on the first stage of implementation of European Union' tabled by Jonker and others on behalf of the EPP Group,[28] a motion tabled by British Labour Members 'on proposed changes to the Treaty of Rome'[29] and, later, a motion tabled by Nord on behalf of the Liberals 'on European Union'.[30] It is possible that the EPP Group, whose motion had been prepared by a special working party, had hoped that their document would form the basis of the Committee's work. The Committee, however, decided to work on the basis of Spinelli's draft.

Such motions for resolution can be seen as 'markers' tabled to express Group positions. Further such markers were produced at later stages by the EPP Group,[31] reflecting their constant preoccupation with the fact that the initiative undermined their claim to be the most federalist.

Spinelli produced a draft 'guidelines' resolution which, after revision and amendment, was adopted by the Committee on 24 May 1982 by 31 votes to 0, with 2 abstentions[32] – a remarkable degree of consensus within the committee whose members were clearly committed to finding the necessary compromises, but would now have to bring along their Groups in the plenary.

The 'guidelines' report again emphasized the need to move beyond the then political and legal framework of the Communities by establishing a Union capable of dealing more effectively with the internal and external problems facing Europe, notably in the fields of general economic policy, monetary policy, policy for society and the gradual framing of a common policy in the field of international relations and security. What was envisaged was not a totally new conception but one based on the Community institutions with adjustments 'to eliminate the existing shortcomings and to enable the Union to shoulder new tasks and to increase its competences'. This would include a strengthening of the Commission 'as the Union's pivotal institution' and executive; the joint exercise of legislative power by the Council and Parliament, 'deriving their mandates respectively from the Member States and the citizens of the Union'; measures to enable the Council, by means of appropriate procedures, to take promptly decisions which lie within its powers; defining and specifying the role and the powers of the European Council; reinforcing the links between EPC and the Treaties; and enabling Parliament to participate in the constitution of the executive (i.e. the Commission). The principle of subsidiarity was considered to be one of the essential principles of the Union.

The 'guidelines' resolution was adopted in plenary on 6 July 1982 by 258 to 35.[33] Few amendments were adopted mainly because the EPP and Liberal Groups had agreed to stick to the compromise agreed in committee. Understandably, therefore, they did not support amendments tabled by other Groups.

Phase II : The Substance of the Reforms

The second phase of the Committee's work was the one in which the major detailed issues were thrashed out. It lasted a whole year, from July 1982 to September 1983.

Six co-rapporteurs were appointed, each responsible for a particular subject under the overall coordination of Spinelli. They were: De Gucht (Lib.) on the legal structure of the Union, Moreau (Soc.) on economic union, Pfennig (EPP) on policy for society, Prag (ED) on international relations, Junot (EPD) (and, following his resignation from Parliament, Seeler (Soc.)) on the finances, and Zecchino (EPP) on the institutions. This allocation was agreed by the Committee after discussions between the Committee's bureau and each Group's coordinator on the Committee. Initially, each Group was given one rapporteur with the exception of the EPP which was given two. This was highly unusual (the EPP being only the second largest Group), and reflected the desire of Ferri and Spinelli to involve the EPP more closely following the earlier disagreements. The proposal was accepted with some misgivings, in particular by the Socialists (the largest Group). When later Junot left Parliament, balance was re-established by appointing Seeler to replace him as rapporteur, there being no new Gaullist candidate.

Each rapporteur drafted a working document. These were discussed in committee between September and December 1982, revised by their authors,[34] discussed again, and then each rapporteur drafted one chapter of the motion for resolution to be submitted to plenary. The drafts were also examined in two seminars held at the EUI in Florence, which involved the rapporteurs, the chairman and the secretariat, together with professors of law, political science and economics from various European universities, and high-ranking Commission officials.[35] This was both a major input into the Committee's work, and a way of involving potential outside supporters.

At the end of this phase, Spinelli, as Coordinating Rapporteur, presented a new text taking up the various paragraphs proposed by the different rapporteurs, but in a different order and with a number of changes wherever there was overlap or contradiction. Despite friction with certain rapporteurs – Spinelli interpreted 'contradictions' to include some conflicts with his own views – his new draft was mostly accepted as the basis for the final round of formal amendments in committee. There were some 350 such amendments. Often, Members wished to give greater emphasis to one or another subject close to their hearts, but several reflected the persistence of important divergences (see next subsection). Following the round of formal amendments, the Committee agreed to hold a second round of amendments, of which there were about 30, for important points, limited to amendments proposed on behalf of the political Groups.

During each round of amendments, Spinelli came up with 'compromise amendments' taking advantage of Parliament's rules which allowed such amendments to be tabled by the rapporteur after the deadline for normal amendments. It was here that Spinelli showed his skill in bringing the various viewpoints together. Without giving up on the points he considered essential, he was able, by cajoling, persuading, compromising and, on occasion using ambiguous language, to bring the Committee round to texts often agreed by consensus.

The Committee adopted the text by 29 votes to 4, with 2 abstentions[36] in a public meeting held during Parliament's Strasbourg session on 5 July 1983. The compromise did not fully satisfy all parties, however, and when it was submitted to the plenary it attracted 185 amendments. Again, many were 'markers' designed to profile party positions or else concerned minor details and favourite hobby-horses. Nevertheless, again, some amendments indicated differences of approach (as we shall see). However, few were adopted and the resolution was approved by Parliament on 14 September 1983 by 202 to 37.[37]

In adopting this resolution, Parliament came down in favour of a new Treaty, replacing (though absorbing) the existing treaties. The project drew on ideas contained in past reports, notably the Commission's 1975 report on European Union[38] drafted in preparation for the Tindemans Report. Its provisions were more 'moderate' than some had expected and were based on the existing Community structure (see chapter 7). It was a political compromise which nevertheless had its own coherence.

Phase III: Putting it in Treaty Format

The final phase of the Committee's work (in autumn 1983) consisted of 'translating' the resolution into a draft treaty worded in proper legal language. The Committee appointed a team of four professors of law,[39] who worked in a series of meetings with Spinelli and the Committee Secretariat, with rapporteurs participating in the discussions on their section. They reported regularly to the Committee.

The work was not purely technical. Some parts of the Resolution were capable of different interpretations and some points had been left open. One particular problem was the procedure by which the new Treaty would enter into force (Art. 82).[40] In political terms what Spinelli proposed amounted to a repetition of the exercise conducted by Schuman in 1950: those countries that so wished should move ahead together without waiting for all countries to agree to do so. The legal basis and method envisaged for this are described in the next chapter. It would open the way for a new Treaty to come into force even if one or two Member States opposed it. If such an event became credible, it would change the dynamics of the bargaining process among the Member States and might induce some States to accept certain proposals reluctantly rather than risk being left out.

This issue had deliberately been left by Spinelli to the last phase. He had wished first to build as broad a majority as possible around the substance of the proposal for a new treaty before introducing this controversial element concerning the tactics for enhancing its prospects. Introducing it at this stage also meant that the lawyers could counter legal arguments that might be used against the proposal. Most important, however, was that by this time the climate of opinion in the EP was ready for such a proposal. MEPs had by then witnessed the watering down of the Genscher–Colombo proposals, largely because a small minority of Member States rejected even its modest innovations. Since at least one Member State was opposed to virtually any reform of the institutional system, any proposal such as the Draft Treaty establishing the European Union (DTEU) had to find a way around that obstacle.

Another problem in the legal 'translation' of the Resolution concerned the section on external political and diplomatic relations. The intention of the rapporteurs had been to integrate EPC more closely into the Community. Prag's working documents had envisaged a fusion of the two frameworks, though leaving most power in this field with the Council. However, the adoption of an amendment by Hänsch in committee had left EPC under the sole responsibility of the European Council working by the method of cooperation: it would be further away from the EC institutions than was then the case. In order to overcome this contradiction, the Committee adopted a formula whereby the European Council remained responsible for political and diplomatic cooperation in general terms, but placed responsibility for its 'conduct' in the hands of the Council. The Commission would be able to propose policies and actions, and could be asked to implement agreed policies.

Other than battles on wording, notably on economic policy where a careful balance had to be struck that was acceptable both to left and right, there were few other controversies at this stage. During final adoption of the text by the Committee some 85 amendments were considered, about 20 of which were either accepted or partially incorporated into compromises proposed by Spinelli and the lawyers.

The issue of how the EP should follow up the draft Treaty was dealt with in a short resolution prepared by the Committee. Spinelli envisaged that the President of Parliament, assisted by the Bureau of the Institutional Committee, should visit national capitals and present the proposals to national governments, asking them to institute the procedure for approval in accordance with their respective constitutional rules. At the same time, the parliaments of the Member States would be asked to put pressure on their governments to start the procedure for approval. The new EP elected in June 1984 would be invited to take all useful initiatives, notably any agreements with national parliaments that would facilitate adoption of the Treaty. This draft attracted some 16 amendments in committee, concerned largely with the degree to which the DTEU should be presented as a proposal ready for ratification or as a first discussion document to be revised following discussions and even negotiations with national authorities and national parliaments. Spinelli's draft hinted at such a possibility, but wished to present the DTEU initially as ready for ratification. He feared that to present it as a discussion paper from the beginning would lessen its impact and risk provoking interminable discussion.[41] He was well aware that adjustments to the text would be inevitable in the process of consideration and adoption, but emphasized that these should be kept to the minimum necessary, and pointed to the fact that the draft Treaty had been drawn up by a Parliament in which all the major political parties of Europe were represented. The Committee adopted a version close to Spinelli's text, but the matter was reopened in plenary.

The Committee adopted its report as a whole, including both the motion for resolution and the preliminary draft Treaty, on 14 December 1983 in Strasbourg by 31 votes to 3, with no abstentions.[42] Only the British Labour and Danish Socialist Members and the Irish Fianna Fáil Member of the Committee voted against.

In plenary, no new articles were added, nor any deleted, the few amendments adopted having, except in one case, been accepted by the committee. The DTEU was adopted on 14 February 1984 by 237 to 31, with 43 abstentions. The resolution accompanying it was adopted by 237 to 32 with 34 abstentions.[43]

THE EVOLUTION OF PARTY ATTITUDES

In view of the complexity and importance of the issue, it was a remarkable feat to have achieved such a degree of consensus, especially a few months prior to the European elections. The final resolution enjoyed the official support of the Socialist, EPP, Liberal and Communist Groups. The Conservatives left a free vote (with the majority supporting) and the EPD (Gaullists) did not take part. It obtained a majority among those voting of every nationality except Denmark.

Such support was far from certain at the beginning of the exercise. There was the continual risk that alliances would break down over the detailed content of the proposals, either on the institutional or on the policy side. As well as differences of emphasis of a party nature, DTEU supporters also divided between maximalists and minimalists (curious alliances appeared in committee between Christian Democrat, Liberal and Italian Communist maximalists on the one hand, and Conservative and Socialist minimalists on the other). Furthermore, there was always a risk that, even with total agreement on method and content, party jealousies over credit for the DTEU would undermine the whole operation. Most of these potential hazards were overcome by patient negotiation and compromise. Others were papered over with ambiguous wording or swallowed reluctantly by the minority on a specific issue. Although the final result was subject to different interpretations concerning the status, importance and follow-up of the DTEU, the broad-based character of the initiative was maintained throughout.

Those opposing the DTEU in the Parliament were also divided. They included opponents of the EC (such as the Danish People's Movement, the Greek Communists and some British Socialists); supporters of the Community who nevertheless opposed any increase in the powers of the institutions (such as the Danish Socialists, Gaullists and Fianna Fáil) and Members who, whilst supporting further integration, disagreed with the method (such as some Conservatives).

The *Socialist Group* was the most divided on the issue of the DTEU, despite the fact that a majority of its members had signed the original Crocodile resolution, and a majority in favour remained throughout the whole exercise. In all the votes it split, usually into national sub-Groups (though there were divisions within these too).

The Italian, Luxembourg and two Belgian parties supported the Treaty throughout – not a single Member voted against or abstained on any of the Resolutions. The bulk of the Dutch and German Members similarly gave full support. Willy Brandt supported the Crocodile Club resolution from the outset[44] and several German Members had been active in the Club. However, two German Socialists, members of the Committee on Institutional Affairs, Hänsch and Focke, repeatedly called for a clearer and more detailed description of what European Union would mean for ordinary citizens and for less ambitious institutional proposals.[45] They put forward an alternative institutional proposal during the second phase of the Committee's work This was a single large amendment seeking to replace a whole chapter of the carefully drafted resolution. It was ruled out of order by the Chairman, himself a Socialist, which led to a heated exchange of opinions within the Group. Although their proposal did not, in fact, differ enormously from the final outcome of the Committee's work, Hänsch and Focke from then on maintained staunch opposition. One article has ascribed this to 'petty personal jealousies',[46] but Hänsch's insistence that European Union would not be attractive to the ordinary citizen if it were seen to be merely institutional tampering did strike a chord among Socialist and other Members. This theme was taken up by Dankert, the Dutch Socialist President of the EP. In a speech marking the thirtieth anniversary of the EP in September 1982, he called upon Parliament to give priority to presenting policies for solving the crisis in Europe and not to 'emphasize the institutional problems unlikely to generate much interest among our voters'.[47] Spinelli responded by having the Committee secretariat prepare a document summarizing the enormous number of resolutions adopted by Parliament, which indeed spelt out its answers to problems facing the Community in virtually every sector of its activities. The fact that almost all these proposals remained without effect illustrated the inadequacy of existing decision-making procedures. The 'policies versus institutions' debate continued throughout the preparation of the DTEU and the Committee was careful to avoid being too academic or purely institutional in its proposals. With the deepening of the Community's deadlock over budgetary contributions, the reform of the CAP and other issues, more and more Members became convinced that institutional reform was necessary so that new policies could be adopted and existing ones reformed.

The French Socialists found themselves in a difficult position at a time when, domestically, they were only recently in power and were still focusing on their national attempts to relaunch the economy. They were also divided internally, with the 'CERES' faction opposing the initiative whilst the 'Rocardiens' supported it. In between, the bulk were willing to go along with proposals for reform, but were cautious about those aspects that could be construed as limiting national sovereignty. They too preferred to discuss policies rather than institutions. The French Socialists decided to vote in favour of the 'guidelines' resolution in July 1982 (despite instructions rumoured to have been given from party headquarters in Paris to the contrary).[48] However, they abstained in the vote on the resolution on the substance in September 1983 (though a minority including Moreau voted in favour), and again in the final vote on the draft Treaty (this time with only one rebel: the party was at that time in the process of drawing up its list for the forthcoming elections). Their caution was to seem excessive – even embarrassing – following President Mitterrand's speech to the EP on 24 May 1984 in which he welcomed the Draft Treaty (See chapter 8).

The Irish Labour MEPs did not take a strong collective position. Their main specific concern was to avoid proposals that might undermine Irish neutrality. In the final vote they divided, with most abstaining, but with Halligan indicating strong support for the DTEU. John Hume of the Northern Ireland SDLP supported the initiative through all its stages.[49]

The Greek Socialist members' attitude was significant for a party which had until recently been totally opposed to the EC, and was one of the early signs of PASOK's subsequent evolution on Europe. They never voted against the proposals, but abstained or did not vote. This may be partly attributable to Spinelli's personal contacts with Papandreou, whom he knew during the latter's period of exile. Spinelli visited Greece in autumn 1982 on the invitation of the Greek government to present the initiative to Papandreou and various ministers. Papandreou himself stated to the EP:[50] 'We have repeatedly stressed the absolute need for certain changes because of the lack of any adjustment of the Community's institutions in the last twenty-five years, despite immense changes in the situation within the Community and outside it. In this framework must be seen the suggestion we made that perhaps the time had come for a new Messina, where we would, without abandoning the spirit of the Treaty of Rome, reclarify our ideas about the important problems of our time'. In a highly centralized party such as PASOK, it is unlikely that the MEPs were left a free vote on such an issue.

The British Labour Members voted against the proposals in all three stages. A majority of the Labour MEPs had originally been elected as 'anti-marketeers'. Although their attitude had evolved to the extent that, by 1984, a majority was no longer for UK withdrawal, they were not yet ready to support major integration initiatives at a time when the Party at home was overwhelmingly hostile. This public position, however, masked a certain sympathy among some of them. Five Labour MEPs had signed the Crocodile resolution and Balfe had invited Spinelli to address his constituency party. In the vote on the 'contents' resolution, it was only by a majority of 2 within their own delegation that they decided to vote against rather than abstain. However, as reselection approached, sympathies for the proposals were discreet.[51]

The Danish Socialists consistently opposed the initiative at every stage, as did most of the other Danish parties, all of whom felt under pressure from the People's Movement against the Community which had won four seats in the previous European elections.

Despite the minorities against, the Socialist Group as such supported the 'guidelines' and the 'contents' resolution. It allowed a free vote on the text of the DTEU (with 46 in favour 12 against, with 32 abstentions), but supported the resolution adopted with the DTEU which explicitly approved the draft and the procedure for following it up. The Group was heavily involved in the work of the Committee, supplying its chairman and two of the six co-rapporteurs. It was also backed by the President of the European Trades Union Confederation (ETUC), Debunne, who had lent his support to the initiative. In his speech to the plenary in the final debate on the DTEU, Group leader Glinne was very specific about the Group's support, speaking of the balance and realism of the draft Treaty which 'is not too far removed from present reality or future possibilities', though the Group did express reservations about Art. 82.

Were the Socialist Members in advance of the positions of their respective national parties? Perhaps as regards detail and strategy, but not on the main principles. The Benelux, German and Italian members reflected long-standing party positions, and in the case of the Flemish and the Germans, the party leaders themselves had gone out of their way to support the draft Treaty. The French, as we saw, were if anything too prudent. We have already mentioned the position of the Greek Socialists. The Danes and the British faithfully reflected their party's hostility.

Of all the Groups, the *EPP Group* was the most united on the initiative. In all three votes, it gave unanimous support to the project. Its problems were of a different nature and concerned their desire to take maximum credit for any European initiatives.

We saw earlier the difficulties the EPP had in launching its own initiatives early in the life of the EP, the sensitivities aroused by the Crocodile proposal and the friction over the nomination of Spinelli as rapporteur. These subsided as its members got involved with the work of the committee, though the EPP was always anxious to underline its own self-conception as the most 'European' party, for instance by tabling a more far-reaching 'constitution'.[52]

The EPP did have some occasional difficulties with the contents, notably over the need for a Bill of Rights to be included in the DTEU.

The EPP Group was keen on this, supported by the Liberals. There was in fact little specific opposition, but Spinelli feared that anything other than incorporating the existing Council of Europe Convention in the Treaty could lead to very lengthy discussions and delay. The work of Parliament's Legal Committee in this area lent weight to this fear.[53] There was simply no consensus on what new rights should be added to the Convention. Pfennig and Luster (EPP), however, argued that such a Bill of Rights would be one of the most attractive features and was essential for obtaining public support. Parliament decided to follow Spinelli's recommendation (later backed by the lawyers) and refer to the existing Convention, though leaving it open to the future Union to adopt its own list.

Throughout the drafting of the Treaty, the EPP Group made sure that it carried national Christian Democratic parties with it. The Group held several meetings with CD members of national parliaments[54] to discuss the DTEU. Successive EPP congresses, which involved leading national politicians, gave it their backing.[55]

The *European Democratic Group* (EDG), almost entirely British Conservatives, was normally the most cohesive Group in the EP. The issue of the DTEU, however, caused a number of internal divisions.

The EDG's approach to reforming the treaties had always emphasized the practical aim of making the institutions function more effectively. Although the Group did contain members who described themselves as federalists, it was always looking over its shoulder to London, where the party leadership was hostile to such tendencies. Nevertheless, over half its members signed the Crocodile resolution and the Group voted in favour of it. Thus the Group did not oppose reform as such, nor the right of the EP to put forward proposals, but was cautious regarding their content, emphasizing the need for pragmatism and realism. With the 'guidelines' resolution, the Group had to take a decision on the extent and direction of reforms it was prepared to go along with. It decided, by a narrow majority, to vote in favour of the resolution, though five Members nevertheless voted against and three abstained. When the 'contents' resolution was debated, the Group decided to support the resolution, provided an amendment was adopted establishing a permanent veto for Member States. It attempted to negotiate with the EPP and ELD Groups on this point but this was not possible: majority voting had been an important issue of principle in the EP for many years, and most MEPs felt that the compromise contained in the resolution (10-year transition period) already went far enough. Their amendment having been rejected, the EDG decided to abstain (but J.D. Taylor (Ulster Unionist) voted against). In spite of this apparent unity, many members put their own position on record in the debate.[56] Newton Dunn, for example, stated: 'I am strongly in favour of the motion on European Union but am abstaining out of loyalty to my political Group,' sentiments echoed by Prag, Jackson and Johnson, the latter even explaining to the plenary that he would stick to the Group position because it had the effect of increasing the majority for the Resolution, as many EDG members would otherwise have voted against! Most speakers gave general support, while expressing reservations concerning specific parts of the DTEU, or the method. J.D. Taylor, on the other hand, described the text as 'the greatest threat by the EP to the sovereignty of the United Kingdom since the first direct elections in 1979'.

By February 1984, and the final vote on the draft Treaty itself, these divisions could no longer be hidden by a bloc abstention. The Group allowed its members a free vote: 22 voted for the DTEU, 6 against and 6 abstained. In the debate, some members announced that they had been convinced of the need for reform by the intervening failure of the Athens summit and would now support the draft Treaty. Whatever the reason, the centre of gravity of the Group did appear to have shifted considerably towards the project.

The *Communist Group* was divided, with the French and Greek 'exterior' Communist Parties opposing the DTEU and the Italians supporting it. Party Secretary Berlinguer spoke personally in the debate on the 'contents' resolution, indicating strong support for the initiative.[57] The Greek 'interior' communist, Kyrkos, supported the 'guidelines' resolution but abstained in the 'contents' resolution and on the DTEU itself, explaining that his Party thought 'highly of Mr Spinelli's efforts and of his vision of a united Europe',[58] but had three reservations on the contents of the DTEU (majority voting, competition policy and the insufficient priority given to regional policy).

The *Liberals* gave consistent support to the project. Only the Danish Liberals, under the same pressure as other Danish parties, abstained in the final two votes (though they had supported the 'guidelines' resolution) except for one of their three members, Haagerup, who voted in favour. The Liberals too used the opportunity of ELD congresses as well as informal contacts[59] to discuss the proposals with national parties.

As to the *EPD ('Gaullist') Group*, Chairman de la Malène summarized their position in the final debate in which he stated that they supported European Union but found the proposals badly timed, unrealistic and procedurally insufficient.[60] The Group decided to abstain on the 'guidelines' resolution and not to participate in the votes on the 'contents' nor on the DTEU itself. This position, however, was not always followed by all members: Lalor of the Fianna Fáil Party voted against the first two resolutions, whereas three Gaullist Members supported the initiative (two in the final vote).

From this examination of Group positions, it can be seen that the only major case of a serious potential conflict between MEPs and their national party was that of the UK Conservatives, and this was one of the reasons why they split.[61] Such divisions also existed among their Westminster MPs, even if the proportions were not the same. Almost all other parties had taken positions that conformed to those of their parties back home, though in some cases they had contributed to shifting or at least defining these positions, and in any case, the DTEU went into more detail. However, just as on domestic issues, the positions of parties was not always identical to the position of their own ministers in government.

Thus, Spinelli's achievement was not to have foisted his own ideas on a reluctant Parliament, but to have enabled the Parliament to come up with a concrete reference point for all parties and Groups able to serve as a focus for formerly disparate action both in and out of Parliament. In his words:

> if the ideas contained in this draft and the resolution had not been in the minds of the great majority of this Parliament, it would have been quite impossible for me to put them there. I have merely practised the art of maieutics, after the manner of Socrates. I am the midwife who has delivered Parliament of this infant. Now we must nurture it.[62]

The exercise embarked upon was considered by some to be close to that of being a constituent assembly (hypothesis 12 in chapter 2), but the majority probably considered it more a strategy to achieve significant treaty changes (hypothesis 11).

The existence of the elected Parliament, with members of all of the main political parties working full time on European issues, frustrated with the failings of the Community and their own relative impotence, building a sufficient *esprit de corps* to work together across party and national divisions, was crucial to the whole exercise.

7 The Draft Treaty

This is not the place for a full legal and political analysis of the draft treaty[1] as we are concerned more with the DTEU's role as a stimulus and a basis for new developments. None the less, a short summary is in order, together with an assessment of the more salient points and political objectives of the EP.

STRUCTURE AND CONTENTS OF THE DRAFT TREATY

The DTEU consisted of a preamble and 87 Articles grouped into six parts. As we have seen, it was a fully-fledged Treaty *ex novo*, rather than a Treaty amending the existing Community treaties, but it contained provisions taking up on behalf of the Union the *acquis communautaire* and adapting it to the Union.

The preamble stated a number of general principles. It specified that the aim of the European Union was to continue and revive the democratic unification of Europe by means of more efficient and democratic institutions and on the basis of the principles of pluralist democracy, respect for human rights and the rule of law. Union action would be based on the principle of subsidiarity. Until then this principle was little known except to students of federal systems, but from this time on it became an oft-quoted principle – though clearly subject to different interpretations. As defined in the draft treaty, it referred to entrusting the common institutions 'only with those powers required to complete successfully the tasks they may carry out more satisfactorily than the States acting independently'. This principle was further spelled out later in the Treaty (Art. 12.2).

Part one ('The Union') laid down a number of principles. The notions of Union citizenship (Art. 3) and territory (Art. 5) were introduced, though it was specified that these depended on the Member States of the Union: citizenship of the Union, or territory of the Union, was by virtue of the citizenship of, or being part of the territory of, a Member State.

That the Union would be based on the principles of democracy and the respect of fundamental rights was not explicitly laid down in the Community treaties. The DTEU Art. 2 (accession of new members)

161

therefore laid down that any *democratic* European state might apply to become a member of the Union; and Art. 4 laid down that the Union should apply the fundamental rights and freedoms derived from the common principles of the constitutions of the Member States and from the ECHR. In this respect, it formalized the Joint Declaration by the European Parliament, the Council and the Commission adopted on 5 April 1977. It then went further, however, specifying that the Union might itself accede to the European and UN Conventions and that it should adopt its own declaration on fundamental rights within five years of the entry into force of the Treaty. Above all, it envisaged penalties and sanctions being applied to Member States in the event of serious and persistent violation of democratic principles or fundamental rights (Art. 44).

Part one also established (Art. 7) that the Union was, in effect, the 'inheritor' of the Communities. All the provisions of the Community treaties, legislation and agreements in the EPC framework that were not altered by the Union Treaty itself would remain in force until modified in accordance with the procedures of the new Treaty. These procedures varied according to the nature of the previous Community measures.

Part two ('Objectives, Methods of Action and Competences of the Union') specified general social ('human and harmonious development of society . . .'), economic ('the economic development of its peoples . . .'), and international ('security, peace, cooperation, détente, disarmament, development . . .') objectives of the Union. It also laid down a basic feature of the Union, namely the distinction made between two methods of action and the attribution of competences within these methods. The two methods of action were *'common action'* where the Union institutions as such could take decisions and act, and *'cooperation'* in which the Member States of the Union reached intergovernmental agreements in the framework of the European Council. When the Union took common action, two types of competence were foreseen: *exclusive competence* whereby the Union alone might act, and *concurrent competence* in which both the Union and the Member States might act, though the latter only in so far as the Union had not adopted its own legislation or action. As a safeguard against overcentralization, the principle of subsidiarity was again reaffirmed here and it was specified that a law which initiated or extended Union action in an area of concurrent competence where it had hitherto not taken action must be adopted in accordance with the procedure for organic laws, requiring special majorities (see below). The distinction between exclusive and concurrent competence was not new. Under the Community treaties the EC had exclusive competence regarding tariffs, for example, and concurrent competence concerning regional policy and, indeed, most areas of EC responsibility.

Throughout the Treaty, the particular type of action and competence attributed to the Union was specified for each policy area. A transfer from cooperation to common action was possible (Art. 11), but this would require the approval of the European Council (presumably unanimous, see below).

Part three ('Institutional Provisions') provided for institutions based on the existing Community institutions. However, the relationships between them, and the procedures by which legislative and executive acts were adopted, were substantially modified, thus affecting also the relative power of each institution.

The European Council was integrated into the framework of the Treaty (this would be the first time it was mentioned in any Treaty). No disposition provided for any change in its working method, which it could decide itself. Although its primary responsibility was in the field of cooperation, it could continue to formulate communications to the other institutions without any limitations on the subject. The role that it had already assumed of nominating the Commission was formalized, though limited to nominating the President.

The Council would continue to be composed of representatives appointed by the governments of the Member States, but each government would nominate a representation led by a minister who was permanently and specifically responsible for Union affairs. This was an attempt to overcome the lack of coordination between the different formations of the Council attended by a variety of ministers. Parliament hoped that a requirement that national representation in the Council should be led on all occasions by a specific government minister would overcome this problem. The minister could still be accompanied by other, specialist ministers and officials.

The DTEU provided for the Council to vote by the same weighted ballot as before, acting either by simple, absolute or qualified majorities or by unanimity, as laid down in the Treaty under the legislative procedure (see below). Nevertheless, it provided for the possibility to invoke a vital national interest, thereby postponing the vote. The 'Luxembourg compromise' would thus be given recognition in a treaty, but subject to two conditions: the Commission had to recognize that a vital interest was at stake, and the grounds for requesting a postponement had to be published. Furthermore, the provision would lapse after a ten-year transitional period.

The role of the Commission would be strengthened. Its term of office would be modified to coincide with that of Parliament. Its appointment would follow each European parliamentary election and would involve the designation of its President by the European Council, his/her constitution of a team and programme, and a vote of confidence by Parliament allowing it to take office. This would preserve an element of involvement by the Member States, through the European Council, in the nomination of the Commission, but also strengthen the possibility of constituting a strong and coherent team by allowing the President to choose the other members.[2] The provision for a final vote of confidence by the Parliament took up the longstanding demand by the EP,[3] partly recognized in the Stuttgart Solemn Declaration. Clearly Parliament intended to have a Commission that, whilst having a President acceptable to the Member States, reflected parliamentary majorities. Once appointed, however, the Commission could be dismissed only according to the same procedure as in the EEC Treaty (Art. 144), namely by a vote of censure by a qualified (i.e. two-thirds) majority in Parliament, a majority sufficiently high to avoid constant instability.

The Parliament remained in its current composition. Provision was made for an organic law to lay down a uniform electoral system. Provisions were laid down for the Court of Justice and the Court of Auditors each to have half their Members appointed by the Council and half by the Parliament. The possibility was provided to the creation of new organs by means of an organic law.

These modifications to the composition and structure of the institutions were not in themselves dramatic. More important were the changes concerning the legislative procedure. First, however, one should note that the Community system of regulations and directives was abandoned in favour of a single type of Community laws, largely to reflect the recent legal developments on the direct effect of directives, and the growing trend for directives to be more and more detailed leaving little scope for national divergence. It was, nevertheless, provided in Art. 34 that laws should, as far as possible, restrict themselves to determining the fundamental principles governing common action and entrust the responsible authorities in the Union or the Member States with setting out in detail the procedures for their implementation. Furthermore, Art. 35 allowed differentiated application of laws: this would allow the exemption of certain Member States or regions from the immediate application of particular laws.

The procedure for the adoption of Union law would place the Council and the Parliament as partners within the 'legislative authority', somewhat akin to their positions as branches of the budgetary authority. The right of initiative remained with the Commission, although on reasoned request from Parliament or Council, the Commission would be expected to submit a draft law conforming to such a request, failing which the Parliament or the Council could themselves take an initiative. Once a draft law was introduced, it was to be submitted first to the Parliament and then to the Council, each body being required to act within a specific deadline, failing which it would be deemed to have approved the draft referred to it. This provision for a deadline was in response to one of the main criticisms of the Council, namely that it consistently took years to act on legislative proposals, whereas under the budgetary procedure time-limits forced it to act promptly. Where the two branches of the legislative authority agreed on a text, it would be adopted. Where they disagreed, unless the Council had rejected it unanimously (or in the case of an organic law by a qualified majority), a conciliation procedure was to be opened in which a delegation from Council met a delegation from Parliament.[4] They would have three months to reach agreement on a joint text, which would be submitted to each branch for approval by an absolute majority (or in the case of organic laws by a qualified majority). Where conciliation failed to reach agreement, a second reading was foreseen in which Parliament might approve the text as adopted by Council or, by absolute majority, adopt amendments to it proposed by the Commission: it could not amend it by itself. This text could then be rejected by the Council by a qualified majority. This complex set of provisions implied that either Council and Parliament finally agreed (co-decision) or else that a text on which an absolute majority of Parliament and the Commission agreed could become law if a minority in Council large enough to prevent it rejecting the text by a qualified majority was willing to support the Parliament and the Commission.

The Commission would play an important role throughout the legislative procedure. As well as having the main right of initiative, it could put forward amendments at any time that had to be put to the vote as a matter of priority, and if it specifically opposed the draft emerging from the Parliament, then the Council would need a higher majority to approve. It would participate in the conciliation procedure and, should that procedure fail, its decision to side either with the Council or with the Parliament would be crucial in determining which of the two was in a stronger position: if it sided with the Council, then Parliament would have to examine Council's text on a 'take it or leave it' basis, whereas if it sided with the Parliament, Council could only reject the outcome by a qualified majority.

Taken as a whole, this legislative system aimed to minimize the scope for filibustering and delay, but nevertheless, provide safeguards for each institution. The difficulty for any given institution to foresee the outcome in the event of the conciliation procedure not producing an agreement was intended to be a powerful inducement to compromise.

Another objective was to strengthen the Commission's executive function. Most Community legislation provides for its implement-ation, execution or the adaptation of its provisions by the Commission as the EC executive (just as national legislation enables governments to adopt statutory instruments). However, over the years, Council subordinated the exercise of these powers by the Commission to the approval of committees of national civil servants. Such a variety of committees and procedures were set up in various items of Community legislation, that the name 'comitology' was invented to describe it. Parliament had consistently criticized this, and in the draft Treaty sought to strengthen the Commission, no longer subjecting it to the approval of national civil servants, on the grounds that the Commission, which is accountable to Parliament, should clearly be responsible for such decisions.

This part of the draft Treaty also sought to strengthen the applica-tion of European law. Art. 43 strengthened the possibilities open to the Court of Justice to ensure uniform interpretation of Union law (quash-ing judgments of national courts that are in breach of Union law), arbitrating on disputes among Union institutions and in safeguarding human rights. Art. 44 laid down a procedure for Council to sanction a Member State failing to fulfil its obligations. Finally, part three also specified Parliament's right to conduct inquiries and to receive petitions.

Part four ('The policies of the Union') mentioned mainly the areas already dealt with – at least partially – within the EC, either by virtue of specific treaty articles, or by virtue of decisions taken under Art. 235 EEC or within EPC. However, the policy provisions that were sometimes laid down in detail in the EC treaties were sketched in outline only in the DTEU, leaving it up to the future political pro-cesses of the Union to determine them. Nevertheless, the references to consumer protection, environment policy, education, research, cultural policy, information policy, and the EMS were more explicit than in the EEC Treaty. Art. 47 laid down a strict *timetable for completing the internal market*: two years for goods and people, five years for services, and ten years for capital. Parliament thereby pioneered the concept of deadlines for completing the single market, an idea that had been developed in its Economic & Monetary Committee and the 'Kangaroo' intergroup. In almost all the economic and social policy areas, the DTEU laid down that the Union should enjoy concurrent competence. The only areas in which it was to enjoy exclusive competence were those in which it already did so by virtue of the EEC Treaty (although it had not always exercised this in practice). The method of cooperation within the European Council would be used for diplomatic and political aspects of foreign policy (formerly dealt with in EPC); for matters related to international terrorism; and measures designed to reinforce the feeling of individual citizens that they were citizens of the Union. However, the implementation of foreign policy decisions could be entrusted to the Union institutions. In addition, these matters – which could themselves be enlarged in scope by the European Council (e.g. to security) – could be transferred from the field of cooperation to that of common action by a decision of the European Council. In that event, the area so transferred to common action (presumably concurrent) would still not be on the same basis as the other areas subject to common action as (1) Art. 23 allowing a Member State to invoke a vital national interest would be applied to these areas without any transitional time limit of ten years; (2) individual Member States would be allowed to derogate from some of the measures taken; and (3) the European Council would be allowed to restore the fields so transferred to the field of cooperation.

Part five ('The finances of the Union') simplified the budget procedure by abolishing the distinction between 'compulsory' and 'non-compulsory' expenditure, subjecting all expenditure to a single procedure. It allowed the Union itself to amend and extend its sources of revenue through the adoption of an organic law: there would no longer be a national veto on extending own resources every time a new ceiling was reached, but a majority of two-thirds of the weighted majority vote in the Council, together with a similar qualified majority in the Parliament, would be needed. Provision was also made for a system of financial equalization in order to alleviate excessive economic imbalances. Here, Parliament was clearly influenced by the long-standing wrangle over the UK's net contribution, and at the same time inspired by the existence of the German federal equalization system among the *Länder*. Long-term financial programmes, adopted according to the procedure for adopting laws, would serve as the basis for drafting the budget. Borrowing and lending would be brought within the budget procedure.

Part six ('General and Final Provisions') contained the controversial procedure for entry into force of the Treaty (see below). It also laid down a procedure for revising the Treaty once in force, which involved the approval of changes by both arms of the legislative authority in accordance with the procedure applicable to organic laws and the ratification thereof by all the Member States. This guaranteed any state acceding to the Union that the body they joined would not subsequently be changed by a majority. An article on the seat of the institutions left matters in the hands of the national governments (European Council), but placed a time limit on the decision after which the competence would revert to the legislative authority; again we see an attempt to settle an issue that had long plagued the Community.

MAIN CHARACTERISTICS OF THE DRAFT TREATY

A striking element of the draft Treaty was that, although it represented a break from the existing Communities with the constitution of a new *ex-novo* Treaty, it nevertheless sought to stress continuity and gradualism. Continuity was ensured by the provisions for the assumption by the Union of the *acquis communautaire* and by the fact that the institutional structure was based on that of the Communities. It was clearly intended that the Union should start off where the Community had reached in the construction of Europe.

Gradualism was enshrined in the allocation of competences; the exclusive competences granted to the Union were no wider than those enjoyed by the existing Community; most economic and social policy areas came under the category of concurrent competence, in which Union measures could be initiated only by the special majority required for an organic law. Foreign policy, security and approximation of civil and criminal law were left to the method of cooperation, requiring consensus in the European Council.[5] They could, by agreement, be transferred to the area of common action, although if and when this happened there were still a number of safeguards including the possibility of returning them to cooperation. Concerning security, even though dealt with by cooperation, it would initially concern only economic and political aspects of security, thus corresponding to the areas already dealt with in EPC. Gradualism permeated the draft Treaty.[6]

Why, then, was a new Treaty necessary if it was only to continue with gradualism? Parliament clearly considered that the possibility for gradualist development by creative interpretation of the existing treaties had reached its limits, or at any rate was proceeding far too slowly. A new Treaty would allow gradualism to go further, or faster. In Spinelli's words, 'it is not a matter of making a big leap but rather a matter of giving the Community legs to walk on'.[7]

The DTEU did not seek to create a centralized state. The Union would strengthen the federal characteristics of the EC but it would have no extensive bureaucracy of its own, relying on Member States' administrations for the implementation and execution of Union law, it would have no army or police force, it would be governed by the principle of subsidiarity, its law might only lay down 'the fundamental principles governing common action and entrust the responsible authorities . . . with setting out in detail the procedures for their implementation' (Art. 34); and a number of important matters were in the hands of the intergovernmental European Council.

In terms of specific changes to the EC system as it stood in 1984, the draft treaty sought three crucial changes and a number of less important ones. The three crucial changes were:

1. A widening of the field of *competence* of the Community/Union and the formalization of foreign policy cooperation and judicial cooperation in the treaty (with the possibility to transfer them later from 'cooperation' to 'common action').
2. An increase in the *efficiency* of the Community system by:
   (a) broadening the scope of majority voting in Council,
   (b) strengthening the executive powers of the Commission.
3. More *democracy* by enlarging the powers of the EP to give it:
   (a) codecision with Council for the adoption of legislation,
   (b) the right to confirm a new Commission after each European election.

These were the key points on which any reform would be judged. Other points were also important, such as the timetable for completing a single market; the new procedures for fixing the seat of the institutions, for appointing judges to the ECJ, and for the budget; the strengthening of the Court's powers of review; the sanctioning of Member States failing to apply judgments; the formal entrenchment in the treaty of the principle of subsidiarity, of basic rights and of the notion of Union citizenship; the new single form of 'law' to replace directives and regulations, and the specification that ministers for EC affairs should lead national delegations in Council. However, compared to the key objectives, they were secondary in terms of fundamentally changing the EC system.

Besides the features of the new Union, the draft Treaty contained a crucial article concerning the setting up of the Union. We have already seen how Parliament hoped, in drafting a treaty itself, to build up political momentum before Member States would negotiate. Parliament also included in the draft Treaty a further device to try to minimize the scope for blocking the reform process. This was the procedure for the entry into force of the new Treaty.

ENTRY INTO FORCE OF THE DRAFT TREATY

The provisions of Art. 82 of the draft Treaty were arguably the most controversial, yet they were central to the strategy that Parliament decided to follow.[8] This article envisaged the possibility of the Union being established, if necessary, without the participation of all the EC Member States. Parliament decided to present the draft Treaty in its own right, and not to use Art. 236 of the EEC Treaty (and its equivalents in the ECSC and EAEC Treaties)[9] laying down a procedure for revision of the existing Treaty, both because it felt that this article was inapplicable to such a project and because it disliked the procedures laid down by Art. 236.

How did Parliament justify avoiding Art. 236? After all, a considerable body of legal opinion maintains that since the Community treaties have called into being a new legal order which limits the sovereignty of Member States,[10] they cannot be amended other than by the procedure prescribed therein.[11] Although amendments have been made in the past,[12] which did not follow that procedure, the controversy this caused later was among the reasons that ensured that subsequent revisions[13] were carried out in conformity with the procedure. Parliament itself had supported the use of the revision procedures, which aim to preserve the *acquis communautaire* from erosion by the Member States and involve the Community institutions in the procedures.

In this case, however, it was argued that it was not just a matter of revision but the creation of a new Treaty, the scope of which was far wider and went beyond simple amendments to the existing treaties. 'The revision procedure must be applied when one acts within the framework of the old system, which one intends to reform. That procedure no longer comes into play when the aim is to constitute institutions with new powers and possessing a different juridical status'.[14] Indeed, the EEC Treaty had been created without reference to the revision article in the ECSC Treaty, and when the *ad hoc* Assembly engaged in the preparation of the Political Community and, later, the Member States studied the Fouchet Plan, no references were made to the revision procedures of the existing treaties. Parliament felt that it too was correct not to invoke these procedures in this case.

But above all, Parliament wished to open the door for the possible adoption of the draft Treaty by a majority of Member States, whereas Art. 236 requires ratification by *all* Member States. Parliament had witnessed the discussions on the Genscher–Colombo proposals in which single Member States were consistently able to block proposals, however moderate. It was conscious that certain Member States were unlikely to accept anything like the draft Treaty, except, perhaps, if confronted with the possibility of being left out with the majority of Members going ahead without them. Some Members may have had in mind the precedent of Schuman's Declaration in 1950 to move ahead with those Member States of the Council of Europe which agreed to proceed further down the path of integration: six of its twelve Member States agreed to do so; others followed later. In this case, the EP defined a 'critical mass' necessary to forge ahead; Art. 82 referred to a majority of Member States whose total population represents two-thirds of the population of the Communities.

Such arguments were politically attractive, but the legal implications of moving in such a way from Community to Union were somewhat different from moving ahead to create the ECSC Treaty 30 years before. Unlike the earlier case, the Union would absorb Community matters and administer them through its own institutions. A harmonious coexistence of the Union and the Community would be difficult to imagine. What then were the possible scenarios if a new Treaty were ratified only by a majority of the Member States of the Community?

The simplest scenario from the legal point of view would be one in which the non-contracting Member States accept the creation of the Union, perhaps safeguarding their interests by means of some forms of association agreement with it. In this case, there should be no obstacle in the way of allowing an abrogation of the Community treaties by unanimous agreement of all its signatories, in accordance with international law.[15]

But if the non-contracting Member States insisted on their rights as established under the Community treaties rather than safeguarding these by an association agreement, what would happen? Legally, there would be side-by-side existence of the Community and the Union. However, the political, practical and even legal difficulties would be prohibitive. There would be costly institutional duplication: Community Parliament,

Council, Commission and Court existing alongside those of the Union. It would entail discussion within both frameworks of a whole range of policy matters, with the Union states presumably acting as a bloc within the Community institutions, probably insisting on implementing the provisions for majority voting wherever possible under the old treaties, and possibly voting to run down Community policies and to cut its budget. It is difficult to see what advantages non-contracting Members would have in the long run in insisting on the maintenance of the Community system alongside that of the Union. The stronger cohesion of the Union and the commitment of its Member States would leave little doubt as to which would in practice become the pre-eminent body. For these reasons it can only be concluded that, whilst non-contracting Member States would juridically be in a position in which they could insist on the maintenance of the Communities alongside the Union,[16] the political and practical difficulties inherent in such a solution would be prohibitive and they would, in fact, eventually prefer either to join the Union or to negotiate an association agreement or a two-tier system protecting their interests.[17]

The EP's strategy of proposing a Union Treaty that could come into effect without the unanimous accord of the Member States of the Community was audacious, but if it ever came to that point, feasible. It felt that the threat of moving ahead, if necessary, without certain Member States was credible, and that this would have an important bearing on the dynamics of any subsequent negotiations. This was a courageous and highly significant position for a Parliament elected in *all* the Member States to take.

8 From the Draft Treaty to the 1985 Intergovernmental Conference

This chapter examines this period in considerable detail. To the author's knowledge, little else has been written on the political dynamic that led from the draft Treaty to the convening of the Intergovernmental Conference (IGC) that negotiated the Single European Act (SEA). Particular attention will be given to the role of the Parliament and its members in this process in order to evaluate how far they contributed to triggering the 1985 treaty revision.

From the outset, Parliament sought to avoid its draft Treaty being drowned at birth in a Council working party. On the contrary, it wished to broaden the debate to circles which – whilst still essentially a political elite – would be far wider than would normally deal with European initiatives. In this respect at least, it was successful.

Already during the preparatory phase Parliament began to interest significant groups in the DTEU. Consultations took place between EP political groups and their corresponding national parties. Seminars were organized by the EUI with the rapporteurs, which sparked off considerable interest in academic circles, with a number of important seminars organized by universities in various Member States. (Spinelli himself was awarded several doctorates *honoris causa* by universities in this period.) The ETUC and the Employers' Organization UNICE both followed the work of the Committee closely and were to adopt positions supporting the DTEU, as did various interest groups.

After the adoption of the DTEU, Parliament pursued four main channels in trying to build up support for Treaty reforms:

1. through political parties which had to take a position on the issue in their policy statements and manifestos for the European elections, having due regard to their MEPs and how they had voted on the DTEU;
2. direct to governments, both individually and collectively in the European Council;

3. through national parliaments which were invited to support the initiative and to each of which the EP sent delegations to explain and seek support;

4. through interest groups, non-governmental organizations and academia.

THE 1984 EUROPEAN ELECTIONS AND NATIONAL POLITICAL PARTIES

An early opportunity to take the Treaty to a wider audience was the European elections. Although some of its more enthusiastic supporters had expected the elections to be a sort of referendum on the DTEU, most MEPs realized that this was not possible. Nevertheless, the elections provided an important opportunity for explanation, information and discussion. It obliged national political parties to take positions on the Treaty in their national manifestos or elsewhere. Political parties at the national level – and not just their MEPs – could not avoid taking a position on the future path of European integration. These positions inevitably had to bear in mind how their Members had voted in Strasbourg. The elections therefore functioned as a 'transmission belt' obliging national politicians to address the issue publicly.

The first element of the 'transmission belt' was the congresses of the European party federations preparing the joint manifestos for the elections. The EPP and the ELD gave full support to the draft Treaty, but the CSP was unable to overcome its divisions on the issue. Their manifesto referred to the need for institutional improvements and, although it was not very specific, footnotes indicating dissent were entered on this section by the British and Danish parties. The PSI and the PSDI insisted that the manifesto contain an annex in which they confirmed their support for the DTEU and declared 'that they will organize their activities and election campaign in support of this proposal'.

Although almost all political parties discussed and had a position on it, it cannot be said that the DTEU featured prominently in the campaign. Essentially ten secondary national elections took place.[1] European issues did creep in, however, and the DTEU was usually among them. Almost every newspaper in the quality press of all Member States devoted some space to the draft Treaty.[2] It featured in televised debates, including a debate between the four party list leaders and Spinelli on German television.[3]

Although it was thus given a good airing, the draft Treaty was not a subject that could easily become a focal point in the party political competitions that dominate election campaigns. In most Member States, the positions adopted by parties precluded, in one way or another, the DTEU from being a major instrument of party political battle. In some countries, such as Italy in which every significant political party had included support for the draft Treaty in its election manifesto, debate on the Treaty could only take place in terms of degrees of support, or emphasizing one or another aspect of it: hardly the stuff of electoral controversy. To varying degrees, this situation applied also in Belgium, Luxembourg, Germany and the Netherlands (though in the latter two countries some criticism of too much emphasis being given to a supposed institutional panacea was forthcoming from the Green Parties as well as some members of the Socialist Parties).

In Denmark there was the opposite phenomenon. The People's Movement against the EEC, which again won 4 out of the 16[4] seats and was perceived as a major threat by the political parties, made a big issue out of the DTEU, accusing other parties of not being vigorous enough in opposing it. As a result almost every party emphasized their opposition to the draft Treaty. Only the small Centre Democratic Party, which again won one seat, raised a timid voice in favour of institutional reform based on the draft Treaty. The Liberal[5] and Conservative Parties did not rule out further progress in European integration, but were not willing to stick their necks out in favour of the DTEU.

In the remaining four countries, the party political mix was such that one might have expected the issue to become the subject of electoral controversy, but in each case there were circumstances which prevented it from doing so. In France, the joint opposition list, including both Gaullists who had voted against the draft Treaty and the UDF coalition of Christian Democrats and Liberals who had voted for, was divided on the issue. The Socialists, however, were not able to exploit this fully, as they had themselves abstained in Strasbourg and if anything this abstention looked embarrassing following Mitterrand's speech welcoming the draft Treaty (see below). The Communists had opposed the DTEU, but others could point out that their Italian colleagues had supported it and in this way underline the differences between the French and Italian Communist Parties. No party, then, had an interest in highlighting the issue during the campaign.

In Great Britain, the governing party under Mrs Thatcher portrayed itself in that campaign as the moderate party on European issues between the 'Euro-fanatical' Liberal-SDP Alliance on the one hand and the largely anti-European Labour Party on the other. The Conservative campaign was run by the party headquarters and leadership rather than by the MEPs and, as we saw in chapter 6, their attitude towards the draft Treaty did not match the 22–6 vote in favour among their Members in Strasbourg. It would certainly have been difficult to point to support for the DTEU at the same time as the party was engaged in attacking the Liberal-SDP Alliance for being too European. The Alliance itself tried to escape the 'Euro-fanatic' image with which the other parties had painted it, and did not draw much attention to the support for the DTEU that it had hinted at in its manifesto. Having had no members itself in Strasbourg other than Labour defector Gallagher, it perhaps felt less committed to the DTEU than would otherwise have been the case. Labour did make some play of attacking the Conservatives for having supported the DTEU, especially when this appeared to contradict statements made by Thatcher in the course of the campaign, but it was unable to make the issue feature prominently in the absence of a strong position on the matter by the other parties.

A remarkably similar situation existed in Greece, with the (Socialist) governing party playing the 'moderate' role between the anti-European Communist Party and the pro-European New Democracy.

In Ireland, the controversial part of the DTEU was the security aspect, and all those who had supported the Treaty had expressed reservations on this point. Again, there was little food for inter-party debate. Attention focused more on the reforms to the CAP being negotiated at that time, and in particular the 'super levy' on milk.

Thus, the DTEU, whilst not being a dominant electoral issue, had in the course of the campaign become a factor of which political elites in all the Member States had become very much aware. They were also aware that it would remain an issue after the elections.

INITIAL REACTIONS OF GOVERNMENTS

Several national leaders had, during and after the election campaign, voiced support of the DTEU, but usually in rather general or cautious terms. President Pertini of Italy on 26 May 1984 stated: 'this is a political signal which Europe and my country have long desired'; the Dutch Prime Minister Lubbers stated on 5 April 1984:[6] 'the draft Treaty on European Union must not become a further disappointment for European citizens'; the Belgian Prime Minister Martens:[7] 'the Belgian government will consider in a constructive manner the Draft Treaty on European Union approved by the European Parliament'; Queen Beatrix, in a speech to the EP on 17 February 1984: 'your initiative will prompt the Government and Parliament to consider the prospects offered by your proposals'. Italian Prime Minister Craxi[8] and Foreign Minister Andreotti,[9] the Portuguese Prime Minister,[10] the President of the Spanish Senate speaking on behalf of the Prime Minister,[11] the German Chancellor[12] all spoke out in support, again in general terms, of the DTEU. By far the most significant statement, however, was that of President Mitterrand.

Speaking to the EP on 24 May as President of the European Council, Mitterrand made a carefully prepared speech on European Union. Expressing his personal commitment to such a goal, he criticized the current workings of the EC and, pointing out that France had initiated the so-called 'Luxembourg compromise', criticized the way that this worked in practice and called for its review. He went on to specify a number of necessary reforms, and his speech culminated in an expression of support for the draft Treaty:

> France, ladies and gentlemen, is available for such an enterprise. I, on its behalf, state its willingness to examine and defend your project, the inspiration behind which it approves. I therefore suggest that preparatory consultations, leading to a conference of the Member States concerned, be started up.[13]

Mitterrand's speech placed the DTEU firmly on the political agenda. The French press, which had not given a very large coverage to its adoption by Parliament, was suddenly full of comments, analyses and interviews with Spinelli. It seemed to be a major turning point in the French attitude towards European integration. In particular, Mitterrand's emphasis on calling a conference of 'Member States concerned' appeared to lend support to the perspective opened by Art. 82 DTEU.

There can be little doubt that Mitterrand knew exactly what he was referring to when he made his speech to the EP, and that he had decided to do so after careful consideration. Immediately after the adoption of the DTEU by Parliament, President Dankert (normally accompanied by Ferri and Spinelli) had toured the national capitals, as instructed by Parliament's resolution, formally to hand over to national governments and Parliaments copies of the DTEU. They had met Mitterrand on 16 April 1984. Spinelli had always argued[14] that France – and therefore its President – was the key to the eventual success of Parliament's initiative. A European Union without France was inconceivable, politically and geographically. In terms of the history of European integration, its position had always been crucial, whether it had been playing an initiating role as at the time of Schuman and Monnet, or a more negative role as under de Gaulle. If France were to espouse a more advanced proposal for European Union, the Benelux countries, Germany and Italy would certainly follow. Spinelli had therefore prepared the meeting with Mitterrand carefully.[15] He handed Mitterrand a memorandum containing some reflections on the possibility of a French initiative in this field. The memorandum repeated once again the reasons why a relaunch of the European enterprise was necessary, described the essential features of the DTEU and pointed out why the French President was in a unique position to set the ball rolling. Spinelli proposed that Mitterrand should seize a suitable occasion (such as his forthcoming speech to the EP) to declare that Europe was in an impasse and that it was necessary to move ahead along new lines; that Parliament's draft Treaty was a viable and realistic basis for such a step; and to invite the governments of interested Member States to prepare to ratify a new Treaty. Mitterrand had promised to answer Spinelli in his speech to Parliament, a promise which he duly kept.

Some[16] thought Mitterrand's speech was an electoral gimmick in the weeks preceding the European elections. As we have seen above, it was a difficult one to exploit, and his continued action *after* the elections implied that there was more to it than that. Others considered that there were reasons connected to the negotiations going on at that time over the British budget refund. The speech took place after the failure of the Brussels Summit to resolve the British budgetary problem, at a time at which confidence in the Community's ability to solve it, after almost five years of negotiation, was at its lowest ebb. Whatever the merits of the case, Britain had scarcely played its cards in a 'European' manner and many voiced scepticism about Britain's commitment to Europe. The repeated adherence of successive British governments to the aim of European Union, the most recent of which was Thatcher's signature to the Stuttgart Solemn Declaration, was not sufficient to overcome this feeling.[17] Mitterrand's speech, and various statements made after it by the French government,[18] implied that France was interested in a new structure involving those countries genuinely committed to Europe. Lending credence to moving ahead without all Member States could have served a tactical purpose, namely to put pressure on the British government. After five years of talks and two successive meetings of the European Council ending in breakdown, it was felt that a failure at Fontainebleau could lead up to the break-up of the Community. If so, an alternative course of action was ready.

In fact, the Fontainebleau Summit (25/26 June 1984) reached agreement on the British budget rebate and related matters. The possibility of Mitterrand inviting only a certain number of Member States to nego-tiate a new Treaty was inconceivable, with the Summit deemed to be a success. Instead, Mitterrand proposed, and the Summit agreed, to establish an *ad hoc* committee on institutional matters modelled on the Spaak Committee, to make proposals on institutional reform. This fallback position had been discussed beforehand with the Germans, Italians and Dutch. This was the only possible way forward in the immediate future, and again emphasized the long-term nature of Mitterrand's commitment.

Before the Summit, there had again been contacts between the French government and Spinelli. Foreign Minister Dumas and his private of-fice had exchanged views with Spinelli, who had himself written again to Mitterrand on 8 June suggesting various ways in which his speech could be followed up. Spinelli proposed calling an intergovernmental Conference of Member States accepting the DTEU as a base, claiming that there would otherwise be no criterion to distinguish those wanting real political Union from those who would attend to participate in endless discussions on the meaning of the word Union.[19] He compared the situation to that of Schuman in 1950 when he laid down as a criterion the acceptance of a supranational authority to govern the coal and steel market. Spinelli argued that the IGC should indicate which articles of the DTEU should, in its view, be modified (with the agreement of the EP) and which additional points should be added, establish procedures to negotiate with Community Member States not wishing to join the Union, and prepare procedures for ratification of the Treaty. He urged that such a conference be prepared at the highest political level, by the heads of government themselves or by their personal representatives, thus repeating his traditional argument that the matter should be kept for as long as possible out of the hands of national bureaucrats.

That Spinelli's arguments were at least partly accepted by the French government was confirmed in a letter from Dumas to Spinelli on 25 July 1984, in which he stated that the *ad hoc* committee should put forward proposals based on Stuttgart and the EP's draft Treaty 'permettant que soit convoquée une Conférence des Etats Membres qui *avaient déclaré leur détermination à progresser dans la voie de l'intégration européenne*',[20] maintaining therefore the option of pushing ahead without all Member States. He also emphasized in his letter, that 'as you requested', the preparatory work was in the hands of personal representatives of the heads of government.

Indeed, the decision of the European Council to model the commit-tee on the Spaak Committee was not without significance. The orig-inal Spaak Committee in 1956 had given new impetus to European integration at a time when the process had appeared to have ground to a halt following the rejection of the Defence Community Treaty. Composed of personal representatives of the heads of government, it had prepared the drafting and signature of the EEC Treaty, as a supplement to the Coal and Steel Community. To have chosen the same name in the current circumstances was felt by many to have been an indication of the intention of at least those heads of governments that were aware of the historical precedent.

THE DOOGE COMMITTEE

Although the heads of government had agreed with the Mitterrand/ Spinelli proposal that the committee be composed of their personal representatives, this did not avoid, in some cases, the nomination of national officials.[21] The Danish Prime Minister chose the top Foreign Ministry official to represent him. In stark contrast, Italy nominated Ferri, the outgoing Chairman of the EP's Committee on Institutional Affairs, and France nominated Maurice Faure, the former Foreign Minister who had signed the Treaty of Rome and a former international President of the European Movement. Mitterrand's choice of Faure again signalled his continued commitment well after the elections and the solution to the British problem. Britain itself nominated Malcolm Rifkind, then a Foreign Office Junior Minister. Belgium and Greece nominated sitting MEPs.

Garret Fitzgerald, succeeding Mitterrand as President-in-Office of the European Council, nominated Senator Dooge, majority leader in the Senate and former Foreign Minister, as chairman of the committee. Although this reflected normal practice, the President of a Committee going with the Council Presidency, it did mark a departure from the supposed Spaak Committee model. Spaak had been an agreed independent chairman who did not represent his country, and several governments were unhappy with Fitzgerald's move. In particular, Kohl had wished to nominate outgoing Federal President Carstens as a candidate for chairman. Once the (quick) announcement had been made, however, it was impossible for Fitzgerald to backtrack for domestic political reasons.

From the outset, the committee established its independence from the Council by holding its meetings elsewhere, in the Egmont Palace in Brussels. It declined Council's offer to provide the secretariat of the Committee, establishing its own secretariat composed of a member of Fitzgerald's private office (Katherine Meenhan, who was chair of the

European Movement in Ireland) and an official from each of the Council and the Commission. Both these officials had previously been responsible for following the EP's Committee on Institutional Affairs on behalf of their own institution. Each member of the committee was allowed to bring an adviser and a note-taker to meetings. Ferri's adviser was Dastoli, Spinelli's personal assistant.

The committee held four working meetings after its preparatory meeting and before the meeting of the European Council in Dublin to which it presented an interim report. Parliament's new President, Pflimlin, and Spinelli were invited to two of these meetings. Each member of the committee prepared papers on particular subjects, but responsibility for drafting the interim report was given to Faure. His draft, which was given the go-ahead by the Elysée in spite of some reticence on the part of the French Foreign Office, was adopted with few amendments as the interim report. Significantly, the advisers of the representatives of the six original Member States of the Community met privately before the meeting to coordinate their position.

During the work of the committee there had again been numerous contacts taking place in the background. President Pflimlin was strongly committed to backing the draft Treaty and lobbied assiduously on its behalf in the meetings that he had with heads of government[22] and with Senator Dooge. Spinelli himself had a meeting with Garret Fitzgerald and he and Dastoli kept in contact with various members of the committee, notably Dumas.

The Committee's interim report was adopted by majority and is therefore littered with reservations expressed by the British, Danish and Greek representatives.[23] The Danish representative expressed an overall reservation. Essentially, the position adopted was approved by the representatives of the six original Member States and Ireland.[24] In view of the pre-meeting which they held, and in voting through a text which they knew would never be acceptable to at least one of the other States, the six implicitly accepted Parliament's analysis that it might be necessary to move ahead without everyone. At the very least, it represented a conscious decision to push through a majority report rather than the lowest common denominator and to expose the division between pro-integration states and the others.

The interim report, after making various considerations on the nature of the problems facing the Community, called for an IGC to negotiate a European Union Treaty. It therefore endorsed Parliament's analysis of the need for a new Treaty. The only specific reference made to Parliament's draft treaty was that this IGC should be guided 'by the spirit and the method underlying [the] draft Treaty adopted by the European Parliament'. However, examination of the report reveals a number of striking parallels with the DTEU:

1. On the policy side it listed almost exactly the same areas as needing further development and indeed followed the same structure as the draft Treaty (Section A, 'a homogeneous internal economic area' corresponding to Title 1 of Part 4 of the Draft Treaty 'economic policy'; Part B, 'promotion of the common values of civilization' corresponding to Title 2 'policy for society', and Part C, 'the search for an external identity' corresponding with Title 3 'international relations').

2. The provision for majority voting in the Council, with unanimity required only for new areas of action or accessions, was similar to the provision in the DTEU for majority voting in all matters subject to 'common action', but with unanimity required for transferring new areas to common action. The report proposed that 'for a transitional period a Member State can plead a vital national interest provided it can objectively justify it to the Council, which in turn must ensure with the help of the Commission that the vital interests of the Community as a whole are respected', procedure which recalls the provisions of the DTEU providing for transitional period in which Member States may invoke a vital national interest recognized by the Commission and justified in writing.

3. The report included a provision corresponding almost exactly to Art. 35 of the DTEU, allowing 'differentiated Community rules, provided such differentiation is limited in time and based solely on economic and social considerations'.

4. The report showed similar opposition to the European Council becoming simply another body dealing with the day-to-day business of the Community.

5. It proposed to strengthen the role of the Commission and put forward a method for appointing a new Commission virtually identical to that envisaged in Art. 25 DTEU.

6. The section of the report on the EP was somewhat vaguely worded, but took up the proposals in the DTEU for joint decision-making with Council as regards legislative power, expanding the supervisory role of the EP to external relations and giving the EP responsibility in decisions on revenue.

7. The report also referred to the need to strengthen the powers of the Court of Justice, although it did not make any specific proposals.

Despite the similarities of content, the report was not, of course, drafted in the same precise legal language as the draft Treaty.

The interim report was submitted to the Dublin European Council on 1 and 2 December, which asked the committee to continue its work and to submit a final report to the next meeting of the European Council at which a preliminary exchange of views would take place, leaving the final decision to the June 1985 meeting of the European Council in Milan, which would be devoted in priority to this subject.

The new EP reacted in a resolution on 12 December, drafted by the Committee on Institutional Affairs, which noted the convergence of ideas between the interim report and the DTEU. It requested the convening of an IGC no later than June 1985, 'possibly with the participation of all the Governments of the Member States', and basing its work on the DTEU. It called for a suitable procedure between the EP and the IGC to be established with a view to reaching agreement on the text to be submitted for ratification. The EP thus accepted the inevitability of its draft going through a procedure involving negotiation among States, but intended to participate in that procedure itself in one way or another, hoping to create an equilibrium between national and European approaches.

The Dooge Committee had six more meetings to produce its final report[25] to the Brussels European Council on 29–30 March. The Dublin European Council had requested it to 'continue its work with a view to securing the maximum degree of agreement'. This implied that an attempt should be made to reach a compromise. In fact, the majority held firm on its position of principle, though accommodations were sought on particular issues. In addition, the Committee filled in a few gaps left in its interim report and had meetings with a delegation from the Economic and Social Committee (which supported the EP's draft Treaty in its submission),[26] and, again, an EP delegation composed this time of Spinelli and Formigoni.[27]

The discussions in the committee centred on majority voting in the Council (with various formulae examined to get around the problem of 'vital interests' ranging from mere declarations of intent to arbitration by other institutions or else proposals for lists of items on which no 'veto' would be allowed), the EP's legislative powers, security, strengthening the Court, economic convergence and the prodecures for the IGC (mandate, preparations, role of EP). The results of these discussions, as presented in the final report, showed that the split between, on the one hand, the original six and the Commission (plus Ireland except on security) and on the other hand the UK, Greece and Denmark remained significant. The report was still subject to reservations on numerous points and in some cases this included new reservations, even by representatives in the 'majority' (e.g. Ruhfus on economic convergence). In some important areas the text had been expanded.

The most significant changes to the interim report were:

1. the spelling out of the majority and minority positions on voting in the Council, with the majority favouring qualified or simple majority decisions except in a few cases in which unanimity would be required, such cases to be fewer than in the current treaties, and the others supporting majority voting where currently provided for in the treaties but with unanimity required should a Member State invoke a very important interest;

2. giving more details as to what was meant by 'joint decision-making' on legislation by specifying that Commission proposals would first be discussed in the Parliament, that Council would deliberate on the text adopted by Parliament, and in the event of disagreement, conciliation would be initiated on the basis of a new Commission proposal (it did not specify what should happen if conciliation failed, but the term 'joint decision-taking', presumably precluded unilateral decision by one side);

3. proposing that association and accession agreements require EP approval;

4. proposing that decisions governing the development of own resources also be taken jointly by the Council and the EP;

5. spelling out that the Court be strengthened as 'supreme arbiter' and also charged with the protection of basic rights;

6. adding a reference in the preamble of the Treaty to 'the principles of pluralist democracy and the respect for human rights';

7. extending the text on 'priority objectives' (i.e. policies) with additions concerning the creation of a technological Community and security (the latter going beyond what the EP had proposed in its Draft Treaty) and,

8. regarding procedure, that the IGC include the prospective Member States (Spain and Portugal) as well as the Commission, that it associate the EP with its work and that the outcome be submitted to the EP.

The report was submitted to the Brussels European Council on 29/30 March. As planned, the heads of government had only a preliminary exchange of views. They 'welcomed both the approach outlined in the report and the content of the interesting proposals put forward' and stated that detailed examination of the proposals would continue by means of bilateral contacts, aiming at final decisions at the Milan summit in June.[28]

THE REACTION OF NATIONAL PARLIAMENTS

During this whole period, the EP had developed a dialogue with national parliaments. As foreseen from the outset, the DTEU was submitted to national parliaments as well as to national governments. Although it is highly unusual for national parliaments to be closely involved in the preparation of treaties before their final ratification following conclusion by governments, the EP felt that for a Treaty of such a character it wished to allow the national parliaments an opportunity to be involved at an earlier stage, though the ease with which this could be done varied with the constitutional system in each Member State. As we have seen, the EP hoped that national parliaments would, in the main, prove to be allies in that it was felt that opposition to European integration had usually emanated from national governments or national bureaucracies. In particular, it argued that national parliaments had already lost considerable power to the Council, a legislative body meeting behind closed doors, and that a strengthening of the EP's position within the institutional system of the Community was part of a common struggle for parliamentary democracy.

The first national parliament to react was the Chamber of Deputies in *Italy*, which adopted a resolution on the same day that the EP adopted the DTEU pledging the Chamber to 'embark on the procedure for the ratification of the revision of the Treaties proposed by the Committee on Institutional Affairs of the European Parliament with a view to establishing European Union' and calling on the government 'to support this proposal henceforth as strongly and promptly as possible in every appropriate political and institutional forum and to take adequate steps to prepare itself for this task in view of the Italian Presidency of the Community in the first half of 1985'. A second resolution adopted at the same time called on the Government to 'arrange for its ratification in accordance with constitutional procedures' and 'to hold talks with the Governments of the other Member States with a view to increasing the number of ratifying parties'.[29] This last provision indicated support for Article 82 of the DTEU.

The Italian Senate adopted a resolution on 10 May 1984 which described the draft Treaty as 'the most appropriate means of creating the necessary institutional conditions to breathe new life into the Community's decision-making processes, which at present are obviously out-dated and inadequate, and of formulating the Community policies which Europe needs at present'. It called on the government 'to approve the draft Treaty without delay, to submit it to Parliament for ratification, to take whatever action is necessary to ensure that it is approved by the largest possible number of Community countries'.[30] This text was adopted unanimously. On 18 July 1984 the Senate described the draft Treaty as 'a minimum but sufficient basis for reform' and reiterated 'the motion already passed by the Senate on 10 May 1984 calling on the Government to approve the draft Treaty without delay, submit it to Parliament for ratification and to take whatever action is necessary to ensure that it is approved by the largest possible number of Community Countries'. Again, we can see an approval both of Parliament's draft Treaty and of the method for its entry into force.

In *Belgium*, identical resolutions were tabled in the Chamber and in the Senate jointly by the floor leaders of the main political parties (Socialists, Christian Democrats, Liberals and the Volksunie) supporting the DTEU and another was tabled in the Chamber by the Ecologists, also supporting it. These were referred to the Foreign Affairs Committees, and on 24 May 1984 the Chamber unanimously[31] adopted its report, which considered that 'it is necessary to develop new policies and to establish a new institutional balance', that this requires institutions that 'have been rendered more efficient and democratic', that the DTEU 'constitutes such an initiative' and called on the government 'to take immediately all steps necessary to open negotiations on the draft Treaty establishing the European Union with the other Member States' and to 'embark on the ratification procedure as swiftly as possible as soon as the Member States have reached agreement on the Treaty, and to urge the governments of other Member States to do likewise'. The Chamber thus indicated its full support for the DTEU, but remained silent on the possibility of its entry into force without all Member States.

The first negative reaction was a resolution adopted on 29 May 1984 by the *Danish Folketing*. The Folketing emphasized that 'the right of veto and the preservation of the existing distribution of powers between the Council of Ministers, the Commission and the European Parliament is fundamental to Denmark's membership of EEC and therefore rejects the draft Treaty'. However, the resolution then went on to list a large number of objectives for the Community, which included combating unemployment; concerted action to reduce working hours in all the Member States; new joint actions in the field of industry, research, technology and energy; efforts to improve the environment and working environment; control over multinational companies; development cooperation.[32] Critics were not slow to point to the contradiction between this ambitious list and the means the Folketing was willing to give to the Community to implement it. The resolution was adopted by 134 votes to 30, with 2 abstentions. The 30 were in fact anti-marketeers opposed to the long list of objectives for the Community: the only support for the draft Treaty came from the two abstentions. The resolution had the merit of making Denmark's position perfectly clear and could be pointed to show how the prospects for the DTEU were linked to Article 82. Later, following the presentation of the Dooge Committee report to the European Council, the Folketing again debated the issue (while an EP delegation was present to discuss the matter; see below). The resolution adopted then[33] allowed the government to participate in negotiations and was interpreted by observers as 'giving the government a little more margin for manoeuvre than it had previously'.[34] It could also be seen as a first sign that Denmark might accept some modifications to the Treaties, at least concerning their scope. Nevertheless, it remained a highly restricted position.

In *Germany*, the Bundestag held a preliminary debate on the DTEU on 13 April 1984, which indicated general support from the CDU/ CSU, SPD and FDP Groups but some reservations from the Greens in particular on the article referring to cooperation in the field of security. A motion for a resolution[35] was tabled jointly by all the parties which 'welcomes the European Parliament's initiative in submitting the draft of a Treaty establishing European Union to all national parliaments for their opinion. The German Bundestag will draw up such an opinion and submit it to the European Parliament within one year'. The text was referred to the Foreign Affairs Committee and other committees were asked for an opinion. In addition, the 'Europa-Kommission' (a Joint Committee of German MEPs and MPs) was involved in the work. Among the rapporteurs nominated by the Foreign Affairs committee was Petra Kelly of the German Green Party, who had been a member of Spinelli's private office when he was a Commissioner. The President of the Bundestag, Dr Jenninger, in a speech in Cologne[36] on 9 December, indicated that he expected the Bundestag to lend its full support to the draft Treaty (which it ultimately did, but far too late to affect events in this period).

In *France*, the responsible bodies in both the National Assembly and the Senate are the 'Delegations to the European Communities' set up to deal with European affairs (the constitution of the Fifth Republic precluding the establishment of parliamentary committees on these matters). Both delegations drew up detailed reports[37] on the various aspects of the draft Treaty, being critical of some aspects, supportive of others, and in some feeling that it did not go far enough. The report of the delegation of the National Assembly was adopted soon after Mitterrand's speech to the European Parliament, whereas that of the Senate was adopted beforehand. The delegation of the National Assembly concluded by considering 'that a new situation calls for a new Treaty and that the construction of Europe cannot be advanced unless the Community is provided with the means to establish an institutional system capable of expressing political will'. The report of the Senate delegation welcomed the draft Treaty and noted 'that the system and the institutional mechanism proposed are flexible and progressive, which would ensure that the European Union would be gradually moulded along the lines desired by the Member States'. However, it felt 'constrained to express its doubts as to the realistic chances of the draft Treaty's success in the foreseeable future, but it would not for this reason deny the value, interest and importance of the work accomplished'.

Following the presentation of the Dooge Report and discussion with an EP delegation, the National Assembly's delegation returned to the subject adopting a new report[38] which, whilst noting that the Assembly was powerless to act until the government included the item on its agenda, nevertheless made a number of remarks. It drew attention to the similarity of the DTEU and the Dooge Report, stating that the latter is an 'echo' of the former. It said that if an IGC were called, the DTEU, being detailed and structured, would be at the centre of the negotiations. It noted that President Mitterrand's speech of 24 May 1984, 'a pris le contre-pied de l'attitude française traditionnelle', and represented a strong commitment of principle. It noted recent governmental documents which, while supporting 'more majority voting' considered it premature to abandon the possibility of invoking a vital interest (on this point the report considered Dooge to be more far-reaching than the DTEU, which maintained a transitional period of ten years) and which considered the increase of the EP's power to be 'inevitable', supporting the Dooge proposals in this respect together with uniformization of the electoral procedure. The report concluded that the opportunity 'must be seized without hesitation' and an IGC convened with 'a precise mandate to be completed within a given period'. It 'considers that the need to improve the efficiency of the Community's decision-making process is indispensable but that it is no less vital that the process be made more democratic'. It called for an increase in the EP's budgetary power, notably on revenue. It 'suggests that, should the notion of "vital national interests" be retained, as the French government seems to wish, any State having recourse to (it) give its reasons for doing so to the Council and the European Parliament'. Finally, it supported the proposals for strengthening the ECJ.

It is interesting to compare these conclusions with those of a report by the same body three years before[39] which considered that the existing institutional system was working adequately, that the EP proposal (then still being drafted) was going too far too soon, that 'l'Union européenne n'est pas si urgente au niveau des institutions que l'on doive remettre en cause les progrès réalisés à propos d'une querelle purement intellectuelle . . .'. and which supported the Genscher–Colombo proposals (which the May 1985 Report considered a failure). The shift of opinion was clear, and cannot be attributed to the 'conjuncture' of day-to-day Community issues as the first report was drafted during the deadlocked British refund negotiations, while the latter followed agreement on a whole range of issues (refund, own resources, IMP, EMS 'mini-package', etc.): one might well have expected the conclusions to be the other way around. The debate on the draft Treaty was apparently helping to reshape attitudes to institutional reform.

In *Ireland*, the Joint Committee of the Dáil and the Seanad on the EC drafted a comprehensive report,[40] having taken evidence from Ministers, MEPs (including Spinelli), European officials (including the author) and the European Movement. The report, adopted on 20 March 1985, considered the DTEU and the Dooge interim report, adopting a generally favourable tone but worried about Irish neutrality and whether the Union would have adequate mechanisms for economic convergence. It concluded that 'the Joint Committee is in favour generally of moves to improve the workings of the European Communities and to move towards genuine European Union, and it welcomes the European Parliament's draft Treaty establishing the European Union'. It was 'aware of the considerable support among European leaders for the draft Treaty' and was 'conscious of the need to prepare Irish political and public opinion' for a conference and for 'the possible entry into force of a European Union'. It stressed the 'economic, social, cultural and political advantages to be gained', but emphasized that these could be at the expense of Irish national interests if there were insufficient commitment to provide the EC with adequate financial resources to promote redistribution and convergence. It stated that 'the degree of solidarity shown to this country [must be] sufficient to offset the risks to our vital national interests consequent on phasing out the veto and allowing greater powers to the Commission and Parliament'. In addition, it insisted on an acceptable formula to allow Irish neutrality to continue indefinitely. With an eye to Art. 82 of the DTEU, the conclusions stressed the disadvantage of exclusion from the Union, considering that 'of all the vital national interests ... none is more vital than Ireland's continued membership itself'. When debated at the Dáil, however, a divergence appeared between the government and the opposition. PM Fitzgerald called for Ireland to be 'actively and constructively involved' in this endeavour, whereas the opposition leader Charles Haughey stressed the need to 'retain the power to pursue national policies to deal with our own problems'.[41]

In the *Netherlands* both chambers of the Parliament adopted resolutions in May 1985. In its resolution,[42] the First Chamber 'heartily welcomes therefore this initiative by the European Parliament to give impetus to the stagnating process of integration' and

> emphasizes that it is imperative to carry through institutional reforms such as:
> - recognition that the Council should take majority decisions.
> - a better balance between the powers of the Council, the Commission and the European Parliament
> - joint legislative power for the European Parliament.

The resolution called for an IGC 'in the near future . . ., taking the draft Treaty as a starting point'. It also states that 'in consideration of Article 82 of the draft Treaty, every effort should be made to ensure that the Member States ratify the Treaty at the same time and only in special circumstances can an exception be made'. The Second Chamber adopted a shorter resolution[43] in which it 'considered and approved' the draft Treaty and noted the final report of the Dooge Committee. It stated that the IGC must include a representative of the Commission and that the EP 'must be closely consulted on all aspects of the conference'. The minimum that the IGC must achieve is the improvement of the decision-making process in the Council, 'the consolidation of the role of the Commission and the improvement of the situation of the European Parliament'.

In the *United Kingdom*, the House of Commons, whose procedures at that time for dealing with European affairs were often criticized as being superficial and inadequate,[44] did not react to the DTEU, and the chairman[45] of the Select Committee on European legislation refused to arrange a meeting with a visiting EP delegation. A report[46] on the Dooge Report was drawn up consisting of the proceedings of the committee meeting of the 15 May 1985 at which evidence was taken from the British member of the Committee, Malcolm Rifkind, who provided a memorandum that was annexed to the report. In this memorandum, originally prepared by the FCO for the Lords Select Committee, the government's main objections to the DTEU were spelled out (though it said it approved of 'some aspects'). These objections were: (1) that Art. 82 was contrary to international law and to Art. 236 EEC; (2) that the EP would be able to adopt legislation 'without the consent of the Council' which would undermine ministerial responsibility to national parliaments, 'make Community decision-making more difficult and cumbersome', and would not 'diminish the frustrations of the members of the European Parliament who would soon be demanding much greater and less hedged-about power over legislation'; (3) that the changed balance between the institutions would 'increase the probability that Member States would find themselves under pressure to accept proposals which they judged to be against their national interest'; (4) that the phasing out of the 'Luxembourg compromise' over ten years 'would be fundamentally damaging to Community cohesion', and (5) that the UK would have to participate fully in a strengthened EMS. In accordance with Commons procedures, the Select Committee did not itself draw up any conclusions in its reports. It simply forwarded the memorandum and the minutes of its discussions to the House. The discussions consisted essentially of questions to Rifkind, none of which challenged the claims made in the memorandum.

The House of Lords decided in February 1985 to set up a special *'ad hoc* sub-committee on European Union' charged specifically with considering the DTEU 'with particular reference to its possible implications for the UK and the Community'. The sub-committee took evidence from ministers, academics, industrialists, former Commissioners and others, and visited the EP in Strasbourg as well as receiving an EP delegation (including Spinelli) in London. Its report[47] was published in July 1985, consisting of a 3 page report, 49 pages of appendixes including the full text of the DTEU, the Dooge Committee's interim and final reports, and some 330 pages of written and oral evidence. Although it concluded that they 'do not believe that the time is ripe for a fully new Treaty of the type proposed by Mr Spinelli', the Lords did recognize that 'the essential steps to improve the functioning of the Community may not be possible without amendment of the Treaty', and 'that the task of amendment should be faced'.

Furthermore, the Select Committee took up a number of the EP's detailed criticisms of the functioning of the existing Community, notably on:

1. The inability of the existing institutional system to deliver a *free internal market*, stating that 'problems that might have been relatively easy to solve when the EEC Treaty was drafted in 1957 have developed wholly new dimensions with which the machinery of the Treaty is not equipped to cope' and that 'the creation and maintenance of a genuinely free common market . . . necessarily involves some incursion into the domain of national sovereignty and is therefore a task for which conventional methods of intergovernmental negotiation and cooperation are inherently inadequate'.

2. The difficulty for the Community to take up *new matters* of common concern to the Member States, considering that 'many of today's problems were not, and could not have been, foreseen by those who drafted the Treaties. The result is that explicit power is lacking in areas important to the internal development of the Community' (para. 86). Articles 235 and 236 are only limited solutions.

3. The *Luxembourg compromise* which 'casts a shadow' over all the proceedings of the Council such that 'it is hard to conceive of a better recipe for inertia', that Member States have 'succeeded in recovering for themselves the possibility (or at least the appearance) of exercising exclusive sovereignty in those areas where they had agreed to allow the Community to exercise collective sovereignty', that the 'Community decision-making process will not be unblocked without more majority voting' and that 'it is clear that abuse of the Luxembourg compromise is the greatest obstacle to the completion of the internal market'.

4. The weakness and lack of autonomy of the *Commission*, stating that it was 'never intended that the Commission should become merely the civil service of the Communities, nor that the terms of every new proposal should be negotiated in detail by the Council' and that the effect of the 'Luxembourg compromise has been to deprive the Commission's power of initiative of much of its practical meaning', that 'the whole scheme of the Treaties has become distorted. It is essential if the Community is to work well that the Commission should be in a position to carry out properly the duties imposed on it by the Treaties and therefore to command respect' and that 'the areas in which the Commission works best and (generally speaking) with least controversy are those in which its freedom of action is greatest' and therefore that 'the Council must be prepared to limit its activities to taking decisions of principle and laying down policy guidelines for the Commission, and to allow the Commission greater scope in detailed implementation, subject

to scrutiny by the Council and the Parliament', and that 'expressions of political will or juggling with institutional arrangements alone will never be sufficient to correct it'.

5. The inefficiency of the *Council* and that the original intention of the Treaties 'was that Council should act as a 'college of delegates' not as a forum for intergovernmental negotiation', that in its work it has become increasingly bureaucratic with national officials able to block progress and decisions on minor points, and that it needs a major reform to change this state of affairs as 'anything in the nature of a gentleman's agreement to be more efficient would be ineffective, given the Byzantine complexity of the present system'.

6. The *Court of Justice* and the fact that 'the right of individuals to bring proceedings challenging actions of Community institutions, or their failure to act, are narrowly circumscribed at present' and that 'the scope for individuals to bring such actions should be widened'.

7. The *European Council* considering that 'the institutional status and functions of the European Council should be clarified and defined'.

The Select Committee made a number of proposals that followed from these criticisms which, in some cases, coincided with the objectives of the DTEU (e.g. on the scope for individual actions before ECJ, more majority voting in the Council, strengthening the Commission, formalizing the European Council). Thus, although negative in its global reaction to the DTEU, the Lords' Report gave backing to many of the key reforms sought by the EP and, in giving the DTEU such comprehensive and serious treatment, gave the whole exercise greater credibility in one of the reticent Member States.

In *Luxembourg* and *Greece*, the national parliaments did not formally consider the DTEU, though they both received the EP delegations.

It is striking that all the national parliamentary reactions – even the Danish one – accepted the need for an increase in the scope of European policies. All but the Danish parliament accepted the possibility of a new Treaty. The EP's 'Article 82' strategy of threatening a move, if necessary, without all the Member States was not rejected out of hand by those who might be called on to do so. Most national parliaments gave explicit support to the two crucial institutional objectives of the DTEU: an increase in *effectiveness* of the Community's institutions, to be achieved largely by more majority voting in the Council (the British and the Danes alone wanting to maintain a right of veto, the French being ambiguous) and an increase in *democracy* through co-decision on legislation for the EP. The value of democratic legitimacy and a stronger parliamentary institution in a European Union was explicitly endorsed by most national parliaments.

THE EP DELEGATIONS TO NATIONAL CAPITALS

In accordance with the resolution adopted with the draft Treaty in February 1984, ('to arrange all appropriate contacts and meetings with the national parliaments'), confirmed in the resolution reacting to the Dublin Summit[48] which extended the mandate to include other politically significant national organizations, the Committee on Institutional Affairs organized visits of small delegations to each national capital.

The Committee had been reconstituted after the election and was now chaired by Spinelli, with Croux (EPP/B), Seeler (Soc/D) and Gawronski (Lib/I) as vice-chairmen. A suggestion that it take responsibility both for European Union matters and for interinstitutional relations within the existing treaties, which had until then been in the hands of a sub-committee of the Political Affairs Committee, was resisted by the Political Affairs Committee and by Spinelli himself, who did not want the Institutional Committee to be distracted by numerous 'small steps' reports, preferring to concentrate on lobbying for the draft Treaty and the issue of European Union generally, closely following the work of the Dooge Committee and stimulating the issue in national capitals.

The Committee first sent to each national capital in the autumn of 1984 a 'scout', i.e. a member of the committee from the governing party in each country.[49] The 'scouts' formally prepared the visit of the delegation, but also did some explanatory work and tested the initial reactions. In early 1985, these 'scouts' led delegations consisting of four members with a spread of parties and countries. When possible, Spinelli joined the delegations too. On occasion, other members accompanied the delegations (at their own expense). The interlocuteurs of the delegation were arranged by the 'scouts' in accordance with their assessment of what would be appropriate according to the customs (e.g. in the UK it would not be appropriate or useful to meet the Speaker), and political situation in each country, as well as what was possible practically.

These visits provided a stimulus to discussion on European Union in the Member States, and were an opportunity for authors of the DTEU to explain and defend it directly. In West Germany, France, Ireland,

Luxembourg, the Netherlands and the UK the discussion with the relevant parliamentary committee took place while they were drafting reports on the matter. In two countries (the UK and the Netherlands) the delegations also furnished written answers to questions submitted by the national parliamentary committees. The impact of the discussions went well beyond national parliaments, however, and often obtained substantial media coverage. For the second time in less than a year, a far wider cross-section of the political elites in the Member States than normally deal with European affairs was brought into a detailed discussion on the future shape of Europe. Some aspects of these visits are worth considering in detail.[50]

In *Copenhagen* the European debate had traditionally been between those seeking withdrawal from the EEC and those wishing to remain inside. The dynamic of such a debate led to pro-marketeers minimizing the importance of any aspect of the EC that 'threatened' national sovereignty. With TV debates carefully balancing pro-marketeers and anti-marketeers, the cleavage in Danish politics was over the issue of withdrawal. The issue of European Union changed this.[51] A few prominent Danish politicians, mainly from the government parties and led by former Foreign Minister and former EP Vice-President Guldberg, set up an 'Action Committee on European Union' in January 1985.[52] Criticizing the way the European debate had been conducted in Denmark until then, they pointed to the dangers of Denmark being left behind by the others if it attempted to block progress. The committee maintained contact with Spinelli. Although the four Ministers who joined were forced to resign from it when the Radical Party threatened a motion of censure against the government, its existence broadened the debate and gave 'moderate' pro-marketeers greater freedom to put forward constructive proposals without appearing to be out on a limb, especially as the anti-European forces had been contained in the 1984 European elections It also stimulated an awareness among pro-Europeans, especially the government, of the possibility of Denmark appearing yet again to be the main footdraggers. The visit of the EP delegation forced these latent tendencies into the open. The Folketing's 'market committee' met the delegation, although its traditional policy had been to avoid direct contacts with the EP. Whilst the Danish interlocutors of the delegation generally stuck to the Folketing resolution's opposition to institutional change, they were also insistent that Denmark was not anti-Europe and were at pains to point out that Denmark had only rarely invoked a formal veto and that it supported an extension of Community policies and finance.

As we saw above, the Folketing adopted a new resolution during the visit that was indicative of a shift in emphasis. Support was announced for the creation of a secretariat for EPC, offering Copenhagen as a seat. This was illustrative of a desire to present constructive proposals, albeit ones that coincided with their intergovernmental view of the EC. The delegation was told that an increase in the powers of the EP was not to be ruled out in the long term, and that there should immediately be more majority voting in the Council when no vital interests are at stake, though each state should be able to define its own vital interests; to overrule it by a vote would simply lead to the non-application of the measure by the state concerned and the gradual breakdown of the Community's legal system. The EP delegation rejected this argument claiming that the recent German cereal price veto showed that Ministers in difficulty are quite capable of defining anything as a 'vital interest'. The delegation continually reminded their interlocuteurs of the possibility of other countries moving ahead without Denmark, but welcomed the signs of a shift in position, which they felt to be an indication of what could be achieved under pressure.

In *Brussels*, the discussions during the delegation visit revealed general support among all parties, coupled with an awareness that Belgium was not in a pivotal position concerning the final outcome of the European Union discussions. It would certainly be among the countries pushing hardest for reforms along the lines of the DTEU, but the outcome would depend on how far certain other countries were willing to go. Some hesitation was expressed with regard to Article 82, but opinion was gradually shifting in favour of such a means of putting pressure on reticent countries, in particular Britain. The Flemish and Walloon autonomist parties expressed dismay that the DTEU did not provide for representation of the regions on the Council. Some MPs expressed the view that the DTEU was far too prudent.

In *Bonn*, the visit of the EP delegation took place two weeks after a working party of spokesmen and ministers responsible for finance and taxation of the three coalition parties (CDU, CSU and FDP) and the Vice-President of the Bundesbank had considered the DTEU. The working party's conclusions,[53] whilst emphasizing that European Union 'remains our political goal', expressed some reservations concerning the financial aspects of the DTEU, which, it was felt, did not take account of the impact of the envisaged Union competences in this field on the FRG with its federal structure. It was felt that 'the provisions of the DTEU concerning financial equalization (Art. 73), loan financing of the Union budget (Art. 75(2)), use of the ECU as a means of payment

(Art. 52(3)) and the concurrent competence of the Union as regards monetary and credit policies (Art. 51), for example, would seem to be appropriate only within a federal European state'. They noted that the DTEU concentrated on economic policy and 'does not, therefore, aim to create a federal European state with extensive responsibilities in areas of foreign affairs, security and law'. It was felt that the discrepancy was not acceptable. The same conclusions also stated that 'the monetary powers of the Member States and their central banks must remain undiminished until an autonomous European central bank system with independent control of the money supply has been established within the framework of a federal European state'.

When the delegation visited Bonn, these views were also echoed by opposition spokesmen and by representatives of the Länder in the Bundesrat. The EP delegation argued that it was contradictory to call for a European federal state while at the same time rejecting a first step in this direction. All the interlocuteurs, however, accepted the need for a new Treaty and were willing to take the DTEU as a basis for discussion. Criticisms were generally accompanied by constructive counter-proposals. For instance, on taxation it was proposed in several different meetings (Finance Minister, SDP leader, Bundesrat), as an alternative to the DTEU proposals, that different sorts of tax should be allocated to the Union and Member States (and *Länder*) respectively: the possibility of the Union being allocated the right to tax mineral oil was suggested a number of times. On the legislative procedure of the Union Parliament's main aim of co-decision with conciliation was approved. The system proposed in the DTEU was similar to the German system[54] providing for conciliation between the Parliament/Bundestag and the Member States in the Council/Bundesrat. However, the DTEU provision on a negative outcome of the conciliation procedure and the high threshold for the adoption of successfully conciliated laws were criticized. Strong support was also expressed for majority voting in the Council, (although the farm price negotiations which were to lead to a German veto were by then underway). The CDU chairman (Dregger) felt the DTEU was inadequate on security matters and the SPD Chairman (Vogel) supported a secretariat for EPC. Concerns were expressed by *Länder* Ministers from the Bundesrat on areas of Union competence that might overlap with *Land* competences (education, research, information, culture), without their participation in Union decision-taking.

On Article 82, opinions were divided; the Chancellor's office said that initially an attempt should be made to achieve progress together and it was not yet time to consider alternatives. The CDU Deputy

Foreign Minister Mertes said that progress need not be at the rate of the slowest participant but drew attention to the fact that a German government must also take account of the quadripartite responsibilities for Berlin before taking any decision affecting relationships with any of those powers. The FDP leader Bangemann (in government) and the SDP/ Bundestag opposition leader Vogel both stated that, if necessary, progress would have to be achieved without all Community states. In the case of Vogel, this represented a shift in position as he had previously stated opposition to this. The SPD Vice-President of the Bundestag, Frau Renger, however said that Art. 82 was problematic and that all the Ten must progress together. In all, it was clear that a number of issues still had to be thrashed out in Germany, and divisions existed even within the governing coalition. Notwithstanding considerable sympathy for the draft Treaty, some issues and tactics appeared difficult to swallow, and the government was not yet prepared to break with the UK.

In *Athens*, the visit of the delegation was overshadowed by a negative reaction, particularly in the media, to the absence of Spinelli. Although Spinelli had undertaken to accompany some delegations when there was a particular interest or request for his presence and when his timetable permitted, he in fact only went to four capitals (Brussels, Paris, Dublin and London). Some absences were due to ill-health (he underwent two operations in the spring and summer of 1985), but he was also anxious to minimize the identification of the DTEU with himself personally rather than with the EP as a whole. In Greece, the press erroneously supposed that he wanted to visit either large or favourable Member States only and that his absence was a snub. (In fact, as we have seen, Spinelli had personally visited Athens for talks with Papandreou and others in 1983.) In spite of this problem, and in spite of the unwillingness of one of the 'scouts', Mavros, to participate in most of the meetings, the delegation felt that the visit was useful. In governing (PASOK) circles, reactions were reticent or hostile to the DTEU, but not opposed to any institutional reform. The Minister attached to the Prime minister, Tzochatzopoulos, told the delegation that Greece's reservations on the veto could be explained in psychological terms by its limited experience as a Member State and its particular problems: once the issue of the IMPs was solved, the government's position might become more flexible. Dooge Committee member Papantoniou said that Greece favoured the non-abusive use of the veto and greater EP powers in respect of the budget, own resources and political control. The President of the Greek parliament said that its position would not be as negative as that of the Danish Folketing.

Among the opposition parties there was a range of opinions. New Democracy, hoping to become the government again in the forthcoming national elections, expressed support for the DTEU through its leader Mitsotakis. The 'external' (pro-Moscow) Communists opposed any strengthening of the EC, except the consolidation of the EMS in so far as this might lessen the hegemony of the dollar. The 'interior' (Euro)-Communist Party favoured institutional reform. Opposition pressures were thus divergent and if the government failed to win the forthcoming elections it would either be dependent on support from the 'exterior' Communists or else lose outright to New Democracy. If it won, all the cards would remain in its hands, which meant, in fact, those of Papandreou.

In *Paris*, the EP delegation discussions with the Assembly and Senate (Legal Affairs and Foreign Affairs Committees) reviewed the reports drawn up by their respective delegations. The lack of a procedure for early dissolution of the EP should it dismiss the Commission worried some French parliamentarians, who felt that the DTEU was a 'parliamentary' constitution (as in the IVth Republic). The discussions allayed some of these fears. The National Assembly delegation later drew up a new report, which went a long way to supporting the EP's position, as we saw above. The delegation discussions with government ministers confirmed previous positions, that the MEPs encouraged, namely that a conference should be convened, even if not all the Ten would be party to it, and draw up a new Treaty based on the DTEU and the Solemn Declaration.

In *Dublin*, the EP delegation met the party leaders (Fitzgerald, Haughey, Spring, McGiolla), and the joint parliamentary committee on European affairs (then drawing up its report on the DTEU and which itself visited Strasbourg for further talks with the EP a week later) and held a public meeting under the auspices of the European Movement. The attitudes encountered were largely those described above in the parliamentary committee's report, with the Labour Party placing particular emphasis on neutrality and economic redistribution, and Fianna Fáil being reticent on voting in the Council. The most striking feature of the visit, however, was the media discussion that it engendered, starting with a leading article in the *Irish Times* on the day the delegation arrived. In the following months, a debate on the aim of European Union and its implications for Ireland raged in the Irish press, further stimulated by the report of the joint committee (20 March), the Brussels Summit (29/30 March), a Conference of the Royal Irish Academy sponsored by the EP (12 April), the EP debate (17 April), a high-level

Conference[55] of the Association of European Journalists in Blarney (26 April) and a symposium of the Irish Economic and Social Research Institute (30 May). For a period of five months the issue of European Union, previously conspicuous by its absence, was never out of the papers.[56]

In *Rome*, the EP delegation had little explaining or convincing to do in its meetings, with parliamentarians and government ministers already committed to support the reform initiative. The visit served to re-emphasize various parties' commitments and to gain publicity. In addition, a meeting with all the main employers' and workers' representatives was organized in which they stated their full support for the initiative. Unique among the visits, a meeting was held with the President and members of the Constitutional Court. They confirmed that Italy could be party to the DTEU even if not all EEC Member States were.

As in Greece, the delegation's visit to *Luxembourg* was criticized locally for the absence of Spinelli, who was ill. The meetings, with government ministers and parliament committees, allowed the Luxembourg side to express general support for the DTEU and institutional reform, including majority voting and co-decision, but reservations on issues of economic concern to Luxembourg, i.e. the issue of the seat of the institutions and monetary and taxation policy.

The delegations to *The Hague* first answered written questions submitted by the political groups in each Chamber of the Dutch Parliament. (The written answers were approved by the EP committee on Institutional Affairs.) The tone of the questions was somewhat sceptical, notably those from Christian Democrats, but when the delegation visited The Hague the scepticism appeared to be dissipated. In all the meetings (parliamentarians, two sides of industry, government, press) strong support for the DTEU was expressed, in particular for its key points on voting in the Council, powers of the EP, strengthening the Commission and enlarging EC competences. The point on which strong hesitation was expressed was Article 82 DTEU. The Dutch had traditionally adopted an anglophile position and there was considerable reticence, notably in the Foreign Ministry (whose Secretary of State Van Eekelen was a member of the Dooge Committee), which did not want to lose the UK. They were aware of the tactical value of the Article, and were reminded by the delegation that the Netherlands had twice before joined in the establishment of Communities without the British, Communities that would never have been established at the time if their agreement had been sought but which they had joined later. This was a point that all the EP delegations to the 'old six' had been making, of course, but it became the major point of discussion in the Netherlands, and the fact that this message was repeated by a British Conservative on the delegation increased the impact.

The visit to *London* was the longest of the delegation visits. It met not only with the directly relevant ministers (Howe and Rifkind), and parliamentary committee, party leaders or European affairs spokesmen, as in other capitals, but also with some dozen junior ministers and PPSs, the two sides of industry (TUC and CBI), the 'think tank' of the governing party[57] and party officials, the European Movement, feature writers from the media, and others. It was thus an attempt to present the case for reform to a very broad cross-section of the British political élite. The delegation was able to note that almost all the groups it met had examined the DTEU and drawn up their own positions. The position expressed by almost all governmental and pro-governmental interlocuteurs, however, was one of professed scepticism concerning the real desire of other countries to push through any substantial reform, dismissing their statements as posturing and rhetoric. Nevertheless, a desire (in the aftermath of the long budget refund dispute) to show that the British were also 'good Europeans', combined with a concern among business circles that the Community's progress towards a genuine common market was insufficient, led to the advocacy of 'pragmatic' proposals for improvements in decision-taking in the Council by means of an agreement to vote more frequently and to make more use of abstentions where the treaties require unanimity. The delegation dismissed *this* as rhetoric, pointing to previous declarations of intent along similar lines which had no real impact and no legal value. The message the delegation continually hammered home was that the Community as it stood was incapable of achieving even the objectives of the existing treaties (pointing in particular to British interests blocked by other Member States), that there was a significant momentum developing for a new departure and that Britain was in danger of 'missing the bus' for the third time.

There were few public signs, however, that these arguments had any impact on government or pro-government circles, which generally continued to oppose Treaty amendment and an IGC. As to the opposition, the Labour Party, in a period of reviewing its previous support for UK withdrawal, preferred to ignore the complicating factor of European Union, though the TUC took it seriously, distributing and discussing the ETUC statement on European Union[58] with the delegation. The Alliance leaders (David Steel and David Owen) were more forthcoming, and tabled a motion in the Commons[59] welcoming the visit of the

EP delegation and calling on the government to support the convening of an IGC to draft a European Union Treaty. They assured the delegation of support for co-decision for the EP but favoured the retention of the ultimate right for a Member State to exercise a veto. Steel, citing recent discussion in ELD meetings, agreed that other states were determined to move ahead, with or without the UK, one of the few to treat this possibility seriously.

The delegation visits constituted the most systematic lobbying of national élites yet undertaken by the elected EP. As politically plural delegations, they emphasized the spread of support in the EP for the reform initiative and confronted most politicians they met in each country with an MEP of their own political persuasion, whose arguments could not lightly be dismissed as a manoeuvre from a rival party. It is, of course, impossible to evaluate precisely what impact they may have had on opinions or on decisions in each country. Nevertheless, it is indisputable that they provoked discussion and study of the case for a new Treaty and that they managed to meet most of those responsible for defining their country's position at a time when all the Member States, aware of the conclusions of the Dooge interim report, were preparing their position on the issue for the Milan summit. In at least some countries, the tactic of going behind the government's back to speak directly to national parliaments, parties and interest groups may have increased the pressure on the government to take a favourable attitude. In some countries, it enabled a reservoir of support for the European idea – very general but normally lacking any concrete proposal on which to focus or an opportunity to discuss the future of Europe in global terms – to be tapped.

INTEREST GROUPS AND NGOs

The many transnational non-governmental organizations on the European scene could scarcely ignore such an issue. In December 1984 the European Trade Union Confederation (ETUC) adopted a statement[60] on European Union in which it stated that:

> the present Treaty already provides, in important areas, that competences of Member States should be transferred to the Communities. Democratic control of opinion is denied to national parlia-

ments in these fields. It is thus essential that the European institutions be democratized so that they do not become bodies where Ministers, officials and diplomats have more decision-making power than the democratically elected members of the European Parliament. Far-reaching reforms are needed to ensure that there is competence at European level to solve problems which will require a solution at that level and which cannot be solved other than at that level. The ETUC considers that the Draft Treaty establishing the European Union, which the European Parliament has adopted, aims in that direction. Although that draft does not provide an adequate answer to all problems it nevertheless indicates the course to be followed.

This statement was approved with only the Danish LO expressing reservations. The British TUC thus approved the document, thereby signalling a significant change in their attitude to European integration. The statement was used as a basis for ETUC lobbying activities (e.g. in the preparations of the Economic and Social Committee submission to the Dooge Committee), and stimulated national Union federations to adopt statements and lobby for the DTEU.

Other transnational organizations were also active. The Council of European Municipalities organized an appeal signed by the mayors of over 150 big cities stating that 'the time has come to finally seal the Union of our States' and calling on 'our governments to convene a conference to draft the Treaty on European Union in agreement with the European Parliament's draft and decide on the procedure for its ratification'.[61] Later, the Conference of Local and Regional Authorities of Europe supported the EP 'without any reservations'.[62] The organization of former resistance fighters (the International Union of Resistance and Deportee Movements) called for 'the rapid adoption and ratification of the Draft Treaty . . . with a view to creating the European Federation or United States of Europe for which we all fought'.

In some countries, newspapers carried appeals by intellectuals in favour of the DTEU. In France, *Le Monde* carried such an appeal the day before Parliament's final debate on the draft Treaty. Similarly, several Italian newspapers carried an appeal on 8 February 1984. A similar appeal was signed by 146 Greek intellectuals. An appeal by French scientists and Nobel Prize winners was presented in September 1984.

Not without significance was the role played by the European Movement. This body was a shadow of its former self and had for many years lacked a coherent strategy acceptable to its diverse components, which included a variety of organizations with their own ideas about the future of Europe. The DTEU provided it with a concrete proposal around which almost all of its components could unite, reflecting the broad unity achieved within the EP itself. Its action became more incisive and it would be fair to say that through its auspices 'European circles' in political parties, unions, pressure groups and academia in most Member States were aware of the DTEU even before its adoption by Parliament. The Movement also organized a large congress in Brussels in March 1984 – a couple of days after the breakdown of the Brussels summit – the main theme of which was support for the DTEU. The congress received considerable publicity[63] as well as the participation of a large number of prominent figures.[64] The Union of European Federalists played a major part in the European Movement activities and was active on its own count, especially in Italy and Germany.

THE RUN-UP TO MILAN

The Brussels summit decided to prepare Milan through 'bilateral contacts'. In fact, such contacts were already well under way since the submission of the Dooge interim report. The whole issue of institutional reform and a possible new Treaty became the subject of talks in the regular bilateral summits (such as the Franco-German Summits); of declarations, statements, speeches and interviews; of planned and unplanned 'leaks'; and of lobbying through various channels – all well beyond what is normal before a European Council meeting. The national governments were the main actors in this process, though the EP, political parties and their transnational federations, interest groups, the Commission, national parliaments and individual personalities all played a part. The resolutions of national parliaments and the systematic visits of EP delegations to national capitals described in the preceding sections were part of this.

Among the national governments, the main dividing lines were those that had become apparent within the Dooge Committee. The Dooge process had identified a package of reforms that was broadly acceptable to the majority of Member States corresponding, in general terms, to the EP's main objectives in the DTEU. In view of the opposition of the minority, what would the attitude of the majority be? Would they push ahead by themselves, as the EP urged, hoping the others, if placed in front of a fait accompli, would follow? Would they do so globally (as envisaged in Art. 82 of the DTEU) or in an additional Treaty (e.g. on political cooperation) that could be signed separately without legally affecting the existing Communities? Would they simply accept the lowest common denominator acceptable to all Ten? If so, what could they do to entice or pressure the minority to raise the level of this denominator? If it included bluffing that they would go it alone, how would they make it appear realistic? Finally, if there were differences of opinion among the 'majority' on tactics, would they be able to reconcile them? How far would they be influenced by other actors?

Within days of the adoption of the Dooge interim report, Belgian Foreign Minister Tindemans set the tone, stating that 'we now know that if we want to go further, there will no longer be ten of us',[65] a position he re-emphasized following the Dublin summit in a meeting under his chairmanship of the EPP policy bureau attended by the Christian Democratic heads of government (Kohl, Lubbers, Martens, Fitzgerald, Santer) and others (Andreotti, Klepsch) in Dublin on 4 December 1984. Immediately after that summit Mitterrand indicated the importance he attached to these matters, declaring in his press conference that 'the institutional debate may now take precedence over the others'.[66] A week later, speaking to the 'Berliner Pressekonferenz', Sir Geoffrey Howe laid down his marker for the British position, speaking of support for 'real and practical steps' that would enhance 'unity' notably of the internal market and in external policy.[67] The theme of 'unity not Union' had previously been developed by Mrs Thatcher in a speech in Avignon in which she claimed not to know what 'European Union' meant, preferring practical unity in policies, and was faithfully echoed in a *Times* leader on 23 October entitled 'Unity not Union'.[68] As if in reply, Chancellor Kohl, in his New Year's Message to the German people, promised that the FRG was 'resolutely determined, with its friend France, to give decisive impetus to the European Union concept in 1985'.[69] This declared determination was echoed by the incoming President of the Council, Andreotti, in his statement to the EP on the programme of the Italian presidency in which he stated:[70] 'In approving the draft Treaty establishing the European Union, the Strasbourg Assembly has clearly indicated the objective to be pursued in order to emerge from the present crisis. . . . For our part, no effort will be spared in seeking agreement by June on a date for convening an intergovernmental conference with the task of negotiating the Treaty on European Union.'

Already, though, differences of emphasis on the tactics to be followed were beginning to appear among the 'majority' countries. Although some were clearly hinting their determination to make progress even without all (though not always being specific as to whether this would be through a global or an additional Treaty), the Netherlands, at least, was reticent on the prospect of leaving the UK behind, and the German statements rarely went beyond general support for European Union. The growing contradiction between Kohl's statements and the actions of his government were striking. As a still weak leader of a coalition in which some Ministers had departmental (e.g. Stoltenberg at Finance, Kiechle at Agriculture) or political (CSU) reservations on increasing the scope or level of integration, whilst others were strong supporters of the reform proposals (FDP, other CDU), he was, as on other issues at that time, unable to impose his authority. Statements such as:[71] 'being the driving force behind European unification is one of the Federal Republic's reasons for existence' and that he and Mitterrand were personally determined 'to make an initial decisive step this year' and that 'the principle according to which one sticks with the pace of the slowest member of the company is not a good one' did not tally well with some of the positions taken by his Ministers in the Council on own resources, on car emissions (with threats to go it alone) or on farm prices (with the first German use of the Luxembourg compromise, over a minor difference in position). Nor could Kohl be pinned down with a more specific statement on reform: his declarations remained general and his actions symbolic (as in the hand-holding with Mitterrand at Verdun). Even in a speech on European Union to the Bundesrat, he remained very general on institutional matters.[72] By February 1985, doubts were being expressed[73] about his ambiguous position, pointing out that Kohl 'must be perfectly aware that his support was essential and decisive for the success' of Mitterrand's initiative, and wondering whether he was only interested in 'a compromise on a compromise [of Luxembourg]' and 'institutionalising cooperation regarding foreign policy and defence, which would be limited to a few countries to give the illusion of having established the pure and hard kernel of Europe, excluding problem countries like Denmark, Greece and Ireland'. Opposition leader Vogel was quick to pick up such criticisms, stressing in a visit to Brussels on 20 February that the SDP was very much in favour of the draft Treaty.

Certainly from the French viewpoint, the continuing ambiguity of the West German position was cause for anxiety. A firm jointly subscribed position would certainly gain the support of the Benelux countries and Italy. In the autumn of 1984 there had been indications on the French side[74] that they hoped to prepare a joint initiative for the Franco-German summit of 29/30 October, which came to nothing. Prime Minister Fabius confirmed to Spinelli on 27 February that France was prepared to take action, but their main worry was to have Chancellor

Kohl's full support.[75] Before the summit of 1 March 1985, on the same day as the Fabius–Spinelli meeting, Mitterrand announced, while decorating Commissioner Cheysson with the 'Légion d'Honneur', that 'in the months ahead, France will take an initiative which will take people by surprise . . . and which will contribute to the transformation of the European institutions'.[76] The Mitterrand 'surprise' was the subject of much speculation over the following months. If, as Fabius seemed to suggest, his intention was to enlist Kohl's support, then the summit two days later did not, at least publicly, come up with anything specific. Mitterrand and Kohl confirmed their intention of taking 'initiatives' in the next few months to speed up the political construction of Europe – another general statement of intent. Kohl added[77] merely that the Milan summit would be of particular importance while Mitterrand said that 'for the second time since the Second World War, Europe must forge its destiny in the years 1985–1990'. The contrast in levels of ambition was striking.

A week after the meeting, *Le Monde* carried an article which some suspected had been 'planted' by the French government. (This was certainly the opinion of the West German government, as the Minister of Finance said to the visiting EP delegation on 26 March.) The article[78] claimed that the Federal Republic was turning its back to Europe and that it had calculated that its best interests lay in maintaining the common market but in resisting policies that would burden it financially or hamper its margin of manoeuvre in economic, monetary or political fields. It was clearly designed to set a cat among the pigeons of the Bonn Marktplatz. At their following meeting at the end of the month (26 March in Paris), the two leaders were reported to have discussed the 'possibility of taking a common initiative with a view to relaunching the Community, should the results of the Milan summit prove unsatisfactory, which would also involve Italy. This initiative (there is talk of a Franco-German 'Treaty') would in the long term be open to all Community partners prepared to accept it.'[79] If Kohl had allowed himself to be committed – as a result of the pressure or otherwise – to a joint initiative, it remained shrouded in mystery as to its nature and was envisaged only if the Milan summit should fail.

Mitterrand, whether disappointed or not, continued to emphasize his personal commitment. On Sunday, 28 April, in the course of a long television interview, he said: 'I am frankly European. . . . Europe enlarged to twelve must provide itself with strong institutions, genuine structures. It must progress towards its political unity or it will be irremediably outstripped by countries such as the USA, Japan and a few others looming on the horizon.'[80] On 9 May, in a special briefing to a restricted group of French and foreign journalists, he reportedly[81] spoke of his 'determination to press forward with European political integration. One option was to press forward in this direction with some, but not necessarily all, of the Community's present membership'. Officials spoke of the Milan summit being 'followed by a smaller heads of government meeting of those states which wanted to move faster towards strengthening the Community institutions'. Although much of the press reported this as a retreat by Mitterrand, as he was dismissive of the possibility of calling an IGC of all Member States,[82] it can rather be seen as a determination to press ahead without all. He had adapted to Kohl's timetable (first to seek results in Milan) but, again in accordance with the EP strategy, indicated a preference for a global approach ('strengthening Community institutions') rather than an additional Treaty on areas that could be dealt with separately (political cooperation or monetary union). His next meeting with Kohl, however (Koblenz, 29 May) was under a cloud of Franco-German disagreements over the recent world economic summit (France felt that the FRG and the UK had rushed to embrace the American position, abandoning previously agreed European standpoints on trade and monetary negotiations), over the American Strategic Defence Initiative and over several Community issues. No mention was made of EC institutional reform.

Meanwhile, the Parliament held a major institutional debate in April 1985 following the publication of the final Dooge report. It was based on two reports from the committee on Institutional Affairs. One was 'on the deliberations of the European Council on the European Union'[83] and covered the work of the Dooge committee. The other was an interim report 'on the progress of deliberations in the national parliaments on the Draft Treaty'.[84] The rapporteurs were respectively Croux (EPP) and Seeler (Soc), first and second vice-chairmen of the committee.

In the resolution adopted as a result of the Croux Report, the Parliament again reiterated its belief in the necessity of a new Treaty which it professed to be all the more urgent with the enlargement of the Community to 12 Member States, and noted that the Dooge Committee, successive presidents of the Council, several heads of government and the parliaments of several Member States also recognized this need. It noted 'that the objectives, powers and institutions of the Union, as proposed by the *ad hoc* committee, are consistent with those described in precise legal terms in Parliament's draft', but found the *ad hoc* committee's final report 'deficient in certain key areas'. It called for the convening of an IGC to negotiate on the basis of the *acquis communautaire*, the Dooge Report and the draft Treaty and proposed that 'acting in accordance with appropriate concertation procedures, Parliament and the Conference should adopt the final text of the draft Treaty to be submitted to the governments for their signature and to the different countries for ratification'.

The resolution was thus largely similar to the one adopted in December. Parliament thus took on board the Dooge Report which it tried to synthesize with its own original strategy. It held firm to the idea that the Treaty might be ratified without all the Member States. The explanatory statement of the committee's report described the Dooge Report and the draft Treaty as 'strikingly similar in a number of respects'. It referred to the fact that the Dooge Report was not unanimously approved, and stated that 'the fact that the majority persisted and retained the proposals of the interim report holds out the hope that the possibilities opened up by Article 82 of the draft Treaty have not passed unnoted'.

The resolution adopted as a result of the Seeler Report was relatively brief, re-emphasizing the EP's willingness to continue its contacts and meetings with national parliaments, calling on them to continue their work on the draft Treaty in cooperation with the EP 'in order to achieve the widest possible parliamentary consensus throughout the Community on the Treaty establishing the European Union'.

The two resolutions were carried by majorities of similar proportions to those which, in the old parliament, had approved the draft Treaty (Croux Report 204 to 52, with 30 abstentions, Seeler Report 201 to 41, with 22 abstentions).[85] The figures mask some significant changes. On the one hand, the number of members from political parties opposed to European Union had increased at the European elections, but on the other hand, there was a shift of certain members and parties in favour of European Union as compared to their previous position. The former phenomenon was accounted for largely by the doubling of the number of British Labour members (accounting for more than half of those who opposed the Croux Report) and the entry into Parliament for the first time of members of the Green Parties and of the French Front National. It was countered by the new explicit support of the French Socialists and by the increase in the proportion of the British Conservatives supporting the Croux Report, despite its reiteration of the need to create a European Union, if necessary, without all the Member States of the Community.

The debate,[86] attended by Dooge and several members of his committee, showed that the majority in the Parliament felt that a certain momentum had been obtained since Parliament adopted its Draft Treaty. It was now difficult for Member States to avoid addressing this issue seriously. The Dooge Report was generally welcomed as a political report that was consistent with the legal terms of the more detailed draft Treaty. This view was confirmed by Craxi, speaking immediately after the debate in his statement on the Brussels meeting of the European Council, in which he stated that the 'Dooge committee report is essentially a political synthesis of the draft Treaty'. Referring to the 'balance, wisdom and . . . farsightedness' of the draft Treaty, he felt that 'its special merit was to install impetus and vigour to an examination which until then had been marked by uncertainty, reticence and certain misgivings'.[87]

Craxi was not very forthcoming during this debate on the plans of the Italian presidency over the next two months leading up to the Milan summit. The first three months of the Italian presidency had been absorbed with successfully finding outcomes to a series of difficult issues facing the Community at that time: the enlargement negotiations with Spain and Portugal, the integrated Mediterranean programmes, the 1985 budget, steel and the 'clean car' regulations. During this period, the Dooge Committee was still at work finalizing its definitive report. Nevertheless, the aim of the Italian Presidency to convene an IGC, proclaimed to the EP in January by Andreotti, was not obscured by these issues. Meeting with the Bureau of the EP Socialist Group on 21 February in Rome, Craxi had stated that Italy intended to 'work as hard as it can so that at the European Council in Milan, an agreement on calling an IGC with a mandate to negotiate a draft Treaty on European Union can be reached'.[88] Craxi repeated this message at the CSP congress in Madrid on 11 April 1985 in which he stressed the need to limit unanimity to an absolutely essential minimum, guarantee the authority and the independence of the Commission and give the EP effective rights to participate in legislation through shared decision-making with the Council.[89] Craxi held an intensive series of bilateral contacts in preparation for Milan, first charging Ferri (the former chairman of the EP's institutional committee) with a discreet exploratory mission to each of the national capitals,[90] and then holding his own series of meetings with other heads of government, and (first) with Presidents Pflimlin and Delors.

The Belgian government was not altogether happy with this procedure. At the end of the Brussels European Council, Tindemans was reported as regretting that the Dooge Committee's task had been terminated and that the responsibility was now entirely in the hands of the Italian presidency which 'now has a great responsibility *vis-à-vis* history'.[91] He added that the approach to the Milan summit would be 'three nerve-racking months'. It seems[92] that Belgium feared that the diplomacy of bilateral contact 'might lead to a more or less ramshackle compromise between the four big countries'. He replied to a parliamentary question in the Belgian parliament[93] that 'in Milan Belgium will support the idea of an Intergovernmental Conference even if the Italian Presidency does not bring it up'. Whatever the reason, the Belgian government sent its Minister for European Affairs, De Keersmaeker, on a consultative mission around smaller Member States.[94] This almost rival set of consultations led to some confusion over the Belgian position, with Tindemans having to deny that Belgium was trying to canvass support for a rival package.

In an attempt to focus the discussions on a concrete proposal, Italy put forward on 21 May a draft mandate for an IGC – over a month before the Milan European Council. This three-page document,[95] formulated as draft conclusions for the European Council, referred to the Dooge Report, the Stuttgart declaration and the DTEU and specified a number of policy objectives (economic, common values of civilization and common external policy) taken from the Dooge Report. In order to achieve them, it specified that it would be necessary to extend majority voting in the Council, strengthen the Commission, provide the EP with effective joint decision-making powers in specifically defined legislative areas, redefine the EP's budgetary powers, grant it the right to vote on the investiture of the Commission, formalize EPC, strengthen existing policies and extend them to new areas. Procedurally, it established an IGC 'to negotiate a Treaty on the full implementation, in the course of time, of the European Union', including both Community areas and 'all forms of intergovernmental cooperation of importance for the construction of the Union'. The EP would be 'associated with the work in an appropriate manner and the conclusions of the Conference will be placed before it'. The IGC should finish before the European Council of 3/4 December.

This draft mandate thus took up the Dooge Committee conclusions, and this despite the fact that Ferri's tours of the national capitals and Craxi's own meeting with Thatcher on the occasion of the G7 Summit in Bonn on the 4 May[96] had confirmed that the UK remained opposed to the calling of an IGC. Belgian fears that the Italian Presidency might compromise too soon with the minority thus proved to be unfounded.

The text was communicated to the Foreign Ministers, and the Presidents of the Commission and the Parliament on the 21 May. President Pflimlin replied immediately on the 22 May[97] recalling Parliament's positions and approving 'without reservation' the proposal of the Italian presidency. Craxi himself wrote a week later to his fellow heads of government, reportedly after a telephone conversation with Mitterrand,[98] emphasizing that the Milan summit should be devoted to these issues and that he and Andreotti would carry out political consultations in order to prepare the European Council meeting. Andreotti, meanwhile, cross-examined by the EP's committee on political affairs, stated that 'Italy was not ready to bargain and has no intention of moving away from its proposal'.[99] It would appear that the consultations were not aimed at finding the lowest common denominator.

Preparations for Milan were due to be discussed by the Foreign Ministers in Stresa on the 8 and 9 June. In the event, a set of counter proposals by the UK stole the limelight. These aimed to avoid an IGC and consisted of three documents. The first was a set of draft conclusions for the Milan European Council on decision-taking in the Community 'which could be implemented without delay' and which 'would make a radical improvement to the Community's ability to take decisions of practical benefit to its citizens'.[100] The essence of these proposals were that the European Council would adopt a set of priorities for action each year, that more use would be made of the treaty provisions for majority voting and for abstention where unanimity is required, that Member States would endeavour not to invoke unanimity in relation to measures necessary for the implementation of specific objectives already agreed by the European Council, that issues should not needlessly be referred upwards from Coreper to the Council or from Council to the European Council, and that the Commission should weed out each year proposals which are hopelessly blocked. It thus amounted to a gentleman's agreement among the Member States to apply the existing provisions of the treaties in a manner conducive to rapid decision-taking. No legally binding or enforceable change would be made to the existing procedures. The second British proposal consisted of a 'draft agreement on political co-operation', consisting of nine articles and three annexes. Essentially, it formalized political co-operation, extended it to the field of security and arms production, and envisaged closer cooperation within international organizations and among representations of Member States in third countries. A small secretariat based in the main place of work of the Community would be established to help with technical matters and to advise the presidency.

The third text was entitled 'completion of the Common Market' and consisted of main targets for action by 1990 (thus outbidding the Commission proposal for a target date of 1992).

The Commission also announced that it would be putting forward proposals at Milan, on the internal market and on the technological Community, and it intended to incorporate proposals on the decision-making procedure for these policies.

Reports of the discussion at Stresa[101] indicate that Andreotti at least felt that the Italian proposals had not been undermined and that, in addition to the support of the Benelux countries, France and West Germany were 'very firmly heading in the direction which we believe to be correct'. He said that the British proposals were a step forward, but that Denmark and Greece still had reservations (namely Greek opposition to an IGC and to a political secretariat and Danish opposition to an IGC and to any attempt to reduce the use of the veto, but support for a political secretariat).

Immediately afterwards, Andreotti reported to the EP on the state of play.[102] In a speech which he described as 'of particular significance' he stated 'that the objective pre-conditions of the European revival have now been established'. He declared that 'we must proceed boldly down the road indicated by this Parliament', make progress on existing Treaty matters, develop new areas, institutionalize EPC (which 'suffered from the method of intergovernmental cooperation'), strengthen the EP (to grant it 'a joint decision-making power with the Council') and to put a 'limit on the areas in which unanimity is required'. He made a clear link between scope and level, stating that 'The aim cannot be attained except through two parallel yet closely interrelated developments. I refer on the one hand to the extension of Community jurisdiction to new fields and sectors of activity and, on the other, to the strengthening of the institutions which is needed to enable them to effect that extension.' It was clear that Italy would not accept a mere extension of the scope of the Community without any strengthening of its institutions. Andreotti did, however, allude to a cloud on the horizon, warning that 'some national time-tables would not enable genuinely significant progress to be made if our work were to go on for too long (and whatever happens, beyond the end of this year)'. No doubt he was referring to the French parliamentary elections of March 1986 in which Mitterrand seemed likely to lose his majority in the National Assembly. The months lost after the Dublin summit could yet be regretted.

Parliament wound up the debate with a resolution[103] in which it welcomed the mandate drawn up by the Italian Presidency, repeated

its demand that the outcome of the IGC should be subject to conciliation with Parliament, and again referred to the need for a conference
to be called even if not all the Member States were in agreement.

During the same session, Italy's commitment was again reaffirmed
by a formal address to the Parliament by the President of the Republic, Sandro Pertini, who spoke of his imprisonment with Spinelli on
Ventotene and paid a glowing tribute to the 'patriarch of the United
States of Europe'.[104] He spoke of the revolutionary nature of the European Unity and the fact that the long path of economic integration
was considered to be a means to the end of political unity, emphasizing the long-term commitment of Italy to achieve this. He stated that
the 'draft mandate for the conference, submitted by the Italian Presidency, was cautiously formulated and is not entirely what Italy would
have wished', but it posed the questions 'without the slightest ambiguity'. He elaborated in particular on the need to give the EP 'joint decision-making powers' with the Council. Such a restatement of the
Italian position, by the highest authority of the Republic, and choosing
the EP as his platform served to emphasize the degree of commitment
of the Italians.

There were, however, growing signs that those states supporting the
convening of an IGC were divided as to how to react to the opposition
of the reluctant three. If the three were to block all prospects of reform, should the others move ahead, as the EP had urged, by breaking
with the Community and creating a new treaty or by the more moderate approach of signing an additional treaty among themselves (e.g. on
foreign policy cooperation)? As Andreotti put it:

> Such a decision, legally speaking, does not require a unanimous vote
> [but] one should not ignore the fact that even those countries whose
> ideas resemble ours very closely, and agree to an approach in con-
> formity with the desire as expressed by the EP, are unsure how ap-
> propriate it would be to create a new legal instrument.[105]

There were again signs that France wished to urge more radical action on Germany but that Kohl was reluctant to respond. Meeting Craxi,
Mitterrand stated that Milan should 'lead us towards progress [but]
this may appear presumptuous when heels are being dragged in Luxembourg' (an apparent reference to German ministers in the Agriculture Council).[106] According to Gazzo, the main reasons for this setback
in preparations for Milan was 'undoubtedly Chancellor Kohl's unreli-
able European policy. [He] has been subject to internal political influ-
ences and strong pressure from Thatcher.'[107]

Kohl did participate in an EPP leaders' meeting in Rome on 20 June along with other Christian Democrat Prime Ministers or Foreign Ministers (Fitzgerald, Santer, Andreotti, Tindemans) and, among others, President Pflimlin, EPP Group leader Klepsch, Dooge and Herman, in which they endorsed a statement prepared by EPP Group in the EP in favour of a new treaty that would amend the Community treaties to provide for co-decision powers for the EP, more majority voting in the Council, a stronger Commission, a deadline for completing the internal market, a widening of Community competence (notably research and environment) and a development of the EMS. Again, this implied major changes to the existing Community treaties, which they were fully aware was opposed by three states. Again, however, there was no explicit indication of a strategy should those states refuse to embark on such modifications of the treaties.

The eve of the Milan European Council saw a curious spectacle: the launching on the same day of a French government memorandum in Paris and a joint Franco-German text in Bonn. The memorandum 'Pour un progrès de la construction de l'Europe'[108] was presented by Elysée Secretary General Vauzelle to the press on the morning of 27 June. It contained a long list of policy areas in which EC action was suggested and a number of institutional proposals that went beyond anything that France had proposed in recent years: an increase in EP powers (such that Council would deliberate on Commission proposals as amended by Parliament which it would not be able to amend without first seeking agreement in a conciliation committee with Parliament) more majority voting (with a requirement to supply supporting evidence to invoke the Luxembourg compromise), an increase in the administrative power of the Commission and the appointment of a Secretary-General to head an EPC secretariat. On the other hand, the Franco-German text launched later the same day in Bonn consisted of a 'Draft Treaty on European Union' limited almost exclusively to EPC and not dissimilar to the Howe draft.

How did it come about that two quite different texts were launched on the same day both in the name of the French government? And how was it that the joint one with Germany reflected traditional French priorities, whereas the unilateral French text contained items which were traditionally more a German preoccupation? The different nature of the texts might provide the clue – the Paris memorandum concentrating on changes to the existing treaties, the Bonn text being a new treaty additional to the Community treaties. Was Mitterrand's ambition still to seek fundamental changes to the Community's system, come what may, but Kohl willing only (should this prove impossible) to add new elements to those treaties? In any case, it would appear that the Bonn text was released prematurely, as a result of a debate in the Bundestag[109] – hence the fact that Vauzelle's presentation in the morning made no reference to the other text about to be presented the same afternoon.

The Benelux governments too met on the eve of the European Council and adopted a 'common position' in favour of majority voting, an increase in the EP's legislative budgetary and control powers, a strengthening of the power and authority of the Commission, increased own resources, a stronger EMS and the completion of the common market by 1992.[110] However, they too did not indicate how these objectives were to be achieved should some states remain opposed to revising the treaties.

The majority of States favouring further integration and a new treaty thus went into the Milan Summit with no agreed strategy on how to deal with the recalcitrant minority. Some, such as the Netherlands, were reluctant to force a split with the minority. Others seemed prepared to envisage a separate Treaty among the majority states in areas that could coexist with a continuing Community. A few seemed prepared to go further along the lines envisaged by the EP and set up a Union that would replace the Community, a course urged by the EP's Bureau which held a special meeting in Milan, and by 100,000 demonstrators in a Federalist rally outside the European Council.

The Milan summit therefore began with much confusion. It soon ran into deadlock. A Commission proposal simply to amend three Treaty articles crucial for completing the single market (Articles 57, 99 and 100) to provide for majority voting where the EP approves a Commission proposal failed to break the deadlock, as did a draft resolution submitted by Genscher calling for Member States to 'return to the decision-making procedure which existed before the so-called Luxembourg Disagreement', to abstain rather than vote against measures they do not like where unanimity is required, to improve the powers of the EP, to complete the internal market and to develop a common foreign and security policy.

Eventually, the deadlock was broken by the unprecedented action of the President of the European Council calling a vote. By 7 votes to 3, Craxi's proposal to convene an IGC was adopted. The vote was taken on the basis that Art. 236 EEC allows an IGC to be convened by a majority – even though its results ultimately require unanimity. The majority states were therefore displaying their determination and giving a signal to the minority states that they would not be blocked, but – at least for the time being – offering a procedure that guaranteed the minority that they could not (yet) be overridden. It at the same time postponed the need for the majority to agree on a strategy if the minority continued to block. The next steps would depend on the reaction of the minority states: would they refuse to participate in the IGC, participate but oppose any treaty amendment, or compromise?

This chapter has provided considerable evidence of how the European Parliament, in launching its draft treaty at a time at which Member States appeared not to be particularly interested in the issue of institutional reform, managed nonetheless to build up a head of steam in favour thereof. Parliament's project, carefully built on the widest possible political consensus within the Parliament, received support from a number of national political parties, national parliaments, NGOs and, ultimately, some governments. This support did not extend to all the details of the draft Treaty, but to many of its principal objectives. The momentum it generated was sufficient to stimulate those governments with a generally favourable attitude to European integration to take initiatives in favour of institutional reform. This in turn obliged the more reticent governments to react. The relationship between the two groups was affected by suggestions and hints – first launched by the EP – that, in certain circumstances, a majority of states might seek to find ways of pursuing the integration process without the minority should the latter persist in opposing all reform. This implicit threat was not as credible as it might have been had there been agreement among the majority on a strategy and method for proceeding in such a way. It none the less featured in the dynamic that led to the decision to convene an IGC.

9 The Intergovernmental Conference of 1985

In this chapter we shall examine the 1985 IGC which produced the Single European Act (SEA). We shall look at the dynamics of the negotiations and explore how some key compromises were obtained. For reasons of space, we shall concentrate on the impact of the EP and the discussions concerning its own powers.[1]

PROCEDURES AND PRESSURES

The three reluctant Member States agreed to participate in the IGC. The threat that, if it came to breaking point, the others – essentially the six original Member States – might just go ahead alone was (especially having regard to the geographical situation of the recalcitrant States) not an implausible hypothesis. A failure by the recalcitrant Members to participate in good faith in a duly convened IGC might provoke such a scenario. At the very least, it would have reopened another lengthy period of bitterness very soon after the British budgetary saga had been resolved. The less dangerous course of action, from their point of view, was to participate fully in the IGC, making enough concessions to keep it running and, therefore, to ensure that it remained in the framework of the treaties where Art. 236 gave them the guaranty of unanimity.

Thus we can see evidence of the dynamic that we examined in chapter 1 and which has so often characterized advances in European integration: the majority was showing its intention to proceed even against the wishes of the reticent minority, yet preferring to keep them on board if possible. The minority preferred to join in, albeit reluctantly, when faced with this determination, rather than risk provoking the majority into going ahead without them.

This dynamic was enhanced by the fact that the European Council had, indeed, approved four different institutional initiatives, two of which could very easily be done with only some Member States. They were the revision of the Treaties according to Art. 236; the drafting of a political cooperation Treaty; a request to the Council to 'study the institutional conditions in which the completion of the internal market could be achieved within the desired time limits'; and the launching of the 'Eureka' process outside the Community framework:[2] the second and the fourth of these could be done outside the EC treaties, and, if necessary, without all the Member States.

As the negotiations proceeded, the majority also offered not just 'stick' but 'carrot'. Linkages were made with some objectives which the UK in particular keenly supported, notably the completion of the internal market. We have seen how awareness had been growing, thanks in part to the efforts of the EP, of the 'Cost of non-Europe' and of the failure to complete what had been an original objective of the EEC. The EP had suggested a target date of 1990. Delors, in his first address to the EP as Commission President in January 1985, had suggested that the lifetime of two Commissions would be an appropriate timescale, i.e. a deadline of the end of 1992. The March 1985 European Council in Brussels had approved the idea and the Commission had prepared its famous White Paper, listing up to 300 measures that required agreement – but in many cases unanimity – in order to eliminate internal frontiers. It seemed unlikely that this could be achieved without treaty amendment, such amendments needing to be part of a package dealing also with other objectives. The IGC would not deal with this issue alone – the Commission proposal to do just that had been rejected at Milan – but it would become one of several key issues. The British found themselves 'under pressure to make concessions towards European union and to the EC policies about which they had serious misgivings, in order to stay in the game and to attain their own specific goals'.[3]

The day after his return from Milan, President Delors reported to the EP's Committee on Institutional Affairs. The Committee unanimously approved a motion for resolution which expressed satisfaction with the calling of the IGC, called for the EP to be an equal partner with the Conference, and again reiterated that, should it be impossible to move to Union with all the Member States, those willing to should do so by themselves. The motion, as approved by Parliament on 9 July,[4] was deliberately worded to represent Parliament's formal opinion, necessary for the IGC to be convened under Art. 236. As the July part-session was the last before September, the EP was keen to ensure that there be no excuse for reticent Member States to delay the start of the Conference. In fact, at the Council meeting of 22 July, the three recalcitrant Member States made no attempt to block or delay the Conference. Council had before it a formal proposal from the new Luxembourg Presidency to revise the treaties,[5] a letter from President

Pflimlin stating that Parliament's resolution of 9 July could be considered as its favourable opinion,[6] and the favourable opinion of the Commission.[7] It was able to convene the IGC.

The Presidency proposal stated simply that revision of the EEC Treaty

> should be undertaken with a view to improving the Council's decision-making procedures, strengthening the Commission's executive powers, increasing the powers of the European Parliament, and extending common policies to new fields of activity.

Four points which corresponded to the key objectives of the DTEU. It stated that amendments should be based on the Dooge and Adonnino Reports and the Commission's proposals on the free movement of persons. In convening the IGC on this basis, Council broke with precedent. In previous revisions of the Treaty,[8] the substance was negotiated within Council, often in close association with the other institutions, and the IGC was a formality at the end. This time the real negotiations took place in the IGC itself, the outcome of which was far from sure when the other institutions gave their favourable opinions.

There was some discussion within the Council as to whether a separate IGC should be convened to draft a political cooperation treaty. It was decided to deal with both matters in a single IGC, headed by the Foreign Ministers, but without prejudice to the decision as to whether there should be one or two treaties, and with each aspect prepared by a separate working group. The political directors (senior officials dealing with political cooperation in the foreign ministries) prepared an EPC Treaty, while a group composed largely of the Permanent Representatives of the Member States and chaired by Dondelinger (the Luxembourg Member of the Dooge Committee) dealt with revisions of the EEC Treaty. Leaving open the question of having one or two treaties also left open the question of the separation of EPC and Community matters. But it also made it easier to sign – or threaten to sign – an EPC Treaty among only a certain number of Member States should negotiations become blocked.

The two working parties met almost weekly from early September. The EPC working party based its work on the British, French and German texts (see previous chapter), and amended versions by the Dutch and Italian governments. The working party on the EEC Treaty, on the other hand, asked for proposals to be submitted by 15 October. It received some 30 proposals from the Commission and every Member State except the UK. The Commission was first off the mark, the Member States generally waiting until just before (or even after) the deadline.

Both working groups reported to the Foreign Ministers who met as an IGC on five more occasions before the Luxembourg Summit, speeding up the frequency of their meetings towards the end, and holding an additional 'conclave' immediately before the Summit.[9] The working groups carried out preparatory work and some compromises were made at the level of the foreign ministers, but progress was slow and the main questions were only settled – and even then sometimes only partially – by the heads of government, who discussed the issue at the Luxembourg Summit for some 21 hours – 11 more than planned. The loose ends were then settled in a final meeting of the Foreign Ministers on 16/17 December.

In addition to the IGC, work began on the two other procedures launched in Milan. Eureka took form as a separate intergovernmental framework that would nevertheless involve the Community, though to what degree would only become clear later.[10] It served as a reminder that it was possible to set up alternative frameworks to deal with major policy initiatives on terms set by certain major Member States, not necessarily involving the same membership as the Community. As to institutional improvements that did not require Treaty amendment, a document was drafted by the presidency[11] concerning four main subjects: altering Council's rules of procedure to provide for a vote to take place when requested by the President, the Commission or a majority of delegations; an undertaking by Member States to abstain rather than vote against proposals requiring unanimity in the Council where the measure concerns an objective laid down by the European Council; an undertaking by those Member States which believe that the 'Luxembourg compromise' gives them the right to block a decision by invoking a vital national interest that they would do so only if they could justify such an interest in writing to the European Council; and the possibility of exempting Member States from certain obligations. Although discussed in Coreper on two occasions, Council soon decided to leave these matters until after the IGC, as their impact would depend on the Treaty reforms.

EXTERNAL INFLUENCES ON THE IGC

Having initiated the reform process, Parliament was keen to maintain the momentum. We have seen that Parliament had a strong mistrust of IGCs, especially when the bulk of their work was carried out at the level of officials:

All previous reports (1972 Paris summit declaration, Tindemans, 3 Wise Men, Genscher-Colombo) concluded that further progress towards European Union, including institutional reforms, was necessary. However, they all suffered the same fate of being sent for further consideration to working groups of national officials and experts which invariably watered down the initial proposals to insignificant compromises.[12]

Parliament was aware that a phase of intergovernmental negotiation and signature was necessary (though not necessarily according to Art. 236): it had called for the convening of an IGC on several occasions leading up to the Milan Summit. However, it was determined that the process should retain its political character and also that the inevitable national perspective of foreign ministry officials should somehow be balanced by a determined European impact. It therefore called for the new Treaty to be approved jointly by the Parliament and the Conference, with appropriate concertation procedures to settle differences of viewpoint, a request it was to repeat several times.[13]

The Member States were divided on how to react to this request. The Council was not able to settle the matter at its meeting of 22 July, and it was left to the initial meeting of the IGC itself on 9 September to reach a compromise. With a letter from President Pflimlin on the table reiterating Parliament's demands, the ministers agreed that the Conference would 'take account in its work of the draft Treaty adopted by the European Parliament' as well as 'any further proposal which the European Parliament may wish to submit' and proposed that 'during the meetings of the Conference its members should meet with' President Pflimlin and whoever else he chose to be accompanied by. The Conference also agreed 'to submit the results of its work to the European Parliament'.[14]

Whilst the statements of intent concerning the use of the DTEU and the close association of Parliament were welcomed by the latter, the assessment of the word 'submit' was more difficult. It seemed to imply more than merely 'inform' the Parliament, but what weight did it give to the EP's viewpoint? Parliament's Committee on Institutional Affairs put forward its own interpretation. Taking together the commitments to submit the text to Parliament and to consider any *further* proposals which the EP wished to submit, the Committee considered that this implied an acceptance of the procedure that it had previously proposed, namely that Parliament consider the outcome of the Conference and, if necessary, vote amendments which would be submitted to the Conference and subjected to a conciliation procedure.[15]

This public interpretation was bound to force the issue within the IGC. At its following meeting, after a long wrangle, the President of the Conference told Parliament's delegation that the minister's interpretation of the word 'submit' was merely to inform the EP and give it the opportunity to express an opinion.[16] There would be 'no second reading' in the IGC. This position was repeated by the Luxembourg Presidency to Parliament's plenary session on 23 October. Parliament continued to push on this point, however, and was supported by Italy which declared that it would only ratify a new Treaty if it were accepted by the EP. This would mean that the negotiations could not be finally closed until Parliament had debated the matter and its views considered by the Conference.

As to its draft Treaty, Parliament repeatedly emphasized that this could serve as a basis for the work of the Conference, since it defined, in precise legal terms, appropriate changes in the competence of the Community and in the powers of the institutions which 'had obtained a very wide concensus of the great majority of the political forces of almost all the countries present'.[17] In practice, the IGC did not use the draft as a systematic basis for its work but, according to the Luxembourg Presidency, the relevant extracts were systematically included in the dossiers on each of the areas considered[18] and President Delors, giving seven examples, assured Parliament that the Commission proposals were based on the draft Treaty.[19]

Parliament monitored the IGC closely. It received the documents tabled (either officially or unofficially).[20] It held two debates on its work. An urgency resolution, tabled by Herman, was adopted on 10 October.[21] A more important debate was held on 23 October on the basis of oral questions to the Commission and to the Council. The Committee on Institutional Affairs and the main political groups all tabled questions which provided an opportunity for the Luxembourg Presidency and the Commission to report on the progress of work in the IGC and for MEPs to express their viewpoints. However, the debate was marked by a clear divergence between the aspirations of the Parliament and the attitude of the Luxembourg Presidency, both on the content of the reform and on the procedures to involve Parliament. The atmosphere was not improved by the poor performance of an inexperienced Luxembourg minister who stated that he was speaking 'in a personal capacity', misquoted several MEPs, and attacked Parliament's position on this and other unrelated issues.[22] The EP responded with a resolution which reiterated its position on the procedures and also gave a mandate to its Institutional Committee to draft comments on the proposals tabled in the IGC and to forward them directly to the President of Parliament for him to use in his meetings with the IGC.[23] This delegation of tasks to a parliamentary committee was somewhat unusual, but enabled a speedy reaction to developments. The Committee entrusted eight of its members with particular subject areas being dealt with by the IGC. On the basis of documents they drew up, and a synthesis put together by Croux, Vice-Chairman of the Committee, it adopted a set of conclusions for President Pflimlin to use.[24]

The meetings between Parliament's delegation and the IGC were of limited value,[25] but not without significance. The delegation consisted of President Pflimlin and Spinelli, accompanied on one occasion by Formigoni, Chairman of the Political Affairs Committee. At the first meeting, the President of the IGC was practically the only one to reply and enter into a discussion with the parliamentary delegation. Only at the last meeting did a real discussion take place in which almost all of the national delegations explained their position in detail. On this occasion the discussion centred on the question of the powers of the EP and the Italian delegation announced that the compromise texts on the table did not constitute an adequate base for Italy to ratify. Andreotti insisted on a strengthening of the texts, in particular as regards the powers of the Parliament, and received some support from the Belgian, Dutch and French delegations. This issue, highlighted by Parliament's presence, was to be among the dominant issues in the final conclave of the IGC and the Luxembourg Summit.

On the eve of the summit, Parliament held an extraordinary meeting of its Enlarged Bureau in Luxembourg and issued a statement[26] expressing its concern and disagreement with the preparatory work submitted to the European Council, warning that it would be dangerous for Europe if the heads of government were to try to conceal their differences behind a compromise without any real content. It stated that it would prefer the heads of government to continue with negotiations rather than abandon the necessary reforms.

The Luxembourg Summit did agree on the bulk of a package of reforms, leaving some matters over to another meeting of the foreign ministers on 16/17 December. Italy formalized its reserve to await the position of the EP and the Italian Parliament. This gave the EP a chance to come back with one final attempt to strengthen the package. The possibility of an Italian veto gave extra weight to the EP's position, though this was limited by the counterweight of a Danish reserve pending the position of the Folketing.

The EP adopted a resolution[27] on 11 December stating that the results were 'unsatisfactory and [it] is unable to accept in their present
form the proposed modifications to the EEC Treaty, particularly as regards
the powers of the European Parliament'. The resolution spelt out a
number of criticisms of the package: the uncertainty of the 1992 deadline; the restrictive definition of Community powers; the failure to touch
on Community finance and the lack of effectiveness and democracy in
the decision-making process. It called on the Foreign Ministers to make
some changes to the texts on the cooperation procedure with the EP
concerning legislation (three amendments were spelt out),[28] on monetary cooperation, on the unity of the treaties and on the executive
powers of the Commission.

The Foreign Ministers met on 16/17 December and made very small
gestures towards the EP's position on these points, finalized the texts
approved in principle at the summit and declared the negotiations closed
– still with Italian and Danish reserves pending and without attempting to deal with a number of issues that were simply dropped. These
events are described below.

The EP was not alone in attempting to influence the IGC. Some
national parliaments also took position during the negotiations. As we
saw in the last chapter, the Italian, Belgian, Dutch, Irish and French
parliaments had given favourable treatment to the EP's draft Treaty.
On 3 October, the Bundestag held a public hearing with Spinelli and
others as part of its (lengthy) study of the EP draft Treaty: on 5 December, it approved a resolution calling on the government to use the
draft Treaty as the basis of its position in the IGC and stating that the
absolute minimum was the introduction of co-decision between Council and the EP on legislation, and generalized majority voting in the
Council.[29] The resolution came too late to have any impact on the
IGC. The Italian parliament took a similar position, but earlier on. In
mid-October, the Senate's Foreign Affairs Committee unanimously
adopted a resolution urging the government to ensure that the EP's
draft Treaty remain at the centre of debate, that legislative and budgetary decision-making powers be conferred on the EP, and that the
EP be associated with the IGC according to the procedure it requested
in the 'Croux' resolution.[30] On 29 November, the corresponding committee of the Chamber also unanimously stated that the proposals then
on the table were unacceptable, that it opposed a shift towards
intergovernmentalism, and that it supported EP Council co-decision,
generalized majority voting and a real monetary and social dimension
to the Community.[31] The support from some national Parliaments for

the DTEU was thus maintained in the form of support for key objectives in the IGC.

Similar support came from the *European party federations*, which continued to act as transmission-belts between the EP's political groups and national leaders as they had done for the launch of the reform process. The European People's Party (EPP) held a 'summit' of all the Christian Democrat heads of government,[32] party leaders, Commission Members, foreign ministers and the Group leader in the EP on 12 November in Brussels. They adopted a declaration confirming their desire to pursue 'the development of the EC towards political Union in accordance with the recommendations of the EP and the Dooge Committee'.[33] They supported the 1992 deadline for the completion of the internal market; extension of Community action in the field of research and technology, energy, environment and development policy; strengthening the EMS; improving cohesion; institutionalizing EPC; creating a legal area to combat crime, terrorism and drug trafficking; and cultural cooperation. On the institutional side, they considered that the EC 'cannot be governed by structures which are less democratic than those of the Member States' and that the EP should have greater powers of control and suitable legislative powers. The Commission should be strengthened and, within the Council, unanimity restricted to a strictly limited number of cases. The EPP leaders thus signalled their presence on the more ambitious side of the debate.

The Confederation of Socialist Parties of the EC (CSP) was divided with the British Labour and Danish Social democratic parties opposing a position supported by all the other member parties. At the Madrid Congress of the CSP, this division had become so clear (with traditionally cautious parties such as the French and Irish Socialists joining the majority) that it was agreed to adopt a policy document on European Union that would not bind the two opposing parties – a highly unusual procedure. This 5-page policy document[34] was presented to Poos, chairman of the IGC, by a CSP delegation led by its president, the former Dutch Prime Minister Den Uyl. It took up virtually all the proposals concerning the institutions contained in the DTEU. Most national parties in the CSP thus formally endorsed the main institutional objectives of the EP.

The Federation of European Liberal and Democratic Parties (ELD) appealed to the heads of government before the Luxembourg summit to extend majority voting, include the monetary dimension in the treaties and extend the powers of the EP. The European Democratic Group, composed almost entirely of British Conservatives in the EP, adopted a resolution on European Union and presented its views in a press conference given by its vice-chairman on 29 November[35] consciously differing from the views of the UK's Conservative government. It supported treaty revision and called for the right of proposal for the Commission in EPC matters, the veto to be restricted to cases where a Member State justifies it in writing and presents it to the EP in plenary session, the Dooge formula for legislative co-decision, the elimination of the distinction between compulsory and non-compulsory expenditure in the budget and granting the EP a right to censure individual Commissioners. This too can be seen as an attempt to push a government further along the path of reform.

Numerous non-governmental organizations also lobbied actively during the negotiations. At European level, apart from the European Movement and the Federalist organizations, it is worth noting statements from ETUC giving general support to the EP's draft Treaty,[36] a declaration from a number of leading industrialists and a statement from the European Conference of Local and Regional Authorities supporting 'the EP's demands without reservation'.[37] Clearly, the DTEU served as a focus and reference for many non-governmental actors.

THE SUBSTANCE OF THE NEGOTIATIONS

The IGC received a wide range of proposals.[38] Indeed, almost all of the main changes proposed by the EP in its draft treaty were covered by treaty amendments tabled by the Commission or Member States, though not always in the same terms. The only major area not covered was the budget, Delors claiming that the EP had not pushed this subject actively.[39] Parliament could thus claim success in that the national governments had been brought to the point of negotiating on all the major areas in which it had proposed reforms.

The Member States, however, had varying priorities. The extension of the *scope* of the Community was broadly accepted, with proposals even from Denmark (partly to show its good faith in areas of least difficulty and partly as an attempt by the Danish government to divide its opposition). On the *level* of integration, there was general resistance from the countries that had opposed the convening of the IGC and specific resistance on certain points from others. It was clear that any strengthening of the institutions would only get through by stubborn insistence from its advocates and as part of a global package.

In this situation it was not surprising that Member States wished to send public 'signals' to each other and lay down markers outside the negotiating room. Early in the negotiations some of these again sought to pressure the reticent states by indicating determination to push ahead, if necessary without them. Others simply set markers on issues. In the *Financial Times*[40] on 10 July, the Secretary General of the Italian Foreign Ministry Ruggiero urged Britain to 'bring itself back into the mainstream of the European Community' stating that Mrs. Thatcher

> must realize that what she regards as 'European unity rhetoric', is serious and in the ascendancy. If not, Britain's opposition will only have the effect of strengthening the unity of the six countries which founded the Community.

A similar message was carried in *The Times* of the same day in the form of a letter from Croux, in which he also criticized *The Times'* editorials, which tended to echo the Foreign Office line.[41] The Dutch Minister Van den Broek put forward a similar view to the foreign affairs committee of the Dutch parliament, stating it was not beyond the bounds of possibility that some of the Ten may move ahead: the others to follow when possible.[42] The Dutch objective was for a single treaty (EPC and EC) with as priority increased powers to the Commission and EP, extension of the Community's scope, and an improvement in the decision-taking process.[43] The same three objectives (but with a specific reference to including security) were listed by Tindemans, who emphasized that an 'original form of federation or confederation' was their final objective.[44] On 19 November, the Prime Ministers, Foreign and European Ministers of the Benelux countries met in Brussels and issued a declaration listing five priority objectives: internal market (broad definition) by 1992, generalized majority voting in Council, additional powers to the EP, EMU and development of Technology in the Community framework.[45] Felipe Gonzalez chose the College of Europe in Bruges to state Spain's commitment to 'go forward with European Union as its goal', seek more majority voting, strengthen the Commission and increase the role of the EP.[46] The French European Minister signalled his determination to make it again possible to decide by majority and for the EP to have all the rights which an elected Parliament should have.[47] The German Federal President addressed the EP on the same day as its 23 October debate on the IGC, calling for a strengthening of the EP's legislative powers, and stating that it was intolerable for the Community to be less democratic than its Member States.[48]

The minority states no doubt felt obliged to reply. Sir Geoffry Howe made a major speech in Bonn on 3 October in which he stated[49] that 'Britain is not afraid of European Union' but defined European Union as 'the process of deepening and broadening the scope of European activities so that they inherently cover a growing proportion of Member States mutual relations and of their external relations', and claimed that in that sense 'such a Union exists now'. He called for agreement on an EPC treaty and did not rule out changes to the EEC Treaty, but emphasized that change should be minimal and 'pragmatic' as 'the founding fathers knew pretty well what they were doing'. He did 'not believe that decision-taking in the Community is paralysed'. Majority voting should take place where provided for in the existing treaties. The signals coming from Denmark, on the other hand, were confusing with political statements from ministers and opposition leaders aimed more at Danish public opinion[50] beginning to concede the possibility of limited treaty amendment, but debated in the context of a complex domestic situation. In early November, the Italian government was reported to have approached the 11 others to adopt a more positive attitude, and to have sought a Rome–Bonn–Paris axis to overcome resistance in London, Copenhagen and Athens.[51] On 23 November, Andreotti delivered the VIIIth Jean Monnet lecture at the EUI, using the occasion again to urge other governments to be more constructive and to warn that Italy would not accept an agreement without substance.[52]

Meanwhile, the negotiations themselves proceeded in the two working groups. For the details, it is better to proceed to an analysis on a subject-by-subject basis.[53]

Two Acts or One?

Although the question as to whether to have a single or two separate acts covering Treaty reform and EPC was left to the end, arguments were presented right from the beginning. Once the IGC was underway and the potential threat of a two-speed Europe receded, arguments focused on the desirability of linking or integrating the EC and EPC frameworks. In its opinion on the convening of the Conference, the Commission argued strongly for bringing them together as a major step towards European Union. In a statement on 19 September, Delors argued for a single Treaty comprising a preamble and three sections (joint provisions, EEC revision, political cooperation). This structure was followed in November in a French proposal for a 'single act', on which the negotiations were then based.

The preamble was similar to that of Parliament's draft Treaty, with general considerations on European Union, and the pursuit of new objectives through a better functioning of the Community institutions. During the final rounds of negotiations other recitals were added to the preamble as a compromise, replacing proposals that had initially been put forward for new Treaty articles on fundamental rights and monetary affairs.

The proposal for a Title I (common provisions) envisaged five articles laying down that the European Union would comprise the European Communities (based on the Treaties and Title II) and political cooperation (based on the Luxembourg, Copenhagen and London Reports[54] and Title III); that the 'Council of European Union' (former European Council) composed of the heads of government and the President of the Commission define general guidelines for Community policies and EPC; and that the European Council be assisted by a secretariat (additional to that of EPC) under the authority of the Presidency. In the end, three articles were approved which were based on the French proposal but did not define the entity as 'European Union' (simply saying that both the EC and EPC contributed towards developing such a Union), and kept the old name for the European Council, which would not have its own secretariat nor be charged with giving guidelines. The specific reference to the existing reports governing political cooperation, to which the Solemn Declaration was added, gave a formal status to them and to the details they contain that were not repeated in Title III. This was the first mention of the European Council in a Treaty, its composition specified to include the President of the Commission on an equal footing with the heads of state or government (thereby making it different from a Council meeting at the level of prime ministers).

Titles II and III included the IGC's conclusions on the revision of the EEC Treaty[55] and on political cooperation respectively. Title IV (final and general dispositions), as well as the usual technical articles, specified that the Court of Justice would only be competent to deal with matters covered by Title II. There would thus be no judicial review of political cooperation, nor matters covered by the preamble or Title I. This considerably limited the import of these sections of the Act, notably those referring to democracy and human rights.

Internal Market

This was the centrepiece of the talks, for both fundamental and tactical reasons. It was an area in which a basic aim of the EEC Treaty was still not achieved. Its importance was generally recognized, partly as a result of lobbying activities by MEPs (e.g. 'Kangaroo' Group) and the Albert/Ball Report. It was of particular importance to one of the reticent states (UK) and the case for improving the effectiveness of the institutions was clear.

The EP had called for the setting of specific deadlines for achieving the internal market (two, five and ten years respectively for free movement of goods and persons, of services and of capital)[56] and had specified that personal checks at internal frontiers should be abolished. The necessary legislation would be adopted by qualified majority voting. An initial Commission proposal to the IGC provided for a single deadline of 31 December 1992[57] to establish an area 'without borders, in which persons, goods, services and capital shall move freely under conditions identical to those obtaining within a Member State'. Council would act by qualified majority voting, except on the free movement of persons, in which unanimity would be required until the end of 1992. Implementing measures would be adopted by the Commission, except where the Council unanimously reserved the right to lay down measures itself in specific cases. There would be automatic mutual recognition by Member States of each other's rules and regulations in so far as common provisions were not adopted by the end of 1992.

The Commission proposal met with various reserves. The *definition* of an area without internal frontiers was opposed by the UK, France and West Germany, which found it too broad and all-encompassing. The automatic 1992 *deadline* was felt to be too rigid by France, Greece and Ireland. *Derogations* were sought in particular fields by particular countries (e.g. the UK and Ireland on measures concerning plant and animal health, notably rabies control). The *decision-taking* procedures (qualified majority voting and delegation of powers to the Commission) were opposed by Denmark and Greece. Greece, Ireland and Portugal were worried about the potential centripetal effects of an integrated market and linked their position to the outcome of the negotiations concerning the chapter on *cohesion*. Denmark, West Germany and others were worried that *harmonization* measures with repercussions on the environment, consumer protection and health could force them to lower their standards. By contrast, the Commission proposal was generally supported by Italy and the Benelux countries.

Work eventually proceeded on the basis of a revised proposal by the Commission.[58] This retained a broad definition of the overall objective, but, instead of the blanket provision for qualified majority voting, substituted a list of specific EEC Treaty articles that would be modified to provide for it. It also took away the automatic element of the mutual recognition of national legislation in 1992, providing instead that the Council, by qualified majority voting on a Commission proposal, should decide by the end of 1992 which provisions should be so recognized and it toned down the powers to decide by qualified majority voting legislation on free circulation of persons.

Much of the discussion centred on the list of articles to which qualified majority voting would apply, with a different permutation of support and opposition to each one. It was only at the summit that most of these issues were resolved, though not without difficulty: the heads of government spent some three hours just on the issue of the British and Irish health regulations.[59] The outcome was a lengthy set of articles and declarations. The definition of the internal market as an *area* (rather than a mere 'market' limited to economic matters) with free circulation of goods, persons, services and capital, was accepted. First France (during the conclave) then Germany and finally the UK came round to this broader definition, but its scope was limited by replacing the phrase 'under conditions identical to those obtaining within a Member State' with 'in accordance with the provisions of the Treaty'.

Concerning the transfer from unanimity to qualified majority voting, provisions dealing with the common customs tariff, provision of services by nationals of third countries and measures concerned with banking, medical and pharmaceutical professions (Arts. 28, 57.2 and 59.2) were so transferred. Art. 70.1 was modified to allow for qualified majority voting decisions on exchange policies and movement of capital, but preserving unanimity if such measures would constitute a step backwards concerning the free movement of capital – an interesting way of entrenching the *acquis communautaire* in this field. For Air and Sea Transport (Art. 84), the switch to qmv was accompanied by the addition (by the Foreign Ministers after the summit) of a new sentence retaining unanimity where the measure concerned is likely to have a serious effect on the standard of living and on employment in certain areas. For harmonization of indirect taxation, unanimity was maintained, but the article (99) was rewritten to place an obligation on the Council to act before the 1992 deadline and to consult the EP. A new Art. 100 (a) would apply in place of Art. 100, except for measures concerning fiscal policy, free movement of persons and the rights of employees, allowing Council to act by qualified majority voting for single market legislative harmonizations. It was complemented with a number of provisions that met concerns expressed by Member States. It was laid down that Commission proposals on health, safety, environment and consumer protection should be based on a high level of protection (i.e. harmonizing upwards). It provided that Member States could apply national measures concerning the environment, the working environment, or where justified under Art. 36 EEC, but such measures would have to be notified to the Commission, which would confirm them after verifying that they were not a disguised restriction on trade between Member States. In such cases, the Commission or a Member State could bring the matter before the Court of Justice directly (i.e. without first going through the Commission's 'reasoned opinion' procedure laid down in Arts 169 and 170). A separate article provided that the Commission should take account of the particular situation of weak economies in its proposals, which could include temporary derogations. In 1992, the Commission would make an inventory of remaining national dispositions not yet harmonized under Art. 100 (a). The recognition of their equivalence would not be automatic, but would be possible by qualified majority voting.

A number of declarations were annexed to the new Treaty. The nature of the 1992 deadline was settled in this way, with an affirmation that it was the firm intention to take the necessary decisions concerning the Commission's 'White Book' on the internal market by then, but that this deadline would not have any automatic legal effects. On the Commission's executive powers in this field, partly dealt with in another chapter of the revision of the Treaties, a declaration requested the Council to reserve a predominant place to the 'advisory committee' procedure which was held to be rapid and efficient.[60] Another Declaration provided that none of these articles would affect the rights of Member States to take measures they consider necessary concerning immigration from third countries, terrorism, criminality and traffic in drugs, works of arts and antiques, though in a separate 'political declaration' the Member States undertook to cooperate in these fields.

Monetary Union

The Commission put forward a proposal that did little more than codify the existing situation and provide for a procedure for further development. The only advantage would lie in mentioning the EMS and the ECU for the first time in the treaties, formalizing their link to the Community. The existing structure of the EMS (with its two-tier system) and its decision-taking procedures would be codified without change.

The Finance Ministers discussed this proposal – the only case of a sectoral Council becoming involved in the IGC. It was felt to be weak by France, Belgium, Ireland and Italy. However, the UK, West Germany and the Netherlands opposed any inclusion of monetary articles in the Treaty revision. The UK Chancellor, Nigel Lawson, was reported as stating that 'the inclusion of Economic and Monetary Union as a goal in the Treaty is unacceptable and pointless'.[61] Stoltenberg dwelt on the problem of referring to central banks in an intergovernmental treaty, whereas such banks are autonomous in some Member States. These positions were strongly criticized by the Commission, which recalled recent declarations by the governments on the development of the EMS and the overall objective of Economic and Monetary Union (EMU).

A few days before the Luxembourg Summit, Anglo-German opposition to including monetary matters in the Treaty revision was confirmed during the Thatcher–Kohl meeting in London on 27 November. This did not augur well for the summit. However, the French and Italian governments announced measures liberalizing their exchange control provisions, which had always been an important demand by West Germany in EMS negotiations. This cleared the way for Kohl to compromise during the summit, leaving Thatcher isolated (she was still reported[62] as saying 'no and no' to any reference to EMU at the end of the first evening session of the summit).

It was eventually agreed to insert three extra indents in the preamble of the new Treaty, which would refer to the objective of EMU as laid down by the Paris Summit of October 1972, to the Bremen and Brussels Summits of 1978 establishing the EMS, and to the measures that had been taken by the Central Banks of the Member States to establish monetary cooperation. Secondly, a new chapter would be added to the EEC Treaty entitled 'Cooperation in economic and monetary policy (Economic and Monetary Union)'. It would lay down that Member States should cooperate to promote the convergence of their economic and monetary policies, in accordance with the objectives of Art. 104 of the Treaty. In doing so, they would take account of the experience acquired through the EMS and in developing the ECU. Any further development requiring institutional change would take place in accordance with Art. 236 after consulting the monetary committee and the committee of Governors of the Central Banks. Thus, although further development was envisaged, it would require, for any institutional development of the EMS, a Treaty revision according to Art. 236.

This point was so strongly criticized after the summit, notably by the EP in its resolution of 11 December, that at the Foreign Ministers meeting of 16/17 December this issue was reopened. A declaration was added to the Acts of the Conference specifying that further (non-institutional) development *was* possible within the existing frameworks. This would not require Treaty revision. However, even this declaration was not approved by all, and had to be incorporated as a declaration of the presidency and the Commission.

Thus, in this key area, the reticences of the reluctant Member States was reinforced by the sensitivities of the normally pro-integration possessor of the strongest currency, the Deutschmark, and little was achieved of immediate value. However, a seed was planted for future developments.

Economic and Social Cohesion

The imminent arrival of Spain and Portugal into the EC combined with a desire to balance the perceived centripetal effects of the single market made this subject a key one in the negotiations. The main argument centred on the strength of the commitment to economic redistribution to be written into the Treaties, with a clear divergence between those countries likely to benefit from such redistribution and some of those likely to have to contribute towards it. The Dutch Foreign Minister spoke of the need 'to buy the support of the Mediterranean countries for the internal market'.[63]

Subsidiary arguments took place on codifying the regional fund in the Treaty, on revising the provisions for the other funds, notably the articles concerning the social fund, on the advisability of new Community loans (which Germany in particular opposed) and on the degree of coordination among the three funds (with France in particular wishing to avoid an 'implicit' fusion of the three).

The compromise worked out was based on a Commission proposal. The Community would contribute to the objective of economic and social cohesion through the structural funds, the EIB and the other existing financial instruments. There would be a unanimous decision within one year on the rationalization and coordination of the three funds, followed by the introduction of qualified majority voting for the regional fund and its maintenance for the other funds. There would be no revision of Arts. 123 to 127 on the Social Fund, which most Member States felt were flexible enough. The question of overall financial commitment was settled by a declaration referring to the conclusions of the European Council meeting of Brussels 1984, which stated that the financial means allocated to the structural funds would be significantly increased in real terms within the limits of financial possibilities. This meant it would effectively be dealt with in the context of a revision of the own resources system, which was, in any case, inevitable within the next year or two. There was, however, implicit recognition of the need for a substantial increase.

Environment

The Commission proposed four new Treaty articles on environmental policy laying down its objectives (quality of the environment, health and rational use of resources), principles (preventive action, polluter pays, integral part of all Community policies, and compatible with economic and social development), a long list of specific areas for Community intervention, a provision allowing more stringent national measures where these did not distort the common market, and for Council to act unanimously on objectives and the principle of Community intervention, but by a qualified majority voting for implementing measures.

The Commission proposal was broadly acceptable, but the UK insisted on references to balancing the benefits and costs to industry of environmental policy, determining scientifically the causes of pollution, and taking into account different geographical conditions. Ireland and Greece wished to balance environmental considerations with those of economic development. The Netherlands and Greece disliked the Commission proposal's long list of specific areas for Community intervention, arguing that it was unnecessary to be so detailed. Denmark, the UK and Greece opposed decision-taking by majority. West Germany submitted a proposal based on Parliament's draft Treaty[64] to add animal protection to Community competences.

The Commission submitted a revised proposal which maintained broadly the same objectives and principles, but dropped the long list of specific areas of intervention. It stated that Community proposals should take 'account of' scientific evidence, costs to industry, different regional situations and the need for economic development. It added the principle of subsidiarity: that the Community should act where the objectives can better be achieved at Community level than at the level of the Member States in isolation. This would be the only explicit phrasing of the principle in the treaties. It maintained its proposal on the decision-taking procedure (unanimous on the principles and objectives, qualified majority voting on implementation).

This new Commission proposal proved broadly acceptable to the Member States, except for the issue of the decision-taking procedures. This was settled by postponing the problem: it was provided that the

Council could decide unanimously what areas can subsequently be decided by qualified majority voting. The IGC also agreed to allow individual Member States to lay down more stringent conditions compatible with the Treaty. It also added a provision, after some controversy, providing for cooperation with international organizations in these fields and for agreements to be concluded in accordance with Art. 228 EEC. A paragraph provided that this would not prejudice the competences of individual Member States to negotiate international agreements in this field, but a declaration inserted in the Acts of the Conference confirmed the existing case law of the Court of Justice to the effect that the Community is competent for the external aspects of its internal policies.[65] A second declaration specified that Community action should not interfere with national policies concerning the exploitation of energy resources. With these specifications, the IGC approved the Commission proposal.

Technological Research and Development

As the discussions on giving Community a formal competence in this field took place at the same time as the discussions on Eureka, the Commission and several Member States were anxious to give the Community a broad range of possible means of action in this field.

General agreement was reached quickly on the Commission proposals for a lengthy list of various sorts of Community action. However, there was a divergence as to which measures could be approved unanimously and what by qualified majority voting. Germany and the UK were particularly anxious that decisions concerning finance should be unanimous. A compromise was negotiated which provided for unanimity in the adoption of the multi-annual framework programme, and qualified majority voting for the adoption of particular programmes and their implementation (except where this required the creation of common enterprises or structures at the European level). However, it was laid down that the framework programme would go into considerable detail and would include the level of finance as well as its division among the various activities proposed. Community expenditure would be approved under the budgetary procedure, but the total amount could not exceed that provided for in the framework programme. This would limit the EP's powers to increase spending in this field, but not its powers to allocate such spending.

Social Policy

Denmark submitted a proposal on 16 October for a new name for chapter 1 of Title 3 of part 3 EEC 'Labour market and working environment'. To this chapter, a new Art. 118(a) would be added enabling Council to adopt directives (by an unspecified majority) laying down minimum criteria for safety and health at work. Member States would be allowed to adopt more advanced criteria. Art. 122 would be modified to lay down that the Commission annual report should include a chapter on social and working conditions. Denmark also put forward a proposal that, should unemployment increase above Y per cent (figure to be negotiated), Council, on the basis of a Commission proposal, should examine the possibilities to modify the economic policies of Member States in view of boosting employment. These proposals aimed at drawing in the Danish opposition parties by putting forward proposals that could appeal to them.

The Commission put forward a proposal which also provided for a new Art. 118(a), to allow directives to lay down standards for *all* areas currently listed in Art. 118. It also proposed a new Art. 118(b) providing for a social dialogue with the possibility for contractual relationships, at European level.

The IGC agreed on a new Art. 118(a) based on the Danish proposal, providing for directives to lay down minimum criteria on the working environment to protect the safety and health of workers, aiming to harmonize conditions in this field. Council would act by qualified majority voting, though the UK at first maintained a reserve on this point insisting on unanimity, but in the end settled for an extra paragraph and a declaration in the Acts of the Conference that the Community will not place unjustified burdens on small and medium-sized enterprises. A paragraph specified that Member States could adopt stricter conditions compatible with the Treaty. The Commission proposal for Art. 118(b) was adopted. The Danish proposals for a new article on unemployment and for a modification to Art. 122 were dropped.

Political Cooperation

As we have seen, the issue of how to organize foreign policy cooperation was a longstanding bone of contention. Only *ad hoc* cooperation (EPC) had been established. The DTEU had pressed for its formalization and its linking to Community institutions, whilst maintaining its character of 'cooperation' among the Member States.

British, Franco-German, Dutch and Italian proposals were tabled,[66] seeking to entrench EPC in treaty form, but without bringing in many changes to existing practices. This approach proved acceptable to the IGC, whilst leaving until the end the question of its incorporation in the same treaty as Community matters (see above). There were, however, different nuances to be ironed out.

On the *aims* the UK proposal referred to 'consultations and exchange of information to secure a broad identity of views'; the Franco-German and Dutch texts to 'the gradual implementation of a common European policy' and the Italian text to 'the systematic formulation and implementation of a common external policy'. This proved to be a difficult point, but the final text spoke of a 'European foreign policy'.

The UK text would oblige Member States to consult each other before adopting their final position in foreign policy questions of interest to them all, to take full account of this when working out national positions, and to refrain from actions that would damage their joint reputation as a coherent force. The Franco-German text was similar, but also referred to 'joint action' (not just national action) and would cover *all* major foreign policy matters. The others were close to the Franco-German proposal. The final text took up the structure of the UK text, but added references to joint action and the development of common principles and objectives.

On the *structure* of political cooperation all texts placed overall responsibility with the European Council (renamed 'Council of the European Union' in the Franco-German text), with day-to-day work carried out by the foreign ministers (the Council in the Italian text). A coordinating and representative role was given to the Presidency. Divergences emerged on the matter of the secretariat: the Franco-German proposal envisaged a Secretary-General appointed for four years by the European Council, heading a secretariat whose other members would be appointed for two years by the foreign ministers. It would assist the Presidency and ensure continuity and coherence with Community affairs. The UK proposal referred to a secretariat in the annexes only and described it as a 'small secretariat, based in the main place of work of the Community' with office space and services provided by arrangement with the Council secretariat, and a 'head' appointed by agreement among the Member States. It provided a detailed list of the functions of the secretariat, which remained technical. The Italian and Dutch proposals broadly supported the UK text, presumably fearing a large intergovernmental political secretariat that could rival the Commission. In the end, it was agreed to have such a small secretariat under the authority of the Council Presidency.

On *decision-taking*, the common assumption was unanimity, but the Italians proposed 'consensus respecting majority opinion', and the final text included an obligation on Member States to refrain, as far as possible, from impeding consensus or joint action. For the rest, existing practices were codified and the text charged the Presidency and the Commission with seeking coherence between EPC and external policies of the Community.

On *international organizations* and conferences, the UK proposed an undertaking not to support resolutions which directly criticize or gravely affect the vital interests of another Member State, and to avoid co-sponsoring resolutions which others oppose. The final text provided for Member States to try to adopt common positions in matters dealt with in international organizations and conferences, and that where not all of them were represented, those that were should take account of positions agreed in EPC. On *representation in third countries*, the final text provided for intensified cooperation among the accredited representations of Member States and the Commission to third countries and international organizations, through mutual assistance and exchange of information.

Security was a touchy matter with particular sensitivities in Ireland (not a member of NATO), Denmark and Greece, and was among the last points to be settled in the negotiations. The final text stated that closer cooperation on matters of European security would contribute to a European identity in external relations and that Member States were disposed to develop further their cooperation on political and economic aspects of security. A reference to technological and industrial cooperation was included. The question of NATO and WEU was settled by providing that this Treaty was not an obstacle to closer cooperation among some Member States in these frameworks.

On the *Parliament*, the UK text provided for the EP to be 'informed', the Franco-German and Dutch proposals provided for its 'association', and the Italian text referred to the 'essential role' of the EP in the 'systematic formulation of the common external policy' and laid down provisions for informing the EP and taking account of its views. The final text contained an article laying down that the EP would be 'closely associated' with political cooperation and charging the Presidency both with informing the EP and with ensuring that its views are 'duly taken into consideration'.

On *future development*, the Italian proposal included an article providing for revision after five years to make further progress, and for the foreign ministers to produce a draft for the European Council which would be submitted to the EP. In the final text, the signatories undertook to examine after five years whether it was necessary to revise the Treaty, but no procedures were specified.

Powers of the Commission and Procedure for its Appointment

A strengthening of the Commission's *executive and management powers* was one of the main issues of the IGC and had been a major objective of the DTEU. Again, positions diverged, but the final text took up a Dutch proposal to modify Art. 145, to oblige Council to confer implementing powers on the Commission, but added a provision allowing the Council to reserve such powers to itself in specific cases, and to lay down modalities for the exercise of such powers by the Commission. The intention of this last point was that Council would draw up, as originally proposed in the report of the Three Wise Men, a number of standard procedures for such modalities. A separate declaration in the Acts of the Conference concerning the internal market recommended the use of the advisory committee system for measures in that field (a point added at the Foreign Ministers meeting of 16/17 December, after the EP expressed fears that the Council would reserve implementing powers to itself).

The Dutch government also submitted a proposal concerning *the method of appointing the Commission*. Resembling the EP's DTEU, it provided for the President of the Commission to be nominated first after consulting the Parliament, for the other members of the Commission to be appointed on his/her proposal, and for the new Commission to present itself to Parliament for a vote of investiture. The Commission's term of office, however, would remain four years and not be changed to five as the DTEU provided. The proposal was not accepted, partly through lack of time. Later, Delors confirmed the Commission's support for the current 'pragmatic' procedure in which Parliament holds an investiture debate and a vote.[67] The Dutch also wished to restrict the number of Commissioners to 12. This was opposed by Germany, Italy and France. It would in any case not require Treaty amendment.

Legislative Powers of the European Parliament

It was clear from the beginning that this would be a difficult area, with Denmark and the UK opposing any formal increase in Parliament's powers. The first proposal submitted to the IGC came from

West Germany, the Commission having held back, wishing first to make progress on policy areas before touching on the difficult issues of institutional change. Aware of the opposition, the proposal put forward the concept of a number of 'baskets' in which Parliament's powers would be adjusted to various degrees. The first basket would consist simply of extending the EP's legal right to be consulted on draft legislation to some articles not already providing for such consultation.[68] The second basket provided for a new Art. 189(a) 'collaboration procedure' which could cover some dozen articles including agriculture, transport, competition policy, social fund and most non-financial aspects of the internal market. Commission proposals would first go to the Parliament, which could approve or amend them within six months. Parliament's version would be forwarded to the Council. If Council amended it, a conciliation committee, composed of 12 members from Council and 12 from the EP, would have three months to adopt compromise proposals by a three-quarters majority; such compromises to be approved by the Parliament (by a majority of members) and by the Council (usually by a qualified majority). Up to this point the German proposal resembled the procedure for the first reading and conciliation contained in the EP's draft Treaty. However, a final, crucial provision took away the essence of Parliament's bargaining position in the conciliation procedure. It provided that should no agreement be reached in conciliation, or should Council or Parliament reject the compromise, it would be up to Council alone to decide. There would thus be little incentive for the Council to compromise in the conciliation procedure. If half of its members did join with Parliament's delegation to reach a three-quarters majority, the proposal could only pass with acceptance by a qualified majority in the Council itself: little change therefore from the previous situation where it was up to Council voluntarily to accept Parliament's position. The EP might gain in that Council would be obliged to deliberate on *its* proposal, rather than that of the Commission, but the Community element as a whole would be weakened by the removal of the Commission's current prerogative to withdraw or amend its proposals at any time, and the requirement on Council either to accept the Commission's proposal or amend it unanimously.

The third basket of the German proposal provided for 'joint legislative action'. Council could adopt texts only if they were approved by the EP by a majority of its members. This would apply to some 'constitutional' measures: Treaty revision, accession of new Member States and association agreements. The German proposal also contained a provision formally recognizing the name 'European Parliament' in the Treaty with a clause stating that it represents 'the citizens of the States united within the Community', a phrase originating in the 1972 Summit communiqué and the 1978 European Elections Act.

The method of working on different baskets was broadly welcomed, but there were numerous reserves on the details of the German proposal.[69] The Commission was highly critical of the implicit weakening of its position and drew up an alternative, divided into four baskets. The first basket, like the first German basket, extended traditional consultation to new fields. A second basket provided for a reference in the Treaty to the conciliation procedure, which would be extended to cover all major items of legislation. However, the procedure would be triggered by joint agreement between Parliament and Council, which implied that without the agreement of the Council there would be no conciliation, unlike the 1975 arrangements,[70] which provide for the automatic opening of the procedure when positions diverge. Furthermore, it would aim merely to ensure that Council be better informed in its deliberations of the significance and meaning of Parliament's opinion, and in view of reaching an agreement with it, whereas the 1975 procedure aimed 'to seek an agreement between the European Parliament and the Council'. Finally, it would be up to Council to take a final decision 'taking into account results of concertation', whereas under the 1975 procedure this is supposed to take place 'when the positions of the two institutions are sufficiently close'. If the aim was to codify existing practice, it did so in a retrograde way.

The Commission's third basket proposed a new 'cooperation procedure' which would apply when Council acts by qualified majority vote. After the traditional Commission proposal, Parliamentary opinion and Council deliberation, Council would adopt a 'common position', which would return to the EP. In a second reading, Parliament could, within two months and by a majority of its members, propose amendments to Council's text or reject it entirely. Council could then adopt these amendments by qualified majority vote if they were approved by the Commission, or unanimously if the Commission did not approve them. Also unanimously, it could modify Parliament's amendments or override a Parliamentary rejection of the text. The procedure thus amounted to a repeated consultation of Parliament, giving it a second chance to amend or reject, but under more difficult conditions. The novelty resided in the EP's ability to oppose a proposal outright, in which case the majority required in Council would change to unanimity.

In its fourth basket, the Commission proposal took up the German text's third basket, adding own resources to their list of areas requiring Parliament's approval.

The Commission proposal met with diverse reactions. The extension of traditional consultation was not very controversial, Parliament being consulted in practice anyway (though it would enlarge Parliament's scope for using the tactics it developed following the 'Isoglucose' Ruling). On writing the conciliation procedure into the Treaty, a number of countries felt that this was better left to interinstitutional agreements and Denmark opposed any extension of conciliation. The proposed cooperation procedure was broadly supported by the Netherlands, Belgium, Ireland and Greece, but other countries felt either that it did not go far enough or that it went too far. As to Parliamentary agreement for constitutional matters, the principle was accepted by all countries except Denmark, but there was disagreement on articles it should apply to: each article proposed met with at least one reservation (e.g. Greece and France re 138, France, UK and West Germany re 201, France and Ireland re 236, Greece re 237).

The German and Commission proposals were put forward as compromises that the authors hoped might prove acceptable to the more reticent countries. Delors was later to acknowledge that this might not have been the best tactic, as the proposals left little room for further compromise when these countries nevertheless expressed reserves. More ambitious countries were left in a difficult tactical position of having to propose strengthening texts that others labelled as too far-reaching. Italy nevertheless attempted this by submitting a new proposal, which referred to the DTEU and the Dooge Report as its sources. Instead of the 'cooperation procedure' Italy proposed a system of successive readings such that the approval (or non-rejection) of both Parliament and Council would be necessary for most major Community policies.[71] This amounted to full co-decision, with procedures for Parliament and Council to consider each other's amendments. Italy also approved the Commission proposal on the 'constitutional basket' and proposed granting Parliament a formal role in receiving petitions and conducting inquiries. Italy's position appears to have been considered as tactical by most delegations in the IGC, who took it as a signal that Italy supported strengthening the Commission proposals. Almost all delegations criticised the inordinately high number of readings (potentially six).

France put forward a proposal containing elements taken both from the Commission and the German texts. Under the 'cooperative procedure' a Commission proposal would first be debated by the EP which could amend or reject it by an absolute majority within two months. If the Commission did not specifically reinstate or modify its proposal, Council would deliberate on the basis of Parliament's text. It the EP rejected the Commission proposal, Council could approve it only unanimously. If Council's version differed from Parliament's, a conciliation procedure would follow in which compromise would be sought. If this failed, Council would be free to act. This text was close to the German proposal, but did not go into so much detail on the conciliation procedure and took up the Commission's text on Parliamentary rejection of proposals. France also proposed that for matters concerning VAT, excise duty and company taxation, Council would act henceforth by qualified majority vote if the Commission proposals were approved by the EP by an absolute majority.

The French proposal appears not to have satisfied any delegation. Positions were becoming entrenched around the previous proposals. After a difficult round of discussions on 21 October, including a meeting with Parliament's delegation, the Foreign Ministers were unable even to agree on a new mandate for the preparatory group. The Presidency drafted a compromise taking up the Commission proposal on the cooperation procedure, but applying it to just nine articles and changing the procedure for dealing with EP amendments in the second reading to leave it entirely up to the Commission to decide which amendments would go to the Council (though the amendments it did accept would be in the text unless subsequently removed by Council). It also retained the 'fourth basket', but only for Arts 237 and 238. The incorporation of the conciliation procedure in the Treaty was dropped. This proposal was sufficiently watered down that only Denmark felt it went too far. The Benelux countries, Germany and France considered it to be the bare minimum.

The draft was discussed on 16 November with Parliament's delegation which considered it unacceptable. Towards the end of this discussion, Andreotti stated that for Italy, the compromise currently on the table, in particular the text concerning EP, was insufficient to justify the whole exercise and that Italy would in any case not ratify a text that was not acceptable to the EP itself. He received some support, though in less categoric terms, from Tindemans and the French European Minister, Lalumière.[72] One Belgian newspaper[73] hailed this as the 'rejection front', putting some counter-pressure on the minimalist Member States.

Subsequent discussions in the conclave and in the meeting of the European Council itself were unable to agree on any changes to the

Presidency compromise, however. With a few drafting amendments, the European Council approved this text, but instructed the foreign ministers to clarify the procedure to be followed should Parliament, in its second reading, reject the common position of the Council, or if Council failed to act within the three months' deadline in its second reading. Denmark and Italy maintained reserves on this text, for opposite reasons. Thatcher was reported[74] as preferring the EP to be 'disbanded rather than see it block EEC affairs as it has done in recent years'.

In its resolution on the results of the summit, Parliament asked for the Foreign Ministers to make a number of changes to the text, namely that the new cooperation procedure should apply to all acts requiring a majority decision in Council (as the Commission had originally proposed); that in the second reading, Parliament's text would stand unless modified by the Council within three months, (acting by qualified majority vote where the Commission did not approve Parliament's position or unanimously where it did); and to fix a deadline for Council to reach a common position in its first reading.

At their meeting of 16/17 December, Foreign Ministers failed to agree on any extension of the cooperation procedure to further articles. As regards Council's second reading, they did agree to allow all of Parliament's amendments to be submitted to the Council, even where the Commission did not approve and incorporate them into its new proposal. However, Parliamentary amendments which were not taken up by the Commission could be adopted by unanimity only. It was also specified that should Council not take a decision by the end of the three months' deadline, then the proposal would fall. Whilst not as far-reaching as Parliament's proposal – supported by the Commission, Belgium and Italy – that its position should stand if Council failed to overrule it, this provision would at least place some pressure on Council to adopt the amended proposal rather than see the whole process come to nought. On the question of a deadline in Council's first reading, it was agreed to add to the acts of the Conference a declaration by the Presidency referring to the proposals to improve Council's internal procedures, and expressing the intention to do so as soon as possible. In presenting the results of the Conference to Parliament in January, the Dutch Presidency stressed the importance of this, which would require amending Council's Rules of Procedure: another strand of reform launched at the Milan Summit but left until after the IGC. Finally, they agreed to change the formal name of the EP from Assembly to European Parliament, thereby giving recognition in the treaties of the name the EP had given itself.

Court of Justice

The ECJ's workload had been growing for a number of years and it was further distracted from its main tasks by being the labour Court for Community officials. The EP, though not in the context of its draft Treaty, had been pressing for a subsidiary Court to be set up to deal with such matters.[75] The IGC was seized with the matter by a letter from the President of the ECJ. With, it seems, little controversy, the IGC approved a new article enabling Council, acting unanimously on a proposal of the ECJ and after consulting the Commission and the Parliament, to set up a subsidiary Court to deal with matters other than those submitted by Member States, Community institutions or by national jurisdictions according to Art. 177 EEC. A right of appeal to the full ECJ would remain on points of law. The internal rules of this Court would be drawn up in agreement with the ECJ and subject to unanimous Council approval. An easier procedure was also approved for reviewing certain aspects of the ECJ's statute. This could henceforth be done by the Council, acting unanimously at the request of the Court and after consulting the Commission and Parliament: no longer requiring treaty amendment.

Human Rights

The lack of any formal provision in the treaties requiring Community institutions to respect fundamental rights or requiring Member States to be democratic had been a subject of concern and was one of the issues addressed by Parliament's draft Treaty. The IGC agreed to include in the preamble to the Act, a reference to the joint promotion of democracy and human rights, and adding the European Social Charter to the list of references mentioned in the 1977 Joint Declaration: in effect taking up the list in Parliament's draft Treaty. However, merely adding the matter to the preamble, which was specifically excluded from the competence of the ECJ, limited the import of this inclusion in the Treaty.

Subjects not Included in the Final Compromise

The IGC failed to reach agreement on some matters, ostensibly because it decided to concentrate on the most important subjects. There was a reluctance to continue negotiations into 1986, with the French elections looming,[76] and some of the matters left open were ones on which agreement seemed difficult. They included culture (proposal by the Commission), development aid (Netherlands and Denmark), voting rights for EC residents (Denmark), energy (Denmark) and differentiation (France). This last proposal would allow the Community, where the unanimity required under Art. 235 for new policies was not attained, to take a decision that would only apply to those countries approving it, where such a decision would not affect the common market. This again flagged up the possibility of proceeding without all Member States.

RATIFICATION

The IGC closed with Danish and Italian reserves for opposite reasons, and every government put a different gloss on the result. Thatcher called the results 'clear and decisive', whilst assuring the House of Commons that the veto remained intact.[77] Delors called it a 'compromise of progress'. Mitterrand stated that 'some countries, including France, wanted more and will continue to demand it'.[78] Kohl stated that his country would have been prepared to go further, particularly as regards the Parliament's powers.[79] Schlüter said that he was satisfied with the results because ultimately they did not signify 'the slightest loss of sovereignty'.[80] Martens expressed satisfaction, but was criticized in Belgium for having accepted such a weak package and for not having taken the same position as Italy.[81] The Portuguese government stated that it would have preferred more progress in conferring new powers on the EP.[82]

In its January 1986 session, the EP was faced with adopting a position on the outcome of the IGC. The reserve of the Italian government implied that the EP's position would determine its acceptance by Italy, though unlike in December, there was little scope to use this constructively. Although it was far from the overall reform Parliament sought, most MEPs wished to avoid jeopardizing the package now that it was clear that negotiations were at an end, either because they felt the prospects of launching a future reform process would be weakened by its failure, or, in the case of MEPs from governing parties, a desire to avoid embarrassing their heads of government. Others felt that Parliament should reject the package as hopelessly inadequate (though not all were convinced that this really would lead to its non-ratification, but those who did hoped that this would provoke a crisis leading to more determined action by the majority states). The few Eurosceptics opposed the package for the opposite reason.

The Commission and a number of national governments exhorted MEPs to accept the package. Council President Van Eekelen travelled to Brussels to 'sell' the package to the bureau of the Committee on Institutional Affairs and the main Group spokesmen.[83] In the end, Parliament[84] reiterated its negative assessment of the package, but did so in such a way as to make it understood that it was not calling for non-ratification. The resolution reiterated Parliament's December assessment ('unable to accept in their present form'), stated that a genuine reform remained necessary (and that the Member States remain bound by their commitment to European Union) which Parliament would continue to push for using its contacts with national parliaments and drawing up new 'proposals for reform to be put to the citizens in the 1989 elections'. In the meantime, the EP announced its intention to 'exploit to the very limit the possibilities offered by the Single Act – if it is ratified', called on the governments to 'amend the internal rules of the Council' so as to compel it to hold a vote 'when the Commission or three Member States so request', thus indicating its expectation that the Act would, in fact, be ratified. Although there were misgivings about the ambiguity of the resolution, reflected in the support for some of the amendments that were tabled to it, the text reflected the dilemma in which MEPs found themselves.

Three crucial amendments[85] spelling out more specific alternative positions were rejected. They were:

1. No. 29 by Mr Hänsch and others: 'Refuses to give its agreement to the results': 77 votes for, 220 against, 7 abstentions. Supported by Italians from all Groups, German and Benelux Socialists, half of the Liberal Group, individual EPP and Greens.
2. No. 5 by Sir Jack Stewart Clark 'accepts with great reluctance . . . the results of the IGC': The vote was not recorded. Supported by European Democratic Group.
3. No 13 by Mr Megahy: 'The Act . . . is unacceptable on the basis that it gives too much power to EEC institutions': 41 votes for, 252 against, 1 abstention. Supported by UK Labour, Greek Communist, Danish anti-EC and some Greens.

This, then, cleared the way for Italy to ratify, though it maintained its reserve until after the debates in the Italian Parliament.[86] What, then, of Denmark? Here, the domestic political divisions were crucial. The minority centre-right coalition was willing to accept the Act. However, it relied in the Folketing on support from the Radicals (Radikale Venstre) on domestic matters, whilst trying to keep Social Democrat support on foreign affairs. Both these parties opposed the Act. In the case of the Social Democrats, the situation was complex. The party was divided on the EC, with the leadership supporting Danish membership but with a large minority opposed. The party as a whole felt pressure from the growing strength of the anti-EC Socialist People's Party. In this situation, there was little incentive to go out of its way to support the government: quite the contrary when it thought it could cause the government to fall on the issue. After intense internal discussion, it decided to oppose the SEA in the Folketing, which rejected it by a majority of five. Schlüter managed to outmanoeuvre the opposition, however, by calling a referendum, for which he had support from the Radicals. The Foreign Minister made a lightning tour of national capitals to establish that the other Member States were unwilling to reopen negotiations, as the Folketing resolution had requested. Indeed the Dutch Presidency emphasized this by calling a signing ceremony for the Act on 17 February – ten days before the referendum – which it hoped would be the occasion for the 11 to show their determination to the Danes. In fact, Greece refused to put such pressure, and Italy saw no reason to lift its reserve before Denmark, so the Act was signed by nine.[87] Both the Commission and the EP were represented by Vice-Presidents, showing their dissatisfaction with the Act.

The referendum campaign in Denmark centred on its continued membership of the Community. The government thought it could win by presenting the rejection of the SEA as a first step down the path to withdrawal. Many anti-marketeers were happy to campaign for withdrawal, thus making the government's tactic easier.[88] Although the Social Democrats tried to present the issue as the SEA alone, with no further implications, they had little success in this. Furthermore, many prominent party members and trade unions disagreed publicly with the party line, calling for a 'yes' vote. The referendum gave a 56 per cent majority for the reforms.[89]

Denmark, Greece and Italy added their signatures to the Act on 28 February. In signing Italy recorded a lengthy declaration in which it spelled out the reasons for its dissatisfaction, supported the revision of Council's rules of procedure, and called for a review before 1988 to extend the Act, particularly with regard to the EP's participation in the legislative process. This was followed by a joint Italo-Belgian communiqué in which they announced their intention to coordinate their action in this direction.

Before it came into force, the SEA suffered one further delay – a ruling of the Irish Supreme Court to the effect that it would require revision of the Irish constitution, and therefore a referendum. The new Haughey government – which in opposition had been critical of the SEA and might have been tempted to oppose the SEA to embarrass the Fitzergald government had the referendum been held earlier – obtained a large majority in favour of it with relative ease (opposition coming mainly from circles fearing the loss of Irish sovereignty or neutrality).

ASSESSMENT

A feature that distinguished this particular episode of reform from previous ones was its initiation by an elected Parliament. The EP aimed to set in motion a political process, avoiding or at least leaving the stage of intergovernmental negotiation until such time as sufficient political momentum had developed. In this respect, it was quite successful. Six of the ten national parliaments gave highly favourable treatment to the draft Treaty, two even calling on their governments to ratify as such. Political parties, trade unions, employers organizations and nongovernmental organizations all gave support to Parliament. Certainly, there was no mass mobilization of the general public (notwithstanding the demonstration at the Milan Summit): the issue was largely confined to political elites. Nevertheless, the political elites in all Member States became aware of Parliament's proposal and the issues it raised. In a sufficient number of Member States it generated enough support for it to become either opportune or necessary for the government to take it seriously and push for reform, in turn obliging other governments to discuss the issues. Thus, supporters of European integration were forced to take a stand, those reticent were obliged to accept debate and, ultimately, negotiation.

In 1981, few people thought that Parliament would get so far, or even that it could draw up proposals backed by its main political groups. When it did so, few expected national governments to take the matter seriously and when Mitterrand did so, many felt that this was a ploy for the European elections. When the European Council established the Dooge Committee on his proposal, and when the Dooge Committee also concluded that a new Treaty on European Union was necessary, it was easy to point to the opposition of three Member States. When the European Council overrode this opposition there were doubts as to whether these Member States would participate in the IGC, and when they did it was not at all clear that a Treaty revision would be approved. Yet, the momentum was sufficient to go through all of these stages, though not to achieve as far-reaching a reform as the EP would have liked.

In terms of the EP's three main objectives that we identified in chapter 7, it can be seen that the SEA did indeed extend the field of Community *competence* in the fields of economic and social cohesion, social policy, the environment, technological research and, potentially, EMU, albeit in a cautious way. The SEA also took up the idea of a deadline for achieving the single market. It formalized and linked to the Community the intergovernmental procedures for foreign policy cooperation, as proposed by the EP. As regards the *efficiency* of the institutional system, it provided for a small increase in the field in which the Council acts by qualified majority vote, and held out the prospect for greater use of qualified majority vote in practice. It provided for only a marginal reinforcement for the Commission's executive powers, the significance of which remained to be seen. Finally, it increased the legislative powers of the EP, albeit in a limited area and still falling short of genuine co-decision. It did not alter Parliament's role in the appointment of the Commission. These changes were small and incremental, and their significance would depend crucially on the implementation in practice, which we shall see in the next chapter. It was at the same time the first significant overhand of the treaties and a disappointment as compared to Parliament's initial aspirations.

If the result was disappointing, this was in part due to two reasons that the EP had itself pinpointed at the outset of the process. The first of these was the need for unanimity. Parliament had envisaged the possible establishment of a European Union without all the Member States of the Community joining. The precedent for this was the creation of the ECSC by six Member States of the Council of Europe in 1952. As we saw in chapter 7, the situation would be more complicated if such a manoeuvre were attempted *vis-à-vis* the Community, but it was feasible if it came to the crunch. Hints were dropped at various times, as we saw in chapter 8 and this one, that a 'hard core' might move ahead without the reticent states, at least in certain fields: it was perhaps because of this threat that the UK, Denmark and Greece prefered to participate and to make at least some concessions. But in doing so, they ensured that the IGC was based on Art. 236 and that the concessions they made would be limited.

The second was the involvement of national officials. There the essence of Parliament's analysis was, perhaps, simplistic. Pointing to the repeated declarations of heads of governments in favour of European

Union, and the opinion polls which consistently showed public support for the concept, it was easy to conclude that the blockage was taking place somewhere in between. Reality is, of course, somewhat more complex. Nevertheless, it is not unreasonable to suspect that national officials do have a vested interest in the status quo, and a preference for intergovernmental procedures in which their role is central.[90] On a number of occasions in the process, indications emerged that this was indeed a factor. In France, for example, Maurice Faure's first draft of the conclusions of the Dooge Committee was rumoured to have been approved by Mitterrand against the wishes of the Quai d'Orsay. French MEPs bemoaned the slowness with which foreign ministry officials took up the instructions of the political leadership.[91] Political statements by French leaders often seemed contradictory to those being taken by officials in negotiations.[92] *Le Monde* on 13 November referred to the distinction between the views of the President of the Republic and those of the administration. Other examples could be given for other countries, but it is clear that this is a factor not to be neglected.

Despite these obstacles, the threat of a majority move to European Union and the political momentum generated before the negotiations were no doubt useful in ensuring that the first general overhaul of the treaties since they were signed was actually carried through. In both these aspects, the EP played a role. Our hypothesis no. 11 would appear to be confirmed, but its significance would depend on the effective implementation of the treaty amendments. It is to this that we shall now turn our attention.

10 Making the Most of the Single European Act

We have seen how the EP's initial reaction to the SEA was far from enthusiastic, but that it resolved, on the one hand, 'to exploit to the very limit the possibilities offered' and, on the other hand, to prepare the way for further reform. This chapter will examine the impact of the SEA, dwelling in particular on how Parliament attempted to exploit it. The next chapter will examine how Parliament relaunched its campaign for European Union.

The institutional changes introduced by the SEA, all partly achieving changes sought by the EP, affected all four institutions. There was an increase in majority voting in Council, a reinforcement of the Commission's executive powers, a strengthening of the Court of Justice's ability to ensure judicial review and to apply the law, and an increase in Parliament's own powers. In all four cases, the importance of the SEA depended on how the limited reforms it introduced would be implemented in practice. We shall now examine these in turn. Did the constitutional changes create new possibilities for integration? Was more space available for incremental advance?

INCREASED MAJORITY VOTING IN COUNCIL

The SEA extended qualified majority voting to a limited number of articles. Many of these concerned the internal market: Arts 28, 59.2, 70.1, 84, 100(a) and 100(b) and the provisions concerning pharmacists, doctors and bankers formerly in Art. 57.2. Others were Art. 56, parts of Art. 118, and the new articles on the regional fund, various implementing measures on research, health and safety at work, and, potentially, environmental matters.

The importance of this extension was not immediately clear. After all, even where qualified majority voting was already allowed under the Treaties, this had been a somewhat rare occurrence, and some governments indicated that they continued to interpret the 'Luxembourg compromise' as giving them a right of veto. The 'Luxembourg compromise' itself, not being part of the Treaties, could not be modified by a Treaty amendment, and was not discussed in the IGC.

Parliament had urged Council to modify its Rules of Procedure in order to encourage the actual use of majority voting. Such a change had been envisaged at the 1985 Milan Summit, but the issue had been left open pending the IGC. Following the signature of the SEA, it still took Council over a year to reach an agreement on a change to its Rules allowing the President or the Commission or the representative of any Member State to request a vote. If this request is supported by a simple majority, then the President is obliged to move to a vote. Notice of items susceptible to a vote is indicated two weeks in advance to Member States.

How did these changes work in practice? There was a striking increase in the number of votes taken in Council. This began in some areas after the signing of the SEA but before its entry into force, thus demonstrating that a political taboo had been broken. The pressures described in our synthesis in chapter 1 would appear to have played a role.

Precise statistics as to the number of votes in Council were hard to come by and Council deliberations continued to be bound by the rule of secrecy. Nevertheless, Council has indicated that in the first half of 1985, there were about 12 votes; in the first half of 1986, there were over 40.[1] During the first ten months of the Single Act, there were over 70 and also many 'decisions without a formal vote where it is clear that the required majority exists'.[2] Nor were these votes confined to non-controversial areas. Votes were taken on emission standards for cars, a ban on hormones in meat (leading to a 'trade war' with the USA), permitted radioactivity levels in foodstuffs, rules for transfrontier television broadcasts, several fishing controversies, foreign aid and some of the crucial reforms in the CAP. Interestingly, there were cases in which Member States in the minority challenged a vote in the Court on the grounds of an incorrect legal base (arguing that an article requiring unanimity should have been used) rather than invoke the 'Luxembourg compromise' during the vote.[3]

Indeed, there was a reluctance by Member States subscribing to restrictive interpretations of the Luxembourg compromise to invoke it, lest they find that the compromise would not be sustained. At the same time the others were reluctant to push them to the point at which they might invoke it. This state of creative ambiguity derived also from the fact that with enlargement to Spain and Portugal, it was not clear whether Member States seeking to invoke the compromise would have sufficient support in Council to constitute a blocking minority.

The Commission and the EP were keen to ensure that, wherever possible, proposals were based on Treaty articles allowing a vote in

Council. There were a number of areas in which the choice was not self-evident. On occasion, Council modified a Commission proposal to adopt as a legal base an article requiring unanimity. This gave rise to a number of cases where the Commission took the Council to the Court of Justice in order to establish that a legal base requiring a majority vote was the appropriate one.[4]

Thus, the SEA treaty changes, the modification of Council's Rules of Procedure, the greater ambiguity surrounding the nature of the Luxembourg compromise, pressure from the Commission and Parliament and the deadline of 1992 to adopt a considerable volume of single market legislation all contributed to a greater willingness within Council to make use of the possibility of taking majority votes. This contributed significantly to improvements of Council's decision-taking efficiency. However, crucial areas still required unanimity including most environmental legislation, harmonization of indirect taxation, the framework programme for research, free movement of persons, workers' rights, coordination of the structural funds, development, cooperation, monetary integration and appointments.

STRENGTHENING THE EXECUTIVE POWERS OF THE COMMISSION

We have seen how, in its draft Treaty, the EP sought to give the Commission full executive powers,[5] in other words to do away with the rigidities of the comitology system. In the SEA, the Member States added a provision[6] obliging Council to confer implementing powers on the Commission. However, at the same time it allowed Council to lay down 'principles and rules' for the exercise of these powers, and also, in specific cases, to exercise implementing powers itself. The IGC annexed to the Single Act a unanimous Declaration[7] in which Member States agreed that priority should be given to the Advisory Committee procedure for matters falling under Art. 100a (internal market). Advisory Committees, being purely consultative, would not have the power to block the Commission.

An implementing decision was thus required to lay down the 'principles and rules' to be followed. The Commission put forward a proposal[8] which would still allow committees of national civil servants to be set up, but which would streamline them into three types: Advisory (purely consultative), Management (able to refer a Commission decision to Council by *opposing* it by a qualified majority) and Regulatory (where the draft decision would be blocked and referred to Council if it were not *approved* by a qualified majority). If a measure was referred to Council, the latter would have a period not exceeding three months to adopt an alternative measure by a qualified majority, failing which the Commission decision would stand (in the case of Management committee procedure) or to approve a Commission proposal by a qualified majority or amend it unanimously[9] (in the case of Regulatory Committee). A decision of some sort was at least guaranteed within a reasonable deadline. In its opinion on this proposal,[10] Parliament sought to delete the Regulatory committee formula.

Council's implementing decision of 13 July 1987[11] took no account of Parliament's opinion and modified the Commission's initial proposal in order to increase the blocking powers of national civil servants. It kept the three procedures (baptizing them procedures I, II and III respectively) but modified them, notably by introducing variants and adding a fourth procedure for safeguard measures (mainly trade). The most important weakening of the Commission's proposal was to introduce a 'variant B' to procedure III such that Council, by a simple majority, could continue to block a Commission proposal referred to it even after the three month deadline, and *even when it could not agree on an alternative decision*. This would open the possibility of no implementing measures to enact principles already agreed in Community legislation. Similarly, under variant B of the safeguard procedure a Commission decision would be annulled if it were not *confirmed* by a qualified majority within Council.

Following this decision, the Commission stated that it was firmly opposed to procedure III (b) and safeguard (b) and that it would never put forward a proposal – nor be party to a compromise – that would incorporate either of these implementing procedures in a piece of Community legislation.[12] It issued a declaration regretting that the Council had adopted these procedures and deploring that Council did not fix a deadline for adapting existing procedures to the new framework. For its part, Parliament decided to take the Council to the Court of Justice on the ground that this decision did not conform to the intention of the Single Act, which was to strengthen the Commission's executive powers. However, the Court ruled that Parliament did not have the right to bring proceedings for annulment before the Court under Art. 173 EEC, and did not deal with the substance of the matter.

The issue therefore had to be fought out in each and every legislative proposal containing implementing procedures. The Commission indeed refrained from proposing procedure III (b) and safeguard (b) which meant that Council, if it wished to use these procedures, had to amend the Commission proposal by unanimity. Parliament too took part in this battle by amending legislative proposals containing unacceptable 'comitology' procedures. In order to avoid the various parliamentary committees adopting a divergent approach, the meeting of committee chairmen agreed on the following guidelines, subsequently endorsed by Parliament.[13]

1. In first reading, Parliament should systematically delete any provisions for procedure III (a) or III (b) and replace it by procedure II (a) or (b), or, for proposals concerning the internal market put forward under Article 100 A of the EEC Treaty, procedure I. Alternatively, when the subject matter is particularly important or sensitive, Parliament could provide for decisions to be made by the legislative procedure instead.

2. In second reading, Parliament should continue to oppose any provisions in a common position for procedure III (b), but III (a) could be accepted exceptionally, as a compromise, except for proposals concerning the internal market put forward under Article 100 A of the EEC Treaty, where II (b) should be the maximum acceptable compromise.

Comitology provisions pursuant to Article 145 are unacceptable for taking decisions concerning expenditure, as Article 205 EEC specifies that the Commission *alone* should be responsible for implementing the budget approved by Parliament.

Parliament generally stuck to these guidelines, although it often accepted Council common positions where they include procedure III(a) as part of a general compromise. The results have been mixed.[14] Despite pressure from the other institutions, Council did not respect the Declaration annexed to the SEA: from the entry into force of the Act until January 1990 it introduced the advisory committee procedure into only 14 Acts under Article 100 A (while the Commission proposed it 40 times) and, for all internal market measures, 32 times (out of 109 proposed). On the other hand, the use of procedure III (b), safeguard (b) or the reservation by Council of executive powers to itself were kept to a minimum.

Despite all this, the Commission has significant leeway. The bottom line is that, when it is determined to see its implementing measures through, the Commission can do so easily under procedure I, relatively easily under procedure II where it needs only a blocking minority in the committee to support it and where, even if a decision is referred to Council, a blocking minority would also be sufficient to see the Commission decision stand. Under procedure III(a), a Commission proposal to Council requires unanimity in Council to amend it. This is paradoxically more difficult than under procedure II as it falls under the provision of Article 149 (1) EEC whereby Council may only depart from a Commission proposal by unanimity. Again, a determined Commission can see its position through at the end of the day unless the Member States are unanimous in wishing to modify it. Only under procedure III(b) can the Commission be blocked by a simple majority.[15] Provided it has a simple majority with it, it can ultimately see its position through.

Thus, as a result of the SEA, the 'comitology' procedures have at least been standardized and implementing decisions of some sort are guaranteed under all but two procedures. Nevertheless, from the EP's viewpoint, the problem of democratic scrutiny remained. Only national civil servants monitored the Commission, and if they were to block a Commission decision, the matter would be referred to the Council alone.

Parliament made attempts to compensate for this lack of scrutiny. In 1988 it reached an agreement with the Commission through an exchange of letters between Presidents Plumb and Delors whereby all draft implementing measures, with the exception of routine management documents with a limited period of validity and documents whose adoption is complicated by considerations of secrecy or urgency, are forwarded to Parliament at the same time as they are forwarded to the 'comitology'-type committees in question. Parliament changed its Rules to require these drafts to be referred to the Parliamentary Committee responsible. When a Committee is dissatisfied with a Commission proposal, the relevant member of the Commission can be invited to the Committee to discuss the matter. In urgent situations, notably between meetings, the Committee chairman may contact the responsible Commissioner directly. If the Committee remains dissatisfied, it may, if the importance of the matter warrants such action, take the matter up in plenary.[16]

On Parliament's other objective concerning the Commission, namely a change in the procedure for appointing it, the SEA introduced no change, leaving on the record a statement by President Delors supporting the previous 'pragmatic' procedure. This was indeed followed again in 1988–9, with the new Commission delaying its oath-taking ceremony at the Court of Justice until after it had received a vote of confidence from Parliament.

STRENGTHENING THE CAPACITY OF THE COURT OF JUSTICE

We have seen how the SEA modified the treaties in order to allow Council to attach to the Court of Justice (ECJ), and at its request, a new Court of First Instance (CFI) with jurisdiction to hear certain categories of cases and with appeals to the ECJ on points of law only.[17]

The ECJ lost no time in taking up this opportunity. Even before the ratification of the SEA, it submitted working drafts to the Presidents of the Council, Parliament and Commission in November 1986. It was able to take into account the initial reactions to these when it submitted its formal proposals[18] to Council on 29 September 1987 – two months after the entry into force of the SEA. Council duly referred them to the Commission and the Parliament for an opinion and to Coreper to prepare its own deliberations. The discussions in the various institutions centred on three main problems: the scope of the CFI's jurisdiction, the number of Judges and the need for Advocates General.

In its initial proposal, the ECJ proposed that the CFI should deal with cases concerning staff, competition law, anti-dumping and subsidy cases and cases arising under the ECSC Treaty. It considered that this area of jurisdiction could be extended later, notably in the area of actions for damages. However, despite support from the EP and the majority of Member States, there was opposition to the inclusion of anti-dumping and subsidy cases from the Commission and at least one Member State. Notwithstanding a special plea put forward by the President of the European Court before Council,[19] the compromise finally reached in Council left these outside the jurisdiction of the CFI. This was strongly criticized on the grounds that such cases raise complex questions of fact which the CFI should be ideally suited to investigate, they are immensely time-consuming, and without them the new Court could be underemployed. Council did agree to add an additional paragraph in which it undertook to review this matter after two years of operation of the CFI. When this review took place, on the basis of a Court of Justice proposal in 1991, the Council took two years to decide to extend the CFI's jurisdiction to hear all actions brought by natural or legal persons, except – still – those concerning anti-dumping and anti-subsidy measures.[20]

The ECJ had proposed that the CFI consist of seven Members sitting in two specialized chambers. The Commission, the Parliament and ultimately the Council agreed that it should consist of 12, but sometimes able to sit in chambers of three or five judges.

As regards Advocates General, the ECJ had proposed dispensing with them as their fundamental role, namely assisting with the development of Community law, was dispensable at the CFI, whose main characteristic would be the verification of facts. Parliament, in its opinion, considered that three Advocates General should be appointed in addition to the Judges. It argued that their absence might lead to the CFI being seen merely as a Court of preparatory inquiry establishing facts, leaving the decision on legal issues to the ECJ on appeal. In that case, the ECJ's workload would scarcely be eased. The presence of Advocates General would enable judgments to be argued in greater depth giving the CFI greater authority.[21] The Commission also supported the inclusion of Advocates General. Council adopted a compromise providing[22] that, in certain cases, members of the CFI may be called upon to perform the task of an Advocate General. They are therefore not additional to the number of Judges but designated among them on an *ad hoc* basis.

The Council decision was adopted on 24 October 1988[23] – less than 16 months after the entry into force of the SEA. The CFI began work at the end of 1989, contributing to an increase in the efficiency of the judicial system of the Community.

THE EUROPEAN PARLIAMENT

We have seen how the SEA also provided for an increase in the powers of the Parliament which fell short of a general right of co-decision on Community legislation. The Act introduced two new procedures for associating the EP with the adoption of Community Acts:[24]

- the *assent procedure*, which required approval by an absolute majority of members of the EP for the accession of new Member States to the Community and for association agreements with third countries;
- the *cooperation procedure* introducing a second reading for certain items of Community legislation, including most of the legislative harmonizations necessary for the internal market.

In line with its stated intention to 'exploit to the very limit' the possibilities offered by the Act, Parliament made use of these procedures, as well as other developments resulting from the SEA, in order to maximize its influence.

The Assent Procedure

Parliament dealt with some 34 assent procedures during the first two years of the Single Act. This number is higher than some governments had imagined when signing the SEA. Sir Michael Butler, UK Permanent Representative to the EC at the time, was of the opinion that there would be no assent procedure before the 1989 elections.[25] However, the procedure applied not only to the initial association agreements with third countries but also to any modifications or supplements to these agreements, including additional protocols such as financial protocols. The Community had association agreements with almost all the Mediterranean countries and one with the 69 signatories to the Lomé Convention, which were thereby brought under these provisions.

Three examples show how Parliament made use of this power. In December 1987, it simply postponed its vote on an agreement with Turkey in protest at the arrest of the leaders of two political parties upon their return to Turkey, accompanied by MEPs, for elections. It later approved the protocol in early 1988. More spectacular was Parliament's initial refusal to give its assent to three agreements with Israel. Parliament was unhappy with the conditions for exports to the Community for Palestinian producers in the occupied territories. The dispute occurred at the time of the beginning of the Intifada in the West Bank and Gaza. Parliament therefore rejected three protocols to the EEC/Israel Association Agreement. The agreements were referred back to Council. Council in turn referred them back to Parliament, which agreed to put the proposals back on its agenda, but postponed consideration of them for several months. During this period the Commission, as well as MEPs, had discussions with Israeli representatives, which produced some concessions on West Bank exports. Parliament then approved the protocols. Finally, Parliament refused its assent to financial protocols with Syria and Morocco in 1992 to protest at the human rights situation in these countries. This caused a serious diplomatic rift with Morocco in particular, which refused, in retaliation, to renew a fishing agreement with the Community.

The assent procedure gave Parliament real power, albeit for one category only of international agreements entered into by the EC, and essentially of an obstructive nature, but which it tried to use constructively. In any case, it put Parliament 'on the map' as far as third countries were concerned, with a corresponding increase in the lobbying of Parliament by their representatives.[26] It also held promise for the future when any enlargement of the EC would require Parliament's approval, which would give it the opportunity to block accession if it felt the conditions were unacceptable. As accessions require changes to the Treaty, they would be an opportunity for Parliament to press for certain Treaty changes.

The Cooperation Procedure

We have seen how the 'cooperation procedure' – limited to ten articles – amounted essentially to a second consultation of the EP in more difficult conditions (needing an absolute majority to propose amendments and unable to use delaying tactics) than traditional practice in its single reading. Yet the EP has managed to squeeze more out of the procedure than may have seemed likely at first sight. Let us look in detail at the options available to Parliament and how it has made use of them.

In the new second reading, Parliament receives Council's 'common position' and has three months to do one of three things:

1. explicitly approve the text, or by remaining silent approve it tacitly, in which case Council must adopt the Act in question in accordance with the common position;
2. reject the text, in which case it will fall unless Council decides unanimously within three months (and effectively with the agreement of the Commission which can always withdraw the proposal) to overrule Parliament;
3. propose amendments which, if supported by the Commission, are incorporated into a revised proposal which Council can only modify by unanimity, whereas a qualified majority will suffice to adopt it. Council has three months to choose one of these options, failing which the proposal falls. Any amendments not supported by the Commission require unanimity to be adopted by Council.

In these last two cases (i.e. rejection or amendment of a common position), Parliament can act by a majority of its members only. The three months' deadline may be extended to four months by joint agreement between Council and Parliament.

Case (1) is straightforward: Parliament finds that it can accept Council's position and Council must adopt the Act accordingly. Case (2) arises rarely, but is important both as a matter of principle (Parliament considers that if it, as the elected assembly, rejects draft legislation then it should fall) and as a matter of tactics: if sustainable rejection is a credible threat, Parliament can put more pressure on the other institutions to accept its amendments. In this respect it is important to note that until 1995 in all but one case when Parliament rejected a common position, either Council was unable to find the necessary unanimity to proceed, or else the Commission withdrew the proposal.

This brings us to option (3) – the most common scenario. At first sight it would appear that parliamentary amendments not incorporated in the text in the first reading seem unlikely to fare better in the second reading, when Council's positions have been fixed. However, Parliament has two extra levers not available in the first reading. The first is to use the threat of rejection as a means of putting pressure on the *Commission*. The Commission is almost invariably keen on seeing the legislation through, and Parliamentary rejection will either cause the text to fall or at the very least will bring back a unanimity requirement in Council, which severely limits the Commission's own margin of manoeuvre. The Commission is therefore likely to incline towards accepting at least some amendments that it would otherwise have refused, rather than risk Parliamentary rejection. In order to maximize this leverage, Parliament revised its Rules to provide for the Commission to announce its position in Parliament in the second reading *before* the final vote on the amendments tabled, thus allowing Parliament to use the option of rejection if it is not satisfied with the Commission's response.

The second lever is time pressure. The three months' deadline on Council is an extra constraint on it. As in its first reading, Council may well be faced with a Commission proposal that incorporates Parliamentary amendments that many Council members do not like. But whereas in the first reading, Council has unlimited time to explore compromises among its members, this is not the case in the second reading. The easy option is therefore to return to its first reading position, but this will only be possible if it is unanimous. If it is not unanimous – even if only one Member State agrees with the Commission/Parliament position – this will be difficult. The other states may be forced to choose under time pressure whether to accept something that is not quite what they wanted, or to lose the proposal entirely – something that, by that stage, is also unattractive. Of course, a qualified majority must still be found to accept the text – nothing can be imposed by a minority that the majority finds totally unacceptable – and Member States supporting the Commission/Parliament position may well back down, especially if they are in a small minority. Much depends on the exact circumstances and how Council divides. But to obtain either the qualified majority needed to approve the amended proposal or the unanimity to change it, there will often be a need for further negotiations and compromise under time pressure, with it being easier to find a qualified majority than to find unanimity.

What evidence is there of real EP impact on legislation adopted under the cooperation procedure? An analysis[27] of the first four years (July 1987–September 1991) shows that, for the 208 procedures:

In first reading:
- Parliament approved 50 of them and amended the 158 others;
- The Commission accepted 1626 of the 2734 amendments adopted by Parliament (i.e. 60%) and modified its proposals to Council accordingly;
- Council approved 1216 of the 2734 parliamentary amendments (i.e. 45%).

In second reading:
- Parliament approved without amendment almost half (90) of the Council common positions;
- In 127 cases, Parliament adopted a total of 716 amendments to the common position, 366 of which (48%) were supported by the Commission and 194 (27%) by Council;
- In one case, Parliament rejected a common position and the text fell as Council was unable to overrule Parliament by unanimity within three months.[28]

Of course, these figures take no account of the importance of various amendments, nor, of course, of the discussion and bargaining that can lead to the withdrawal of amendments before they are voted on, or conversely, the adoption of 'no-hope' amendments merely to put pressure on for a compromise. Furthermore, the Commission or Council sometimes agree to take up Parliament's amendments in another way such as in another or a new directive, or simply give a political undertaking to Parliament. Often it is the *backing* given to a Commission proposal by Parliament that is politically important. None of this can be reflected in the figures. What is clear is that Parliament entered the traditional Commission–Council dialogue, and had a perceptible impact. The take-up rate for parliamentary amendments bears comparison to certain individual chambers in national parliaments.

In any case, the second reading gave Parliament a chance to react to Council's position, provided some added scope to use public opinion, and introduced a more publicly visible way for dealing with parliamentary amendments. The ritual of two readings helped create an impression of classic bicameral legislative procedure being followed at European level – an important consideration in view of the next set of reforms.

A good example of how Parliament used these powers was when in 1989 it considered exhaust emission standards for small cars. Here, it was faced with a Council common position that fell below the standards it supported in its first reading. Parliament was keen on raising these standards to levels equivalent to those required in, for instance, the USA and Sweden, and it was known that some Member States shared Parliament's concern, but had been in a minority in Council. Parliament's committee on the environment therefore prepared second reading amendments for higher standards. Pressure was put on the Commission to accept these amendments before Parliament took its final vote, by making clear that if the Commission did not do so, Parliament would instead reject the common position, and the legislation would fall as there was clearly no unanimity within Council to overrule Parliament. The Commission therefore accepted Parliament's amendments which were duly incorporated into a revised proposal. Council then had three months in which either to approve it by a qualified majority, or to amend it by unanimity (which it could not do as at least three Member States agreed with Parliament) or to see it fall (which would have created havoc in the car industry with uncertainty and division in the internal market while the whole procedure started again). A reluctant majority in Council therefore adopted the revised text.

Less spectacularly, but with notable impact, Parliament used these powers among other things to strengthen consumer protection in package holidays, to tighten rules on insider trading, to provide for greater transparency in the pricing of pharmaceuticals, to limit advertising on transfrontier broadcasts to 15 per cent of transmission time, to raise minimum standards for safety and health at work (and to provide for information and consultation procedures for workers in this context), to modify the content of Community research programmes (notably to boost research on cancer and AIDS), to ensure transparency in methods of calculating and advertising consumer credit, to make car insurance regulations when travelling abroad more favourable to victims, to ban hormones in meat, and to support the proposed ban on tobacco advertising – all examples affecting both major sectoral interests and the wider public. MEPs at last had examples to show that the EP was not just a talking shop.

Other Developments Arising from the Cooperation Procedure

Legal Base of Proposal

The choice of the Treaty article on which to base legislative proposal now became crucial. It determined whether the matter would fall under the cooperation procedure or not. In most cases, the choice clearly followed from the text of the treaty. In some cases, however, there was a scope for interpretation. For instance, emission standards could be either a legislative harmonization necessary to ensure fair competition within the internal market (legal base Art. 100 (A): cooperation procedure and majority voting in Council) or a purely environmental measure (Article 130 (S): simple consultation of Parliament and unanimity in Council). Parliament was naturally keen to ensure a broad interpretation of the scope of the cooperation procedure and when it revised its Rules to take account of the SEA, it laid down a procedure for challenging the legal base, allowing the committee responsible, after consulting the Committee on Legal Affairs, to report straight back to the plenary on this point alone.

Parliament and Commission usually reached agreement on the legal base. For instance, they agreed on all but seven of the 145 proposals outstanding when the SEA came into force.[29] In 1990 in the context of the 'code of conduct' (see below) the Commission and Parliament agreed to contacts 'between their legal services by far-reaching exchanges of view, whenever the Commission is preparing to take new initiatives in new areas',[30] to try to avoid disagreements on their legal base. However, some important disagreements led to Parliament challenging both the Commission and Council.

A spectacular disagreement arose on a proposal for maximum permitted radioactivity levels for foodstuffs,[31] where the limits agreed after Chernobyl needed to be replaced by a permanent measure to avoid separate national measures fragmenting the internal market for foodstuffs. Here, the Commission avoided the cooperation procedure by using a Euratom Treaty legal base, requiring only the consultation of Parliament. Parliament first sought to amend the legal base and then, when the Commission refused to accept this, delayed giving its opinion. This forced Council to prolong the existing (temporary) regulation with its stringent limit values. Parliament then gave its opinion rejecting the Commission's proposal. This allowed Council to take a decision which Parliament then attacked in the Court of Justice on the ground of an incorrect legal base. However, it lost.[32]

The Commission and Parliament did agree on using 100 (A) as the basis for harmonizing environmental standards applicable to the titanium dioxide industry, but *Council* modified it to 130 (S), which not only avoided the cooperation procedure but also required unanimity in Council and reduced the resultant legislation to the lowest common denominator. The Commission, with Parliament support, successfully challenged Council's decision in the Court. Parliament was also successful in challenging the legal base imposed by Council for adopting the directive on the right of residence for students and their dependants. Council had (by unanimity) changed the legal base proposed by the Commission (Art. 7 requiring cooperation procedure with Parliament and qualified majority voting in Council) to a more restrictive one (Art. 235 requiring only consultation of Parliament and unanimity in Council).

Thus, Parliament was not without success in preventing the scope of the cooperation procedure from being eroded by the other institutions.

Reconsultation of Parliament

When Council adopts a common position which contains new elements on which Parliament did not express an opinion in first reading, it must *reconsult* Parliament. Parliament then carries out another first reading. Moving straight to the second reading would not allow Parliament to exercise its full rights under the cooperation procedure, especially as it has limited itself in second reading to tabling amendments that conform to its first reading position or represent compromises. Despite initial reluctance, Council accepted in principle to reconsult Parliament in such circumstances. None the less, Parliament has often had to go to the Court when Council failed to reconsult it when substantially modifying a Commission proposal, often winning its case.[33]

Parliament managed to convince Council to reconsult Parliament whenever it decides to amend a legal base to an article that would otherwise not require a second reading.[34] In these cases, Parliament receives a 'common orientation' (instead of a 'common position') of Council.

In April 1990, the Commission undertook to 'ensure that Council respects [its obligations] for reconsulting Parliament' and to 'bring proceedings before the Court of Justice to annul any act adopted by the Council without duly reconsulting Parliament'.[35]

Council and Commission Explanations to Parliament

The SEA introduced a requirement for Council and Commission[36] to inform the EP fully of the reasons which led Council to adopt its common position. However, the first justifications received were deemed to be unsatisfactory by Parliament.[37] Following a formal statement to the House by Parliament's President Lord Plumb on 28 October 1987 and two resolutions on 18 November 1987 threatening Council with legal action,[38] Council's explanations improved to the extent that they provide an account of its viewpoint on each of the substantive issues raised. This was a considerable improvement but still fell short of the request by President Plumb that 'as a minimum, the Council should provide a specific and explained reaction to each of Parliament's amendments'.[39] Parliament also pressed for Council to reveal the positions taken by each of its members during votes, and this was eventually conceded in 1992, though in practice, this information was usually available informally.

Contacts, Negotiations and Dialogue with the Council and the Commission

The increase of its formal powers strengthened the EP's position in the discussions with other institutions that inevitably accompany consideration of legislative proposals. The only *formal* procedure for negotiating with Council was the 1975 conciliation procedure but its limitation to legislation with financial implications meant that it could only be combined with the cooperation procedure in two areas (Research Programmes and Regional Fund). Parliament pressed for an extension,[40] but Council was reluctant to combine the two procedures, and only one case arose where the conciliation procedure was used during a cooperation procedure, namely for the review of the Regional Fund.

Dialogue with Council also takes place through the regular appearances of the Presidents of the various specialized Councils before the responsible Parliamentary Committees. These have become an opportunity to discuss – formally in the meeting or informally in the corridor – parliamentary amendments to legislative proposals being considered by Council. The Commission also reports to parliamentary committees on developments in Council.

Parliament also explored new forms of dialogue with Council. A provision to this effect was added to Parliament's Rules. Meetings and correspondence between committee chairmen/rapporteurs and Council presidents have increased.[41] Contacts between officials in the committee secretariats and their counterparts in the Commission and Council have also improved, especially after the transfer of most such EP officials from Luxembourg to Brussels.

After the signing of the SEA, the Commission reviewed its mechanisms for contact with the EP. In this review, it stated that the establishment of the cooperation procedure 'exigera une approche qualitativement différente, garantissant que chaque proposition tienne compte dès le stade de la conception de la nécessité de receuillir l'approbation du Parlement'.[42] It therefore encouraged 'consultation préalable' with the Parliament whereby the Commission would sound out MEPs before formalizing the Commission's initial legislative proposals. This would be done informally by contacts with the responsible parliamentary committees, rapporteurs, spokespersons of political groups and their staff.[43] It was further decided that the Commission officials following discussions in parliamentary committees should be the same as those following discussions in Coreper, and that Commissioners themselves should participate more systematically in EP committee discussions on legislative proposals.[44] It was agreed that every Directorate General in the Commission should have a parliamentary officer to assist and coordinate relations with the Parliament and in particular the competent parliamentary committee. An interinstitutional working party at the level of officials was instituted to cooperate at a technical level in the application of the legislative procedures.[45] All these measures enhanced the dialogue between MEPs and the Commission[46] and expanded the network of contacts that we identified in chapter 3 as an important feature.

For its part, when revising its Rules of Procedure to take advantage of the SEA, Parliament provided for a procedure to negotiate with the Commission on an *annual legislative programme* and timetable. Arguing that this was needed to manage its workload, Parliament was exploiting the fact that (unlike some national parliaments) it is master of its own agenda, and this persuaded the Commission of the advantages of negotiating an agreed programme with it. The first such programme was agreed in March 1988. This opened the door for Parliament to influence the priorities in the Commission's programme and to press for the inclusion of new items (e.g. following up parliamentary 'initiative' reports) or even the exclusion of items.

Most years have seen discussions centre on a joint declaration of priorities and on the scheduling of proposals, but in 1990 they spilled over into a revision of Commission–Parliament relations generally. Agreement was reached on a '*code of conduct*' in which the Commission accepted a number of improvements to its cooperation with Parliament. Besides the commitments mentioned earlier (concerning the choice of legal base for proposed legislation and the requirement to reconsult Parliament when proposals are significantly modified by

Council), the Commission undertook to support extended use of the assent procedure for international agreements, to include MEPs as observers in delegations negotiating major international agreements, to keep EP Committees informed of 'the main positions arising from discussions in the Council', to act in Council meetings to ensure that no political agreements are reached until the Council has 'had a reasonable period of time to consider Parliament's opinion' and that, upon request, a member of the Commission will explain to the competent EP Committee at its next meeting the reasons for failing to accept amendments at second reading.[47]

Parliament and European Political Cooperation

The SEA[48] charged the Presidency with informing Parliament on EPC matters and ensuring its views are taken into account. This was spelled out in more detail in the 'Decision of the Foreign Ministers on the occasion of the signing of the Single European Act' which specified that the Presidency reports to Parliament at the beginning and end of each six-month term of office; holds colloquies four times a year with Parliament's Committee on Political Affairs as well as special information sessions as required; sends an annual written report to Parliament; forwards texts adopted by the Ministers and replies to resolutions of major importance on which Parliament requests its comments.

These provisions were largely a codification of previous practices. The first year of the Single Act brought no innovations other than the regular attendance of the new EPC Secretariat, usually its head, at meetings of Parliament's Committee on Political Affairs. Under the Spanish Presidency of Council in 1989, better procedures were developed for responding to Parliament resolutions and for improved liaison between the Presidency and Parliament between the 'colloquies'. Parliament also sought to involve the Commission in reporting on and discussing EPC matters on the basis of the Commission's full participation therein and its joint responsibility with the Presidency for ensuring consistency between EPC and the Community's external policy. This was in line with Parliament's objective of bringing EPC more into the Community framework. Parliament's use of its new competences under the assent procedure in the Community framework to pursue political foreign policy objectives (as in the rejection of the Israeli protocols) was also a way of developing the overlap between the two frameworks. Parliament also tried to encourage a broad interpretation of 'political and economic aspects of security' by adopting reports on security matters, and by maintaining a security and disarmament sub-committee.

Budget Procedure

The SEA did not amend the budgetary provisions of the Treaties but its commitments to greater economic cohesion, research and new policies necessitated an increase in the ceiling of Community resources. This was approved on the basis of the 'Delors package' agreed at the European Council of February 1988 in Brussels. It took over a year of intensive negotiations among Member States, the results of which, under Art. 201 EEC, required national ratification – virtually a small IGC and treaty revision. The outcome was very close to the order of magnitude of increased Community resources sought by the Commission[49] and backed strongly by Parliament, which had set up a special Temporary Committee on this. This Committee gave a higher profile to the issue and, again, a pattern emerged of Parliament's Groups and MEPs making the case for an increase in resources towards national political parties in parallel to the Commission's efforts towards national governments and administrations.

Some of the increases in expenditure foreseen required an increase in the level of the maximum rate applicable to increases of non-compulsory expenditure (NCE) for which Parliament has the final power to allocate funds. Theoretically, Parliament could have used its power to allocate new resources for the expansion of other policies than those intended by Council. As we saw in chapter 4, this was among the considerations which induced Council to agree in June 1988 to an *interinstitutional agreement* proposed by Parliament. Under the terms of this agreement,[50] expenditure ceilings were agreed laying down ceilings on six categories of expenditure covering the whole of the Community's general budget for each year until 1992. Where these would result in increases beyond the maximum rate, Council and Parliament would be deemed to have jointly agreed on the new rate necessary. Parliament effectively agreed to use its powers to allocate non-compulsory expenditure in such a way as to allow the orderly doubling of the structural funds as sought by the European Council (something Parliament had in any case strongly argued for) in return for a guarantee that other sectors of interest to Parliament would not be frozen. Parliament also gained, for the first time, a veto over excessive increases in agricultural expenditure as the ceilings could only be raised with the assent of both Council and Parliament. The agreement made the annual budgetary discussions less conflictual, with ceilings and the main pattern of expenditure agreed in advance. Nevertheless, the framework has not prevented Parliament and Council agreeing jointly to revise the ceilings when necessary, for instance, in response to developments in Eastern Europe requiring Community financial aid.

Change in Balance of Parliament's Activity

The increase in its legislative work, arising both from the introduction of two readings and from the growing volume of Community legislation generally, led to a shift of emphasis in Parliament's work. The number of legislative resolutions (opinions, second readings and assents) doubled between 1985 (132) and 1989 (264) rising further to reach 311 in 1991, whereas the number of non-legislative resolutions fell (352 in 1986, 341 in 1989, 271 in 1991) despite recourse to delegated adoption of some such resolutions by committees.

ASSESSMENT

In this chapter, we have concentrated on the main institutional changes brought about by the SEA. A few words must be said about the strengthening of Community competences and how the SEA affected the development of policies in practice. This varies from one domain to another.

The single market process certainly gained a momentum of its own. By 20 May 1992, 83 per cent of the necessary measures listed in the Commission's White Paper had been adopted. The internal market, as we saw in chapter 1 and will return to in the next chapter, created its own dynamic with further consequences for the integration process. Policies for economic and social cohesion also made considerable progress once the new agreement on Community finance had been reached in February 1988. This doubled the structural funds between 1987 and 1993.

Social policy became an increasingly conflictual issue within the Community. Despite attempts such as the Social Charter proposed by Delors and approved by 11 Member States at the December 1989 European Council in Strasbourg, and continual pressure from the EP, especially after the 1989 European elections, social policy measures, notably the Social Action Programme to implement the Social Charter, made little headway, except precisely in the area of health and safety at work where the SEA had added the new Art. 118 (A) to the treaty providing for Community action, and qualified majority voting, in this area. The new Art. 118 (B) was also used by the Commission to develop social dialogue.

Research and technological development was another area where difficulties arose. The 1987–92 Framework Programme which under the terms of the SEA had to be agreed unanimously before the individual programmes could then be approved by qualified majority voting, was held up for over a year, while the UK held out for a lower level of expenditure than wanted by any other Member State. Indeed, the level the UK wanted was little above its previous levels and would have prevented many of the new programmes taking off. In the end, a compromise was reached in late 1987 at a level of 5.6 billion ECUs over five years: only 0.1 billion ECUs different from an offer rejected by the UK in December 1986,[51] but with considerable delay and bitterness created in the meantime.

Environmental policy continued to develop in the EC framework, the new Title VII of the treaty giving greater legitimacy to EC action. However, many of the most important environmental measures were in fact introduced on the basis of internal market legislation, where Art. 100A of the treaty, also introduced by the SEA, required measures to be based on a high level of environmental protection and, unlike Title VII, allow qualified majority voting. As with social policy, the availability of qualified majority voting proved to be crucial when it came to the practical development of policies and the adoption of legislation.

As to EPC, its formalization was an objective of the DTEU. Although its incorporation within the SEA did this and linked it formally to the Community, as did the provisions for Commission participation in EPC, no possibility was laid down for transferring items from the method of intergovernmental cooperation to the more integrated Community method, which the DTEU had explicitly envisaged. The danger of it developing as a separate institution in its own right remained. The establishment of an EPC secretariat, whilst contributing to the effectiveness of political cooperation as such, potentially reinforced its separation from the Community. The provision that it be based in Brussels at least guaranteed its links to the Community system and when it was eventually set up, it was agreed to locate it within the Council Secretariat. This diminished the chances of it developing as a rival institution. As to the other innovations to existing EPC practice, they did not change its character which remained a loose coordination of national policies.

The SEA and measures flowing from it brought about significant changes in the 'constitution' of the EC. All of the institutions were affected to some degree and the overall impact, increasing the EC's efficiency and democratic accountability, strengthened its supranational features. At the same time, the SEA widened its scope. The integration process itself and Community policy-making moved forward in several areas. The 'constitutional' reforms initiated by the EP's 1984 proposal may not have achieved European Union but they certainly helped the Community regain momentum in that direction.

The changes were, however, limited. Substantial areas of policy remained subject to the rule of unanimity in Council, and developed far more slowly. The Commission's executive powers were not strengthened to the extent that was implied by the SEA. The cooperation procedure with Parliament fell short of a right of co-decision and in any case only applied to certain categories of legislation. Parliament's role in the appointment of the Commission was not recognized. For these and other reasons Parliament was determined that the SEA should not be the last word this century in EC constitutional reform. Let us now examine how it was to go about relaunching a campaign for European Union.

11 Relaunching the Ship

PUTTING REFORM BACK ON THE AGENDA

Spinelli summed up the attitude of the Parliament after the adoption of the SEA:

> When we voted on the draft treaty of union, I mentioned to you the short story by Hemingway about the old fisherman who catches the biggest fish in his life, which then gets eaten up by sharks so that he arrives home with only the bones of the fish. Well, we have arrived home too, and all we have left are the bones of the fish. This is no reason for Parliament to give up the struggle. We have to get ready to venture out again, with better tackle to catch our fish and to save it from the sharks.[1]

In this chapter we shall examine how Parliament sought to reopen the prospects for further constitutional reform, what alliances it sought to build, whether it was successful in shaping perceptions and attitudes, and what results it achieved. It will take us from the initial attempts to reopen the issue of reform in 1987 to the beginning of the Maastricht IGC in 1990.

Already in its January 1986 resolution, besides resolving to exploit the SEA to its limits, Parliament requested its Committee on Institutional Affairs to prepare new proposals in time for the 1989 elections. The Committee appointed Fernand Herman, a Walloon Christian Democrat, and ex-member of the Dooge Committee, as rapporteur. The Committee decided that he should first produce an interim report while the committee also drew up a series of reports aimed notably at showing the insufficiencies of the Community as it resulted from the Single Act. It envisaged reports on:

- the democratic deficit (Toussaint Report)
- the cost of non-Europe (Catherwood Report)
- fundamental rights (De Gucht Report)
- an analysis of the first year's application of the SEA (Graziani Report)
- Council's decision-taking procedures (Stauffenberg Report)
- relations with national parliaments (Seeler Report)
- the procedures for consulting European Citizens on European political Union (Bru Puron Report)
- WEU (Boesmans Report).[2]

These reports would culminate in a final report on Parliament's strategy for European Union (Herman Report).

The theme of the '*democratic deficit*' was a traditional concern of Parliament. In the Toussaint resolution it stated:

> The Community's powers, and consequently the Council's legislative powers, are the outcome of a process of transfer of powers which has been under way between the Member States and the Community since it was set up. This transfer has reduced or limited the powers of the Member States and, as a result, the powers of the national law-making bodies – the national parliaments. At Community level . . . this loss of powers has not so far been offset by any transfer of those powers to (the European) Parliament.[3]

The Toussaint Report argued that the SEA had been another step in this direction. Jacques Delors gave added pertinence to this point when he asserted that, by the late 1990s, some '80 per cent of our economic legislation, and perhaps even our fiscal and social legislation as well, will be of Community origin'.[4]

It claimed that the Council was not the appropriate body to exercise alone the legislative powers of the EC, and criticized its procedures for their secrecy, inefficiency and unaccountability. These last points were also a matter for the Stauffenberg Report, but in the end the Committee confined itself to holding public hearings with constitutional experts on the subject of Council's procedures, without finalizing a separate report.

Emphasizing the democratic deficit was an attempt to draw attention to the importance of strengthening the EP's powers.[5] It was also aimed at forging an alliance with *national parliaments* by reassuring them that the EP was only after those powers that they had lost, and asking them to make common cause in defence of parliamentary democracy. The Seeler Report took up these arguments and Parliament approved a resolution supporting closer ties and cooperation with national parliaments. Among the closer ties developed were nine visits by delegations from national parliaments to the EP's Institutional Committee in 1988–9 in order to discuss strategy for European Union. These formed the basis for increasingly regular contacts which, as we shall see, culminated in the November 1990 'Assizes' in Rome.

In fact, several national parliaments had taken up the EP's critisisms of the SEA. The Belgian Senate and Chamber adopted identical resolutions in July 1986 stating that the SEA was insufficient and calling for the EP to 'prepare, in agreement with the other Community institutions, a draft Treaty for the Union to be submitted to the national Parliaments for ratification'.[6]

The Italian Senate on 1 October 1986 approved a resolution in which it affirmed that the 'Single European Act is quite incapable of producing the European Union to which the Heads of State and of Government of the Member States have repeatedly and solemnly pledged themselves' and calling on the government 'to support the European Parliament in its efforts to accelerate the process of European unification and ensure that an explicit mandate is given to the European Parliament to be elected in 1989, also authorizing it to hold a poll among the citizens of the Member States, if necessary'.

The Italian Chamber of Deputies approved a resolution of similar tone on 17 December 1986.

In the Irish parliament, the report of the Joint Committee (of the two Houses) on the Single Act stated that the 'principles of democracy are not served if the European Parliament's role is restricted to a consultative one'.

The Dutch parliament in November 1986 reconfirmed 'its support for the draft treaty adopted by the European Parliament on 14 February 1984' and considered 'that the Single European Act fails to meet the real requirements'. It considered 'it essential and urgent to encourage appropriate measures to reactivate the fight for European Union' and considered

> that there must be adequate support for the strategy recommended by the European Parliament's Committee on Institutional Affairs to ensure that the Assembly elected in 1989 is entrusted with the task of preparing the draft of an act of union for subsequent ratification by the national parliaments.

The Belgian parliament organized an interparliamentary conference on European Union in May 1987 in which the parliaments of all the Member States except Ireland[7] participated along with MEPs. The general theme was that the SEA was insufficient and further reform was necessary. The conference did not formally adopt any declaration, but most participants subscribed to a text supporting 'the idea of holding public consultation on the feasibility of strengthening European democracy by reinforcing the European Parliament's legislative powers'.

This last point was taken up by the EP in the Bru Puron Report,[8] and subsequently in a paragraph of the Herman Report, in which it called for the principle of Parliament drafting a constitution for European Union to be submitted to the electorate in a referendum, either at

European level 'or failing that in the Member States where possible'. One Member State was to react to this invitation, namely Italy, which held a referendum in conjunction with the 1989 European elections. This committed the Italian governement to seek European constitutional reform, to be based on EP proposals.[9]

Parliament did not dwell exclusively on constitutional questions. It also sought to highlight the potential advantages of further European integration. This was done notably through the Catherwood Report on the *'Cost of non-Europe'*. This term had been coined by Albert and Ball in their study commissioned by Parliament in 1983,[10] but was used by Sir Fred Catherwood, a former chairman of the UK's National Economic Development Council, to show the cost, to industry, consumers, governments and taxpayers of the failure fully to integrate the EC economy. He came up with a rough figure of ECU 120 bn p.a., accruing from the non-completion of a single market; the existence of 12 separate currencies; lower growth resulting from a plethora of different economic policies instead of a single, concerted one; separate national military procurement policies; inability to reform the CAP and a range of other causes, including duplication of Research programmes and the non-coordination of public aid programmes.[11] The Report went on to argue that to address the economic problems facing the Community would require fundamental institutional reform. There was, said Catherwood,

> no successful precedent for running a complex Economic Community as a continuous arm's-length negotiation between twelve national governments'.... no organizations expert would have set up a final decision-making body which has a different chairman every six months, has powers of veto without responsibility for suggesting alternatives, is composed of members who can only give it 10% of their time and whose most pressing work [on which their job depends] is at home . . .[12]

The corresponding resolution[13] made the case for institutional reform on the very practical grounds that economic management and prosperity demanded reform.

The Committee also looked at the *protection of fundamental rights*. As we have seen, this was a long-standing concern of Parliament, which considered that a European Union would be incomplete – and possibly dangerous – without basic rights being entrenched in its constitution. The Committee therefore drew up a White Paper[14] under the rapporteurship of the Flemish Liberal De Gucht. It held a symposium on the subject with the European University Institute in Florence and, aided by a team of legal experts, drew up a Declaration on Fundamental Rights and Freedoms, adopted by the EP in April 1989,[15] capable of constituting an EC Bill of Rights. The exercise stimulated much academic interest, raised again the issue of fundamental rights, and produced already one of the elements of future proposals.

The Committee also examined the issue of *WEU* and *defence policy* in a future Union. It adopted a report by Boesmans (Flemish Socialist) which, for timetabling reasons at the end of the 1984–9 Parliament, did not get onto the agenda of plenary. The report called for gradual integration of WEU into the Community, a virtually taboo subject until then, listing a set of measures in ascending order of importance:

- transfer of WEU to Brussels,
- exchanging observers at level of Assembly, Council and Secretariat,
- changing the composition of the WEU Assembly to include MEPs,
- a Merger Treaty providing for a common set of institutions,
- a full takeover of WEU functions by the EC (albeit with transitional provisions including exemptions for some Member States).

The Graziani Report on the *first year of operation of the SEA*, approved in October 1988, recognized that the SEA had opened 'the way for a degree of development on the part of the Community which should be exploited',[16] but that it had nevertheless left the Community 'deprived of adequate means of action in the areas of the common foreign policy, security, a common currency with a central bank, energy, development aid, cultural cooperation, education and European citizenship'. Meanwhile, Parliament's experience with the SEA's new legislative procedures during this time, as we saw in the previous chapter, demonstrated its ability to act constructively and rapidly, regularly securing the necessary majorities in cooperation procedure votes. This helped to lessen the misgivings of sceptics. Failure to make full use of its limited SEA powers in a competent manner would have prejudiced Parliament's credibility when it demanded full legislative co-decision.

The *interim* Herman Resolution, adopted along with some of the above mentioned sectoral reports in June 1987,[17] already took up some of the points they developed, and reiterated a number of principles contained in the DTEU. Its main purpose, however, was to address the next step forward on *strategy* that Parliament intended to follow. It defended Parliament's right to draw up a new 'draft for European Union'. But it did not define precisely *what* it wished to draw up, referring merely to a 'draft', a 'plan', or simply 'preparations'. This ambiguity reflected the differences of view about Parliament's 'constituent' role.

A number of 'Constituent assembly federalists' took the view that the SEA was a failure, and that this was because, despite the EP's input, it had been drafted by governments. They felt that the only way to go further was for the new Parliament elected in 1989 to be a Constituent Assembly, drafting a constitution for direct ratification by national Parliaments or by referendums. Indeed, referendums could also be used to confer a constituent mandate upon the EP. Such a strategy had been aired by Spinelli shortly before his death in 1986. It was subsequently taken up and developed by a large part of the federalist movement (UEF) and in the 'Federalist Intergroup' – set up in the EP in 1987 as the successor to Spinelli's 'Crocodile Club', which argued that Parliament should ask for a 'constituent mandate' from as many countries as possible for the 1989 election. This school of thought did achieve the organization of the 1989 referendum in Italy, called by popular initiative.

Others were not convinced that this was a realistic scenario – even as a means of upping the stakes in order to fall back on a different approach later. Some felt it was unnecessary to ask for a 'mandate' – Parliament had not done so to prepare its draft treaty and there was no reason not to act on its own initiative. MEPs' 'mandates' came from their electorate – what was required was an *undertaking* from governments that they would take up any new EP 'draft'.

Many felt that another draft Treaty so soon after the DTEU and the SEA would be premature, and there was no reason to draft anything new while the DTEU remained largely unfulfilled. What was needed was a new window of opportunity which seemed most likely to arise in 1992, as this was the year in which the SEA envisaged the possible revision of EPC, in which the budgetary perspectives agreed in 1988 would run out, and last but not least, the year in which the single market was due for completion and its consequences would be apparent. These points were made by Lord Plumb, President of Parliament, when he met the Foreign Ministers during their 'conclave' in Grenada in April 1989 and argued for some immediate pragmatic improvements (such as extending the conciliation procedure) whilst Parliament should prepare global proposals for early 1992. A premature initiative might be counter-productive, and other avenues might arise earlier and be used to help pave the way, such as an 'interinstitutional conference', an idea put forward by Felipe Gonzalez in his speech to the EP during the Spanish Presidency of Council.

These divergences of views had not been entirely resolved by the time of the adoption of the final Herman resolution on 16 February 1989,[18] which contained similar ambiguous references to a 'draft' or 'comprehensive proposals in the form of a draft' without specifying its legal form: treaty amendments, new treaty, constitution. By then, there was another reason for ambiguity: the Member States had agreed, in the June 1988 European Council, to set up a committee composed mainly of the Governors of the Central Banks of the Member States but chaired by Delors, to draft proposals for EMU and this was due to be discussed at the June 1989 European Council in Madrid. It was becoming conceivable that the newly elected Parliament in July 1989 might be confronted with the prospect of a sectoral reform process, much earlier than initially expected. This would obviously affect what sort of proposals Parliament might make.

On the other hand, the Herman Report at least signalled that agreement had been reached in Parliament on what the basis for a new 'draft' should be. It should

> be based on the acquis communautaire, the draft treaty establishing the European Union adopted on 14 February 1984, the comments on this draft treaty submitted by the national parliaments, the experience of operating the Single European Act, the need for effective functioning of a single, barrier-free market and any constructive contributions put forward in public debates at the time of the 1989 European elections.[19]

It would be drawn up with the full involvement 'of the other institutions and the national parliaments'. The resolution ended with a threat: Parliament would refuse to 'approve any further accession treaty with a new Member State without the institutional reforms necessary to make the Community more effective and more democratic and unless significant progress towards European Union were made'.

The 1989 European elections were, like those of 1984, fought on a variety of issues, most of them national. This time there was no specific project on the table, but the new momentum in European affairs together with criticism of the inadequacies of the EC did mean that, at a general level, the issue of further integration was among those debated. Again, parties had to take a position partly influenced by how their MEPs had voted in Strasbourg and the arguments MEPs used within their party discussions.

Two countries stand out as worthy a mention. One is Italy because of the referendum mentioned above and the 90 per cent support in it for giving a 'constituent mandate' to the EP, which could only strengthen the commitment of the Italian government. The other is the UK where, unlike 1984, the Labour Party campaigned on a pro-European stance. This was not a federalist stance, but it contrasted with the perceived hostility to further integration of Thatcher and the Conservative party campaign.[20] It resulted in a large victory for the Labour Party, which reinforced its European commitment and left Thatcher looking bereft of public support for her stance on Europe. Her Bruges speech of September 1988 envisaging a Europe very different from that sought by the EP had echoed across Europe. It now seemed that the echo from her own country contradicted her; Conservative MEPs were among those to criticize her afterwards, and splits in the Cabinet, notably over joining the ERM, became a public secret.

By the Madrid meeting of the European Council just after the European elections, the time was ripe for a decision to move forward on EMU. In most countries, the election campaign had, if anything, helped prepare opinion, and Thatcher was in a weak position should she attempt to block a decision. Thus, the European Council 'restated its determination progressively to achieve economic and monetary union' and agreed that the first stage of EMU should begin on 1 July 1990. An IGC 'to lay down the subsequent stages' would 'meet once the first stage had begun and would be prepared by full and adequate preparation'.

The decision of the European Council to hold an IGC on EMU meant that events were moving somewhat faster than Parliament had expected, but only in the field of EMU. When the new Parliament convened, it was, of course, pleased that the Member States had agreed to such an IGC but was concerned to ensure that its scope should not be limited to EMU. It immediately called for the mandate of the IGC to be extended to include institutional reform (Resolution of 27 July 1989), a position which it elaborated further in a Resolution on the IGC adopted on 23 November 1989, spelling out an agenda for institutional change which it asked the IGC to address. This included an enlargement of Parliament's powers, insertion of fundamental rights into the Treaty, strengthening social policy provisions, strengthening regional cohesion and more majority voting in Council.

Parliament undertook in this Resolution to prepare its own proposals and it laid down the first markers for a strategy for building support for them, envisaging 'an *interinstitutional conference*' at the beginning of 1990 'in which an equal number of representatives of the Commission, the Council and the European Parliament will take part and which will draw up specific proposals for the necessary reform of the Treaty' and inviting the Parliaments of the Member States to participate in 'European *Assizes*' – an Assembly of the Parliaments of Europe – to 'discuss the next stages in the implementation of European Union'.

Let us now turn to the events leading up to the start of the IGC, and examine the interaction between Parliament's proposals and these of other actors.

WIDENING BEYOND EMU

During 1990, Parliament gradually developed its positions. It appointed Labour MEP David Martin, a Vice-President of the European Parliament, as rapporteur and, on his suggestion, agreed to three phases of work. The first phase (Martin I Report), prepared by the committee from November 1989 to February 1990, which led to a parliamentary resolution adopted on 14 March 1990, laid down general principles and guidelines of Parliament's approach, listing the subjects which Parliament asked the IGC to address (at a time when Member States had still only agreed on an IGC on EMU alone). The second phase (Martin II Report), which led to a parliamentary resolution adopted on 11 July 1990, spelt out Parliament's proposals in detail (by which time the Member States had just agreed to the principle of calling a second IGC on political union). The third phase consisted of 'translating' this resolution into the legal language of draft Treaty amendments (Martin III Report) which were duly adopted by Parliament on 22 November 1990, just before the opening of the IGCs, and consisting of the only draft Treaty articles to be tabled before the opening of the political union IGC. This three-step approach was similar to that used in 1982–4 for the adoption of the DTEU (Spinelli Reports), but was telescoped into a far shorter time span of 11 months – by now Parliament was not starting from scratch but had a basis to build on.

What were the issues that Parliament pressed for inclusion in the Treaty revision and what were its precise proposals? The first Martin Resolution[21] of March 1990 established a list of demands, aiming to transform the Community into a 'European Union of Federal Type' – the word 'federal' was no longer felt to be taboo. Besides monetary union, Parliament advocated the integration of EPC into the Community framework, more extensive Treaty provisions in the social and environmental sectors, incorporation into the Treaties of fundamental rights, the provision of systematic majority voting in Council, a strengthening of the Commission's executive powers, a reform of the budgetary resources system and, last but not least, increasing the powers of the EP (specifying co-decision with Council on Community legislation, involvement in the appointment of the Commission, the right to initiate legislative proposals and extending the assent procedure to all major international agreements entered into by the Community and to constitutional decisions requiring national ratification).

In the parliamentary debate, Parliament's proposals received strong support from President Delors, who added only the point that security should become a full part of foreign policy considerations. The Commission thus swung behind Parliament's proposal to deal with these issues in the current round of Treaty revision, whereas previously it had prefered to concentrate on EMU.

The Italian parliament responded immediately, adopting a resolution on 21 March 1990 which specifically endorsed the EP Resolution. At the same time it offered to co-host the 'Assizes'.

The Belgian government was the first national government to give backing to this strategy. It published a memorandum in March 1990, which it drew up after following closely the preparation of the Martin Report in Committee[22] and the debate on it, and produced a remarkably similar set of conclusions. The memorandum argued for an extension of qualified majority voting in Council to all policy areas, for Parliament to elect the President of the Commission and approve the whole of the Commission, to modify the cooperation procedure by giving Parliament a right in a third reading to reject by a majority of its Members legislation adopted by Council, and to extend the assent procedure to revisions of the Treaty, own resources and all major international agreements. It supported the entrenchment of human rights in the Treaty and supported Parliament's definition of subsidiarity. Concerning political cooperation, however, it proposed only to bring this closer to the Community domain, and not fully to integrate it. It was open on the issue as to whether there should be a parallel IGC or whether these issues should be dealt with together with EMU in a single IGC.

The European Parliament, followed by the Commission, the Italian Parliament and the Belgian government, thus placed firmly on the agenda a whole series of further treaty reforms, notably institutional changes, that they wished to be dealt with alongside EMU. Although the UK Foreign Secretary, Douglas Hurd, made a sarcastic remark to the effect that Belgium had been the first to dive into the swimming pool, even if there was no water in it, decisive support was forthcoming from Chancellor Kohl and President Mitterrand in their joint letter to the heads of government of the other Member States in April 1990, before the meeting of the European Council that month in Dublin. In this letter, they called for a second IGC on political union 'to be held parallel to the conference on economic and monetary union', aiming to enter into force at the same time on 1 January 1993 after ratification by national parliaments. They proposed that the IGC should deal with democratic legitimacy, the efficiency of the Community institutions, the unity and coherence of the Union's economic and monetary and political action, and the definition of a common foreign and security policy. This was an agenda, albeit in headline terms, which matched that of Parliament.

The Dublin European Council of 28 April 1990 asked the Foreign Ministers to study the need for treaty amendments and report back to the second Dublin European Council in June which would decide on whether a second IGC parallel to that on EMU would be necessary.

Between the two meetings of the European Council, two more governments joined the ranks of those pressing for reform. Spanish Prime Minister, Felipe Gonzalez, wrote to his colleagues backing the idea that European citizenship should also be dealt with during an IGC on political union, and the Greek government published a memorandum on 15 May which backed most of the proposals contained in the Martin I Report.

The Foreign Ministers considered the issues in Parknasilla on 19/20 May. They cautiously produced a report which consisted of a list of questions and issues to investigate. It fell short of putting forward specific items for Treaty revision. It took up all the issues listed in the Martin I Resolution, putting them in the form of questions: should the field of competence of the Community be enlarged? Should citizen's rights be entrenched? Should foreign policy come under the Community method? What should be the role of the Commission in foreign policy? It listed a number of points to be examined concerning the powers of the EP, including co-decision, strengthened powers of control and participation in the designation of the President and Members of the Commission. It also stressed the need to examine the extension of majority voting in the Council and the powers of the Commission.

The meeting of the European Council in Dublin on 25/26 June 1990 agreed on convening an IGC on political union running parallel to that on EMU. Parliament's pressure to widen the agenda for reform had been successful, helped, no doubt, by the dramatic changes in Eastern Europe at the end of 1989 creating a climate of opinion ready to envisage major changes.

PARLIAMENT'S DETAILED PROPOSALS

The EP was able to adopt its detailed proposals within one month of the European Council having agreed to an additional IGC. Parliament's Committee on Institutional Affairs was already working on elaborating detailed proposals to fill in the 'headlines' put forward by Parliament in March. The Martin II Report was adopted in plenary[23] in July 1990, setting out in detail proposals for treaty reform. Parliament was therefore ahead of the governments and the Commission in terms of spelling out detailed proposals. It hoped to shape the agenda and its proposals are worth examining in detail.

Parliament's resolution first provided a definition of European Union. According to Parliament this would comprise:

- 'economic and monetary union with a single currency and an autonomous central bank;
- a common foreign policy, including joint consideration of the issues of peace, security and arms control;
- a completed single market with common policies in all the areas in which the economic integration and mutual interdependence of the Member States require common action notably to ensure economic and social cohesion and a balanced environment;
- elements of common citizenship and a common framework for protecting basic rights;
- an institutional system which is sufficiently efficient to manage these responsibilities effectively and which is democratically structured, notably by giving the European Parliament a right of initiative, of co-decision with the Council on Community legislation, the right to ratify all constitutional decisions requiring the ratification of the Member States also and the right to elect the President of the Commission.

The Resolution then spelled out the particular treaty changes, except as regards EMU which was dealt with in a separate resolution (Herman Report, see below). A large number of changes were sought by Parliament, but they can be broadly grouped under three headings: (1) widening of Community *competences*, (2) making the Community's decision-taking more *efficient*, and (3) rendering it more *democratic*. These were the same three objectives as we identified in chapter 7 as the main changes sought by the EP's draft Treaty of 1984.

Enlargement of the field of *competences* of the Community was considered necessary in three main areas (economic and monetary union, foreign and security policy and citizenship) and a number of smaller ones.

Parliament was a long-standing advocate of EMU which had featured in its 1984 DTEU and in several reports since then. Just before the 1989 European elections, its Economic and Monetary Committee had prepared a blueprint for EMU (Franz Report), and this committee now defined specific proposals following the same three-phase approach as the Martin Reports on political union: principles, details, legal form. The rapporteur was Mr Herman.

Parliament defined monetary union as 'the circulation of a single currency, the conduct of a single external and internal monetary policy and the establishment of a European System of Central Banks including an autonomous European Central Bank'. The Bank's autonomy would be guaranteed by a requirement that it 'may not request or receive instructions', but it would have to 'support the economic and social policy guidelines' of the Community. Its Governing Council would consist of the national Central Bank Governors and the Board of Directors, the latter being the Governor, Deputy Governor and between three and five others appointed by Council on a proposal from the Commission with Parliament's assent for a five year term. EMU would be phased in by New Year 1996, but 'certain Member States may be granted at their request and in light of their specific situation, longer time-limits'.[24]

Concerning foreign policy, Parliament felt that the time had come to integrate EPC into the Community framework, although it acknowledged that specific decision-taking procedures, protecting Member States' interests, would continue to be necessary in this field. It envisaged a system of qualified majority voting, but with the possibility of granting derogations to individual Member States or, in exceptional circumstances, the right of individual states to opt out. The Commission would take on a role in external representation for all areas of foreign policy and not just for the economic areas as hitherto.

Concerning citizenship, Parliament advocated the granting of voting rights in local and European elections in the Member State of residence and the entrenchment of basic human rights in the Treaty. Citizens of Member States would become at the same time citizens of the Union.

Parliament also advocated the strengthening of existing Community competences in the fields of the environment, social matters, economic and social cohesion, development policy, education, culture and transport. In all these areas it was felt that the existing Treaty provisions were inadequate or, in some cases, totally absent and that the addition of new articles would serve a useful purpose.

In order to demonstrate that, despite this large increase in the field of Community competence, it was not advocating a centralized super-state, Parliament also advocated the entrenchment in the Treaties of the *principle of subsidiarity*. This principle had been mentioned in Parliament's 1984 draft Treaty. However, as the interpretation of the principle is always a matter of judgement, it was perfectly possible for opponents of European integration to use this principle to advocate minimal competences for the Community. Indeed, Thatcher and a group of Eurosceptics known as the 'Bruges Group' began to do precisely this. Parliament therefore decided to draw up a special report on this matter and charged former French President Valéry Giscard d'Estaing to be its rapporteur. This was dealt with in parallel to Martin II Report (and its translation into legal language in parallel with Martin III). Giscard, leader of Parliament's Liberal Group at the time, had been pressing for a role in the institutional debate, and the other Groups agreed to give this report to the former President of the European Council. There was broad agreement on the idea of spelling out the principle of subsidiarity in the Treaty, but in view of the highly divergent interpretations given to the term, the exact formulation became a matter of controversy. Some advocated a 'positive' definition ('the Union shall carry out those tasks . . .'), whilst others felt that a 'negative' definition ('the Union shall carry out *only* those tasks . . .') was more reassuring to the Member States without really loading what would in effect always be a political judgement. In the end, Parliament opted for the 'negative' definition.

There was also controversy over the procedures invoking the principle of subsidiarity in front of the European Court. Giscard had proposed allowing a preliminary reference to the Court of any Commission proposal to check whether it conformed to the principle of subsidiarity, but this would have been an open invitation to filibustering and delaying tactics. A majority of Parliament felt that the existing procedures for bringing matters *post facto* to the Court were sufficient. Indeed, bringing a Commission proposal to Court would have been futile as it can be changed considerably during the legislative procedures. As a compromise, a majority was willing to accept a suspensive effect on the entry into force of the final decision on legislation if the Court ruled by urgent procedure. The Giscard Resolution was heavily amended along these lines[25] before being adopted by Parliament. The Martin Report duly took up the principle.

The second main area of Parliamentary proposals related to the *effi-ciency* of the Community's institutions. This concerned first the issue of qualified majority voting. Parliament argued that applying qualified majority voting only in some areas led to an anomalous situation. Single market liberalizations, most of which could be adopted by qualified majority voting, were proceeding far more rapidly than the laying down of minimum social and environmental standards to apply in that market, most of which required unanimity. Some matters were blocked entirely due to the opposition of a single government. Martin called this 'the dictatorship of the minority'.

Parliament advocated the use of qualified majority voting for all areas where the Treaties give the Community competence. Unanimity would be retained only for constitutional matters: Treaty revisions, accessions, enlargement of Community competences or increasing budgetary resources. In addition, as we saw above, special provisions would apply in the field of foreign policy.

Extending qualified majority voting in Council was not the only way of increasing the efficiency of the Community system advocated by the EP. It also called for a strengthening of the Commission's executive powers, criticizing the 'comitology' system which we examined in chapter 10. Parliament argued for the Commission to be given less restricted implementing powers, but subject to scrutiny and, where major political problems occurred, recall to the full legislative authority (i.e. Council *and* Parliament at either's request).

Parliament also advocated strengthening the Court of Justice by giving it the right to impose penalties on Member States failing to comply with its judgments.

The third main area of Parliamentary concern was *democracy*. As regards its own powers, it put forward proposals for specific procedures that would meet its two main requests: co-decision with Council on legislation and involvement in the appointment of the Commission.

Parliament's co-decision proposal built on the cooperation procedure that had been introduced by the SEA, which it proposed to modify and to extend to all legislation. The procedure would be modified so that legislation could only be approved with the explicit approval both of Council and of Parliament. The conciliation procedure would be used to thrash out compromises. Conciliation would come in after its second reading if Parliament failed to approve Council's position. It also envisaged changing the practice whereby the Commission has discretion as to whether or not to accept Parliamentary amendments, by providing that any amendment approved by a majority of members of Parliament would *have* to be incorporated into the Commission's proposal at first reading. The Commission would retain discretion over amendments adopted only by a simple majority of those voting. The cooperation procedure would be simplified by providing that where Parliament and Council agree at an early stage (i.e. through Council adopting the same position as Parliament in its first reading, or through Parliament in its second reading approving Council's position) for the procedure to be successfully concluded at that stage, thus obviating the need for further readings where both branches have already agreed.

This procedure differed from the co-decision procedure put forward by Parliament in its 1984 draft Treaty, but did so in a way intended to build on the intervening experience of the cooperation procedure. Parliament presented it as a moderate proposal,[26] pointing out that it would not give the EP the right to impose anything on national governments that they did not want, as Council's approval would continue to be necessary, but that it would mean that the decisions taken by Ministers behind closed doors in Council meetings would only become law if they were also explicitly approved in a public vote in the assembly that the electorate had chosen to act at Community level. It would thus be an additional democratic safeguard and would resemble the system applicable in Germany where most legislation requires the approval both of the elected Bundestag and of the body composed of Ministers from State governments, the Bundesrat, with a conciliation procedure to reconcile differences.

As regards the appointment of the Commission, Parliament went further than in the DTEU (simple vote of confidence by Parliament in the Commission as a whole). It now took up Mitterrand's proposal that the President of the Commission should be elected by the EP, and proposed a two-stage procedure in which Parliament would first elect the President on a proposal of the European Council and second (once the full team of Commissioners has been settled by agreement between the President and the national governments) would hold a debate and a vote of confidence on the Commission as a whole before it could take office.

As we have seen in chapter 5, the vote of confidence had become an established Community practice. Entrenching it in the Treaty would, Parliament hoped, be a mere formality. Electing the President, however, was more ambitious, though here too Parliament could point to the precedent of the Assembly of the Council of Europe which elects the Secretary-General of that organization on a proposal of the Committee of Ministers, which sometimes submits one and sometimes more than one candidate.

The prominence of the position of Commission President had been restored by Jacques Delors and there was a strong argument for a greater democratic element in its appointment. It was also a job in which there was no 'buggin's turn' among the Member States, normally sorted out by agreement by heads of government in which national parliaments were not and could hardly be involved. Parliament felt that its case was good.

Besides these 'big two' there were a number of other items on Parliament's shopping list for its own powers. Parliament proposed to formalize in the treaties various rights that it had acquired in legislation or in practice. This included the right to set up committees of inquiry in order to investigate cases of maladministration or alleged contravention of Community law; the obligation on the Commission to respect Parliament's requests in the budgetary discharge procedure; recognition in the Treaties of the rights of members of the public to petition the European Parliament; and the right to bring cases to the European Court for annulment of Community Acts. It also sought the right to initiate legislative proposals where the Commission failed to respond to its requests.

Parliament did not consider that adjusting its own powers was the only way to improve democratic accountability in the Community. It also proposed that Council should meet in public when adopting legislation, that national parliaments should have better access to information (a separate resolution, based on a report by Duverger but heavily amended, was adopted on relations with national parliaments), that a consultative Committee of Regions should be set up to allow regional authorities a direct input into the Community system, and that the EC should entrench fundamental rights in the treaty and accede to the ECHR.

Globally, Parliament's proposals appeared to fulfil the intentions expressed in the February 1989 Herman resolution of being based on the *acquis*, the DTEU, the experience of the SEA and the consequences of the single market. Although the main thrust of Parliament's demands were identical to those contained in the DTEU, the details and emphasis were adapted to take account of what had happened in the intervening years.

Parliament's Resolution was adopted by an overwhelming majority reflecting the consensus achieved among the major political groups. This consensus was now wider than at the time of the DTEU. Since then, the UK Labour and Greek PASOK members had come around to supporting further integration and the French socialists had dropped their inhibitions about using federalist vocabulary. The new members from Spain and Portugal were almost exclusively supporters of the integration process. The consensus achieved meant that broadly the same points would be made by MEPs within all the main political parties of the Member States and towards the national governments and parliaments.

This is not to say that Parliament was monolithic, even within the majority supporting the Martin proposals. There were, naturally, differences on a left–right scale on, for instance, the degree of emphasis to be given to economic and social cohesion, social policy, environmental policy, and so on. There were differences over strategy, with some who believed that Parliament should threaten to use its various negative powers (e.g. its right to reject the budget, to delay legislation and to block association agreements or accession by new Member States) as a means of exerting pressure on the governments. There were different approaches to federalism. Finally, the existence of rival political families naturally led to occasional friction and jealousies.

On this last point, the Christian Democrats again found themselves in an awkward position. Just as in 1984–87, when Spinelli had been the driving force behind Parliament's draft treaty and Mitterrand had been prominent in ensuring that the governments then embarked on an IGC, Christian Democrats seemed again to be concerned that the leading figures in this reform process were from other parties. Parliament's rapporteur, David Martin, was a socialist, as was its President, Enrique Baron, who had the important task of speaking for Parliament at ministerial and European Council meetings. Three successive presidencies of the PU-IGC were Socialist: De Michelis (Italy), Poos (Luxembourg) and Dankert (Netherlands, usually replacing Foreign Secretary Van den Broeck, who was largely embroiled on behalf of the Community in the Yugoslav crisis), not to mention President Delors.

The Christian Democrats therefore wished to highlight their own role and, if possible, to outflank all others in the 'European' stakes. They saw their chance with the issue of a European 'Constitution'. The Committee on Institutional Affairs had agreed that it would be appropriate for Parliament to draft a 'Constitution' on European Union in response to the referendum held on this subject in Italy at the time of the 1989 elections. Colombo, former Italian Prime Minister, had been appointed rapporteur. However, once the Member States agreed to call IGCs to revise the treaties, Parliament felt that it was inappropriate to start drafting constitutions at that stage. Unlike 1984, when the drafting of a new Treaty had started off a process of reform, this time the Member States had already agreed to embark on a Treaty revision and Parliament was already preparing proposals in that context. To put forward at the same time specific proposals to amend the existing constitution (i.e. the Treaties) and also a separate global proposal for a new constitution – even if contradictions could be avoided – would be a confusing and time-consuming exercise. Parliament wisely decided to leave the drafting of a proposal for a global constitution until after the IGCs, when such a process could be used either to relaunch the reform process if the IGCs were unsuccessful or to consolidate the results if they were successful.

However, in order to raise their profile, Colombo and the Christian Democrats insisted on producing 'interim reports' on the draft constitution. Furthermore, he timed the submission of his drafts to coincide with consideration of the Martin Reports. It was difficult for the other groups to prevent this without causing a dangerous row with the Christian Democrats. But, in allowing this to happen, Parliament created unnecessary confusion by adopting, at the same time as the Martin II and Martin III reports, completely different resolutions on what might go in a future constitution. In some circles, and in particular, some countries such as Italy, these proposals inevitably achieved as much if not more publicity as what was supposed to be Parliament's own submissions to the IGCs.

Despite this, Parliament was largely successful in maintaining a broad consensus on the substance and therefore in submitting the same arguments on the same key points within most national political parties and towards governments. Being the first to put such detailed and specific proposals on the table, the EP was again at the forefront of agenda-setting for the IGC.

THE INTERINSTITUTIONAL PREPARATORY CONFERENCE

Parliament was able to bring its proposals direct to the national governments in the interinstitutional preparatory conferences (known by their French acronym, CIP) that met at Parliament's request four times before the start of the IGCs. On three occasions, Parliament's delegation met the General Affairs Council (Foreign Ministers) to discuss political union and on one occasion it met the Finance Ministers to discuss EMU. The first CIP took place just after the April meeting of the European Council in Dublin had envisaged the possibility of calling an IGC on political union, but before the Foreign Ministers had finalized their report to the subsequent European Council meeting in June. Indeed,

the Foreign Ministers had their key meeting in this process at a special meeting in Parknasilla over the following two days. This first interinstitutional meeting consisted largely of exhortations by MEPs to the
Foreign Ministers to ensure as broad as possible a scope to be included
in an eventual IGC on political union. The three other ones took place
after the principle of two IGCs had been agreed at the second Dublin
Summit, on 8 October 1990 in Luxembourg (on EMU), on the 23 October
1990 in Strasbourg (on political union) and on 5 December 1990 in
Brussels (on Parliament's involvement in the IGCs and on co-decision).

Parliament's delegation was a high-level one. Besides Parliament's
President, it included the Chairmen of the five largest political groups
(Cot, Klepsch, Giscard d'Estaing, Sir Christopher Prout, Aglietta), the
Chairman of the Institutional Affairs Committee (Oreja), the rapporteurs
on European Union generally and EMU in particular (Martin, Herman)
and four prominent members of the Institutional, Economic or Social
Affairs Committees (Hänsch, Colombo, Von Wogau, Buron). Thus, the
delegation included one former Head of State, a former Prime Minister, two former Foreign Ministers and a former Finance Minister. This
remained the basis of Parliament's delegation for all subsequent meetings, though the individuals were replaced by others from the same
political group for particular meetings where individual expertise was
required (e.g. when discussing social affairs or EMU).

Each CIP lasted half a day and was usually accompanied by opportunities for informal dialogue (e.g. lunch).[27] The conferences ensured
that Ministers were not only aware of Parliament's demands in general
terms, but also had to listen to detailed argument and explanation by
MEPs, and, to a certain extent, respond. For instance, the German
government representative announced at the first meeting that it supported
the co-decision formula contained in the Martin Report, and the Dutch
government announced that it would not accept increased responsibilities for the EC without an increase in its democratic legitimacy.

At the last meeting, the CIP discussed Parliament's involvement in
the IGCs. Parliament had been pressing to be allowed to participate
in the IGCs, arguing that although Article 236 did not envisage this,
nor did it envisage participation by the Commission, yet the Commission was present. There was therefore no formal reason why another
European institution could not be present too. Parliament also pointed
out that in the previous IGC in 1975, its President, accompanied by
Spinelli, had participated in two of the five Ministerial-level meetings,
and that IGC had agreed to 'submit its results' to Parliament. To press
Parliament's case, its committee on institutional affairs at one stage

went so far as to suggest that Parliament should vote against convening the PU IGC.

This argument was not accepted by several national governments. As a compromise, an understanding was reached that the President of Parliament would be invited to address the start of IGC Ministerial-level meetings, that there would be a 'trialogue' of the Presidents of the three institutions, and that the CIP would be transformed into an 'interinstitutional parallel conference' meeting during the course of the IGCs. Indeed, it was to meet almost monthly, alternating between political union and monetary union. Finally, it was understood that sufficient time would be available between the conclusion of the IGCs and the beginning of national ratification to allow the EP to pronounce on their results, which would be particularly important in view of the linkage that some national parliaments had made between their positions and that of the EP.

THE PARLIAMENTARY ASSIZES OF NOVEMBER 1990

Never before has a major international negotiation been preceded by a conference of the very parliaments that would later have to approve the outcome of the negotiations. The fact that they did so and concluded with a Declaration approved by an overwhelming majority (150 to 13) in which their expectations of the IGC were clearly expressed, was highly significant.

It was President Mitterrand, in a speech to the EP, on the 25 October 1989, who launched the term 'Assizes'. He asked 'why should the European Parliament not organize assizes on the future of the Community in which, alongside your Assembly, delegations from national parliaments, the Commission and the governments would participate?' Parliament seized on this idea, conceiving of the 'Assizes' as a joint parliamentary preparation for the IGCs,[28] and an opportunity to gain wider support for its proposals.

The idea was discussed in the regular meetings held by the presidents of all the national parliaments and of the EP. The Italian Camera dei Deputati offered to host the meeting. Preparations were also discussed in Conference of European Affairs Committees of national parliaments that had begun to meet regularly in 1989, but most preparation was done via the offices of the respective presidents.

It was agreed that approximately two-thirds of the participants would be from national parliaments and one-third from the EP (a compromise between those who thought there should be an equal number of European and National parliamentarians and those who thought that the EP should have a delegation of similar size to the largest national parliaments). Each national parliament would have a number of delegates equal to one-third the number of their country's MEPs, rounded to the nearest whole number (but with a slight adjustment for the smallest three parliaments leading to the national parliaments having, in fact, *over* two-thirds of the delegates: 173 to 85). For various reasons of protocol, the question of who formally convened the conference was left ambiguous, with most parliaments considering that it was 'self-convened' by all the parliaments collectively. Although the meeting was formally entitled 'Conference of the Parliaments of the European Community', the term 'Assizes' soon gained usage in ordinary conversation despite its ambiguous meaning in the English language.

Each national parliament (though not necessarily each Chamber: in the UK for instance only the Lords) prepared written submissions to the Assizes, usually consisting of any resolutions adopted by that parliament on the matter or else of reports from the specialized committee. The EP contribution consisted of its proposed Treaty amendments. Debates took place on the floor of the Camera dei Deputati over a four-day period. Besides the actual participants, speeches were made by President Cossiga of Italy, Commission President Delors and the Council President Andreotti. Debates were presided over by a triumvirate consisting of the presidents of the two Italian Chambers (Iotti and Spadolini) and EP President Baron.[29]

The final Declaration was prepared by a drafting committee consisting of the Chairmen of the European Affairs committees of the national parliaments together with eight MEPs. Originally, it had been agreed (by the preparatory meeting of presidents) that five MEPs only would take part in the drafting committee, but this was changed at the opening plenary meeting of the Assizes in order to achieve roughly the same proportion of national and European MPs as in the Assizes as a whole. Under the rules agreed beforehand by the presidents, and approved by the plenary at the opening, the drafting committee would submit a text which could be approved by the plenary only by an absolute majority of participants. Amendments tabled in plenary would similarly require an absolute majority to be adopted.

The issue of seating arrangements in the Assizes was a matter of some controversy. The initial seating consisted of each national parliamentary delegation sitting as a bloc, with the EP delegation in the centre of the hemicycle, divided into its political groups. At the opening of the first session of the Assizes, however, participants voted by a large majority to sit instead according to political affiliation, based on the EP political groups. It was argued that this was a more 'European' arrangement and that differences of point of view were more on a political than a national basis.

This decision did not meet with universal approval. The British Conservatives – not then part of any Europe-wide grouping – had opposed it. Laurent Fabius, President of the French Assemblée Nationale but also an MEP and member of Parliament's Committee on Institutional Affairs, had initially also opposed the idea, but following a dinner of Socialist delegation leaders the evening before the Assizes organized by Jean-Pierre Cot, at which almost all leaders spoke in favour of sitting by political family, he not only accepted the idea, but agreed to Cot's proposal that he, given his unique position as MEP and President of a national parliament, should formally move it in the plenary the following day.

This decision was to prove important for the dynamics of the Assizes. The political groupings met before or after the daily sittings of the Assizes in order to consider jointly their position on different questions, not least the final declaration and amendments thereto. The secretariats of the EP political groups provided facilities for these meetings, and the core of MEPs within each grouping, having the best international contacts and, frequently, the best linguistic skills, were among the key actors in such meetings.

Some of the EP political groups organized pre-meetings with their counterparts in the national parliaments the day before the Assizes. This was the case for the Socialist, Christian Democrat, Liberal and Green Groups. Indeed, the Socialists' meeting adopted a 'declaration' of Socialist participants in the Assizes, equipping Socialist participants – both national and European – with a set of positions before entering the Assizes. This text was negotiated by consensus among the various Socialist Party delegation leaders, with more cautious parties being encouraged to shift position. The acceptance by the Labour Party delegation of full economic and monetary union, for instance, was endorsed two days later by the Party's National Executive Committee.

The drafting committee worked on the basis of an initial draft prepared by Charles Ferdinand Nothomb, President of the Belgian Chamber of Deputies (and former Foreign Minister and MEP).[30] As Chairman of the Belgian Chamber, he was *ex-officio* Chairman of its mixed committee on European Affairs, and was therefore the one person present both at meetings of Presidents of Parliaments and of the Conference of European Affairs Committees, both of which had been involved in the preparation of the Assizes. His offer to chair the drafting committee and to submit a first draft was accepted.

Nothomb submitted his first draft to the drafting committee only on the evening of the first full day of the Assizes (Tuesday, 27 November). He had used the previous day to hold informal consultations with delegation leaders. The draft was then examined by the drafting committee which fixed a deadline of 22:00 that same evening for its members to submit amendments. These amendments were then examined and voted on the next day by the drafting committee, a simple majority being enough to adopt them. Some 80 amendments were submitted, about half of which were adopted.

Within the drafting committee, there were naturally differences of opinion. The Chairmen of the national parliamentary committees largely reflected the position of the majority in their parliaments and were therefore close to the position of their respective governments, but sometimes the differences went beyond this. The House of Commons Committee, for instance, was chaired by Nigel Spearing (Labour), a long-standing anti-marketeer. The French Senate's Committee was chaired by Jacques Genton, a Gaullist Eurosceptic. That of the Assemblée was chaired by Charles Josselin who, whilst a mainstream French Socialist pro-European, was among sponsors of a proposal to establish a 'Congress' of national parliamentarians at EC level, an idea which in the end did not receive majority support at the Assizes.

The text of the drafting committee was submitted to the plenary, where it had been agreed that amendments could be tabled if signed by five or more members. Some 222 amendments were submitted, largely as a result of discussions in meetings of the political groupings, but also by some national delegations (though some were later withdrawn). The votes took place in the final sitting on Friday morning. By then – and all the more so as the morning progressed – many members had left to catch planes or for other reasons. Absences particularly affected German delegates (who were a few days away from a General Election) and Italians (who, being local, were particularly prey to domestic political distractions). As a result, the requirement that an amendment secure a majority of participants (i.e. 130 votes to be adopted) meant in practice some three-quarters of those present, and only 25 amendments were adopted. When it came to the final vote only 189 members were still present and the text was adopted by 150 votes to 13. Looking at those who were absent, however, it can safely be said that it would otherwise have been adopted by an even larger majority.

The Declaration endorsed the objective of remodelling the Community into a European Union on a federal basis and backed a single currency governed by an autonomous central banking system, taking the view that this required stronger instruments of economic and social cohesion. It supported the incorporation of EPC into the Community structures and the inclusion of European citizenship and fundamental rights in the Treaties. It backed extension in Community competences in the social and cultural fields, and also endorsed the EP s institutional requests concerning co-decision on legislation, appointment and term of office of the Commission, right of initiative, scrutiny powers and assent procedure for Treaty modifications. It called for the EP and the national parliaments to prepare a constitution, with the Commission becoming the executive and Parliament and Council exercising legislative and budgetary functions.

Thus, the Assizes also served to re-emphasize a number of key issues and to help build a body of support for them on the eve of the IGCs.

THE COMMISSION'S OPINION

The Commission produced its opinion, required under the treaties to convene the IGC on political union, on 21 October 1990. It confirmed that the Commission had now swung firmly behind the holding of a second IGC, no longer fearing that this might undermine the EMU process, and showed that the Commission backed a substantial agenda for reform which matched largely that put forward by the EP, though diverging on some crucial points.

The Commission argued for a single Community with a common institutional structure, albeit with flexibility with regard to decision-taking procedures. This treaty would not see the final shape of European Union, but should leave the door open to developments in a federal direction. Qualified majority voting should apply in foreign policy matters in areas determined unanimously by the European Council.

It favoured extending Community competence to largely the same fields as those proposed by the EP as well as introducing the notion of Community citizenship (free movement, voting rights in local and European elections) and incorporating a reference to the ECHR. Extensions of competence would be balanced by incorporating the principle of subsidiarity which it would link notably to Article 235. Within the areas of Community competence qualified majority voting would apply to all except constitutional issues and a restricted number of sensitive issues such as taxation, social security or treatment of third country nationals.

Institutionally, it favoured strengthening the Commission's executive powers in the way that Parliament had proposed but opposed undermining the exclusive right of initiative of the Commission. It supported giving the Court of Justice the right to impose sanctions. As regards Parliament's powers, it did not support co-decision, but merely an extension of the cooperation procedure and its modification such that the Commission's second reading proposal, taking account of Parliament's amendments, would stand unless rejected by a simple majority in Council. It supported giving Parliament the right to confirm the appointment of both the President and the College of Commissioners.

Thus the Commission now took up most of Parliament's main proposals, diverging from them mainly on the right of initiative and co-decision.

THE PREPARATORY WORK AMONG GOVERNMENTS

The governments discussed their approach to the political union IGC at meetings of the Foreign Ministers in Asolo on 6/7 October, of the General Council in Luxembourg on 22 October and Brussels on 5/6 November, and of the European Council (Rome I and Rome II) of 27/28 October and 14/15 December 1990.

At the same time, further memoranda or position papers emerged from individual governments. At one end of the spectrum, the Danish government approved a memorandum on 4 October which many felt was rather encouraging, showing how far one of the most reticent countries was willing to go. Denmark's memorandum, approved by the market committee of the Folketing, called for the extension of qualified majority voting in environmental, social and research matters; an extension of Community competence in the fields of indirect taxation, consumer protection, development aid, health, education, energy, telecommunications and cultural cooperation and exchanges; an EP right to initiate legislation where the Commission fails to act and the extension of the cooperation procedure to all areas of internal policy decided by qualified majority voting. It proposed the creation of an Ombudsman and a Committee of the Regions. It called for some Council meetings to be held in public. It called for strengthening foreign policy cooperation, but not its extension to military cooperation. In this area, unanimity should remain the norm, but it favoured merging the EPC secretariat and Council.

At the other end of the spectrum, the Dutch government published a paper on 26 October stating that the Netherlands was 'quite prepared to be pragmatic provided that the ultimate aim of a federal Europe remains intact'. 'Democratic legitimacy' was the key issue for the Netherlands: 'new steps were impossible without simultaneously extending the powers of the European Parliament'. It was for extending and strengthening the cooperation procedure in the way proposed by the Commission in its opinion, but reinforced by combining it with the conciliation procedure. It supported an extension of the assent procedure to Arts 113, 138, 201 and 236, giving the Parliament a 'right to request' form of initiative, and the right to appoint and censure *individual* Commissioners. It had reservations regarding the intergovernmental approach favoured by some other states concerning CFSP and JHA, as well as on strengthening the role of the European Council. It supported extending qualified majority voting and expanding the list of Community competences.

Some national parliaments again took position between the second Dublin and Rome European Councils. The Belgian Senate on 13 July gave explicit backing to the EP Martin II Resolution, called for integration of EPC into the EC system and backed the creation of a Committee of the Regions. The House of Lords' European Committee adopted a report on 30 October,[31] which pleaded for constructive UK participation in the process (drawing attention to the benefits of a single currency which outweighed the loss of national control), for a limited extension of qualified majority voting and of the cooperation procedure and for making EPC more efficient and effective. It preferred to avoid debate on federalism, arguing that 'the constitution of the Community is unique and will remain unique'. The Italian Camera (Committee III) adopted a position on 20 November such that Italian ratification of the new treaty would depend upon its approval by the EP, a position accepted by the Italian government.

During this period, first ideas were exchanged among the governments at permanent representative level. Italy put forward a paper on 18 September proposing that the competences of the WEU be transferred to the future European Union. The UK submitted proposals for technical improvements in EPC, for improving budgetary control, and for allowing the Court of Justice to fine Member States failing to respect its judgments. Germany took up the idea of a Committee of Regions and put forward a formulation for inserting the principle of subsidiarity in the treaty. Spain followed up Gonzalez's letter on citizenship with a more detailed paper.

The deliberations of the Foreign Ministers culminated in the two Roman European Council meetings. It is a measure of how far the debate was carried forward during this period that the conclusions of Rome II – fewer than 7 weeks later – were already far more extensive than Rome I, which was itself more forthcoming than Dublin.

In Rome I, the European Council 'confirmed the will progressively to transform the Community into a European Union by developing its political dimension . . .',[32] but references to extending EC competences, EP powers, defining European citizenship, the objective of a common foreign and security policy and the need to go beyond the present limits with regard to security were all subject to UK reservations in what was to be Thatcher's last summit. The conclusions recorded that 'on these points the United Kingdom delegation prefers not to preempt the debate in the intergovernmental conference'. The conclusions made no specific reference to extending qualified majority voting or to involving the EP in the appointment of the Commission.

The Rome II conclusions[33] saw the European Council agree to a long list of issues for the IGC, asking the latter to give them 'particular attention'. This was the culmination of all the agenda-setting exercises of the European Parliament, the Assizes, the interinstitutional conference, the Commission and national governments and parliaments. The European Council's list began with the heading 'democratic legitimacy' where it asked the conference to consider extending and improving the cooperation procedure, extending the assent procedure, involving the EP in the appointment of the Commission and its President, increasing Parliament's powers of budgetary control and consolidating the right of petition to the EP and the latter's powers of inquiry. It also asked the conference to consider developing a co-decision procedure for acts of a legislative nature. It noted the support for creating arrangements enabling regional and local authorities to be consulted.

Under the heading of a common and foreign security policy, (henceforth CFSP), it asked the IGC to examine an institutional framework based on one decision-making centre, namely the Council, a unified secretariat (EPC and Council), a reinforced role for the Commission, adequate procedure for consulting and informing the EP and procedures ensuring that the Union speaks with one voice towards the outside. Decision-taking would be based on the rule of consensus for 'defining general guidelines' (with abstention or non-participation to be encouraged to facilitate consensus) and qualified majority voting for 'the implementation of agreed policies'.

On security, the European Council emphasized that the prospective role for the Union in defence matters should be considered including the idea of a commitment by Member States to provide mutual assistance (as in Article 5 of WEU Treaty). It committed the IGC to examine the future of WEU, without going as far as the Italian Presidency had proposed which was the gradual absorption of WEU by the European Union by the 1998 expiry of the WEU Treaty.

Under the heading of extending and strengthening Community action, the European Council noted that there is 'a wide recognition of the need to extend or redefine the Community's competence in specific areas', citing notably the social dimension, cohesion, environment, health, research, energy, infrastructures and cultural exchanges. It asked the IGC to examine how to bring intergovernmental matters in the field of justice and home affairs into the Union framework. It emphasized the importance of the principle of subsidiarity without specifying this should be incorporated into the treaties. Under the heading of European citizenship, the IGC was asked to consider voting rights in European and municipal elections, joint consular protection and freedom of movement, as well as the creation of an Ombudsman.

Finally, under the heading of 'effectiveness and efficiency' the European Council 'emphasised that extending the responsibilities of the Union must be accompanied by a strengthening of the Commission's role and in particular its implementing powers' and asked the IGC to examine the extension of qualified majority voting in Council, in view of 'making it the general rule with a limited number of exceptions'.

As regards EMU, preparations among the governments had followed a different and well-prepared course. The blueprint drawn up by the Delors Committee of Central Bankers specified all the issues needing negotiation in the IGCs. For 11 states it was quite clear that EMU meant the establishment of irrevocably fixed exchange rates (with the probable option of a single currency), common monetary policy, free circulation of capital and the establishment of a central banking system. Negotiations would therefore be about the timetable for achieving these targets, conditions that needed to be fulfilled for transition to the final stage of monetary union, the provisions for external relations of the monetary union, the structure of the banking institutions and filling out the economic side of EMU. The UK did seek to redefine what EMU meant, first by floating a proposal for competing currencies (i.e. that all national currencies should be legal tender throughout the EC, competing for usage) and then by putting forward its 'hard ECU' proposals (i.e. that the ECU should be 'hardened' by making it impossible to devalue against the strongest national currency, and that it should become a 13th currency in parallel to national currencies). These were looked at politely by the other Member States, but the UK was unsuccessful in persuading the others that monetary union meant anything less than the ultimate establishment of a single currency.

Before the IGC started, preparations began in the monetary committee, the Committee of Central Bank Governors and in a high-level working group chaired by Elizabeth Guigou, then a member of the Secretariat of the Élysée, and later to become European Affairs Minister. The work revealed some differences of emphasis among the 11 Member States supporting monetary union.

Germany was initially isolated (apart from Luxembourg) in its insistence upon very strict convergence criteria being met before any transition to EMU could proceed. Germany, and the Bundesbank in particular, were not prepared to accept any form of EMU that might endanger the high monetary stability.

The work of the Committee of Governors consisted mainly in producing (as instructed by the Madrid summit) the draft statute for the proposed European Central Bank. This was eventually to be attached, almost unamended, as a protocol to the Maastricht Treaty. It envisaged in the final stage of EMU, a European System of Central Banks (ESCB) consisting of a European Central Bank (ECB), endowed with its own legal personality, and the Central Banks of participating Member States. Reflecting German pressures, the primacy of monetary stability and the independence of the ESCB were enshrined as sacrosanct principles in the Committee's Report. Despite the stated position of the UK government that it did not accept the case for a single currency, the Governor of the Bank of England participated fully in all of the Committee's discussions.

By the time of the Rome I meeting of the European Council in October 1990, all Member States except Britain were able to agree that the IGC should aim for an *independent* Central Bank and that the three-phase timetable contained in the Delors Report should be followed, with the second phase beginning in January 1994 and the third phase some three years later.

This growing consensus among the 11 on fundamental principles of EMU made the UK's isolation more and more apparent. On 5 October, Thatcher, under pressure from her Cabinet, agreed to allow sterling to join the ERM, though annoying other Member States by unilaterally announcing the (high) central rate for sterling against the ECU, and continuing to argue that EMU was not necessary to achieve the full benefits of the single market. Any hopes that the gesture of joining the ERM might gain more sympathetic treatment of the UK's position and its 'hard ECU' plan, at least on the part of the Germans, were dashed when the Rome I Summit (confirming the views of the EPP leaders' pre-summit a few days before) essentially decided to proceed without the UK. Thatcher was furious.

Her criticisms of the other Member States, her accusations against the other leaders for having 'ambushed' her, her assertions that EMU proposals were in 'cloud cuckoo land' and the isolation – yet again – of the UK, provoked the resignation of her Deputy PM Sir Geoffrey Howe and the challenge to her leadership of the Conservative Party, which led to her own resignation on 22 November after failing to obtain the necessary majority for re-election. The most prominent opponent of EMU was sidelined, and although the attitude of her successor John Major was not yet clear, it was apparent that the other Member States were determined to press ahead on the basis agreed in Rome.

ASSESSMENT

It can be seen that from a few sketchy headlines in the early months of the year, the agenda for the IGC had been thrashed out to cover a wide series of potentially important reforms. Almost all of the points initially listed by the EP, and subsequently spelt out in its specific proposals, had found an echo and were supported either by particular governments, or backed by the conference with national parliaments or by the Commission in its opinion or else taken up directly by the Foreign Ministers via the interinstitutional conferences. Placing issues on the agenda of the IGC was, of course, no guarantee as to the final result. Nevertheless it was an essential first step.

Parliament had been the first to press for a conference on political union and had defined as early as November 1989, well before such a conference had even been proposed by any government, both a list of subjects which it wished to be see pursued and a strategy for building up support for them. In devoting the whole of 1990 to the gradual formulation of specific proposals, and at the same time beginning a dialogue with the other institutions, with national parliaments and, at the level of its political groups, with national political parties, the EP was able to help formulate much of the preliminary thinking that went into the preparation of the IGCs. Its detailed proposals were ready within a month of the decision to hold a second IGC. Its suggestions for a pre-conference with Council and Commission and for the European Assizes with national parliaments met with positive responses. The pre-conference met four times in the course of 1990 with the participation of all the Member States and the Commission. The Parliamentary Assizes took place just a week after the adoption of the Martin III Report, and three weeks before the start of the IGC. Both were useful vehicles for Parliament to gain support for its views. Indeed the declaration adopted by the Assizes by an overwhelming majority, endorsed almost all the main proposals that Parliament had put forward. For the rest, its influence was more indirect, though none the less significant. As the meeting place of all of Europe's major political parties, and the forum in which discussions on the future of the Community took place at party-political level (rather than at the level of Ministers and officials), the Parliament's deliberations played a role in shaping the climate of opinion of political circles in the Member States, albeit in some more than others, partly via the European party federations whose pre-meetings before summits were becoming increasingly important. In terms of shaping the agenda for the forthcoming negotiations, the European Parliament, through these various means, was strikingly successful.

12 The IGCs on Economic and Monetary Union and on Political Union

In this chapter we shall, as in chapter 9 concerning the 1985 IGC, examine the dynamics of the IGCs which produced the Treaty on European Union. We shall look again at the negotiations and explore how the key compromises were obtained. We shall look in particular at the discussions concerning the EP's key objectives.

PROCEDURES AND METHODS

Both IGCs began the day after the second Rome European Council. It was agreed that they should conclude in time for the Summit due under the Dutch Presidency at the end of the following year, eventually held in Maastricht. In the end, some final legal work meant that the IGC, technically, finished in 1992 under the Portuguese Presidency. Politically, however, Maastricht can be seen as the final point of the negotiations.

The general scheme of the IGCs was monthly ministerial meetings (except August), though this intensified in the run-up to the Maastricht Summit. In all there were some ten formal and two 'informal' ministerial sessions each on EMU and on political union before the final Maastricht Summit. In between, the detailed work was carried out in weekly meetings of the personal representatives of the Ministers. For the most part, these comprised the Permanent Representatives of the Member States in Brussels. The Ministers also met nine times (alternating monthly EMU and political union) with the delegation of 12 MEPs in the parallel interinstitutional conference.

As we have seen, the nature of the two IGCs was somewhat different. Whereas the EMU IGC dealt with a specific subject matter, and most participants had a clear idea of what issues were to be negotiated with a blueprint existing in the form of the report of the Delors Committee of the Central Bank Governors, the same was not the case in the political union IGC. Here, there was no limitation as to the number of subjects, no jointly prepared blueprint (although there were the comprehensive submissions of the Parliament, the Commission and the Belgian, Dutch and Greek governments) and the objectives of the Member States diverged on a great number of points. The EMU IGC was therefore able to get to grips relatively quickly with the key issues, whereas the political union IGC first went through a three-month phase of collecting and studying a multitude of individual proposals.

It was agreed at the outset that the results of both IGCs should be sent for ratification together, which implied a parallelism in their work. Coordination and cohesion of the two IGCs was the responsibility of the Foreign Ministers, and for this reason their personal representatives were allowed to attend EMU IGC meetings as well.

All matters in the PU IGC were prepared by the same group at the level of officials, unlike the 1985 IGC where one working party (again, mainly the permanent representatives) prepared modifications to the Community Treaties and another (the political directors in each foreign ministry responsible for EPC) prepared the provisions on political cooperation. Not too much should be read into this exclusion of the political directors – it would have been impossible to sideline figures so close to Ministers' ears – but it did mean that the overall approach was likely to be more cohesive and, as regards foreign policy, less wedded to EPC vocabulary. Indeed, since the first months of the IGC took place while ministers (and political directors) were preoccupied with the Gulf War, the personal representatives were left considerable leeway at the early stages.

This early phase in the PU IGC was an opportunity for Member States and the Commission to table formal treaty amendments reflecting their approaches or anticipating possible compromises. Altogether, some 2000 pages of draft treaty articles[1] were submitted.

Following this phase of presentation and discussion of the numerous treaty amendments submitted, the Luxembourg Presidency prepared a global 'non-paper' which constituted a global draft as regards political union. This was submitted to the Foreign Ministers on 15 April and communicated at the same time to the EP, with Foreign Minister Poos participating in a debate in Parliament on 17 April, using the opportunity for informal discussions with leaders of the Socialist Group, whilst his coalition partner Ministers did likewise with the EPP.

This non-paper was subject to intense discussions over the next few weeks both within the IGC and outside. The Commission and the EP and several governments including Luxembourg's Benelux partners were particularly critical of the 'pillar' structure introduced whereby new treaty provisions in the field of foreign affairs and internal police matters would not be added to the EC Treaty but would be carried out in a separate legal framework. The EC as such would be just one element of a wider European Union, the other elements being largely intergovernmental. These issues will be examined in more detail below. It was, however, the conviction of the Luxembourg Ministers that their approach was the only one capable of reaching the necessary unanimity. The critics argued that it was too early in the IGC to offer compromises to the reticent Member States, and that it was better first to put pressure on for a more satisfactory solution.

Following a special meeting of Foreign Ministers in Dresden which examined the main criticisms of the non-paper, the Luxembourg government produced a 'draft treaty' in time for the June European Council. It was only slightly different from the non-paper, taking some account of the criticisms, as we shall see. The European Council, as planned, did not enter into detailed discussions on the IGCs, merely taking note of developments so far, conducting a general exchange of views and concluding that the draft was a good base for negotiations.

The Dutch Presidency, due partly to the Yugoslav crisis, only gradually got to grips with the IGCs. It too produced a global draft, but only in September – over two months into its Presidency. The Dutch paper, *inter alia*, brought foreign policy and internal affairs into the Community framework, producing a unitary structure for European Union albeit with modulated decision-making procedures.

A draft version of the Dutch document had been circulated informally at the very beginning of September and had even been discussed by Dankert with the spokesmen on European Affairs of the Socialist Parties in all the national parliaments who were attending a Socialist Group conference in Brussels. Despite some support from these quarters, and although the final version published later in September was a watered-down version, it met outright hostility from several governments. At a meeting of Foreign Ministers on 30 September which became known in the Netherlands as the 'Black Monday' of Dutch diplomacy, the text was rejected as a basis for further negotiations. Only Belgium lent it further support. Although the Dutch text reflected the majority opinion on most issues, it alienated not only the traditionally reticent countries, but also France (on its CFSP provisions) and Luxembourg (on the dumping of its own work). Even those who thought that the Luxembourg text should have been more advanced felt it was too late at this stage of the IGC to try to regain lost ground.

The IGC thus proceeded with the Dutch submitting, on an issue-by-issue basis, modifications of the Luxembourg text, to the regular meetings of the personal representatives, culminating in a new working draft tabled on 8 November. A special conclave of the Foreign Ministers in Noordwijk on 12/13 November was intended to iron out the main remaining divergences before the Maastricht Summit. In fact, it managed to tackle only a proportion of them despite reconvening in Brussels two weeks later. The issues requiring settlement at the Summit itself were at least narrowed down to a smaller number, albeit crucial ones.

Similarly, in the IGC on EMU, steady progress had led, as we shall see, to agreement on most of the main issues with only a handful needing settlement at the Summit. Among these were ones where the outlines of a settlement were clear, but where there was a reluctance to finalize them before a global agreement was reached at the Summit.

The Dutch Presidency, like the Luxembourg Presidency, reported on developments to the EP not only through the interinstitutional conference but directly to plenary. Indeed, the EP held a debate almost monthly on one aspect or another of the IGCs. Minister Dankert also appeared before Parliament's Committee on Institutional Affairs and the respective Socialist and Christian Democrat Ministers were in contact with their corresponding EP groups. As a result, there was no danger of the issues of major concern to the Parliament, including the issue of its own powers, being forgotten or sidelined in the last few weeks.

The Maastricht European Council Meeting was held on 9/10 December. Most participants arrived in Maastricht already on 8 December, to be confronted by large international rallies and demonstrations in favour of European Union. Indeed, the rally organized by the Union of European Federalists included several thousand participants from Central and Eastern Europe as well as from the Community.

Agreement was far from certain when the Summit opened with an address from the EP President, nor even when it embarked on its final session of the evening of the second day. Only in the early hours of the morning on 11 December was a final compromise reached. At the price, notably, of special provisions to apply to the UK for EMU and for social policy, the Summit agreed on the establishment of a European Union including the notion of Union citizenship, the principle of a common foreign and security policy, a single currency and an increase in the powers of the EP. Key issues in the negotiations will be examined below.

EXTERNAL ATTEMPTS TO INFLUENCE THE IGC

Throughout the IGC, there were of course attempts to influence it from the outside. Among others, these included statements and actions by non-governmental organizations, pressure from governments from third states, national parliaments, political parties (or factions thereof) and, as we have seen, the European Parliament.

Indeed, the latter was the only external body to be given a permanent and formal channel of communication to the IGCs. As we saw in chapter 11, the governments agreed to continue the interinstitutional conferences that had been held in the preparatory stage of the IGCs. As a result, a total of ten meetings were held between the IGC ministers and the delegation of parliamentarians, generally alternating monthly between EMU and political union subjects. Parliament retained the high-level delegation it had for the previous CIP meetings.

Parliament's delegation to the interinstitutional conference also embarked on a tour of the national capitals where they met successively each of the prime ministers. These were important not so much in terms of presenting Parliament's arguments to the more reticent leaders, but in terms of putting pressure on those who were on record as being in agreement with Parliament's requests in order to ensure that they lived up to their public statements and felt obliged to fight on the Parliament's behalf, such as Kohl, Gonzalez, Andreotti, Martens and Lubbers.

Besides these contacts Parliament's President spoke at a number of the ministerial meetings of the IGCs, notably at the conclave in Noordwijk, as well, of course, at all the European Council meetings. Parliament's global level of direct contact with the IGC therefore exceeded with the 1985 IGC.

Pressure from national parliaments was largely directed towards their individual participants in the IGCs. There were no new parliamentary Assizes during the IGCs to permit a collective approach, although this had been suggested just prior to Maastricht by a number of parliamentarians. Generally, it was felt that the Declaration adopted at the Assizes in Rome was sufficient as a collective statement. However, the presidents of seven national parliaments and the EP met on 6 December, just before the summit, in Brussels, under Dutch chairmanship. On the initiative of Fabius, Süssmuth and Nothomb (Presidents of the French Assembly, the German Bundestag and the Belgian Chamber respectively), they issued a statement recalling the Assizes Declaration and calling on the heads of government to be particularly attentive to the democratic dimension of the envisaged reforms. The text was signed, apart from the above-mentioned, by the Presidents of the Italian, Luxembourg and Portuguese Parliaments.

Separate pressure each towards individual governments in a domestic political context would clearly not be as coherent as that produced by the Assizes. Indeed, national parliamentary debates tended to throw up a host of reservations on particular subjects and to warn governments of potential difficulties in ratification. In France, for instance, it showed that although the Gaullist Party was no longer so hostile to Europe as in the past, it would, for the most part, oppose supranational developments. Even part of the Socialist Party (the CERES faction of Chevènement) was also likely to oppose the new Treaty. The most spectacular parliamentary debates were in the UK, where attention focused on the divisions within the Conservative Party, with Margaret Thatcher joining with the traditional anti-European elements to send warning shots over the bows of John Major. With an election looming, this limited Major's margin for manoeuvre with his overriding preoccupation becoming the unity of the Conservative Party. It would be difficult to steer any course that would satisfy all the currents in his party, but it became clear that this was what he would attempt to do.

The social partners were also active. ETUC issued further statements in the course of the IGCs dwelling in particular on the social chapter. The employers' organization, UNICE, did the same. ETUC and UNICE jointly negotiated a series of treaty articles on the involvement of the social partners in preparing social legislation. This was taken up by the Commission and served as a basis for negotiation on this subject in the IGC, despite the CBI repudiating what its representative in UNICE had agreed.

The European party federations – the CSP, EPP and ELDR – all met regularly before and during the IGCs. Congresses and six-monthly summits of party leaders and prime ministers each issued declarations, normally quite federalist in inclination. As we have seen, their internal dynamics tend to put pressure on the more reticent or cautious parties to move forward. Members of the Commission belonging to the corresponding political grouping, and the Chairmen of the corresponding EP Groups, also participate in such summits. The most striking texts emerging from these party federations were those adopted on the eve of the IGCs, spelling out in detail objectives they wished to see attained.[2] Significantly, all three took up all the main objectives of the EP as outlined in the Martin Reports. The heads of government of most of the Member States were involved in one or another of these meetings, and signed up to the Declarations, as did other party leaders. The governing parties (and leaders, including prime ministers) of the UK, Denmark and Ireland were alone in not taking part in such processes.

THE SUBSTANCE OF THE NEGOTIATIONS

For reasons of space, it is not possible to examine here the negotiations on all the subjects dealt with by the IGCs. The author has done so in another context.[3] This section will therefore concentrate on only two aspects of the negotiations: the structure of the Treaty and the federal objective on the one hand, and the powers of the EP on the other. These two issues are particularly relevant for the subject of this book. But in examining the proceedings of the IGC, it must be pointed out that at a general level, one important feature overshadowed the whole process. This was the contrast in attitude between the majority of Member States and the United Kingdom. As Ambassador Philippe de Schouthete de Tervarent (Belgian Permanent Representative to the EC, and personal representative of the foreign minister in the political union working party) put it:

> It seems that most Member States shared these preoccupations [for strengthening integration], to various degrees. In the negotiations, France and Germany focused on foreign policy and security, Spain on citizenship and cohesion, Italy and Belgium on the powers of the Parliament and majority voting, Denmark on the environment. . . . But it is important to underline that one of the principal partners was convinced by none of these arguments. The United Kingdom had participated with reluctance in the first analyses concerning EMU [and for political union] the whole exercise seemed to it to be pointless, . . . The final result cannot be correctly appreciated if one ignores the fact that one of the principal participants had no objectives and was seeking no results. This was without doubt the principal difficulty in this negotiation which can, in a way, be analysed as debate between supporters of movement and supporters of the status quo.[4]

Structure of the Treaty and the Federal Objective

Many felt that the time had come fully to integrate EPC into the Community framework, albeit with appropriately modulated decision-taking procedures. This view was reflected in Parliament's proposals to the IGCs and in the memoranda of the Belgian and Dutch governments. When the IGC got underway, the Commission tabled a specific proposal whereby foreign policy, along with development policy and external trade, would become chapters of the EC Treaty. Early discussions in the IGC, however, showed that this view was far from obtaining unanimous support. The UK in particular objected to bringing EPC fully into the Community framework. However, it was not alone on this. France, although in the integrationist camp on most issues, had misgivings about this.

There was similar reticence in another equally sensitive context. This was cooperation in the field of justice and home affairs (JHA). Over the years a number of intergovernmental frameworks for cooperation had emerged, notably TREVI which had an elaborate structure of its own. These procedures were often criticized as being secretive and not being subject to any parliamentary scrutiny be it national or European. The definition of the internal market in the Single Act as an 'area without internal frontiers' had given cooperation in these areas greater importance, and linked the subjects more directly to the Community as such. Again, there was a feeling that these practices should be given treaty status, codified, linked to the Community and subjected to at least some scrutiny by the EP. However, many governments were reluctant to bring these matters fully into the Community's legal framework where the case law of the Court of Justice, applying due process, proportionality, non-discrimination on the grounds of nationality, etc. might have unforeseen consequences not likely to appeal to interior ministries.

Consequently, the Luxembourg 'non-paper' of April 1990 proposed a similar structure to the SEA, with EPC and JHA kept outside the Community framework under separate treaty provisions not part of the EC legal system, with no legal review by the Court and with the Commission enjoying a lesser role in initiating proposals and in implementing policies. The European Union would thus be founded on three 'pillars'. This structure was therefore baptized as the 'Greek temple' approach.

None the less, the CFSP would be more *communautaire* than EPC had been. Council (rather than a separate meeting of Foreign Ministers) would be primarily responsible for determining policy. The EPC secretariat would be absorbed by Council secretariat. Even the language changed, referring to 'Member States' rather than the 'High Contracting Parties' and to 'common policy' rather than 'cooperation'.

At the same time, the Community 'pillar' itself was strengthened, even in the field of external relations (where development policy was made a new chapter of the EEC Treaty rather than a matter for CFSP) and given more federal characteristics such as the notion of common ('Union') citizenship and the objective, under the EMU provisions (which might instead have been made a fourth pillar), of a single currency. The name of the EEC Treaty was changed to EC Treaty, to indicate its political, not just economic, finality.

This 'pillar' structure was criticized by the European Parliament, the Commission and the more federalist-minded governments. The Commission tabled a set of amendments to it, designed to ensure a unitary structure of the Treaty, by providing for the European Union to 'take the place of the European Communities' and by adding provisions on foreign policy cooperation and internal affairs to the modified Community Treaties. This corresponded to the Commission's original proposals, but this time the Commission took over the operational details of the Luxembourg draft regarding foreign policy, thus giving a stronger role for the Council and its Presidency and a lesser role for the Commission than in its initial proposals. The Commission attached an explanatory memorandum in which it stated that the IGC

> should be guided by the basic thinking which has been behind the construction of Europe for forty years now, namely that all progress made towards economic, monetary, social or political integration should gradually be brought together in a single Community as the precursor of a European Union. This being so, it is somewhat paradoxical that the current trend . . . would depart from this general unification process and keep the Community no longer as the focal point but simply as one entity among others in a political union with ill-defined objectives and a variety of institutional schemes.

The Commission argued that, like EMU, the CFSP provisions could have particular characteristics, but that this should not preclude their integration into the Community framework. This model was baptised the 'tree' approach.

The Foreign Ministers discussed the issue at several meetings in May and June. A majority of Member States (Belgium, Germany, Greece, Ireland, Italy, Spain, the Netherlands) supported the 'tree' approach rather than the 'temple' approach. The Luxembourg Presidency, however, was not convinced that the majority view was capable of gaining the necessary consensus at the end of the day.[5] Nevertheless, it did make some adjustments in its new text 'Draft Treaty on the Union' of

20 June. These were designed to reassure the majority that the pillar structure would not be the beginning of the end of the Community system but, on the contrary, could represent a step towards communautarization of the two non-Community pillars. The main changes were as follows:

- to specify that the Union 'shall be founded on the European Communities *supplemented* by other policies and cooperations established by this treaty', thus indicating a priority to the Community system;
- adding two specifications to the effect that the *acquis communautaire* could not be undermined by the new pillars but, on the contrary, should develop further;
- to specify that 'the Union shall be served by a single institutional framework', thus ensuring an *institutional* merger of EPC with the Community (i.e. it would be run by the Community institutions, albeit predominantly the Council), even if it would remain *legally* separate;
- to state that the Treaty 'marks a new stage in the process leading gradually to a Union with a federal goal';
- to include a revision clause specifying that a new IGC would be convened in 1996 'in the perspective of strengthening the federal character of the Union';
- transferring some 'constitutional' clauses of the EC Treaty (concerning Treaty revision and accession of new Member States) to the final provisions of the Union Treaty, thus assuring the unity of the whole in these respects;
- to specify that the Union was responsible not just for relations among its Member States, but also its 'peoples': this again to underline that the process was not merely intergovernmental.

These changes did not fully satisfy the federalist camp. The Belgian Chamber of Deputies adopted a resolution on 27 June 1991 supporting 'a Union with a democratic system and a federal structure; rejects the tripartite structure proposed by the Presidency of the EC Council'. The EP also called (14 June) for 'the unicity of the Community's legal and institutional system [to] be safeguarded and extended to other sectors which currently enjoy inter-state cooperation such as foreign policy'. But nor was the other camp satisfied, the UK and Denmark objecting in particular to the reference to the federal goal.

The European Council meeting on 28–29 June in Luxembourg agreed that 'the Presidency's draft forms the basis for the continuation of negotiations', but also considered 'that the Union should be based on the following principles: ... full maintenance of the *acquis communautaire* and development thereof, [and] a single institutional framework'. The Dutch Presidency, which took over on 1 July, made another attempt to reopen the issue, but unsuccessfully, as we saw above.

The Dutch thus reverted to the Luxembourg structure. However, visa policy was transferred from the JHA pillar to Community competence, and an evolutive clause provided for the possibility of subsequent transfers to be made by Council, acting unanimously. The new text also spelled out that a number of EC treaty articles (those defining the composition of the institutions and certain of their prerogatives) would apply directly to CFSP and JHA, and that administrative expenditure would (and operational expenditure could) be charged to the Community's budget. All these changes enmeshed the CFSP and JHA further into the EC. The specific reference to the 'federal goal', however, continued to be contested by the UK government, which maintained that it would not sign a Treaty containing such a reference.

Most of the other Member States insisted on keeping the reference, as part of the compromise on the structure of the Treaty. Indeed, the UK's focus on the word, rather than on substantive 'federal' developments, convinced many that the opposition had become a symbol for reasons to do with internal divisions within the UK Conservative Party. Its removal could best be left to the Maastricht Summit itself, thus allowing John Major to claim victory on that point, leaving the substance intact. There, the federal objective was replaced by a reference to the new Treaty marking 'a new stage in the process of creating an ever closer union among the peoples of Europe in which decisions are taken as closely as possible to the citizens'. Although it was pointed out that an 'ever-closer Union' must logically imply a more centralized Union than a federal one, this text satisfied the UK delegation. In exchange, a reference was incorporated into Art. B to the effect that the 1996 IGC should review the pillar structure.

Overall, then, the new Treaty maintained the largely intergovernmental character of CFSP and JHA, but brought them within the EC institutional framework. At the same time, the Community pillar was extended both in scope (with new provisions on EMU, consumer protection, culture, education, public health, industry, trans-European networks, social policy and, even in the field of external relations, development policy) and in level (with an extension of qualified majority voting to several new areas and greater involvement of the EP).

The Legislative Powers of the European Parliament

The IGC faced a situation in which a majority (Belgium, Netherlands, Germany, Italy, Greece, Spain and, to a certain extent, France) accepted, in principle, the EP's request for co-decision powers with Council, whereas two (UK, Denmark) were strongly against, and two (Portugal and Ireland) were far from enthusiastic.

As we have seen, Parliament proposed a procedure whereby if, after two readings, Parliament and Council still diverged, a conciliation committee would be convened to negotiate a compromise. The compromise would have to be approved by both institutions. Texts would then be signed into law by the President of Parliament and the President of Council jointly. The German government tabled a proposal that was virtually identical. The Italian government proposed one that was similar and the German and Italian Foreign Ministers issued a joint public statement emphasizing the importance they attached to increasing Parliament's powers. The Commission, which, in its opinion on the convening of the IGCs, had been against co-decision, came up with a proposal that was superficially similar to Parliament's, but differed in a number of details. It would maintain the Commission's discretion in whether or not to accept Parliament's amendments, whatever the majority they are adopted by. Amendments rejected by the Commission could be adopted only by unanimity in Council, as is the case with Member States' amendments. The Commission argued that this was fundamental to the equilibrium of the Community and was supported by Belgium, Germany, Ireland, Portugal and the UK – an unusual coalition!

The Luxembourg Presidency non-paper contained a proposal for a 'co-decision procedure' that would apply only to a few items of Community legislation (environment, research, development cooperation and economic and social cohesion). Furthermore, it would be used only to adopt a new category of Community 'laws', which would, in these fields, lay down the framework for subsequent Community action that would take the traditional form of regulations or directives adopted pursuant to existing procedures.

This, of course, was a long way from satisfying the EP as it would amount to about one co-decision procedure each year. Parliament was also critical of the precise procedure put forward because it provided that if the conciliation procedure failed to find an agreement between Council and Parliament, Council could then adopt its own text and this would become law unless Parliament rejected it within two months by a majority of its members. Parliament felt that this weighted the procedure in favour of Council. Council would not be obliged to negotiate in good faith in the conciliation committee, as it could simply wait for the deadline, adopt its own text and challenge Parliament to reject it. Parliament would be unlikely to make frequent use of its right to reject, not simply because this requires a majority of members to do so, but because it would leave Parliament in the negative role, being blamed for blocking Community action.

The Dutch Presidency took a different approach, proposing to take the existing cooperation procedure, to use it in almost all cases in which Council adopted legislation by qualified majority voting, and strengthen it by giving Parliament the right to reject the final outcome of Council's second reading.

An early draft of the Dutch text (circulated informally for consultation in September but never formally tabled in the IGC) had envisaged a second modification to the cooperation procedure such that when the Council considered the Commission's revised proposal in second reading, it would be deemed to have *approved* it if it failed, by the three-month deadline, either to amend it (by qualified majority) or to change it (by unanimity). (At present, if Council fails to do either by the deadline, the text falls.) It was soon clear that this second modification stood no chance of being accepted by the IGCs – it would, after all, mean that the Commission's reviewed proposal, taking up Parliament's amendments, could become law if only one Member State agreed with it and was willing to prevent a decision in Council before the deadline.

Thus, the text actually tabled by the Dutch Presidency envisaged simply giving Parliament a right of rejection or veto of Council's decisions at the end of the cooperation procedure. Whilst this would undoubtedly reinforce Parliament's bargaining position in the procedure, it would place Parliament under the same constraints regarding the rejection of texts as were described above in relation to the Luxembourg proposal, and without any provision for a conciliation procedure. On the other hand, the proposal applied to virtually all Community legislation and not to a small category only (though the Luxembourg proposal reappeared too in this version of the Dutch text, for the four areas that the Luxembourgers had envisaged).

As we saw above, the whole of the Dutch draft Treaty was withdrawn after two weeks. In October and early November, the Dutch proceeded to produce new texts, based largely on the old Luxembourg text, for each and every subject, leaving the issue of how the various elements would be put together to a later stage. Concerning the powers of the EP, they produced a new text which took the old Luxembourg text as its basis, but which applied the co-decision procedure to a wider area: multi-annual programmes for the environment, the framework programme for research, indicative programmes for trans-European infrastructures and all the areas previously subject to the cooperation procedure.

Discussions in the IGC then revealed opposition by different Member States to different items on this list – and by the UK to all of them. Spain and Portugal opposed co-decision for the research framework programme and for the environment; Luxembourg for Arts 100(a) and 100(b); France and Spain regarding the objectives of the structural funds; France as regards development cooperation programmes; and even the Commission expressed reservations concerning Articles 100(a) and 100(b) (internal market harmonizations) arguing they were sometimes used for highly technical matters.

This list of objections was, however, gradually whittled away, notably at the Noordwijk Conclave of 13 November. The Commission, in particular, having been strongly criticized by MEPs, withdrew its opposition concerning Arts 100(a) and 100(b), without which the scope of the procedure would have been minimal. In the end, some 15 items were accepted for co-decision – a number higher than those previously falling under the cooperation procedure.

The IGC also returned to Parliament's objections to the provisions allowing Council to act unilaterally in the event of conciliation failing. Italy, Spain, Greece, Germany, Belgium and the Commission all supported Parliament's view that the negotiation of an agreement in conciliation should be the *only* way forward when positions diverge, but this view did not reach consensus. Council's right to act unilaterally, provided Parliament does not subsequently reject the text outright, was preserved. The Commission's right to vet Parliament's amendments (those that it rejects needing unanimity to be accepted in Council), was also maintained, except in the context of the conciliation committee where Council's delegation can accept Parliament's amendments by qualified majority voting, irrespective of the position of the Commission.

Curiously, part of the compromise among the governments was to avoid calling the new provisions the 'co-decision procedure'. The UK government, which had been vocal in its opposition to co-decision, hoped to camouflage its concession by avoiding the term. The treaty therefore refers only to 'the procedure laid down in Art. 189(b)', though the UK government tried using the term 'negative assent procedure' (sic) when describing it to the UK parliament. Similarly, the term 'cooperation' procedure was deleted in the treaty, referred to as the '189C' procedure. This would now apply to most of the areas not covered by co-decision where Council acts by qualified majority voting. The main exceptions were agriculture and trade, where Parliament would, as before, simply be consulted.

Finally, the IGC examined Parliament's request to extend the *assent procedure* to further categories of international agreements as well as to Treaty revisions and to constitutional matters where Council acts by unanimity. The Dutch Presidency proposed in October that it should be extended to cover measures concerning the right of residence of Union citizens (this was initially opposed by Luxembourg and the UK); rules for the structural funds (opposed by the UK and the Commission); the uniform electoral system; and further categories of international agreements. Other delegations proposed to add the definition of own resources (supported by Italy, Spain, Greece and Germany), Art. 235 (supported by Italy, Spain, Greece, Germany, Belgium, the Netherlands and the Commission), Treaty revisions (supported by Italy, Spain, Greece, Germany, Belgium and the Commission) and the introduction of the final phase of EMU (supported by Italy, Greece and Belgium). Only the proposals of the Dutch Presidency were incorporated into the final package, the other four falling. However, two areas from EMU were added at the end: amendments to the Protocol of the Central Bank and conferral of special tasks on the Central Bank.

The overall outcome was a substantial step forward for the European Parliament's powers in the Community's legislative procedures. However, it is an uneven one, leaving a confusing variety of procedures (assent, co-decision, cooperation, consultation) mostly complicated and with variants (qualified majority voting, unanimity in Council, simple or absolute majority in Parliament).

The Parliament and the Commission

As we have seen, Parliament proposed to the IGC that the term of office of the Commission should be linked to that of Parliament and that, following each European parliamentary election, the President of the Commission should be elected by Parliament on a proposal of the European Council. Once he/she and the European Council had agreed on the rest of the College of Commissioners, they should be subjected to a collective vote of confidence by Parliament before taking office (as Parliament had done without treaty provision since 1980).

Parliament received early support from Germany which tabled a similar proposal (but proposing that the Commission President be reconfirmed after 2 1/2 years). The formalization of the vote of confidence in the treaties appears to have met with early acceptance in the IGC despite initial Danish and British resistance. Even Member States not enthusiastic about increasing Parliament's powers were prepared to accept this change, which could be presented as being little more than entrenching existing practice.

The proposal that Parliament should also elect the President of the Commission on a proposal of the European Council was, however, more problematic. Several Member States (the UK, Ireland, Portugal, Denmark and the Netherlands), considered that this 'dual investiture' of both the President and the College was too much. The Commission itself, supported by Germany, Belgium, Italy and Spain, was prepared to accept the proposal. As to the suggestion that the term of office of the Commission should be changed from 4 to 5 years to coincide with that of Parliament, this met initially with support only from Germany, Italy and Spain, and hostility from Ireland, France, Greece, Portugal and the UK. Nevertheless, Parliament continued to press the point, which featured prominently in the discussions held in the interinstitutional conference and in the discussions held by Parliament's delegation touring the national capitals to meet the various heads of government. The point was finally added to the text at Maastricht itself, not having achieved even majority support at the Noordwijk meeting of the Foreign Ministers the previous month. This was, perhaps, one of the clearest examples of Parliament's involvement in the IGC producing a specific result.

The new Treaty thus took up Parliament's proposal almost entirely. The term of office of the Commission was linked to that of Parliament. The Commission can only take office following a vote of confidence. Instead of electing the President of the Commission on a proposal of the European Council, Parliament would only be 'consulted'. But 'consultation' in such circumstances – a public vote on an individual politician by an elected Parliament – is surely tantamount to an election or confirmation, as it is inconceivable that any politician would wish to proceed should Parliament reject their candidacy. A more serious departure from Parliament's original proposal was that the President-designate was not given a stronger role in the choice of Commissioners. Member States will be obliged to *consult* the President of the Commission, but not, as Parliament proposed, to choose the rest of the Commission in *agreement* with the President.

This new procedure began after the 1994 European elections, so the Commission appointed in January 1993 served only a two-year term. Any Commission censured by the EP would be replaced by a new one which would only serve out the term of office of the previous Commission.

The IGC declined to take up a Dutch proposal to give Parliament the right to dismiss individual Commissioners – a right which Parliament had not requested, supporting the doctrine of collective responsibility. The IGC initially agreed (Noordwijk conclave) to reduce the number of Commissioners to one per Member State and to allow the Commission, with the approval of Council acting by qualified majority voting, to appoint up to five 'junior Commissioners', but this did not survive the Maastricht Summit which instead agreed to review the issue in the course of 1992.

Other Powers of the Parliament

Parliament had also asked for a number of its powers of scrutiny and control to be reinforced, and to be given a limited 'right of initiative' (i.e. the right to submit legislative proposals to Council).

On this last point, Parliament had asked 'to be given the right to initiate legislative proposals in cases where the Commission fails to respond within a specified deadline to a specific request adopted by the majority of Members of Parliament',[6] a view which received the support of the parliamentary Assizes in Rome. Such a formula would have preserved the Commission's right, in normal circumstances, to initiate legislation, but would have provided a safeguard should it refuse to do so. Within the IGC, the Commission strongly opposed this watering down of its monopoly on the right of initiative. It was already facing an erosion of this monopoly in the CFSP and JHA pillars as well as in the field of EMU, and did not wish this to be added to in the traditional Community fields. Although Parliament's proposal met with some sympathy, the Commission was able to persuade other Member States to oppose it. The resultant compromise was to add a new Article 138(b) to the EEC Treaty allowing Parliament to 'request the Commission to submit any appropriate proposal'[7] but without providing Parliament with a right to act itself should the Commission fail to respond. Presumably, Parliament would have to have recourse to its right of censure should it be sufficiently dissatisfied with the Commission's response.

Concerning the reinforcement of scrutiny and control powers, Par-

liament had asked in particular for a treaty right 'to establish committees of inquiry to investigate alleged contraventions of Community law
or instances of maladministration with respect to Community responsibilities';[8] for its rights of information in the budgetary control procedure to be enhanced; for the observations it makes in the discharge
decisions to be binding; the right to request the Court of Auditors to
carry out investigations and to submit reports; for the right to take the
other institutions to Court for annulment and to enshrine in the treaties
the right of Community citizens to petition it. Most of these requests
related to the entrenchment in the treaties of existing practice or of
provisions laid down in secondary legislation. Most of them were backed
by the parliamentary Assizes in Rome.

Agreement was reached quickly on all these points. Member States
opposed to increasing Parliament's legislative powers were quick to
endorse this increase in its scrutiny powers hoping to divert pressure
in this direction. The IGC also reached rapid agreement on the principle of Parliament electing an Ombudsman, something which Parliament had not asked for. The first Luxembourg non-paper incorporated
provisions on these points that remained virtually unchanged throughout the IGCs. Only on the number of MEPs needed to request a committee of inquiry (changed from one half to one quarter of Parliament,
to bring it into line with Parliament's internal rules) and the reporting
requirements of the Ombudsmen were there any further changes. On
the right to bring cases for annulment, however, Parliament was only
given the right to do so to protect its own prerogatives, not a general
right.

Proposals were also brought forward, originating with some members of the French National Assembly, for a *'congress'* of national
parliamentarians. The proposal gained some support from the UK,
Portugal, Spain and Greece. It was strongly opposed by the EP, which
considered that the creation of an additional body, alongside the Council
(representing national governments) and the Parliament (representing
the electorate) was superfluous and would render the decision-making
procedures even more complex. The parliamentary Assizes in Rome
did not support the French proposal and it ran out of steam in the
IGCs, though the French government persisted until the very end. Finally,
it was agreed on the basis of a UK proposal, to add to the Treaty a
simple Declaration encouraging national parliaments and the EP to
cooperate with each other and another Declaration inviting them to
meet as a Conference of Parliaments on appropriate occasions to discuss the main features of European Union.

OVERALL RESULTS

The British Foreign Secretary, Douglas Hurd, in presenting the Maastricht Treaty to the House of Commons,[9] stated that 'Maastricht was an important step away from an increasingly centralized – and potentially arthritic – Community'. He and the Prime Minister drew attention to the new 'pillars' that were not incorporated into the Community treaties and claimed that Europe had turned its back on the federal model.

Such an interpretation stretches the bounds of credibility. The sphere of competence of the European Community as such was extended by the Treaty of Maastricht, and within those competences an extended use of qmv was provided for. The powers of the supranational Parliament were enhanced. The Commission, with its extended term of office and with its greater dependence on the Parliament for its appointment, became slightly more independent from national governments. Even the CFSP and JHA, although still separate from the more federal Community, were drawn closer to it than before, managed through the Community institutions, financed partially under its budget, and subject to the same revision clauses. To the extent that there is conflict or overlap in their competences, Community provisions prevail. Last but not least, a single currency was provided for.

Yet, there were still some features to comfort intergovernmentalists. The Union/Community still required a basic consensus of its component states to function, not just because Member States still exercised sole responsibility for coercive force, but because even the basic operation of the EC required consensus, for instance, to appoint a new Commission, to agree a date for European elections, to modify own resources or to appoint a new member to the Courts. A single state could cause the Community to grind to a halt as regards its very functioning, let alone as regards the several policy areas that still require unanimity.

The Community was still far from even a federal system, let alone a centralized state, in other respects too. Its budget was still scarcely more than 1 per cent of GDP. The 'Brussels bureaucracy' was smaller than most local authorities, with fewer than 10,000 civil servants (after taking away linguistic and related staff) serving 350 million inhabitants. The bulk of public policy-making remained at national or subnational level, including most issues which continue to gain the bulk of public attention: health, schooling, law and order, local and regional transport, taxation and housing.

The Treaty of Maastricht can best be seen as another constitutional compromise in the long and complex process of incremental integration in Europe. Again, a compromise was reached between the integrationist majority (itself more consciously and more outspokenly federalist in intent than for a long time) and the more reluctant minority. Again, a new round of negotiations would not be long in coming – indeed was scheduled for 1996. Again, the compromise reached contained ambiguities and was presented with different nuances to different constituencies. Again, it disappointed many and aroused fears in others. Yet, the Treaty on European Union was the most significant step forward since the treaties of Rome. In terms of sheer volume, it contained over 150 new or modified articles in the EEC treaty and with some 35 other articles outside the Community treaties. In terms of its vocabulary it broke new ground with concepts of Union citizenship, and a common foreign and security policy. In terms of its objectives, it contained an element of extraordinary importance for integration, namely the single currency. In terms of the powers of the European Parliament it made a significant breakthrough. In terms of the determination of the majority, it demonstrated their will to press ahead, despite the opposition of one Member State, which they allowed instead to opt out of two key areas.

EVALUATING THE IMPACT OF THE EP

In terms of the influence and impact of the European Parliament, the Maastricht negotiations revealed a powerful agenda-setting role and an important influence over some of the issues being negotiated (not least those concerning its own powers), but less over others. Like most of the other actors – be they the Commission, national governments, national parliaments, or interest groups – the EP did not achieve full satisfaction at Maastricht. Yet, it fared better than most in seeing some of its initial aspirations reaching fruition.

In order to evaluate the EP's impact, we shall compare the outcome of the IGCs with the requests made by the European Parliament (Martin Reports), by the Conference of Parliaments ('Assizes') held in Rome in December 1990, and the political party federations' Leaders' Summits or Congresses. The latter comparisons are based on the Declarations made by the Socialist party leaders, notably in Madrid in December 1990 and in Brussels in December 1991, the Congress held by the EPP in Dublin in November 1990 attended by most Christian Democrat leaders, and the Declaration issued by the Liberal leaders' summit in Berlin on the 23 November 1990.

Such an approach enables us to evaluate the 'transmission' of the EP's original proposals via the 'Assizes' to national parliaments and via the Party Federations to national parties and governments and to see whether the IGC responded.

Principles and Structure of the Treaty

The *EP* called for a 'European Union of federal type' (Martin II Resolution, para. 4) which 'must be based on a single institutional framework' with EPC matters 'to be dealt with in the Community framework' (Martin II, para. 8).

The *Rome Assizes* wished 'to remodel the Community into a European Union on a federal basis' (Recital C) and took the view that 'European Political Cooperation must be incorporated into the treaty and into the Community structures' (para. 4).

The *Summit of Socialist Party Leaders* agreed that 'it will be necessary to integrate political cooperation in the work of the institutions' (Madrid Declaration, para. 19) and that the new treaty must 'allow us jointly to establish in the Community framework the necessary mechanisms . . .' (para. 20).

The *Christian Democrats' Dublin Congress* stated that 'the basis for European Union must be one of federation among its Member States' (para. 20) and 'the integration of EPC into the Community system' (para. 33).

The *Liberal Leaders' Summit* urged the IGC 'to take substantial steps towards transforming the Community into a genuine European Union based on a constitution of a federal type' and called for EPC to 'enter the formal EC framework'.

The Maastricht Treaty provided for a 'pillar' structure whereby one part of the treaty amends and adds to the Community treaties, but the provisions concerning foreign policy and security (and those concerning cooperation on internal affairs and justice) are not incorporated into the Community treaties. They stand in their own right with largely intergovernmental procedures not subject to ECJ judicial review. It would at least be the Council (rather than 'the Foreign Ministers meeting in political cooperation') which conducts the policy, with a degree of involvement from the other institutions: the process is therefore brought closer to the Community framework. The reference to the 'federal destiny' of the Community was, in the end, not incorporated into the treaty.[10]

Common Foreign and Security Policy

The *EP* called for EPC to be dealt with in the Community framework (Martin II resolution, para. 8); for Council 'to be given the prime responsibility for defining policy'; for the Commission 'to have a right of initiative' and 'a role in representing the Community externally'; for the EPC secretariat 'to be absorbed by the Commission and Council'; for foreign policy to be the subject of EP 'scrutiny' (Martin II, para. 9); for the scope of foreign policy to include security, peace and disarmament (para. 10) and for the Community 'to have common policies in all matters in which the Member States share essential interests' (para. 11). Qualified majority voting would be the norm, but Member States could be granted derogations or, exceptionally, opt out (Martin III).

The *Assizes* considered 'that a political Union comprising a foreign and security policy of matters of common interest must be established and that EPC must be incorporated into the treaty and into the Community structures' (para. 4).

The *Socialist Leaders* called for 'the implementation of common foreign and security policies to enable the Community and its Member States to maintain their roles on the world stage. . . . It will be necessary to integrate political cooperation into the work of the institutions; to consider an appropriate concept of European security and gradually to define priority subjects for joint action . . .' (Madrid Declaration, para. 19).

The *Christian Democrats* stated that EPC must 'turn into a common foreign policy' (para. 31) and that the EPC secretariat should be 'integrated into the Council Secretariat' (para. 34).

The *Liberal Leaders* call for 'a common foreign and security policy implying a common defence policy'. There should be a member of the Commission 'charged with security and defence matters'. There should be 'a European defence force under a common military command' and 'WEU should be gradually absorbed by the EC'.

The *Maastricht Treaty* provisions on CFSP remain separate from the Community treaties, as was Art. 30 of the SEA. However, it is the Council (rather than 'the Foreign Ministers meeting in EPC') which lays down policy. The Commission has a non-exclusive right of initiative, but the Union is represented externally by the President of Council. Decisions are taken by unanimity, but, in cases where it is agreed to follow 'joint action' Council may define (unanimously) those matters on which implementing decisions can then be taken by a qualified majority vote. The EPC secretariat was absorbed by the Council secretariat. The CFSP includes 'all questions related to the security of the European Union, including the eventual framing of a common defence policy, which might in time lead to a common defence'. However, defence matters are subcontracted to WEU, whose membership will be enlarged to all those Member States wishing to accede to it. WEU secretariat and council will be moved to Brussels and close working relationships will be established with the Community institutions (sychronized presidencies, contact with the Commission, cooperation between the EP and WEU Assembly).

Citizens' Rights

The *EP* called for the incorporation into the treaties of its Declaration of fundamental rights and freedoms and the Joint Declaration against racism and xenophobia; for the Community to accede to the ECHR; and for the development of common forms of European citizenship through 'such measures as voting rights for Community citizens in municipal and European elections in their Member State of residence' (Martin II, paras 18 and 19).

The *Assizes* called for 'the inclusion in the treaties of provisions to establish the idea of European citizenship, including the right for Community citizens to vote in European elections in the Member State in which they reside' and called for the inclusion in the treaties of the EP's declaration on fundamental rights and EC accession to the ECHR (Rome Declaration, para. 10).

The *Socialist Leaders* called for 'the development of European citizenship as a sum total of the rights and duties of European citizens which go beyond the freedoms of movement, residency and establishment' and measures such as 'the right to participate in local and European elections in the state of residence and a common system of consular protection for Community citizens abroad, and possibly other things besides the common passport and common driving licence' (Madrid Declaration, para. 13).

The *Christian Democrats* called for 'Community citizens basic rights' to be enshrined and for voting rights in European elections.

The *Liberal Leaders* called for a European citizenship to be 'the cornerstone of European Union'. They requested that 'the Declaration on Fundamental Rights and Freedoms adopted by the EP on 12 April 1989 should be enshrined in the treaties and the EC should adhere to the European Convention' (ECHR). They called for the 'right to vote for all EC citizens in their place of residence' for European elections.

The *Maastricht Treaty* added a new section on citizenship to the EEC treaty. It opens with the statement that 'citizenship of the Union is hereby established'. Citizens of Member States are citizens of the Union, enjoying the rights conferred by the treaty, including the right to move and reside freely within the territory of the Member States, the right to vote in local and European elections and the right to enjoy consular protection abroad by the diplomatic authorities of other Member States where his/her own is not represented. These rights must, however, be exercised in accordance with detailed arrangements to be adopted by the end of 1994 by Council (assent of Parliament required regarding residence rights). Union citizens are also given the right to petition the Parliament or apply to a Community Ombudsman to be elected by Parliament. An article states that European political parties 'contribute to the forming of a European awareness and to expressing the political will of the citizens of the Union'. The treaty does not comprise a declaration of fundamental rights but the 'common provisions' (Article F) of the Union Treaty, which are not subject to enforcement by the Court of Justice, states that the Union shall respect fundamental rights as guaranteed by the ECHR.

Subsidiarity

The *EP* proposed to add a new Article 3(a) to the treaty specifying that the Community 'shall act only to fulfil the tasks conferred on it by the treaties and to achieve the objectives defined thereby. Where powers have not been exclusively or completely assigned to the Community, it shall, in carrying out its tasks, take action wherever the achievement of the objectives requires it because, by virtue of their magnitude or effects, they transcend the frontiers of the Member States or because they can be undertaken more efficiently by the Community than by the Member States acting separately' (Martin III, Article 3(a)).

The *Assizes* took over this definition of Parliament virtually without change, but took the view that it should be enshrined in the *preamble* to the treaties (Rome Declaration, paras 23 and 24).

The *Socialist Leaders* stated that 'political union should not develop into a European centralized state. This is why the principle of subsidiarity as well as decentralized decision-making should be laid down in the new treaty' (Brussels Declaration, para. 4).

The *Christian Democrats* agreed that 'the subsidiarity principle must be explicitly enshrined in the treaties' (para. 16), that 'the Union will have powers in those areas where it can act more effectively than the Member States working alone, particularly where the scale or the effects of the action go beyond national frontiers' (para. 15).

The *Liberal Leaders* stated that Union 'policies should be subject to subsidiarity and advance decentralization and deregulation'.

The *Maastricht Treaty* includes a new Article 3(b) which reads: 'The Community shall act within the limits of the powers conferred upon it by this Treaty and of the objectives assigned to it therein. In areas which do not fall within its exclusive jurisdiction, the Community shall take action, in accordance with the principle of subsidiarity, only if and insofar as the objectives of the proposed action cannot be sufficiently achieved by the Member States and can therefore, by reason of the scale or effects of proposed action, be better achieved by the Community.

Any action by the Community shall not go beyond what is necessary to achieve the objectives of this Treaty.'

Strengthening Community Competences: (i) Social

The *EP* requested an extension of Community competences and powers in the social field, in particular to provide for the adoption, with qualified majority voting in Council, of policies concerning employment, labour law and working conditions, vocational training, social security, health and safety at work, the right of association and collective bargaining, as well as for the establishment of a legal framework conducive to negotiations of collective conventions at Community level (Martin II, paras 13, 14 and 15).

The *Assizes* stated that the treaties 'must provide for a common social policy' and 'this requires not only strong assertion of the objectives in the treaties but also decision-taking in these areas by qualified majority'. It also called for a European system of concerted action involving management and labour (Rome Declaration, para. 5).

The *Socialist Leaders* called for the Social Charter to have mandatory effect and for the new Treaty to make it possible to make progress 'on such essential issues as establishing minimum rights for all workers with regard to contracts of employment, working hours and conditions, training, access to public employment services, collective bargaining and industrial democracy . . . Measures under new Community competence must be adopted by a qualified majority. However, decisions pertaining to the level of salaries and social benefits should be taken unanimously' (Madrid Declaration, para. 14).

The *Christian Democrats* called for 'broadening, upgrading and supplementing the social policy objectives laid down in the treaties'. A series of measures were listed including, *inter alia*, the adoption of 'a basic core of Community provisions concerning welfare and social security, trade union rights and collective bargaining, without forgetting the needs of citizens in extreme poverty' and the 'recognition of worker's rights to be informed and consulted and to participate in all decisions in their firm which concern them' (para. 70). Qualified majority voting should apply (para. 27).

The *Liberal leaders* appear not to have addressed this issue, but supported qualified majority voting in all legislative areas.

The *Maastricht Treaty* contains no modifications to the social chapter of the treaty as this was not accepted by one Member State – the UK. However, protocol 14 allows the other Member States to use the Community framework to adopt measures that do not apply to the UK, and the UK does not vote within Council (10 votes fewer needed for a qualified majority). Measures can be adopted by qualified majority voting concerning working conditions, information and consultation of workers, equal opportunities and equal treatment and integration of persons excluded from the labour market, and by unanimity concerning social security, redundancy, workers representation and co-determination, employment of third country nationals and financial aid for employment and job creation. It provides for management and labour to negotiate and agree at European level, with the possibility to follow up such agreements with legislation. New chapters on education and vocational training were added to the EEC Treaty.

Strengthening Community Competences: (ii) Environment Policy

The *EP* considered that Community competences regarding environment policy were adequate (except as regards Community participation in international action and the absence of an environment fund) but that a switch from unanimity to majority voting was the key reform needed in this area. It also called for Article 2 of the Treaty to be amended to support the goal of sustainable development (Martin II, para. 15 and Martin III, Articles 2 and 130(r)).

The *Assizes* asked for the EC to be given 'additional competences in the field of the environment and that decision-taking in this area should be by qualifed majority voting'. It called for Article 2 of the treaty to be amended to support the goal of sustainable development (Rome Declaration, para. 9).

The *Socialist Leaders* called for 'a much stronger emphasis on environmental protection', calling on the IGCs 'to provide the Community with adequate instruments to play a leading role'. They also called for 'the principle of sustainable development to be included as one of the tasks of the Community', for qualified majority voting and for 'introducing ecological elements in the structural funds' (Madrid Declaration, para. 15).

The *Christian Democrats* called for qualified majority voting for the environmental sector (para. 27).

The *Liberal Leaders* called for policies which 'give due respect for the environment' (with qualified majority voting).

The *Maastricht Treaty* amended Article 2 to refer to sustainable growth and amended Article 130(s) to provide for qualified majority voting on environment policy, except for fiscal measures, land use planning, management of water resources and choice of energy supply. It also provided for the establishment of a 'cohesion fund' devoted partly to environmental matters.

Strengthening Community Competence: (iii) Economic and Social Cohesion

The *EP* requested a strengthening of policies for economic convergence and actions for economic and social cohesion in particular to 'aim at overcoming the disparities between the various regions' (Martin III, Art. 130(a)).

The *Assizes* called for the treaties to 'include adequate provisions for economic and social cohesion' (Rome Declaration, para. 5) and for regional policy to 'aim gradually to eliminate the disparities between the regions and considers that the resources at the disposal of the Community, notably the structural funds, must be reinforced'.

The *Socialist Leaders* stated that 'a strengthened cohesion policy has to be a core element of the implementation of EMU' and called for 'the adjustment of the instruments for cohesion, such as the regional policies and the EC structural funds, together with the adoption of complementary measures (to) encourage the integration of the least favoured regions in the EC' (Madrid Declaration, para. 6).

The *Christian Democrats* called for 'greater economic and social cohesion, especially by means of Community policies to reduce regional imbalances (para. 62).

The *Liberal Leaders* called for EMU to be 'accompanied by policies which guarantee economic and social cohesion'.

The *Maastricht Treaty* listed the strengthening of economic and social cohesion as one of the objectives of the European Union (Article B) and of the Community (Article 2). The chapter of the treaty on economic and social cohesion was revised, strengthening its references to the need for cohesion, and providing for the establishment of a new *cohesion fund* providing financial contributions to projects in the fields of the environment and trans-European networks in less prosperous Member States. Protocol 15 looked toward the review of the structural funds and of the Community's system of own resources due to take place during 1992 and stated the intention of the Member States 'to take greater account of the contributive capacity of individual Member States in the system of own resources and to examine the means of correcting for the less prosperous Member States degressive elements existing in the present own resources system'. It stated 'their willingness to modulate the levels of Community participation in the context of programmes of the structural funds' and to review the size of the structural funds, all of which was eventually agreed in Edinburgh in December 1992.

Strengthening Community Competences: (iv) Other Areas

The *EP* called for provisions to be added to the treaty giving the Community strengthened competences in the fields of transport (in particular to add safety provisions and trans-national infrastructures to the existing competences), consumer protection, culture, women's rights and development cooperation (Martin II and III).

The *Assizes* called for a separate article on cultural policy to be inserted into the treaty (para. 11), and for 'the Community to pursue active policies' in the fields of social and civil rights, education, etc. (Rome Declaration, para. 6). The *Party Political Federations* did not focus on this.

The *Maastricht Treaty* added new titles and chapters to the EEC treaty concerning trans-European networks for transport and telecommunications, consumer protection, culture, education, vocational training, public health, industrial policy and development cooperation. New articles were added to existing chapters (e.g. safety added to the transport chapter).

Judicial System and Application of Community Law

The *EP* called for the ECJ to be given powers 'to impose sanctions, including financial sanctions on Member States which fail to apply

Community legislation or implement Court judgments' (Martin II, para. 29). Parliament also requested the right to go to the Court of Justice for annulment (para. 38).

The *Assizes* took the view 'that it is essential for the decisions taken by the Community to be implemented both by the Member States and the Community and calls on the Member States to take whatever legislative and executive action is required to ensure that Community legislation is transposed into domestic law on schedule' (Rome Declaration, para. 15).

The *Socialist Leaders* appear not to have covered this aspect.

The *Christian Democrats* stated that 'the Union must be able to take direct action to implement the Court's decisions where national authorities refuse to do so' (para. 28).

The *Liberal Leaders* called for 'financial penalties [to be attached] to decisions of the Court of Justice'.

The *Maastricht Treaty* enabled the ECJ to impose 'a lump sum or penalty payment' on Member States that have not complied with its judgments. It added to Article 173 a new sentence allowing the EP (and the Central Bank) to bring cases for annulment, but only 'for the purpose of protecting their prerogatives' and provided for Parliament itself to be taken to the Court (entrenching case law).

Qualified Majority Voting in the Council

The *EP* considered 'that unanimity should no longer be required for decision-taking in Council, except for constitutional matters (revision of the treaties), accession of new Member States and extension of the field of Community responsibilities (Article 235)' (Martin II, para. 20).

The *Assizes* considered that 'the Council must be able to take its decisions by simple or qualified majority according to the circumstances; unanimity will only be required in the limited cases provided for by the treaties' (Rome Declaration, para. 12).

The *Socialist Leaders* called for 'an improvement of decision-making by extending the application of majority voting in the Council of Ministers: this extension must cover legislation defining certain fundamental social rights guaranteed to all, rules laying down minimum standards of environmental protection and, in general, decisions where the Community level is the most appropriate level at which decisions should be taken. Unanimity must be retained, however, for all modifications of the treaties and in cases where the Council wishes to override the advice of the Commission' (Madrid Declaration, para. 16).

The *Christian Democrats* called for Council to legislate by qualified majority voting 'on all areas covered by the treaties' (para. 37).

The *Liberal leaders* called for qualified majority voting 'in all areas of Community legislation'.

The *Maastricht Treaty* extended qualified majority voting to some aspects of environment policy, development policy, consumer protection, educational measures, public health, trans-European networks and some minor matters. It will extend as of January 1996 to the determination of which third country nationals require visas. No change was made in the social field, except under the protocol to a limited number of areas. In some areas, (CFSP, JHA and other areas of environment policy) Council may agree unanimously to use qualified majority voting for certain matters.

Appointment of the Commission

The *EP* called for 'Parliament to be given the right to elect the President of the Commission on a proposal from the European Council: the President should, with the agreement of Council, choose the members of the Commission'; and Parliament should then have a 'vote of confidence' in the new Commission as a whole before it takes office (Martin II, para. 35). This procedure should follow each European parliamentary election with the Commission's term of office therefore being changed to five years (Martin III, Article 158).

The *Assizes* took the view 'that the President of the Commission must be elected by the European Parliament on a proposal from the European Council by an absolute majority; that the President of the Commission, in agreement with the Council, should appoint the members of the Commission and that the incoming Commission as a whole should present itself and its programme to the European Parliament for a vote of confidence; believes that the Commission's term of office should start at the same time as that of the European Parliament; the same procedure should be followed if a new Commission has to be appointed during the parliamentary terms'; (Rome Declaration, para. 18).

The *Socialist Leaders* stated that the EP 'should be involved in its appointment by investing the President of the Commission on a proposal of the European Council and by taking a vote of confidence on the incoming Commission as a whole' (Madrid Declaration, para. 18). They agreed that the term of office of the Commission 'should normally coincide with that of the Parliament' (Brussels Declaration, para. 6).

The *Christian Democrats* called for the 'election of the Commission President by an absolute majority of Parliament's Members at the start of each parliamentary term, candidates being put forward by the European Council' and the 'appointment of Commissioners by the Commission President from a list of three candidates put forward by each Member State', with the Commission as a whole being subject to 'investiture by the Parliament' (para. 40).

The *Liberal Leaders* considered that 'Parliament must have the right to elect the President of the Commission on a proposal of the European Council and to submit the Commission to a vote of confidence'. The members of the Commission would be 'appointed by the President-elect on the basis of proposals by each of the Member States'.

The *Maastricht Treaty* provides for the Member States to consult the EP on the person they intend to appoint as President, to consult the nominee for President on the other persons whom they intend to appoint as members of the Commission and for the 'President and the other members of the Commission thus nominated' to 'be subject as a body to a vote of approval by the European Parliament'. The term of office of the Commission was changed to five years, to be appointed in the months following each European parliamentary election.

Co-decision Powers for the EP on Community Legislation

The *EP* had asked for Council and Parliament to be given 'equal rights and equal weight in the legislative process' with two readings in each body, a conciliation procedure to reconcile differences, and the approval of both bodies necessary to adopt Community legislation (Martin II, para. 33).

The *Assizes* considered that 'Parliament must play an equal part with the Council in the legislative and budgetary functions of the Union' (Rome Declaration, para. 12) and that 'as regards the European Community's legislative powers, co-decision arrangements between the European Parliament and the Council must be devised' (para. 19).

The *Socialist Leaders* called for 'a strengthening of democratic control by giving the European Parliament the right of co-decision with the Council, in those fields where the Council takes majority decisions' and that 'co-decision could be achieved by, for instance, a procedure where the final approval of both institutions is necessary' (Madrid Declaration, para. 17).

The *Christian Democrats* stated that 'it is essential that there should be set up ... a decision-making procedure ensuring equal participation by Parliament and the Council as . . . proposed by Parliament' (para. 54).

The *Liberal leaders* called for a qualitative leap forward to democracy by granting full co-decision powers to the directly elected EP in all areas of Community legislation'.

The *Maastricht Treaty* introduced a procedure providing for two readings each in Council and Parliament followed, if necessary, by a conciliation procedure. Both Parliament and Council have to approve the outcome of conciliation. However, if conciliation fails, Council can adopt a text unilaterally which will become law unless it is rejected within six weeks by the EP acting by a majority of its members. This procedure applies to some 15 EEC treaty articles. The treaty also extends the parliamentary *assent* procedure to six new areas and introduces the old cooperation procedure (two readings but final say in Council if it is unanimous) to some 15 new areas and maintains it in three. Finally, the procedure for consulting Parliament is introduced in some 24 new areas.

Right to Initiate Legislation

The *EP* called 'for Parliament also to be given the right to initiate legislative proposals in cases where the Commission fails to respond within a specified deadline to a specific request adopted by the majority of members of Parliament to introduce proposals' (Martin II, para. 34).

The *Assizes* took the view that 'a right of initiative must be established in the event of the Commission failing to act' (Rome Declaration, para. 19).

The *Socialist Leaders* considered that the European Parliament should be given 'the right of initiative over legislation *vis-à-vis* the Commission' (Madrid Declaration, para. 17).

The *Christian Democrats* called for the 'protection of the Commission's right and duty of initiative, without prejudice to any right granted to the EP to initiate legislation' (para. 39).

The *Liberal Leaders* considered that 'Parliament and Council should have the right of initiative if the Commission fails to respond to its requests for draft legislation'.

The *Maastricht Treaty* lays down that the EP 'may, acting by the majority of its members, request the Commission to submit any appropriate proposal on matters on which it considers that a Community act is required for the purpose of implementing this treaty'.

The EP's Right to Establish Committees of Inquiry

The *EP* asked for 'a right, enshrined in the treaties, to establish committees of inquiry to investigate alleged contraventions of Community law or instances of maladministration with respect to Community responsibilities' (Martin II, para. 40).

The *Assizes* believed 'that the European Parliament's supervisory powers must be enhanced and formally enshrined in the treaties' (Rome Declaration, para. 20).

Neither the *Socialist Leaders* nor the *Christian Democrats* appear to have addressed this issue.

The *Liberal Leaders* called for the EP 'to have the right of inquiry'.

The *Maastricht Treaty* provided that Parliament may 'set up a temporary committee of inquiry to investigate, without prejudice to the powers conferred by the treaty on other institutions or bodies, alleged contraventions or maladministration in the implementation of Community law, except where the alleged facts are being examined before a court and while the case is still subject to legal proceedings'. It provided for detailed provisions governing the exercise of this right to be determined by common agreement among Parliament, Council and the Commission.

Powers of Budgetary Control

The *EP* called for greater information rights, for its powers of budgetary control to be enhanced and for 'the principle that the observations made in the discharge decisions are binding on all the institutions to be enshrined in the treaty and for the discharge authorities' right to ask the Court of Auditors to carry out investigations and submit reports to be enshrined in the treaty' (Martin II, para. 37).

The *Assizes* called for Parliament's supervisory powers to be enhanced and the position of the Court of Auditors to be strengthened (Rome Declaration, para. 20).

The *Party Federations* appear not to have addressed this issue.

The *Maastricht Treaty* specified that 'the Commission shall submit any necessary information to the European Parliament at the latter's request' and that 'the Commission shall take all appropriate steps to act on the observations in decisions giving discharge and on other observations by the European Parliament relating to the execution of expenditure' and that 'at the request of the European Parliament or the Council, the Commission shall report on the measures taken in light of these observations and comments, and in particular on the instructions given to the departments which are responsible'. It also specified that the Court of Auditors may issue special reports on specific questions at the request of other institutions. The Court of Auditors is elevated to the rank of a Community institution.

Role of National Parliaments

The *EP* expressed 'its readiness to assist the parliaments of the Member States with access to information' and to 'cooperate with the parliaments of the Member States in the now regular meetings that take place at various levels'. However, it considered 'that it would not be useful to set up a new institution' of members of national parliaments (Martin II, para. 23).

The *Assizes* supported 'enhanced cooperation between the national parliaments and the European Parliament, through regular meetings of specialized committees, exchanges of information and by organizing conferences of parliaments of the EC when the discussion of guidelines of vital importance to the Community justifies it, in particular when IGCs are being held' (Rome Declaration, para. 13).

The *Socialist Leaders* took the view that the strengthened EP establish 'closer cooperation with national parliaments: their roles are not in competition with each other, but rather are complementary. National parliaments will play their role in exercising effective scrutiny over their individual ministers who are members of the Community's Council' (Madrid Declaration, para. 17).

The *Christian Democrats* called for national parliaments to 'be more closely involved in the decision-making process. In particular they should have proper access to the information needed to enhance democratic control of the Council members representing their country' (para. 46).

The *Liberal leaders* did not mention this subject.

The *Maastricht Treaty* did not set up any new institution. Two declarations were annexed to the Union treaty. In declaration 12, the national governments undertake to ensure 'that national parliaments receive Commission proposals for legislation in good time for information or possible examination' and took the view that it is important 'for contacts between the national parliaments and the European Parliament to be stepped up, in particular in the granting of appropriate reciprocal facilities and regular meetings between members of Parliament interested in the same issues'. In declaration 13, the EP and the national parliaments 'are invited to meet as necessary as a conference of the parliaments (or "Assizes")'. This will be 'without prejudice to the powers of the European Parliament and the rights of the national parliaments'.

Representation of the Regions

The *EP* called for the creation of 'a body consisting of representatives of the regional authorities in the Member States whose function would be comparable to that of the Economic and Social Committee in its specific field' (Martin II, para. 22).

Neither the *Assizes* nor the *Socialist Leaders* nor the *Liberal Leaders* dealt with this subject.

The *Christian Democrats* called for a 'Regional Consultative Council to be set up, through which the regional institutions of the Member States would be able to take part in the Community decision-making process'.

The *Maastricht Treaty* established a 'Committee of the Regions' with advisory status, with the same number of members as the Economic and Social Committee with which it shares a common secretariat. It is consulted on matters affecting the regions and may also give an opinion, wherever the Economic and Social Committee is consulted.

The above comparison illustrates some striking cases of Parliament's proposals being taken up by others and, frequently, by the IGC itself. The IGC only rarely took up proposals without making any changes to them, but this was also true for proposals originating with the Commission and with Member States. In some areas, the EP could claim little satisfaction, such as on the pillar structure of the treaty and on the CFSP provisions, despite support obtained outside the IGC for its views. In other areas, including citizenship, several extensions of competence and, above all, its own powers, the EP saw a relatively good response in the IGC, despite the limitations (especially in scope) of the co-decision procedure.

As in 1984–5, Parliament's early formulation of a precise and detailed set of proposals was crucial in providing a focus for all those concerned with preparing or discussing the IGC. Again, MEPs were able to obtain a large degree of support from some political parties, some national parliaments and some governments. In the compromises that emerged from the IGC, it obtained a far from negligible proportion of its aspirations.

13 Making the Most of Maastricht[1]

As with the Single Act, much of the true impact of the Treaty on European Union would depend on its implementation and on how the institutions would be able to make the most of the new possibilities afforded. From an integration perspective, the single most important issue will be the process of Economic and Monetary Union. However, a number of other aspects were important, not least for the European Parliament.

A NEW GENERATION OF INTERINSTITUTIONAL AGREEMENTS

The Maastricht Treaty provided for the European Parliament to adopt the regulation governing the duties of the Ombudsman, with the approval of Council acting by a qualified majority. It also specified that the rights of parliamentary committees of inquiry shall be determined by common accord of the Parliament, the Council and the Commission. In both these areas, the EP therefore adopted a set of proposals to discuss with the other institutions in interinstitutional conferences. Parliament also called for interinstitutional conferences to discuss other matters such as the application of the co-decision procedure.

A single interinstitutional conference began at the end of 1992 to seek an agreement on all these issues. It brought together 12 ministers on the Council's side, 12 MEPs on Parliament's side, and members of the Commission, modelled on the interinstitutional conferences that prepared, and later accompanied, the 1990–1 Intergovernmental Conferences. Council wished to raise the issue of subsidiarity, to which Parliament agreed on condition that it was accompanied by discussions on democracy and transparency in EU decision-taking. With the help of the Belgian Presidency in the second half of the year, Council also came round to accepting the benefits of an agreement on the operation of the conciliation committee.

Negotiations were difficult, and finished somewhat later than originally expected (the Danish Presidency of the Council having hoped to finish it during their term of office). In the event, an agreement was reached on 25 October comprising the following elements.

Interinstitutional Declaration on Democracy, Transparency and Subsidiarity

Here, Parliament had been seeking an undertaking by Council always to meet in public when adopting or voting on Community legislation. It also sought to bring Council into legislative planning. However, not a great deal emerged in this part of the interinstitutional agreement. Parliament extracted an undertaking that the three institutions would respect 'the democratic principles on which the systems of government of the Member States are based' and reaffirming 'their attachment to the implementation of transparency'. A set of measures taken by the three institutions to increase transparency was listed in the declaration. On Council's side this included the opening of some debates to the public, publishing records and explanations of voting, and providing greater access to its documents. On the Commission's side this included greater use of Green and White Papers before pressing presenting proposals, wider pre-consultations with interested parties, better access of the public to data bases, documents, etc. The declaration also drew Council for the first time into the discussions on the annual legislative programme, hitherto a bilateral matter between the Commission and the Parliament. The Council committed itself to indicating which parts of the programme it considered to be a priority, thereby offering a way to national parliaments to exert greater influence over their governments in shaping the Community agenda.

Parliament considered that the text on democracy and transparency represented 'merely a minimum first step towards a fully democratic and transparent European Union which the citizens demand' and re-iterated its view that 'the adoption of all legislative texts by a public vote is a *sine qua non* of democracy and transparency'. It recorded this view in a unilateral declaration annexed to the agreement.

Council subsequently changed its Rules of Procedure (see below) to provide that voting records would be published systematically (instead of on request of a Member State, which was as far as Council had been willing to go before the interinstitutional meeting).

On 20 December, the Commission and the Council agreed on a Code of Conduct for public access to their documents, laying down a set of criteria and procedures.[2]

Interinstitutional Agreement on Procedures for Implementing the Principle of Subsidiarity

The three institutions agreed on procedures whereby they each undertook to take into account the principle of subsidiarity in exercising the powers conferred upon them, but they specified that this would 'not call into question the *acquis communautaire*' nor the 'powers conferred on the institutions'. They agreed that the explanatory memorandum of any Commission proposal will include a justification under the principle of subsidiarity. Any amendment to the Commission's text, 'whether by the European Parliament or the Council, must, if it entails more extensive or intensive intervention by the Community, be accompanied by a justification under the principle of subsidiarity'. An annual report will be drawn up by the Commission on compliance with subsidiarity to be debated in Parliament with the participation of the Council and the Commission. Compliance with subsidiarity will be ensured through the normal Community process but, in the event of difficulties, an interinstitutional conference may be convened to consider the matter.

Ombudsman

The initial draft produced by the EP on the role and position of the Ombudsman met with the opposition of the Council and, to a lesser extent, the Commission on a number of points. Some of these were relatively minor (e.g. should the Ombudsman take his oath of office in front of the Parliament or the Court of Justice? The latter was eventually agreed), whereas others were more important. The Council and the Commission, for instance, wanted a time limit of one year after an event for a complaint to be registered; Parliament's position was three years. In the final text, a two-year limit was agreed.

The most important disagreement was on access by the Ombudsman to documents of the Member States in the possession of the Commission. The Council was most reticent to allow such access when confidential or secret documents were concerned, but Parliament considered it to be fundamental. This issue prevented agreement during the Danish Presidency, with one meeting breaking up with mutual recriminations. The final agreement, however, resolved the issue by limiting the Ombudsman's access only to documents classified not merely as confidential but 'classed as secret by law or regulation'. In such cases, (s)he will still have access, but only where the Member State has given its prior agreement, which may include the condition that the Ombudsman shall not divulge the content of such documents. In all other cases, 'the Member States' authorities shall be obliged to provide the Ombudsman . . . with any information that may help to clarify instances of maladministration'. If such assistance is not forthcoming, the Ombudsman 'shall inform the European Parliament, which shall make appropriate representations'.

The Ombudsman's budget is to be annexed to section I (Parliament) of the general budget, and the seat of Ombudsman is to be that of the European Parliament.

Interinstitutional Agreement on Arrangements for the Proceedings of the Conciliation Committee

Under this agreement, the institutions clarified that the conciliation committee in the co-decision procedure is to be chaired jointly by the President of Parliament and the President of Council who shall jointly set dates, agree on agendas and approve minutes, and alternately chair meetings. The committee will meet alternately on the premises of each. Crucially, in view of the difficulty in conducting negotiations with 12 on each side of the table, it was agreed that the co-chairmen can submit joint texts to the committee or propose to it that rapporteurs be appointed. Furthermore, in the phases of the co-decision procedure preceding conciliation, it was agreed that practice developed under the cooperation procedure whereby the Council Presidency, the Commission and the chairman and/or rapporteur of the relevant parliamentary committee hold talks, 'should continue and could be developed' under the co-decision procedure. It was agreed that joint texts agreed at conciliation meetings would be finalized by the legal-linguistic experts of both the Council and the Parliament and submitted to the co-chairmen for formal approval before publication in the *Official Journal*.

Interinstitutional Agreement on Parliamentary Committees of Inquiry

On this point, negotiations only concluded on 20 December 1994. Parliament and Council had diverged in particular on the issues of Parliament's right to oblige national officials to appear before committees of inquiry, access of the committees to confidential documents and the term of office of such committees. In the text agreed, the right to determine the time limit for a committee was left to the EP, provided it did not exceed 12 months, twice renewable by three months.

Member States and Community institutions are required to designate officials to appear before a committee of inquiry upon the request of the committee, unless grounds of secrecy or public or national security dictate otherwise by virtue of national or Community legislation. Member States and Community institutions must similarly provide the committee with 'the documents necessary for the performance of its duties'. Where national or Community legislation provides for secrecy, this must be 'notified to the European Parliament by a representative authorized to commit the Governments of the Member States [or Institution] concerned'. Hearings and testimony at the committee of inquiry will take place in public except when requested by a quarter of the members of the committee, by Community or national authorities, or by witnesses and experts.

THE CO-DECISION PROCEDURE AND ITS SPIN-OFF

The first 'Acts of the European Parliament and the Council' were adopted in 1994, when 30 co-decision procedures were completed. In 18 cases, agreement was reached between the two institutions without needing to convene the conciliation committee. In 11 cases, the conciliation committee agreed a text which was then approved by Council and Parliament. In one case, the conciliation committee failed to reach agreement, Council reconfirmed its common position but this was rejected by the EP by an absolute majority, and consequently failed (voice telephony directive, see below).

In these 30 cases, there was relatively little difficulty in negotiating compromises on the substance of the legislation in question, important though some of it was. Nor were there insurmountable difficulties as regards the application of the procedure. The six-week deadlines proved to be flexible with Council and Parliament agreeing that the conciliation committee's deadline would run as of the first meeting of the committee and that the deadlines for the institutions to vote would run only after discounting a time lag for translations. It was also established that the conciliation committee is not limited to negotiating on amendments adopted by the Parliament by an absolute majority, but can introduce any new text capable of facilitating a compromise. This included points on which the majority – but not an absolute majority – of Parliament had approved amendments.

Where major difficulties did arise between the two institutions was on two 'horizontal' issues: provisions for Commission implementing measures or secondary legislation arising from co-decision acts, and the fixing in legislative acts of volumes of expenditure estimated to be necessary.

On implementing measures, Parliament had objected for many years to the so-called 'comitology' system, as we saw in previous chapters. With the co-decision procedure, Parliament was in a stronger position to oppose unacceptable comitology provisions in legislative texts, and also argued that there was a new legal situation in that the traditional comitology provisions were based on Article 145 of the EC Treaty which allowed Council to lay down conditions for the exercise of implementing measures for legislation adopted *by Council* – but co-decision legislation was not adopted by Council but *by Parliament and Council*, a distinction clearly made in Article 189 of the EC Treaty.

This interpretation was not accepted by the Council and the issue was fought out on each individual item of legislation containing comitology provisions. Although some compromises fudged the issue, Parliament refused to back down and went so far as to reject the voice telephony directive on these grounds. Council was eventually persuaded to negotiate, leading to the adoption of a *modus vivendi* on 20 December 1994. This *modus vivendi* provided for all draft general implementing acts to be sent to the Parliament at the same time and under the same conditions as to the comitology-type committee. The Commission must take into account of any comments by the EP and 'keep it informed at every stage of the procedure of the action which it intends to take on them'. Where a matter is referred to the Council, the latter may not adopt an implementing act without first carrying out a consultation procedure with the Parliament and, in the event of an unfavourable opinion from Parliament, 'taking due account of the European Parliament's points of view' and trying to 'seek a solution in the appropriate framework'. Whilst not fully satisfying the Parliament, the *modus vivendi* goes well beyond all previous provisions for giving Parliament a role in scrutinizing implementing measures. It was also agreed that the 1996 Intergovernmental Conference (IGC) should re-examine the issue.

The question of 'amounts deemed necessary' (fixing in legislative acts amounts which, in the view of the Parliament, should instead be determined in the annual budgetary procedure), also gave rise to conflict. When this threatened to prevent the adoption of the 'Socrates' and 'Youth for Europe' exchange programmes, Council eventually agreed to negotiate a joint declaration whereby Council accepted that 'amounts deemed necessary' would only be incorporated into legislation (pursuant to the co-decision procedure *or otherwise*) when jointly agreed by Parliament and Council. Even then they should serve only as a reference from which the budgetary authority could depart if it could justify doing so by objectively valid reasons. In all other cases, legislation would no longer refer to such amounts.

The resolution of these two 'horizontal' problems illustrated the knock-on effect of co-decision into areas where Council was initially reluctant to concede ground, but where it was ultimately obliged to negotiate a compromise solution.

APPOINTMENT OF THE COMMISSION

The TEU brought in a new procedure for appointing the Commission whereby the Member States first agree on a candidate for President, on whom they must consult the EP, and then the Commission as a whole is subject to a vote of confidence by the Parliament. Both phases gave rise to important innovations.

The choice of a President in 1994 was clouded by the UK's veto on the candidacy of the Belgian Prime Minister, Jean-Luc Dehaene, at the Corfu European Council. Although all other member States agreed to Dehaene's candidacy, the requirement for unanimous agreement among the Member States allowed the UK to prevent his name going forward. An extraordinary European Council convened in Brussels a month later agreed on the compromise candidacy of Jacques Santer, the Luxembourg Prime Minister.

Given the circumstances, the debate and the vote in the EP on Jacques Santer was no formality. A combination of those opposing Jacques Santer, and those who had major reservations about the procedure and the UK veto, threatened his approval by the Parliament. This opposition was not overcome by his meetings with the main political groups in the Parliament prior to the vote. In the event, Parliament approved his appointment only by 260 votes to 238, with the majority composed mainly of Christian Democrats, Gaullists, Forza Italia and a minority of the Socialist Group (largely from governing parties whose representative in the European Council had approved the nomination). The process at least confirmed that the 'consultative' vote in the Parliament amounts to a vote of confirmation as both the President of the European Council (Chancellor Kohl) and Jacques Santer himself confirmed that a negative vote in the Parliament would require the European Council to find another candidate.

The second phase of the procedure required a vote of confidence from the EP once the Commission as a whole had been put together by the national governments in consultation with the President-designate. Parliament sought to build on this Treaty provision by providing in its revised Rules of Procedure that the individual members of the Commission-designate must appear before the relevant parliamentary committees corresponding to their prospective portfolio for a public confirmation hearing. This provision was not universally popular within the Commission and, indeed, the outgoing Commission expressed grave reservations. None the less, it became clear that the EP would simply not schedule a vote at all on the new Commission until it had complied with this requirement. Jacques Santer and his colleagues therefore accepted to go through the procedure, which in turn required a prior agreement on the distribution of portfolios – something that no previous Commission had managed to do before taking office. The Commission-designate reached agreement on the distribution of portfolios in early November, thereby leaving adequate time for Parliament to conduct the hearings.

Parliament none the less postponed the hearings and the vote of confidence until January 1995 – thereby prolonging the life of the Delors III Commission – in order to allow MEPs from the new Member States (who only became members on 1 January) to take part in the vote. Parliament felt that a Commission governing 15 Member States and including representatives from each of them should be voted in by MEPs from all 15.

The hearings, when they took place in January 1995, focused considerable media attention on the aptitude of the candidates. There was strong criticism of the performance of some candidates, but short of rejecting the Commission as a whole, MEPs could only press for a reallocation of responsibilities. This took place in the case of Commissioner Flynn whose chairmanship of a Commission committee on equal opportunities was reallocated to President Santer. Following this, and an undertaking by the incoming Commission to renegotiate the 'Code of Conduct' that governs EP–Commission relations, the EP gave a vote of confidence to the new Commission by 417 votes to 104.

CODE OF CONDUCT

During the process of confirming the new Commission, President Santer had agreed to renegotiate the Code of Conduct governing Parliament–

Commission relations first agreed in 1990. These negotiations took place in the early months of 1995 with the President of Parliament (liaising with the political group leaders) and Commissioner Oreja playing the key role at a political level, while the detailed work was carried out by a small group of officials (from the Santer and Oreja's *Cabinets* and the legal service on the Commission's side and from the Parliament secretariat and certain political group staff on the EP side).[3]

The new Code of Conduct agreed in March referred to the new relationship between the two institutions arising from the vote of confidence which 'exemplifies the relationship of trust which should bind the two institutions'. Under the terms of this Code, the Commission undertook notably:

- to guarantee absolute equality of treatment between Parliament and Council concerning the forwarding of any legislative or budgetary proposal or any other Commission document relating to such proposals throughout the decision-making procedure;
- not to make public any important initiatives before informing Parliament;
- to maintain contacts between the Commission and the Parliament's legal services as regards the choice of legal basis for Commission proposals;
- to forward Green and White Papers to Council and Parliament on an absolutely equal footing and, if they are accompanied by a draft resolution, to submit such a resolution both to Council and Parliament;
- to take 'utmost account' of Parliament legislative initiatives pursuant to the new Article 138B (which enables the EP to request the Commission to submit legislative proposals) and to respond with a reasoned argument in each case;
- to brief the relevant parliamentary committee regularly on discussions within the Council on legislative proposals and to forward to the parliamentary committee any amendments that the Commission drafts in the context of Council's discussions;
- to remind Council of the need to avoid reaching a political agreement before Parliament has given its opinion and to reconsult Parliament if the Council substantially amends a Commission proposal;
- to take 'utmost account' of amendments adopted by Parliament at second reading and to decide not to support an amendment adopted by Parliament only after deliberation at the level of the full College of Commissioners, in which case it would have to explain its reasons before Parliament or at the next meeting of the competent committee;

- 'having regard to the democratic legitimacy of the elected Parliament, to withdraw, where appropriate, a legislative proposal which Parliament has rejected' and only maintain such a proposal 'for important reasons and after consideration by the full College', in which case it shall 'explain the reasons for that decision in a statement to Parliament'; (this point was the most difficult point in the negotiations and will be further examined below);
- to give confidential briefings to parliamentary committees throughout the process of international negotiations.

For its part, Parliament undertook to step up bilateral contacts with the Commission on the timetabling of parliamentary debates; to appoint rapporteurs on future proposals as soon as the legislative programme is adopted; to consider requests for reconsultation as a matter of absolute priority; and to take greater account of the priorities indicated by the Commission (notably in the annual legislative programme).

The crucial issue was that of Commission response to parliamentary rejection of a legislative proposal. Parliament sought (as in 1981) an undertaking from the Commission to withdraw *any* legislative proposal (whatever the legislative procedure) rejected by Parliament. The Commission pointed out that such a provision would amount to a treaty revision and that it could not make such an undertaking without being open to legal and political attack by the Council. Indeed, Council was already expressing disquiet on the issue of the Code of Conduct, which was discussed in Coreper even before it was finally agreed between the Commission and the Council. Parliament, however, insisted that in a democracy, it was unthinkable for legislation to be adopted if rejected by an elected Parliament. The final text of the Code of Conduct reflected a compromise capable of being interpreted by Parliament as a tacit understanding that the Commission would *normally* withdraw any draft legislation rejected by it. The words 'where appropriate' provide a legal safeguard for the Commission and a gesture to the Council. The references to the democratic legitimacy of the elected Parliament, to the need for a consideration by the whole College of Commissioners and to a public statement in Parliament should it decide to overrule Parliament's rejection, all gave weight to this interpretation. Furthermore, President Santer agreed in talks with parliamentary group leaders to make the following statement in plenary: 'in the democratic procedures which are common to our Member States, the rejection of draft legislation by the elected Parliament puts an end to the legislative procedure. We all know that this is not the case under the terms of the Treaty on European Union. As I have said, the Commission cannot go beyond the limits imposed by the Treaty without laying itself open to legal and constitutional challenges. Nevertheless, the Commission fully acknowledges the democratic legitimacy of the elected parliament, and will thus attach very special importance to Parliament's rejection of the proposals in question.'

CHANGES TO RULES OF PROCEDURE

Both Council and Parliament amended their Rules of Procedure to adapt to or take advantage of the possibilities offered by the Maastricht Treaty. Council's new rules were adopted on 7 December 1993. The main innovations:

- catered for the fact that the Council henceforth acts not only pursuant to the Community treaties but also to the second and third pillars of the Maastricht Treaty;
- laid down (following the Joint Declaration agreed with Parliament on transparency) that Council would hold public debates on the six-monthly work programme submitted by its President and on the Commission's Annual Work Programme, and that it could (unanimously) decide to hold other debates in public (in both cases 'public' means that the debate is transmitted to the press room by audiovisual means);
- provided for the results of its votes to be made public when it acts as a legislature 'unless the Council decides otherwise' (which requires a simple majority), and for voting records to be made public by a unanimous decision when Council acts pursuant to Titles V (Foreign Policy) and VII (Justice and Home Affairs) of the TEU;
- arranged for technical adaptations to the wording of legislation and for the signature of legislative acts, so as to cater for acts adopted under the co-decision procedure – which are not to be 'acts of the Council' but 'acts of the Parliament and the Council'.

Parliament adopted a revision of its Rules in September 1993. On the *legislative* front, the main change was to make provision for the new co-decision procedure, but Parliament at the same time laid down provisions concerning all procedures, seeking to ensure that it has at all stages in the procedure equality with the Council as regards access to information and documents – failing which Parliament will bring the procedure to a halt. As regards the co-decision procedure, two aspects

of Parliament's rules seek to interpret the Treaty in a way not necessarily to the liking of Council. The first of these concerns the stage of
'intention to reject' where the Treaty provides for Council to convene
the conciliation committee to explain its position further, following
which Parliament either confirms its rejection or amends Council's
position. Parliament's new rules provide that if Council fails to convene the conciliation committee, then the legislation is dead because
Council has failed to take the process further. This obviates the need
for a second vote by an absolute majority in Parliament to confirm the
rejection. The second matter concerns the eventuality of Council attempting to adopt legislation in the absence of an agreement in the
conciliation committee. The Treaty allows Council to do so, provided
Parliament does not reject the outcome within a six-week period. The
new rules of procedure provide that Parliament will automatically vote
on a rejection motion should Council attempt this. Furthermore, the
rules oblige the President of the Parliament to call upon the Commission to withdraw its proposal should conciliation not reach agreement
and, failing that, to call upon Council not to act unilaterally. The im-
plication is clear: Parliament will not accept unilateral action, and considers that conciliation and agreement should be the only way to adopt
legislation under the co-decision procedure.

As regards the *non-legislative* changes to Parliament's powers made
by the TEU, the main adaptations to the rules concern the involvement
of Parliament in various appointments, from the Ombudsman to the
President of the Central Bank and, as we saw above, to the Commission, in each case providing for public hearings in committee before
Parliament votes. This was first put to the test with the appointment of
Baron Lamfalussy as President of EMI in the autumn of 1993.

Finally, the *general* revision of Parliament's procedures involved a
large number of adaptations tightening up the rules and aiming at making
Parliament work more efficiently. Among them:

- Abolition of the 'Enlarged Bureau' – the managing body of Parliament composed of the President and Vice-Presidents, the group chairmen and the Quaestors – and its replacement with a compact
  'Conference of Presidents' composed simply of the President of Parliament and the chairmen of the political groups. If a vote is necessary, the group chairmen have the same number of votes as there
  are members of their group. The Conference of Presidents will deal
  with all the political aspects of organizing Parliament's business
  (drawing up draft agenda, authorizing committees to draw up re-

ports, handling relations with other institutions, national parliaments and third countries, etc.), whereas the Bureau (President and Vice-Presidents only) will deal with administrative matters (staff, budget, rapporteurs' missions within the EU, organizational questions, etc.).
- Limitation of the number of reports by requiring committees to request authorization from the Conference of Presidents to draw up any non-legislative report.
- Streamlining the procedures for adopting Parliament's agenda and for dealing with procedural motions.

RIGHT TO VOTE IN EUROPEAN ELECTIONS

To implement Article 8(b) of the EC Treaty as amended by the TEU, Council adopted on 6 December a directive[4] laying down detailed arrangements for the exercise of the right to vote and stand as a candidate in the European elections in the Member State of residence. The directive allows EU citizens to exercise their right to vote and to stand for election in their Member State of residence, and includes provisions to prevent individuals from voting or standing for election in two countries at once. Derogations contained in the directive were criticized by the European Parliament. These apply to Luxembourg which is allowed to subject the right to vote and to stand to stricter residence qualifications (5 and 10 years respectively) and to lay down rules on the composition of party lists (no list may contain a majority of non-nationals).

NUMBER OF MEPs

During the Noordwijk conclave of the IGC before the Maastricht Summit, provisional agreement had been reached on increasing by 18 the number of German MEPs to take account of German unification. This was taken out of the package in Maastricht itself, where it was agreed to return to this issue in the course of 1992. The EP, which had made the original proposal for 18 extra German members, returned to the issue following the Maastricht Summit and adopted a proposal for a more comprehensive revision.[5] This proposal was adopted without modification by the European Council. It provided for 18 extra seats for Germany making a total of 99, 6 extra for the other 'big' Member States, 4 extra for Spain, 6 extra for the Netherlands which was curiously under-represented hitherto, and 1 extra each for Belgium, Greece and

Portugal, giving a grand total of 567. The new allocation made the membership of the EP somewhat more proportional to the populations of the Member States without taking away entirely the bias in favour of smaller countries, especially Luxembourg.

SEATS OF INSTITUTIONS AND ORGANS

The Maastricht Treaty envisaged a decision being taken on the seat of the future Monetary Institute and Central Bank during the course of 1992. However, it was impossible to treat this in isolation from the wider question of seats of Community institutions which had been a running sore for many years.

The Member States had never managed to fulfil the obligation placed upon them in the original treaties to agree on a single seat for the institutions. The provisional allocations of 1965 spread them over three towns: Luxembourg, Brussels and Strasbourg. The EP in particular was dissatisfied with this situation, but its attempts to get around this through the gradual concentration of parliamentary activities and staff in Brussels gave rise, over the years, to a number of Court cases. The construction of the new parliamentary chamber in Brussels, allowed by the Court, caused a strong reaction from France which blocked any decisions on the seats of new organs (such as the trademark office, and the environment agency) until it gained satisfaction on the seat of the Parliament. Clearly, it was prepared to do the same concerning the crucial monetary institutions.

In the negotiations it became clear that this matter was not a priority for any Member State other than those with a direct interest in having the institutions on their territory. The EP request (and the Treaty obligation) for a single seat might have the sympathy of some Member States, but none was willing to go to the stake on this issue. France continued to press hard, and Belgium felt rather weak at a time at which the Commission had been forced to move out of the Berlaymont building, and was scattered in several buildings across Brussels, due to the need to remove dangerous asbestos.

The result was that France largely gained satisfaction at the Edinburgh Summit of having Strasbourg declared the seat of the EP and the normal venue for its monthly part-session. The decision recognized the right of the EP to hold additional plenary sessions in Brussels, where its committees would also meet. The secretariat, however, would remain based in Luxembourg! Belgium gained the satisfaction of seeing the seats of the Council and the Commission fixed officially in Brussels, recognizing the *de facto* situation. Luxembourg similarly saw a formalization of the *de facto* seats of the Court of Justice, Court of First Instance, Court of Auditors and the European Investment Bank in Luxembourg. Indeed, except for the arrangements concerning Parliament, the decision remained faithful to the provisional decision of 1965.

The EP declared (resolution December 1992) that it did not feel bound by this decision, questioning its legality. Indeed, not only does the decision not respect the treaty requirement for a single seat, but it also entered into extraordinary detail about the internal organization of the Parliament, specifying that there should be 12 monthly sessions, including a special budget session, and that they should be in Strasbourg. Until now, the Court has always ruled that Parliament is entitled to arrange its own internal organization, including the length of its sessions and how they are broken down into part-sessions. It is equally doubtful whether a decision imposing such a spread of its activities and secretariat is compatible with the duty of loyal cooperation spelt out in the case law of the Court. This will now be tested in the Court in a case brought by France against Parliament when the latter decided to hold only 11 part-sessions in Strasbourg in 1996.

ADAPTATION OF THE WESTERN EUROPEAN UNION

As envisaged in the Maastricht Treaty, Community States not yet members of WEU had the opportunity of joining it. In November, Greece duly joined as a full member and Denmark and Ireland as observers. European members of NATO not members of the Community became associate members of the WEU (Turkey and Norway). The WEU secretariat was moved to Brussels.

As for the development of WEU's own role, the foreign and defence ministers of WEU countries, meeting in Bonn on 19 June 1992, adopted the 'Petersberg Declaration' in which the Member States declared that they were 'prepared to make available military units from the whole spectrum of their conventional armed forces for military tasks conducted under the authority of WEU'. The decision to take part in specific operations will still be taken at national level. The military units could be employed for the common defence of the allies, humanitarian tasks, peace-keeping, tasks of combat forces in crisis management or peace-keeping operations. A planning cell will be established in Brussels and will be responsible for preparing contingency plans for the deployment of forces under WEU auspices. Among the units made available to WEU will be the Franco-German brigade (or 'Eurocorps'), intended to be the nucleus of a European unit.

INSTITUTIONAL ASPECTS OF ENLARGEMENT

The enlargement of the Union to Sweden, Finland and Austria gave rise to a number of institutional discussions. Although agreement was reached without difficulty on the number of votes to be attributed to each applicant state in the Council, the issue of what should constitute the new threshold for obtaining a qualified majority (previously 44 out of 76 votes) had to be defined for a new Council with a total (it was thought before Norway decided not to join) of 90 votes. Most Member States wanted the new threshold to be 64, which represented the same proportion (71 per cent) as the previous level, as with each previous enlargement. The UK wanted the threshold to be 68, representing the same blocking minority of 23 votes. This, however, would have made decision-taking more difficult and was vigorously opposed by a majority of Member States and by the European Parliament, where MEPs made it clear that Parliament would not give its assent to enlargement if the Accession Treaty contained such a weakening of the Union. The issue deadlocked the enlargement negotiations just at the moment when agreement had been reached on all the outstanding policy questions. Eventually, a special meeting of the Council in Ioannina on 27–29 March approved a compromise whereby the threshold was indeed adapted to 64 votes in the Treaty, but an accompanying political declaration stated that, where a measure was opposed by 23–26 votes, then discussions would continue to try to reach a larger majority of at least 68 votes 'within a reasonable time'. It was specified that this 'reasonable time' was without prejudice to time limits laid down by the Treaties and by secondary legislation, notably the time limits in the co-operation and the co-decision procedures, and that the Council rules of procedure (which provide for a vote to be taken at the request of the Commission or a single Member State provided a simple majority agrees) remained in force. It was agreed that the whole system of qualified majority voting would have to be re-examined in the 1996 IGC.

As regards the number of seats in the EP, the EU forwarded in the negotiations the figures proposed by Parliament itself, namely 15 for Norway, 16 for Finland, 20 for Austria and 21 for Sweden. However, Sweden made a strong case for having a greater number on the basis of recent population trends, but its argument that it should have 25 seats (like Belgium, Portugal and Greece) was not accepted. The EP accepted that Sweden should have 22 members and this figure was eventually accepted in the enlargement negotiations. Austria, however, argued that if Sweden was increasing to 22, then it should increase to 21 and this too was accepted. As a result, Austria is now the only Member State of the EU not to have the number of MEPs that EP had itself proposed.

The Accession Treaty also made provision for a change in the rotation of the Council Presidency, as had been suggested by the EP. The new order of rotation seeks to obtain more balanced troikas which nearly always include one of the larger Member States. Furthermore, Council can now agree (unanimously) to change the order of rotation.

FINANCE

The new policies envisaged in the TEU, and the trend in previous policies, required a new agreement on the development of EU finances. An agreement between the Council, the Parliament and the Commission was reached on 29 October 1993. It can be seen as the successor to that of 29 June 1988. It established financial perspectives for the years 1993–9 'intended to ensure that, in the medium term, Community expenditure, broken down by broad category, develops in an orderly manner and within the limits of own resources assigned to the Community'.

Council's position in the negotiations was largely determined by the outcome of the Edinburgh Summit. Indeed, the Edinburgh Summit had entered into such a degree of detail that it effectively pre-empted discussion on the ceilings of the main categories of expenditure.

Many of the features of the 1988 agreement were taken up again in this new agreement. However, there were some important innovations. A new *ad hoc* conciliation procedure for compulsory expenditure was set up whereby, if the Council intends to depart from the preliminary draft budget, this procedure can be invoked in order to secure an agreement between the two arms of the budgetary authority. Such a conciliation is preceded by a 'trialogue meeting' composed of the President of the Council, the chair of Parliament's Budget Committee and the relevant member of the Commission. This thus gives Parliament an extra opportunity to press Council on compulsory expenditure, where Council has the final say on allocation to individual items.

The agreement also specified that *all* expenditure under headings II (structural operations, including the Cohesion Fund) and III (internal policies) would be categorized as non-compulsory expenditure, where Parliament has the final say over its allocation. Non-compulsory expenditure now amounted to some 44 per cent of the budget. The institutions undertook 'not to allow any revision of the compulsory expenditure in the financial perspective to lead to a reduction in the amount available for non-compulsory expenditure' thereby ring-fencing the non-compulsory section of the budget from encroachment by compulsory expenditure. Parliament and Council agreed that the maximum rates of increase under the Treaty are deemed to comprise whatever amount is set under the ceiling. The agreement therefore effectively constitutes an undertaking in advance to raise the rate, obviating the need to obtain each year a qualified majority in Council and an absolute majority in Parliament to do so. Parliament's position is also preserved as far as future enlargement of the Community is concerned by a provision that the financial perspective will be revised by joint agreement in such an eventuality. If no agreement is reached, the existing agreement will no longer be binding.

14 Overall Conclusions

We began this book by examining the main theoretical approaches to European integration, noting that they corresponded in part to the preferences of some of the individual actors in the process itself. From this survey we constructed a preliminary synthesis which drew in particular on the gradual constitutional federalist approach and on neofunctionalism. We highlighted the significance of the constitutional framework provided by the treaties in creating space for the development of policies, networks of actors and other aspects of integration that have been highlighted by neofunctionalists. We saw how the treaties at the same time limit the degree to which these processes can carry the integration process. A new 'federal bargain' is required to create the space to take the process further. This bargain takes place in an IGC and is in the hands of the national governments who, here more than at any other point in the dynamics of the system, retain a gatekeeping role. Nevertheless, the pressures built up in the previous phase of development of common policies and actor networks help put pressure on the governments for a new bargain that will take the process towards a higher level of integration. Some governments are more receptive to these pressures than others with the result that the bargain struck is a compromise between those Member States wishing to proceed further and those reluctant to proceed at all beyond the previous level. The need for unanimity to change the treaties builds in a minimalist bias into such negotiations which can be overcome only by a general willingness to compromise, by an evolution in the attitudes of the reluctant states or, at certain crucial junctures, by an explicit or implicit threat by the integrationist majority to move ahead without the minority.

Into such a pattern, the insertion of a directly elected Parliament was likely to have significant consequences. None the less, expectations of how it would impact on the system and what it would be able to achieve were extraordinarily diverse prior to the first European elections. The diversity, indeed, did not correspond to the different theoretical approaches to integration but was to be found in each one. From the variety of expectations expressed in the writings at that time, and in the expectations of the main political parties expressed in their manifestos for the first European elections, we distilled 12 hypotheses formulated to express these various expectations. Some of these hypotheses concerned the process of the elections themselves, which we have not focused upon for reasons of space, noting only some important characteristics *en passant*. Thus, the rest of the thesis concentrated on examining the impact of the elected Parliament:

- on the one hand, in exploiting the space provided by the treaties through processes close to those developed by neofunctionalist theorists; and
- on the other hand, in attempting to extend the constitutional framework within which it acted, thereby creating further space for a development of policies, networks and channels of influence.

In so doing, we concentrated on examining hypotheses 7 and 11. At least some attention, however, was paid to all the hypotheses formulated, which enables us to reach the following conclusions with regard to each one.

Hypothesis 1:   'That the directly elected Parliament cannot achieve anything as only national authorities have the necessary legitimacy and power. It will remain purely symbolic.'

This hypothesis has been largely disproved. Although national authorities retain the bulk of legitimacy and power, the EP has not remained purely symbolic and has been able to chalk up significant achievements both by using the powers given to it by the treaties and in terms of contributing to pressure to reform the treaties.

Hypothesis 2:   'The elections therefore will produce nationalist whiplash.'

Although there was a degree of nationalist opposition to European integration achieving popular success in the European elections in some Member States, this remained a minority phenomenon and did not exceed, in any case, the levels of such sentiment expressed in national elections. The sole exception was Denmark[1] which produced a nationalist whiplash peculiar to the European elections, although there is some evidence in the UK and France that traditional political parties adopted more cautious positions in the first elections than they had had before. None the less, it remained a minority phenomenon.

Hypothesis 3:   'The elections will achieve little public interest with a low turnout and national issues dominating.'

This hypothesis has been largely borne out by events, though not nearly to the extent that some writers (foreseeing a turnout of 25 per cent) had predicted. Turnout has been low as compared to national elections, but not as compared to local elections nor when compared with federal elections in some other systems. National issues have indeed dominated the campaigns, but European issues have crept in to a greater degree than in national elections and to an extent that parties are obliged to formulate detailed European policies.

Hypothesis 4: 'The elected MEPs will have less influence than the nominated ones who were members of their national parliaments.'

The loss of the influence MEPs previously had by virtue of being members of national parliaments has been compensated by the full-time nature of the job, the greater use made of the Parliament's powers, the development of new channels of influence. These were then enhanced by the increases in the powers of the European Parliament.

Hypothesis 5: 'The elected Parliament will be much the same as before.'

Although the structure and pattern of activities of the Parliament when it first became directly elected was indeed much the same as prior to the elections, these soon developed for the same reasons indicated above for hypothesis no. 4.

Hypothesis 6: 'The elected Parliament will carry greater weight, authority and legitimacy simply by virtue of being directly elected and this will in itself lead to Council and Commission following its recommendations.'

There is only little evidence to show that the simple fact of being directly elected gave the Parliament greater weight, authority and legitimacy. Although the Council and Commission adapted their working practices to pay greater attention to the EP, there is no evidence of a major attitudinal change in the sense of either institution feeling obliged to follow Parliament's recommendations.

Hypothesis 7: 'The elected Parliament will be more effective simply by virtue of being full-time and professional. This in particular will lead to:
(a) the EP being an important 'lobby' for integration and institutional reform.

(b) the development of European parliamentary practices, habits and networks.'

We have found much evidence to show that the full-time and professional character of the elected Parliament, despite some limitations such as the high turnover in membership, has led to it being more effective. This has indeed resulted in it being an important lobby for integration and institutional reform and to it developing European parliamentary practices, habits and networks. In particular, we found in chapter 3 considerable evidence of the commitment of the full-time MEPs and their likely support for the European integration process. We found some support for Cotta's theory that they would have a predisposition or, indeed, a 'vested interest' in the strengthening of the EP and the promotion of European integration. We noted the networks and channels of communication that MEPs developed within their national political parties, their constituencies and the trans-European party political federations. Contacts with national parliaments were developed and able partially to compensate for the loss in direct linkage that existed prior to direct elections. We found evidence to suggest that the EP became a focus for interest groups and lobbying activities, thereby providing another non-national vehicle for such lobbying and developing new channels of interaction for MEPs. We found further evidence of the full-time MEPs developing networks of contacts with the Commission both at the political level of Commissioners and at the civil servant level. Altogether, these developments led to MEPs being the centre of a wide network of contacts and channels of communication making them an asset for their political parties and a target for the activities of interest groups. However, they were unable to develop a great public awareness of their work nor a high level of media attention to it.

In making use of the powers given to them by the treaties at the time of the first direct elections, MEPs were able to develop the legislative, budgetary and scrutiny powers to a limited but significant degree. We saw in chapter 4 how various techniques were developed more fully to exploit the budgetary powers and the legislative consultation procedure. This helped develop perceptions of a functioning political system at EC level that was not merely intergovernmental and in which MEPs fulfilled the role that Haas attributed to them of 'furthering the growth and practices and codes of behaviour typical of federations'.

The role of being a 'lobby' for integration has proved correct in a number of ways connected to hypotheses 10–12 which we will examine below.

Hypothesis 8: 'The elections and the activities of the elected Parliament will stimulate the development of transnational
political parties which will in turn be a factor for integration by influencing their national components and by
substituting national divisions with ideological ones.'

Transnational political parties have indeed developed, albeit to a lesser
degree and much more slowly than had been predicted by many scholars. Direct elections did provide a stimulus to their development and
in particular to the elaboration of common electoral platforms encouraging national political parties from the same political family to embark on a process of common policy formulation. However, a greater
stimulus was provided by the activities of the Parliament itself in
terms of the infrastructure supplied enabling the transnational party
federations to develop their activities, and in the vanguard role
played by the political groups of the Parliament in stimulating the
further development. There is some evidence that this has resulted in
the trans-party federations playing a 'transmission-belt' role from the
EP political groups to national political parties. Furthermore, they have
begun to play a role in bringing a party political element into the
proceedings of the European Council through the partisan pre-summits
they organize.

Hypothesis 9: 'The elections themselves will stimulate public debate
and interest and will mobilize public support for European unification, putting pressure on governments.'

There is little conclusive evidence in our cursory look at the election
campaigns to indicate that they have significantly mobilized public support
for European unification thereby putting pressure on governments. It
is conceivable that in countries where an overwhelming majority of
political parties support the integration process, the European elections
then put some pressure on parties to show that they have or can achieve
results in terms of carrying this process further. The particular case of
the referendum held in conjunction with the European elections in 1989
in Italy can also be mentioned in this context. However, the evidence
in favour of this hypothesis, on the basis of our brief glance at the
elections, is modest.

Hypothesis 10: 'The elected Parliament will force a re-adjustment of
the balance of power among the European institutions,
but without being able to obtain changes to the treaties.'

The elected Parliament was able to force a modest readjustment of the balance of power among the European institutions, but the limited nature of this readjustment was one of the reasons that incited MEPs to seek changes to the treaties, some of which it was eventually able to obtain. Chapter 5 illustrates how Parliament made a major effort to obtain reform within the treaties, but that the response from the other institutions did not result in a major change in the balance of power among the institutions.

Hypothesis 11: 'The elected Parliament will be able to obtain significant changes to the treaties, advancing European integration and also increasing its own powers.'

We have found considerable evidence that the two sets of changes to the treaties negotiated in the first dozen years following direct elections, and which constituted the most significant steps since the signing of the EEC and EAEC treaties in 1958, took place in no small part thanks to the actions of the Parliament and its elected members.

The hammering out of a major reform proposal backed by members from most of the main political parties represented in the Parliament was a strategy that Parliament only managed to develop with difficulty (starting only after two years of following other strategies, and with the help of a non-party 'catalyst' in the form of Spinelli). None the less, it stimulated a reform process that, while not meeting the ambitions of its initiators, produced significant results in terms of European integration.

We have found that the stimulation provided by the DTEU was among the factors which led to the negotiation of the SEA. The draft Treaty provided a focus for supporters of the integration process and was backed explicitly by a number of national parliaments, by the declarations of national leaders in transnational party federation summits, by a number of national political parties in the European election campaign and was the focus of attention of a number of NGOs active in the field. The momentum it generated was sufficient to induce those governments generally supportive of the process of integration to take up the issue of treaty reform to an extent not seen for over 25 years. The clash that this produced with more reticent governments was such that speculation, stimulated by the Parliament, about the possibility of the pro-integration countries moving ahead by themselves (or the more modest alternative of a two-tier system) began to feature in the debate, ultimately helping to persuade the more reticent countries to negotiate and compromise rather than face isolation.

A similar process took place in 1989 to 1992 when the Parliament played a major role in enlarging a reform process already embarked upon by the Member States concerning EMU so that it would be extended to include institutional reform and other aspects of political union. On this occasion too, the transmission belts and channels of communication used at the time of the draft Treaty again provided a vehicle for the EP's proposals to gain wider support. New channels of communication, such as the Assizes and the interinstitutional conference were also developed. The European Union Treaty contains, as a result, a significant number of elements for which the EP had pressed, not least concerning its own powers.

Hypothesis 12: 'The elected parliament will be able to act as a constituent assembly, preparing a constitution for a European Union.'

A number of federalists have laid great store on the EP's potential as a constituent assembly and one of the 'big four' Member States has been committed by national referendum to supporting such a role. In practice, the EP's Treaty/constitution-drafting activities have not resulted in the adoption of a European constitution. These activities have, in practice, fallen more under the terms of reference of hypothesis 11. The language and rhetoric of constituent assembly federalists has rather (intentionally or otherwise) served a tactical role helping to obtain more modest (though none the less significant) achievements.

Underestimated by many in the early years following direct elections, the new full-time Parliament that emerged in 1979 has, in ways not always initially predicted, been a significant contributory factor to the increase in the speed of European integration that took place from the mid-1980s onwards.

It remains to be seen whether this process will continue or whether a new equilibrium has now been found. Given the nature of the dynamics, networks and features we have analysed, it is likely that the European Parliament will continue to bring a degree of stimulus for further integration for many years to come. Whether such a stimulus will be sufficient to produce significant new results in an enlarged Union with a greater number of 'gatekeepers' remains to be seen. As in 1985 and 1991, this may well depend more on the determination of the majority of the Member States than on the lowest common denominator.

The EP is unique as the world's first transnationally elected Parliament. This 'political miracle'[2] has also found the means to be extraordinarily dynamic in a way in which many national parliaments have ceased to be. A distinguishing feature of the EP is that it does not regard itself as part of a finished institutional system, but as part of one requiring evolution or even transformation into something different. In this respect it acted as a stimulus and helped to reinvigorate the process of European integration in the 1980s and early 1990s.

15 Postscript: The Treaty of Amsterdam

As this book went to press, the 1996–7 IGC was drawing to a close. It provides another opportunity to examine – perforce briefly – the impact of the European Parliament on a new step in the European integration process.

The Maastricht Treaty had envisaged a new IGC in 1996. As we saw earlier, this was in order to return to issues left open in 1991. By 1996, however, it was the prospect of enlargement to a dozen new states that provided the main incentive, together with a growing sentiment, amid continued public debate about the role of the Union in the controversial run-up to monetary union, that the Union needed to be made more citizen-friendly, more effective, more open and more democratic.

To prepare the IGC, the European Council meeting in Corfu in June 1994, agreed to establish a 'Reflection Group' to work as of June 1995 to prepare the IGC and to be composed of 15 'personal representatives' of the foreign ministers, together with a member of the Commission and two MEPs.

Eight governments appointed their European Affairs ministers (or the equivalent). This was the case of the UK, with David Davis from the Eurosceptic wing of the Conservative Party. Belgium and Portugal appointed academics, the latter a former foreign minister. Austria appointed their Permanent Representative to the EU, and Luxembourg a former Permanent Representative. Denmark appointed a former Secretary-General of the Council, Finland appointed a former defence minister, and Greece an ambassador.

The European Parliament appointed Elisabeth Guigou and Elmar Brok. This was a balanced choice: Socialist and Christian-Democrat, French and German, woman and man, one with many years' ministerial experience and the other with many years' parliamentary experience. The European Commission appointed Manuel Oreja, previously a chairman of the EP Institutional Affairs Committee and a former foreign minister.

Each member of the Reflection Group was allowed to bring one adviser to the meetings (and a 'note-taker' who could sit at the back). Participation at the meetings was strictly limited to this and a small number of Council officials (including, from time to time, the Secretary-General of the Council). Elisabeth Guigou's adviser was the author of this book.

The European Council also invited each of the institutions to prepare a report for the Reflection Group. Parliament's report was prepared by its Committee on Institutional Affairs. The rapporteurs were David Martin again (Socialist), and Jean-Louis Bourlanges (EPP/France). Parliament's report was the only one to contain specific proposals to change the treaties.

Parliament stressed the institutional challenges facing the Union: tackling the democratic deficit, reforming the decision-making process and preparing the Union for future enlargement. Among the principal deficiencies of the Treaty, Parliament cited the lack of openness and full democratic accountability, the failure to implement effective and cohesive common foreign and security and justice and home affairs policies, and institutional mechanisms designed for a Europe of six which had not been properly adapted since. It also advocated a single, unified and simplified Treaty.

Parliament considered that there should be a more effective EU foreign policy, integrating the common commercial policy, development co-operation, humanitarian aid and CFSP matters within a common framework under the Community pillar and that the Union should inherit the Western European Union's powers. It should be possible for a qualified majority of Member States to undertake humanitarian, diplomatic or military action, which would qualify as a 'joint action'. No Member State could be forced to take part if it did not wish to do so, but nor should it be able to prevent the majority from taking such action.

In the fields of justice and home affairs, Parliament wanted decisions on asylum and immigration policy, the crossing of the Member States' external frontiers and action against drug abuse to be brought progressively within the Community domain.

Parliament also called for an Employment Chapter to focus attention on the need to work towards full employment. Parliament considered that the Union should also strengthen its existing policies on the environment and economic and social cohesion. Greater substance should be provided for the concept of EU citizenship through the development of special rights. Furthermore, the Treaty should contain clear rejection of racism and xenophobia. It also called for tougher measures to combat fraud and other infringements of Union law.

On the institutions, Parliament emphasized the importance of reasserting the role and independence of the Commission. It accepted that there should continue to be at least one Commissioner per Member State, but the President of the Commission should be strengthened, and Parliament itself should elect the President from a list of names put forward by the European Council. Turning to the Council, Parliament called for greater transparency, improved public access to documents and further extension of qualified majority voting. Concerning itself, Parliament wanted the number of Members not to exceed 700, a common statute to be established for MEPs and equal status with the Council in all fields of EU legislative and budgetary competence.

Parliament considered that its own involvement in decision-taking should be through only three procedures: co-decision, assent and consultation. The assent procedure should be restricted to Treaty revision, international agreements, enlargement and adjustments to own resources; the consultation procedure should be used for CFSP decisions; and the co-decision procedure should apply to all legislation. The co-decision procedure to be simplified, notably by:

- eliminating the possibility for Council to adopt a text unilaterally if there is no agreement in the conciliation committee;
- consolidating the phase of 'intention to reject' and 'confirming rejection' into a single rejection vote by Parliament;
- providing that when Parliament and Council agree in first reading, there is no need for a second.

In the case of the Court of Justice, Parliament called for its powers to be extended to the areas covered by Titles V and VI of the Treaty on European Union and to the Schengen Agreement.

Lastly, Parliament again felt that if it proved impossible to reach a positive conclusion at the IGC owing to failure to reach a unanimous decision, consideration should be given to the possibility of proceeding without the minority.

The Reflection Group was chaired by Spanish EU Minister Carlos Westendorp. After the inaugural meeting in Taormina (Messina) to coincide with the ministerial commemoration of the 40th anniversary of the Messina Conference, the Reflection Group met almost three times a month (except August) right up to the Madrid meeting of the European Council in December. The meetings were normally held on the Council premises in Brussels or Luxembourg, but one meeting took place at the invitation of the Spanish Council presidency in Toledo, and another took place in Strasbourg during an EP session.

Discussions proceeded in three phases. In the first phase, each meeting was devoted to a particular theme and Westendorp sent out questions in advance to all the participants, encouraging them to address these questions when they spoke. Following that phase, Westendorp drew up (during the August break) a 'progress report' summarizing the discussions so far and laying down the main orientations or options that the Group had examined. The Group then proceeded to a second round of discussions, again devoting each meeting to a particular theme using the Westendorp text as a basis, especially where this text had indicated – for each subject – items requiring further examination. Finally, in the third phase, the Group finalized its text for the Madrid meeting of the European Council.

All participants agreed that the Reflection Group was not a negotiation or pre-negotiation, but an opportunity to think freely and openly and identify issues that could be dealt with by the IGC, examining the options available in each case. The Group agreed to work in a relatively open manner and with all members free to talk to the press, on the understanding that they would give an account of discussions without, however, directly quoting any other member.

In the early rounds of the discussion, the EP representatives were the only ones with a concrete set of proposals for modifying the treaties. No national government had yet prepared its proposals for changing the treaty and even the Commission, in its report for the Reflection Group, had restricted itself to analysing the Maastricht Treaty and refrained from putting forward specific proposals for change. This enabled the EP representatives to perform an agenda-setting role, outlining Parliament's proposals and explaining them. Elisabeth Guigou, as a former European Affairs minister knowing most of the other ministers present, and having had the experience of negotiating the Maastricht Treaty, was able to present Parliament's position in a way that attracted considerable sympathy. Furthermore, Parliament's two representatives were able to co-ordinate their interventions so that one would speak near the beginning and the other near the end of each *tour de table*, the second speaker being able to respond to points made in the discussion – an advantage enjoyed by no other delegation.

The Group issued its report, in time for the Madrid summit, on 5 December. The report – entitled simply *Reflection Group's Report* – consisted of two parts: a 10-page overview, and a 50-page summary of the main deliberations. These showed that, although there was wide agreement on broad principles and on many specific issues, there were clearly deep divisions with a minority – often of one and almost always the UK. The positions advanced by individual members of the Group were not identified, but the Report was studded with such phrases as 'one of us believes . . .', 'one of us is opposed to . . .', 'some of us thought . . .', 'some members consider . . .', and 'a broad majority of members of the Group favours . . .'.

The majority of the Group recommended that the IGC should focus on trying to achieve results in three main areas:

- *Making Europe more relevant to its citizens*: Strengthening the Union's capacity to deal with international crime; simplifying the TEU; reinforcing the subsidiarity principle; EU involvement in safeguarding human and civic rights and social protection; pillar three of the TEU to be clarified and strengthened (with some JHA policy areas to be made a Community competence); and a clearer Treaty commitment to promoting economic and social integration and cohesion, and job creation.

- *Enabling the Union to work better and preparing it for enlargement*: Making EU processes and instruments more efficient and democratic by consolidating the single institutional framework throughout the TEU; giving national parliaments a greater opportunity to consider EU legislation before it is examined in the Council; reducing the number of legislative procedures to three – co-decision, assent and consultation; the extension of qualified majority voting in the Council (with a large majority prepared to make this a general rule); and reducing the size of the Commission while strengthening its President.

- *Giving the Union greater capacity for external action*: Greater use of qualified majority voting on CFSP matters; structural changes to promote greater synergy between the economic, political and security dimensions of the EU's external relations; and gradual absorption of the Western European Union (WEU).

The Report showed that there was majority support for almost all the main points that the European Parliament had put forward, but that there was unanimous support for almost nothing. On many subjects there was a minority of one (normally the UK), but on some two, three or four Members States jointly formed a minority. In such a situation, the discussions served to clarify the respective positions and to put some pressure on the minorities: those in a minority who nonetheless want a positive outcome from the IGC were likely to re-examine their position on the issues in which they were in a minority in order to see how far they could go in seeking a compromise. However, for any minority not necessarily hoping for a significant package of reform to emerge from the IGC, the situation was entirely different. Largely in recognition of this, it came to be generally accepted during 1995 that the IGC would be unlikely to complete its work before the middle of 1997, i.e. until after the UK Conservative government, whose representative created the greatest difficulties in the Reflection Group, had faced a general election – which opinion polls suggested it could well lose.

The IGC itself began at the Turin European Council on 29 March. It held monthly meetings at foreign minister level and met weekly at the level of the ministers' representatives. The latter were usually the country's permanent representative in Brussels or European Affairs minister. Greece enabled the EP to get an extra channel of information back from meetings of the ministers' representatives in that it appointed an MEP, Yannos Kranidiotis.

Agreement was also reached at Turin on how the EP would be formally involved. France and Britain had opposed giving Parliament a role in the IGC, but all other Member States accepted Parliament's argument that it should have a similar role to that of the Commission in IGC meetings. After lengthy discussions, a compromise was agreed whereby Parliament's involvement would take the form of the President of the Parliament having an exchange of views with the foreign ministers at each of their monthly meetings. Furthermore, Parliament would appoint two representatives to hold monthly detailed exchanges of views with the ministers' representatives. They would also be briefed by the Presidency after each IGC meeting. Elisabeth Guigou and Elmar Brok took on this task. The Parliament's representatives obtained copies of all the working documents and position papers that were produced, and also submitted their own texts. This was a significant improvement in Parliament's position compared to previous IGCs.

Preceding the beginning of the IGC, the Commission and the Parliament produced opinions on the IGC pursuant to Article N of the Treaty. They used the occasion to set out their priorities as to what they wanted to see addressed, and endorsed the convening of the IGC.

The Commission advocated an ambitious IGC to prepare the Union for enlargement. It called, *inter alia*, for majority voting in the Council to be made the general rule; for the WEU to be incorporated into the Union; for the external policy to be made more consistent and to that end the Council and the Commission to be entrusted with more responsibilities in this field; for the number of EP decision-making procedures to be reduced to three (consultation, co-decision and assent); for the establishment of an area of security through better co-operation in the field of justice and home affairs; and for the inclusion in the Treaty of a specific chapter on employment.

The EP (Dury/Meij-Weggan Report) reiterated and confirmed the positions it had adopted in the Martin/Bourlanges Report. It stressed in particular the need to address citizens' concerns. This could be achieved through giving a Community dimension to certain aspects of justice and home affairs; developing the social, ecological and employment aspects of the single market; strengthening citizens' rights; reinforcing the Union's external role; ensuring greater openness in the working of the institutions; and striving towards a more democratic Europe, by extending and improving the co-decision procedure and qualified majority voting in the Council.

At the June Florence European Council meeting, the incoming Irish Presidency was asked to produce, on the basis of the IGC discussions, a general outline for a draft revision of the Treaty. The 140-page paper was ready by December, just in time for the Dublin European Council. It was in general well received. The aim of the Presidency was to reflect in a balanced way the discussions that had taken place while still being quite ambitious as to the level of reform that should be achieved, as the national leaders had requested. The draft was subsequently used as a working document for further detailed discussions at the Conference. However, it remained clear that no agreement would be reached on any IGC issue before the UK election in May 1997.

This last aspect meant that it was important to keep the opposition party – and likely new government – in the UK on board. The EP's representatives in the IGC,[1] with their access to documents, were important in this regard. Also important was the mechanism through which the Labour Party adopted its position on the Intergovernmental Conference. This was done by a working group chaired by the party leader, Tony Blair, and comprising Shadow Chancellor Brown, Foreign Secretary Cook, Deputy Prime Minister Prescott and European Minister Quinn on the House of Commons side and Socialist Group leader Green, EPLP leader David and deputy leader Crawley and EP Vice-President Martin on the European Parliament side. The position drafted by this working group was endorsed unanimously by the party conference in 1995. It differed radically from the Conservative government's position on issues like the Parliament's co-decision powers, the extension of qualified majority voting, the Social Chapter and the Employment Chapter. This is another instance of national party policies being significantly influenced by their MEPs.

There were only six weeks between the election of the Labour government and the crucial Amsterdam summit. This period of intense diplomatic and political activity was further complicated by the unexpected change of government in France, with Lionel Jospin's Socialists seeking at the same time to change the emphasis of decisions concerning EMU, which were also due to be finalized in Amsterdam. None the less, after negotiating until 3 am on the second night of the summit, the heads of government again emerged with a new treaty.

Yet again, the new treaty did not go as far as many had hoped, but none the less contained significant changes to the European treaties, including further steps forward in the integration process. However, on the crucial institutional changes necessary to prevent an enlarged Union of 20-odd Member States becoming paralysed, the Amsterdam Summit was unable to find a solution, agreeing to come back to these issues in the enlargement process itself.

The more significant institutional changes agreed included the following:

- the UK signing up to the Social Protocol which could now be integrated into the Treaty as a revised Social Chapter;
- stronger provisions on employment policy (new chapter), public health, consumer protection and the environment;
- the extension of the co-decision procedure to more than double the number of articles than it previously applied to;
- procedural changes to the co-decision procedure which coincided exactly with those recommended by Parliament (see above);
- greater openness through an obligation to publish results of votes taken in the Council, and statements made in the Council minutes, as well as a right of public access to EU documents;
- giving the Union the power to adopt anti-discrimination legislation concerning gender, race, sexual orientation, disability, age and religion;
- a provision (originating from the Spinelli draft treaty) enabling the Union to suspend a Member State that ceases to be democratic or to respect human rights;
- turning Parliament's vote on the President-designate of the Commission from a consultative vote to a full legal confirmation;
- a transfer of most of the 'third pillar' issues to the Community pillar, albeit with a unanimity requirement and a somewhat limited role for the Court of Justice.

The new Treaty also made a limited extension of the field of qualified majority voting. It introduced the possibility of 'flexibility' whereby, if a Member State or a small minority does not wish to proceed further in an integrative policy area, the majority may proceed without it rather than see the Union be blocked entirely. However, such a procedure would not be possible if a single Member State objected.

It is the limited scope of these last changes, and the failure of Amsterdam to agree a new weighting of the votes in Council, that raised questions concerning the ability of the Union to proceed to a further enlargement.

Seen globally, the Treaty of Amsterdam, if ratified, represents another incremental step, reinforcing some of the federal characteristics of the Union. In particular, the European Parliament has benefited from a substantial increase in its co-decision powers and a strengthening of its position within the co-decision procedure. Yet again, the Parliament itself and its Members played a major part in the reform process. This latest episode therefore confirms the conclusions we drew after examining the impact of the Parliament after direct elections and in particular its influence on the genesis of the Single European Act and the Treaty of Maastricht.

Notes

1. THEORETICAL APPROACHES TO EUROPEAN INTEGRATION

1. The term used by Carole Webb, in Wallace, Wallace and Webb (1983, p. 1).
2. Burgess (1989, p. 20).
3. Weiler (1981, pp. 267–306; 1982).
4. See, for instance, Partan (1993), in which he states that 'in this respect, the Treaty of Rome establishes the European Community as a federal system'.
5. Puchala (1972).
6. Lindberg, in Lindberg and Scheingold (1971).
7. Ibid., p. 46.
8. On the classical federal model see Wheare (1963).
9. Monnet indeed never used the term 'functionalist' or 'neofunctionalist', but did use the word 'federal' to characterize the ECSC and frequently referred to the objective of a 'United States of Europe'. Having lived and worked in America, he was well acquainted with the US federal system.
10. Some writers exaggerated the differences between Monnet and the constituent federalists, e.g. Stephen George claims that Monnet 'must have expected' the collapse of the EDC, preferring 'incremental steps in areas where national sovereignty was not seriously threatened' (George, 1985, p. 19). Yet Monnet was one of the main movers behind the EDC plan, and he announced that he would not seek re-election as President of the ECSC High Authority within two months of its rejection.
11. For an account of the early movements and organizations supporting European Unity, see Lipgens (Vol. 1, 1984; Vol. 2, 1986).
12. For a moving, if less academic, account of the growth of European federal ideas in this way, see Pirlot (1984).
13. English edition by the A. Spinelli Institute for Federalist Studies ISSN 0394 4204 distributed in Great Britain by the Federal Trust for Education and Research.
14. Ibid., p. 31
15. Political Thesis. Foundation of MFE. Reprinted ibid., p. 45.
16. Pentland (1973, p. 158).
17. For example: King Podiebrad of Bohemia in the fifteenth century; Hugo Grotius, Dutch jurist and diplomat, in *De Iure Belle et Pacis* (1625); the Duc de Sully a few years later; William Penn in his 'Essay towards the present and future Peace of Europe' (1693); Abbé de St Pierre in his 'Mémoires pour rendre la paix perpétuelle en Europe' (1712); King Stanislas Leszczynski of Poland in his 'Memorial de l'affermissement de la paix générale' (1748); Saint-Simon in his 'De la réorganisation de la société européenne' (1814); Jeremy Bentham in his 'Plan for a Universal and

Perpetual Peace' (posthumously published in 1843); Immanuel Kant in his 'Zum Ewigen Frieden' (1795); Mazzini and the 'Young Europe' Movement (from 1834); Victor Hugo at the Paris Peace Congress in 1849; John Seeley, Regius Professor of Modern History at Cambridge, in his 'United States of Europe' (1871).

18. Statement by Lord Salisbury on the occasion of Queen Victoria's Jubilee, quoted in Critchley in Bond, Smith and Wallace (1996).

19. Federal Union centred around Lord Lothian, William Beveridge, Barbara Wootton (Head of the Labour Party's Research Department and later Labour leader in the Lords), Lionel Robbins (Director of the Economic Section of the War Cabinet) and Lionel Curtis (Head of Foreign Office Research Unit). It also involved Harold Wilson, Friedrich Hayek, Kim Mackay and Kenneth Wheare, Ivor Jennings (later Vice-Chancellors of Oxford and Cambridge respectively). For an account of Federal Union, see Pinder (1990).

20. Spinelli (1984, pp. 307–8). English translation of this section in *The Federalist Year*, XXVI, No. 2 (1984), p. 158.

21. MFE Foundation Political Thesis, p. 48.

22. Interview, Altiero Spinelli with Sonia Schmidt (1981), published in annex to Ventotene Manifesto, p. 61. In fact, Spinelli withdrew from the Federalist Movement, considering the chance for European Unification had been missed, until 'the issue of European Unification was reopened' with the Marshall Plan, in which the USA offered aid to Europe on condition that the European states agreed to formulate a common programme for European reconstruction.

23. MFE Congress 1950 Strasbourg. Quoted in English in The *Federalist Year* XXVI, No. 3, p. 249.

24. Montani (1982).

25. Resolution of Committee III of the Camera de Deputati, 20 November 1990. Available in English in the EP, Committee on Institutional Affairs, PE 150.302.

26. Quoted in Short (1991).

27. The Hague Congress brought together supporters of European integration and was organized by a coordinating committee of European NGOs. Its size, unprecedented character, timing and the participation of numerous key figures made it a highly significant event in gaining momentum for European integration.

28. An amendment by Reynaud and Bonnefous calling for a European Parliament to be elected on the basis of one MEP for 1 million inhabitants was rejected by 29 votes to 19 in the political commission of the Congress and attempts to reintroduce it in plenary were crushed overwhelmingly (only six votes in favour). see Burban (1991).

29. See Short (1991) and Posselt in Bosco (Vol. II, 1992, p. 126).

30. See Gerbet (1987) and Levy (1989).

31. Though an international conference of Socialist Parties on European unity in Paris in April 1948 supported an increase of the powers of the OEEC to make it 'the nucleus of a federal power to which would accrue that part of national sovereignty voluntarily waved by the states composing it'. Quoted in Short (1991).

32. Posselt went so far as to say: 'Parliamentarians for the first time participated in (external representation) of the State. Parliamentary action began to replace diplomatic action. This gradually changed relations in Europe from a character of foreign policy to a character of home policy, from international law to constitutional law and thus undermined the foundations of the dogma of national sovereignty' (in Bosco, 1992, p. 187).
33. Signed 27 May 1952. Foreign Ministers' invitation to Assembly, 10 September 1952 (their first meeting as the ECSC Council).
34. Resolution no. 14 of the Consultative Assembly of the Council of Europe, May 1952. This is itself illustrative of another phenomenon: the assembly of a wider Europe urging some countries to go ahead, if necessary, by themselves. We shall return to this phenomenon later.
35. See Cardozo (1987).
36. Notably Friedrich and Bowie (1954), produced at the request of the Spaak Committee of the European Movement, which presented proposals to the *ad hoc* Assembly.
37. Mario Albertini, Report to the MFE Central Committee, Paris, 1 July 1967.
38. Some 10,000 people at the Rome European Council of 1975.
39. My translation.
40. Minutes of the EP, 12 December 1990 (OJ C19, p. 65). Colombo then became Italian Foreign Minister and the report was taken over by Oreja, former Spanish Foreign Minister and Chairman of the EP's Institutional Affairs Committee. When he became a member of the Commission, the Report was taken over by Fernand Herman, and finally submitted to the EP in February 1994.
41. Published by the European Parliament in its Bulletin No. 4/S-90.
42. See, for example, the German SPD's Sofort Programme, adopted at the Extraordinary Party Congress held in Bonn on 16–17 November 1992, para. 60.
43. But not all: former German Foreign Minister Scheel in 1975 refuting the automatism of gradual integration stated that 'we cannot wait for European Union to fall into our lap one day like a ripe fruit. Therefore, Europe must give herself the institutions and the necessary competence to be able to act and must do so without delay. She needs a clear constitution which serves as a basis for common foreign economic and defence policy.' Cited in *The Times*, 23 April 1975.
44. Joint Statement on 4 June 1991 by Hans Dietrich Genscher and Hans van den Broek; see Agence Europe, No. 5506 (6 June 1991).
45. Gormley, Kapteyn and Verloren van Themaat (1989, pp. 1–2 and 8).
46. Schuman Declaration of May 1950, para. 5.
47. Brugmans (1989).
48. Debate of the Common Assembly, September 1952, p. 21 (author's translation).
49. Ibid., pp. 18 and 20.
50. Gormley, Kapteyn and Verloren van Themaat (1989, p. 9).
51. The term 'supranational' itself does not appear in the EEC or Euratom Treaties, unlike the ECSC Treaty, where it appeared in Art. 9 (which lapsed with the 1965 Merger Treaty).

52. The French Assembly approved the EEC treaty by 340 votes to 236 whereas EDC vote had been lost by 319 to 264. Yet few members had changed position. The intervening election of January 1956 had changed the strength of the parties, but Communists, Poujadists (among whom Jean-Marie Le Pen) and Gaullists remained opposed, whereas most Socialists and Centrists were in favour.
53. Case 26/62 *van Gend en Loos* v. *Nederlandse Administratie der Belastingen* ECR 1963) p. 1.
54. Case 6/64 *Costa* v. *ENEL* ECR (1964) p. 585.
55. Weiler (1982, p. 350).
56. Ibid., p. 350, n. 28.
57. Federal Constitutional Court, First Chamber, Decision of 18 October 1967 AWD (1967) pp. 477–8.
58. See in particular: 9/70 *Grad* v. *Finanzamt Traunstein* ECR (1970) 825; 41/74 *Van Duyn* v. *Home Office* ECR (1974) 1337; 51/76 *V.N.O.* v. *Inspector der Invoerrechten en Accijnzen* ECR (1977) 113.
59. See e.g. Hanson (1976).
60. Lord McKenzie Stuart, former President of the ECJ, quoting Judge Donner at the 'Scotland in Europe' conference 1990. Reprinted in *Facts* (European Movement, 1990), p. 4.
61. In *Van Gend en Loos* the Advocate General and the lawyers of all the states intervening in the case (half the then Member States) argued the other way.
62. Weiler (1982).
63. These terms are also Weiler's (1982). This is one area in which lawyers and political scientists sometimes diverge.
64. See Weiler (ibid.), who argues that they were and that their combined effect was a balance.
65. *The Times* (London), March 1965, quoted in Heathcote (1965, p. 17).
66. Isoglucose cases 138/79 (*Roquette Frères* v. *Council*) and 139/79 (*Maizena* v. *Council*) ECR (1980) pp. 3333 and 3393.
67. Debates of the EP (14 February 1984), p. 77.
68. *Financial Times*, 20 June 1991.
69. Pinder (1986, p. 50).
70. Ibid., p. 51.
71. Corbett (1984) and Sbagria (1992, pp. 283–91).
72. Debates of the European Parliament, 6 July 1988.
73. Pinder (1992).
74. Mitrany (1943).
75. Taylor (1983, p. 3).
76. Carole Webb, in Wallace, Wallace and Webb (1983, p. 33).
77. Tönnies (1940).
78. A view recently reiterated by Emanuele Gazzo (Editorial Agence Europe, No. 5963, 19 April 1993): 'It is not true that the federalist approach requires a high degree of centralized power, nor a highly uniform society. . . . It is enough to share certain important *values* and important *interests*.'
79. Delors (1990, p. 5).
80. See notably Haas (1958, chapter 1). Haas's use of the term 'loyalty' sits

uneasily with the general neofunctionalist emphasis on *Gesellschaft* (discussed above). He defined 'loyalty' as 'habitually and predictably over long periods [obeying] the injunctions of their authority and turn to them for the satisfaction of important expectations'. Such a definition is some way from a *Gemeinschaft* view and is, perhaps, closer to the German notion of *Bundestreu* if applied in the EC context. However, he went on to say that 'political community is a condition in which specific groups and individuals show more loyalty to their central political institutions *than to any other political authority*' (my emphasis), which seems to be more far-reaching than his arguments generally needed.

81. Lindberg and Scheingold (1970). Englewood Cliffs, N.J., Prentice-Hall, 1970.
82. Haas (1966).
83. Indeed, the treaties never refer to Council (or even an IGC) 'negotiating': it 'lays down', 'approves', 'determines', 'makes regulations', etc. The term 'negotiate' is used for talks with *third* countries by the Commission.
84. Haas (1966, Preface).
85. Ibid., p. 13.
86. Ibid., p. 20.
87. Ibid., p. 128.
88. Ibid., pp. 490 and 522, respectively.
89. Schmitter (1969, pp. 161–6).
90. Haas (1966, p. 10).
91. See notably Hoffman (1986).
92. Pinder (1992). See also Coombes (1970).
93. Spinelli (1957).
94. E. Haas, in Lindberg and Scheingold (1971).
95. Lindberg (1971).
96. Schmitter, in Lindberg and Scheingold (1971).
97. For a (later) analysis of the variety of interests at stake and the *diversity* of their preferred outcomes, see Holland (1980). He disaggregated different types of enterprise which would be likely to have different attitudes to integration.
98. Haas (1976).
99. Taylor in Lodge (1989, p. 24).
100. George (1985, pp. 24–7).
101. See Corbett (1992).
102. See, for instance, the case studies in Wallace, Wallace and Webb (1983); George (1985); and Holland (1980).
103. For a case study of how even groups not particularly affected by EC decisions and initially hostile to working with EC institutions can be drawn into a structural and permanent relationship see Corbett (1988).
104. Agence Europe, No. 5935 (8 March 1993) p. 9.
105. O.J. L 247 (6 September 1988) pp. 23–4.
106. See Corbett (1988).
107. Sally Watts, in *The Times*, 24 February 1995.
108. These are the advisory, management and regulatory committee composed of national civil servants, which assist the Commission with implement-

ing measures and in most cases can cause the matter to be referred to Council, for a description of the mechanics, see Corbett 'Comitology: what it is, why it matters', (1989).

109. Regulation 4064/89 OJ L 395 (1989), corrected in OJL 257 (1990).
110. e.g. cases 184/87 (*Portugal* v *Council*), 68/86 (*UK* v *Council*) and 51/89 (*UK* v *Council*).
111. Taylor (1983).
112. Busch and Puchala (1976, p. 235).
113. Webb (1983, pp. 8–9).
114. George (1985, p. 196), felt that the Community was 'possibly on the brink of collapse'.
115. Keohane and Nye (1977).
116. Puchala (1972).
117. Puchala quoted in Webb (1983).
118. W. Wallace 'Walking Backwards towards Unity', in Wallace, Wallace and Webb (1977).
119. Featherstone (1983, p. 23).
120. Webb (1983, p. 33).
121. W. Wallace: 'Less than a Federation, More than a Regime', in Wallace, Wallace and Webb (1977).
122. Webb (1983, p. 33).
123. See Hoffmann (1986).
124. Presidential press conference, 9 September 1965.
125. Speech for the inauguration of the academic year at the College of Europe, Bruges, 20 September 1988.
126. Kirchner (1992).
127. See Weiler et al., in Hayward (1995), and see notes 78 and 80.
128. German unification might change this perception if combined with conspicuously better economic performance or with heavy-handed political actions by Germany.
129. Tore Nedbrebö: 'Whence Europe? The Political Culture of European Unification', Hovudfag Thesis, University of Bergen, Norway, 1986. However, Nedbrebö also found party sympathies were the most important factor in public attitudes, supporting the view that, on complex issues, people use their preferred party as a reference point.
130. Negotiations on treaty texts or other 'constitutional' documents took place in 1950–1 (ECSC), 1952 (EDC), 1953–4 (EPC), 1955 (Spaak Committee), 1956–7 (EEC & EAEC), 1961, 1962 (Fouchet Plan), 1963–5 (Merger Treaty), 1969, 1970 (1st Budget Treaty), 1971, 1972 (1st Treaty of Accession), 1974, 1975 (2nd Budget Treaty), 1976 (Tindemans Report discussions), 1977–9 (Greek Accession Treaty), 1981–3 (Genscher–Colombo proposals), 1984 (Dooge Committee), 1985–6 (SEA), 1987–8 (Delors I package) 1988–9 (Delors Committee), 1990–2 (EMU and PU IGCs), 1992 (Edinburgh Agreement and Delors II Package), 1994 (Nordic and Austrian accession Treaty and Ioannina Compromise), 1995 (Reflection Group), 1996 (IGC).
131. Agence Europe, No. 6767 (10 July 1996), p. 3.
132. Duchêne in Bond, Smith and Wallis, 1986.

2. WHAT TO EXPECT OF THE EUROPEAN PARLIAMENT

1. Webb, in Wallace, Wallace and Webb (1983).
2. In George (1985).
3. Taylor (1983).
4. Debates of the EP, 18 July 1979, p. 40.
5. View described by Wallace (1972, p. 293).
6. Haas (1958, pp. 390–450). The quotes in the following five paragraphs are all from this chapter.
7. Concerning the IGC on the EEC and EURATOM he felt that the Assembly's results were 'far from impressive', but that it did help ensure that these Communities would have supranational Commissions, that there would be a common Assembly and Court for the three Communities and that the common market would be complemented by active common policies. He points out that it was also the Assembly's idea that the IGC should be led by an independent political personality (in the event, Spaak).
8. Which he deemed to be 'extremely positive' in the case of the ECSC Assembly.
9. In the ECSC Assembly he felt that 'not only does the Socialist Group conduct itself thoroughly in accordance with federal principles, but its policy acts as a potential stimulus for the other groups to do the same'.
10. Haas, ibid., pp. 413–14, n. 36.
11. Quoted by Burban (1978, p. 306; my translation).
12. Quoted ibid., p. 308 (my translation).
13. Morand in Colloquy of the Institut d'Etudes Juridiques Européennes (IEJE) of the University of Liège (1976, p. 87; my translation).
14. Goriely in ibid., p. 113 (my translation).
15. Mansholt in ibid., p. 167.
16. Brugmans in ibid., p. 287 (my translation).
17. Goossens in ibid., p. 239 (my translation).
18. Burban (1978, my translation).
19. Georges Vedel, 'Mythes de l'Europe et l'Europe de Mythes', in *Revue du Marché commun*, October 1967 (my translation).
20. Pierre Henri Teitgen; 'Le Parlement européen au lendemain de son élection directe', in *The European Parliament* (Athens, 1978) (my translation).
21. In IEJE (1976, p. 121) (my translation).
22. Christophe Sasse, 'Le renforcement des pouvoirs du Parlement', in ibid., p. 63 (my translation).
23. Speech to the Congress of Europe organized by the European Movement, Brussels, 6 February 1976.
24. J.J. Schwed, 'La Commission des Communautés européennes et le Parlement européen', in *The European Parliament* (Athens, 1978, Greek Parliament).
25. Jean Rey, 'Réflexions sur l'Union européenne', in IEJE (1976, p. 265) (my translation). The opposite possibility is described by Steed (see below).
26. Christophe Sasse, '*Le renforcement des pouvoirs du Parlement, et spécialement ses nouveaux pouvoirs budgétaires*', in ibid. (my translation).
27. Schelto Patijn; '*L'élection du Parlement européen au suffrage universel direct*', in ibid., p. 157 (my translation).
28. Wallace (1979).

29. Helen Wallace, 'The European Parliament: The Challenge of Political Responsibility', in *Government and Opposition* (special edition 1979), pp. 433–43.
30. Hans Nord and John Taylor, 'The European Parliament before and after Direct Elections', in ibid. (pp. 411–32).
31. France: Law 77–680 of 30 June 1977 authorizing direct elections; UK: European Assembly Elections Act 1978 (ch. 10, section 6).
32. Steed (1971, pp. 462–77).
33. Mary Robinson (later President of Ireland) in IEJE (1976, pp. 175–6).
34. Jean Victor Louis in ibid. (p. 311) (my translation).
35. Wallace (1979, p. 293).
36. Nord and Taylor, in *Government and Opposition* (special edition 1979).
37. Karlheinz Reif, Roland Cayrol and Oskar Niedermayer, 'National Political Parties, Middle Level Elites and European Integration', in *European Journal of Political Research*, Quorum, Berlin, 1980.
38. See *Tribune*, 3, 10 and 17 March 1979.
39. Kirk Draft Report, later the Lord Reay Report of the Political Affairs Committee (Doc.148/78).
40. Georges Vedel, 'The Role of the Parliamentary Institution in European Integration' in *European Integration and the Future of Parliaments in Europe* (Papers and Reports of Symposium, European Parliament, 1975), p. 241.
41. *Documentation* (EPP, Brussels, 1979), pp. 27–8.
42. Ibid., pp. 31–4, 'Electoral Platform' adopted by IInd Congress on 22–23 February 1979 mentions decentralizing political power on the 'principle of subsidiarity', but does not attempt to define it.
43. *Programme for Europe* (Brussels: ELD, 1978) pp. 18–19.
44. *European Programmes* (Brussels: CSP, 1980) pp. 211–18.
45. Ibid., p. 218.
46. Electoral Programmes of the Belgian Socialist Parties. English translation in *European Programmes* (Brussels: CSP, 1980) pp. 10 and 32.
47. Quoted in Featherstone (1988, p. 157).
48. Electoral Programme of the SPD. English translation in *European Programmes*, pp. 44–85.
49. Ibid., p. 142.
50. Featherstone (1988, p. 277).
51. *L'Unité* (January 1976).
52. *European Programme*, p. 120.
53. Lowe (unpublished).
54. Featherstone (1988, pp. 94–5).
55. Ibid. (pp. 205–6).
56. *Campaign Guide for Europe 1979*, Conservative Research Department (London: Conservative Central Office, 1979) p. 51.
57. *Programme du Parti Communiste Italien – 10 juin 1979 élections directes du Parlement Européen* (Luxembourg: Communist Group Secretariat, 1979) 17, pp. 23–5.
58. G. Amendola, *The Italian Communists and the European Elections*, (Luxembourg: Communist Group secretariat, 1978) p. 25. This view echoes that of J. Rey (see above).

59. *Bull. des Communistes Français à l'Assemblée des CE*, 'Les Communistes Français et l'Europe' No. 3 (1979) pp. 16–20.
60. European Parliament DG III Summary of Results.
61. Though several have tried.
62. With the possible exception of the National Front in France in terms of seats won – but this is due to the difference of electoral system with national elections not being run on a proportional system.

3. A NEW POLITICAL NETWORK

1. Cotta (1984, p. 126).
2. Marquand (1979, p. 67).
3. Kirchner (1984). Kirchner also states incorrectly that this meant that they were former members of the Council of Ministers, but many will have been from ministries not involved with the Council and some will have held office before their Member State joined the Community.
4. Own research based on DGIII figures, but confirmed in Westlake (1994, p. 21).
5. Kirchner (1984, p. 67).
6. Westlake (1994, p. 267).
7. Ibid. (pp. 79, 87 and 105).
8. Westlake (1994, p. 19).
9. Kirchner (1984, p. 6).
10. van Schendelen (1984).
11. Westlake (1994, p. 250).
12. William Newton Dunn MEP (later chairman of the Conservative MEPs) wrote that the EP 'held an emergency debate and accepted an amendment from this author (which was supported by a majority of Conservatives who voted) that Britain's attempted veto over agricultural prices should be overruled' in *Greater in Europe* (London: Regency Press, 1989).
13. Agence Europe, No. 6800 (30 August 1996).
14. Castle (1993).
15. Westlake (1994, p. 136).
16. Interview with the author, 14 January 1992.
17. Interview with the author, 4 April 1992.
18. Interview with the author, 1 July 1993.
19. Survey 'Labour Parliamentarians and European Integration', Sheffield and Nottingham Trent Universities, 1996.
20. Marilisa Xenogiannakopoulou, PASOK official in the secretariat of the EP Socialist Group (and candidate in the 1994 European elections). Interview with author, 8 September 1993.
21. Interview with author, 11 October 1985.
22. Westlake (1994, pp. 83 and 85).
23. For which he won *The Guardian's*. Parliamentarian of the Year award.
24. David Curry (Ministry of Agriculture) and Eric Forth (DTI).
25. I disagree with Westlake, however, on this as he feels that 'previous European Parliamentary experience among members of the government and the Commons has made very little difference' (Westlake, p. 110). How-

ever, he was writing before the appointment of J. Quin and the Maastricht Debate.

26. David Curry MEP, in Foreword to Kirchner (1984).
27. Debré, Messmer, Chirac, Mauroy, Fabius, Rocard, Cresson and Juppé. Another, Barre, was previously a Vice-President of the Commission.
28. Poher (interim President), Giscard, Mitterrand, Chirac.
29. Some former prime ministers sitting in the EP subsequently returned to hold high office again in national politics: Colombo and Tindemans, for example, both became Foreign Ministers, Chirac became Prime Minister again and later President.
30. Interview with senior Conservative official, 9 September 1994. The official wishes to remain anonymous.
31. Ibid.
32. Ibid.
33. Interview David Martin, 14 January 1992.
34. Agenda for 90th Annual Conference. Constitutional Amendments (Labour Party, 1991) pp. vii–xiii.
35. David Martin, correspondence with the author 30 October 1991.
36. Questionnaire sent by the author to officials of these parties, May 1994. Responses obtained from German SPD, French Parti Socialiste, Italian PDS, Spanish PSOE, Belgian SP and PS, Dutch PvdA and Greek PASOK.
37. Westlake (1994, p. 61).
38. Castle (1993, pp. 532–45).
39. See Jacobs et al. (1982, p. 83).
40. Correspondence with the author 31 October 1991. He went on to quote point by point the major items of his report that now featured in Labour's policy documents 'Opportunity Britain' and 'Looking to the Future' and in Party Conference resolutions.
41. Owen and Dynes (1992).
42. Tindale (1991).
43. Interview with J. Moermans, Liberal Group Secretariat, June 1994.
44. The list of subjects covered is enormous but not all are necessarily political. Some deal with regional problems, some with religion, some with particular countries (Chile, South Africa) and others with organizational problems (fund raising, press work). A large number are devoted to allowing front-benchers an extra platform besides their (often short) conference speech.
45. Unfortunately, it proved impossible to obtain any fringe guides for the early 1980s, even from the archives at Walworth Road.
46. The President of the EP, Enrique Baron, speaking at a Labour Party Conference fringe meeting in 1991, paid 'tribute to the efforts made by MEPs in this country to influence the approach taken by their parties at home', which had helped change attitudes to Europe (Speech to EPLP fringe meeting, 29 September 1991, Brighton).
47. The rapporteur for drafting the common manifesto was Gerd Walter, Minister for Europe in Schleswig-Holstein and former leader of the SPD MEPs in the EP. He was chosen partly because of his experience as an MEP.
48. Interview with Dankert quoted in Kirchner (1984, p. 151).
49. And the difficulty of convincing selection conferences that they could.

50. Interview with Michael Shackleton, EP official responsible for relations with national parliaments, 8 September 1993.
51. Including 33 per cent of the German delegation being former Landtag members, probably the most powerful of the regional tier assemblies in Europe.
52. Interviews carried out during 1994 with the following MEPs: Newton Dunn, Martin, Donnelly, White, Morris, Crawley, Tongue, Read, Tomlinson, Titley, Pollack, Collins, Ford, Wynn, David, Green and two who wished to remain anonymous (both Conservative).
53. See Jacobs et al. (1992, pp. 256–7).
54. Ibid.
55. Figure supplied by EP security service.
56. Rudolf Hrbek, 'The European Parliament, the Citizens and the Political Environment', Paper for Tapser Symposium, Strasbourg, 17–18 November 1988.
57. Ibid.
58. Interview with David Earnshaw, Assistant to Ken Collins MEP, Chair of the Environment and Consumer Protection Committee, 4 May 1991.
59. Jacobs et al. (1992, chapter 9).
60. I am indebted to John Peterson for this term.
61. Jenkins (1992, pp. 513–14).
62. Commission document 'Relations with Parliament: Administrative Arrangements', SEC 79, 1163, p. 3.
63. Ibid., Annex 2.
64. Westlake (1994, p. 12).
65. A Commissioner responsible for relations with the EP has been designated in each Commission since 1973.
66. During the first half of 1990, the Commission calculated the number of Commission officials who spoke in committee meetings. The most frequent instances over the six-month period were for the following committees: Environment 202; Economic and Monetary 180; Petitions 137; Research 131; Legal Affairs 119; External Relations 101; Budgetary Control 97; Transport 90; Budgets 64 (quoted in Westlake, 1994, p. 18).
67. Altiero Spinelli was one of the few examples, before direct elections. Since then, Claude Cheysson, Willy De Clercq, Abel Matutes and Carlo Ripa di Meana have all followed that route.
68. Thus, the US Congress followed up requests by Parliament's delegations to scrap US visa requirements for citizens of EC countries (none of which required visas for US citizens).
69. None of these figures includes the ACP Assembly.
70. Interview with Peter Brown, National Secretary of the National Organization of Labour Students 1982–3, 20 January 1990.
71. van Schendelen (1984, p. 99).
72. Westlake (1984, p. 23).
73. Jacobs et al. (1992, p. 259).
74. Westlake (1994, p. 270).
75. Information provided by DG. III of the European Parliament.
76. Ibid.

77. The next 12 years saw a further 62 per cent increase for Group As and 43 per cent for Parliament As, partly as a result of enlargement of the EC.
78. Sweeney (1984).

4. EXPLOITING ITS EXISTING POWERS

1. Arts 96 (ECSC), 236 (EEC) and 204 (EAEC).
2. The second phase of the 1970 Treaty had actually diminished Parliament's powers as regards reductions in CE by reversing the majority needed in Council to accept EP modifications. This was described as an 'anomaly' by the Commission in its proposals for the 2nd budget treaty (see COM(73) 1000 p. 4).
3. It is also interesting to note the elements contained in the Commission's proposals for the new budgetary treaty that were *not* eventually incorporated into the 1975 treaty. These included a proposal that Parliament modifications increasing CE should be decided upon by a simple majority within Council, that an explicit decision on the VAT rate be part of the budgetary procedure, that Parliament's assent by a majority of its members be required to authorize Community borrowing, that Parliament's assent be required for the adoption or modification of the financial regulation, that the Community's 'own resources' can be modified by a unanimous Council decision without national ratification, but with the approval of a 3/5ths majority in the European Parliament, and that Parliament's assent be required for appointments to the Court of Auditors (COM (73) 1000 final).
4. If it does not act within 45 days, or if it explicitly approves Council's draft, the budget is adopted as Council established it. This has never happened.
5. The Community Budget: The facts in the figures, EC Commission, document SEC (93) 1100. It is, however, worth recalling that the US federal budget was 2.8 per cent of GDP as late as 1929.
6. *The Budget: Facts in Figures*, 1993 SEC(93) 1100-En p. 13.
7. Described in Pinder (1992, p. 35).
8. *The Budget: Parliament's Case*, European Parliament DGIII 1987.
9. Technically, it was at that time European units of account (EUAs) rather than ECUs, but for convenience the term ECU is used throughout the text.
10. Case 34/86.
11. Council was unable to find a solution in time for the deadline on its first reading (5 October). Both Parliament and the Commission took Council to Court for failure to respect the Treaty. By the time the Court came to rule on the matter, the budget procedure had been resumed and the only sanction applied to Council was that it had to pay the costs of the case.
12. OJ L 185 (1988) p. 33.
13. *The Community Budget: The Facts in Figures*, 1993 edition, Official Publications Office, Luxembourg.
14. It is in any case, statistically, difficult to reduce a figure comprising a high percentage without effecting other changes: for instance, if an item comprising 80 per cent of the budget were halved in absolute terms, it

would still comprise 67 per cent of the budget if no other changes were made.

15. Wyldavsky (1994).
16. Calculated from *The Community Budget: The Facts in Figures* (1988 edition), p. 27.
17. Ibid., p. 42.
18. In 1973 when the distinction between NCE and CE had been mooted in the Treaty but had still to take effect, it was estimated that NCE would be a mere 5 per cent of the budget: see Cocks (1973).
19. The years listed are the years of *creation* of the item, which may well have been kept in subsequent years.
20. For van Schendelen (1984, p. 118): 'There is not a single parliament in West Europe that enjoys such budgetary possibilities' (my translation).
21. Westlake (1984, p. 79).
22. Joint Declaration EP Council. European Treaties (Official Publication Office of the EC), 1987 edition, p. 900.
23. Though it did work as regards the proposal for what became the 1975 Budget Treaty, see above.
24. 'Isoglucose' Ruling. See chapter 1, n. 66.
25. Parliament has at least once delayed a proposal in order to obtain concessions on another matter. In 1991 it repeatedly referred back to committee a Commission proposal on the insurance sector on the ground (carefully never expressed formally) that single market liberalizations were progressing far more quickly than the implementation of the Social Charter. The insurance proposal was of particular interest to the UK, which was the country perceived as holding up the social legislation.
26. The number of non-legislative resolutions rose from an average of 83 per year from 1973 to 1978 to an average of 229 per year from 1980 to 1985. The number of opinions given under the consultation procedure actually declined over the same periods from 161 per year (1973–8) to 146 a year (1980–5). Figures calculated from EUROSTAT General Statistics, section 1 (various years).
27. Jacobs et al. (1992, p. 180).
28. See chapter 3 for figures.
29. Articles 140, 143 and 144, respectively.
30. Article 206(b).
31. Figures calculated from EUROSTAT General Statistics (various years).
32. Figures obtained from secretariat of DGII of the EP.
33. Debates of the EP, 7 July 1977.
34. The nominated Parliament failed even to take Council to court for failing in its duty to adopt the necessary act for direct elections when the latter failed to respond to Parliament's initial proposals on this.
35. Case 13/83.
36. On comitology.
37. Interview, Francis Jacobs (Secretariat, Economic and Monetary Affairs Committee), 15 November 1989.
38. Haas (1958, p. 390).
39. Debate of the EP (25 May 1984), p. 319.

5. REFORM WITHIN THE TREATIES

1. For an account of this, see Jacobs et al. (3rd edition 1995, pp. 212–14).
2. Debates of the EP, 7 July 1981, p. 79.
3. Mariano Rumor, Chairman of the Political Affairs Committee, in an introduction to a summary of the Committee's work in this field ('Growing Together', *Research and Documentation*, D.G. of EP, 1982).
4. Van Miert Report (Doc 1-207/81). Resolution, EP Minutes 9 July 1981, p. 64.
   Hänsch Report (Doc 1-216/81). Resolution, EP Minutes 9 July 1981, p. 52.
   Rey Report (Doc 1-71/80). Resolution, EP Minutes 17 April 1980, p. 52.
   Diligent Report (Doc 1-206/81). Resolution, EP Minutes 9 July 1981, p. 81.
   Elles Report (Doc 1-335/81). Resolution, EP Minutes 9 July 1981, p. 68.
   Baduel Glorioso Report (Doc 1-226/81). Resolution, EP Minutes 9 July 1981, p. 60.
   Antoniozzi Report (Doc 1-739/81). Resolution, EP Minutes 18 January 1982, p. 192.
5. COM (81) 581 fin.
6. 15th General Report, p. 288.
7. The first one to do so was Mrs Thatcher, on 17 December 1981.
8. i.e. involving the chairmen of EP political groups.
9. Bull. EC 11-1981, item 2.3.1.
10. EP Bulletin PE 78.554. Letter of 8 April 1982 by Mr De Keersmaeker to Mr Dankert.
11. EP debates of 19 November 1981, p. 217.
12. Croux Report, Political Affairs Committee, doc. 1-1328/82.
13. Debates of the EP, 29 June 1983, p. 4.
14. COM (81) 581 fin. pp. 10–11.
15. Ibid., pp. 8–11.
16. Not all: the French National Assembly has virtually no right of legislative initiative and the House of Commons, *in practice*, gives its members very little scope (e.g. the lottery system for 'Private Member's Bills').
17. Ibid., p. 10.
18. COM (81), 816 fin.
19. De Pasquale Report, 1983.
20. This is a possible case of a rapporteur's close relation with key government actors paying dividends (though at the same time channelling influence the other way?). Lady Elles was a prominent member of the same political party as the Council President (Lord Carrington), who helped steer through the London Report.

6. PARLIAMENT TURNS TO TREATY REVISION

1. For a more detailed account of the events described in this chapter, see Cardozo and Corbett (1985).

2. EP Working Document, 1-889/80/rev., known as Abens/Crocodile Resolution.

3. Spinelli (1983).

4. Resolution on European Union (Bertrand Report), EP Minutes, 10 July 1975.

5. EP Working Document, 1-347/79.

6. 'Growing Together', *Research and Documentation*, D.G. of E.P. 1982, pp. 7–8.

7. EPP Group Document, G/27/80.

8. EPP Group Document, JE/31/80

9. EP Working Documents, 1-476/80 Geurtsen and Delorozoy on extending human and social rights in the EC, and 1-297/81 De Gucht and others on institutional problems.

10. Stanley Johnson, MEP (UK/EDG), to Cardozo 16 September 1983.

11. This note cannot do more than point to Spinelli's numerous works amongst which the autobiographical 'Pourquoi je suis Européen', *Preuves*, No. 81, November 1951, and *The Eurocrats: Conflict and Crisis in the EC*, (Baltimore: Johns Hopkins, 1966) are appropriate in this context. See also 'Une Constituante Européenne', *Pensée Française*, Fédération Nos. 9–10, 1957; *L'Europa non cade dal cielo* (Bologna: Il Mulino, 1960); and *L'avventura Europea* (Bologna: Il Mulino, 1972).

12. Spinelli (1978, p. 88).

13. See Spinelli (1957).

14. Crocodile Letter to MEPs, 2 December 1980.

15. EP Working Document, 1-889/80/rev.

16. EPP Group Document, 106/81, p. 32.

17. *European Digest* 44, June 1981, Section II, EPP Group.

18. Crocodile Letter to MEPs, 4 March 1981, 5 June 1981.

19. OJ., C. 234/48, 14 September 1981.

20. Debates of the EP, 7 July 1981, p. 77.

21. Some 20 of the 37 full Members were also members of one of these two committees.

22. Hänsch, Van Miert, Blumenfeld, Antoniozzi.

23. Group leaders: Fanti, De la Malène and Pannella. Committee chairmen: Moreau, Veil, De Pasquale, Ferri.

24. Author's own observations, having attended all meetings of the committee during this period.

25. Selection of texts concerning institutional matters of the Community 1950–82 (Luxembourg: EP, 1982).

26. These included: Thorn, Commission President; Tindemans, President-in-Office of the Council; Roseingrave, President of the Economic and Social Committee; Debunne, President of ETUC; Carli, President of UNICE; Petrilli, President of the European Movement; Pinder, Director of the London Policy Studies Institute.

27. Ibid.

28. EP Working Document, 1-940/81/rev., tabled on 12 February 1982.

29. Ibid., 1-926/81.

30. Ibid., 1-301/82.

31. Ibid., 1-635/83/rev., notably a draft 'European Constitution', tabled during the September 1983 'contents' debate.
32. EP Working Document, 1-305/82/A, p. 2.
33. OJ., C.238, 1982, pp. 25–31.
34. EP Working Document, 1-575/83/c, contains the revised working documents.
35. EP Working Documents, PE 81.387, contains summary record.
36. EP Working Document, 1-575/83/A.
37. OJ. C.277, 1983, p. 95.
38. Bull. EC, supplement 5/75 (Spinelli was a Member of the Commission at that time).
39. Professors Capotori of Rome University and former Advocate General of the European Court of Justice; Hilf of Bielefeld University; Jacobs of King's College London; Jacqué, President of Strasbourg University.
40. See also Corbett and Nickel (1985).
41. Interview with Spinelli, 20 February 1986.
42. Spinelli Report, 1-1200/83/A.
43. OJ C.77, 1984, pp. 33–54.
44. DEP, 1-273, 1981, pp. 105–6.
45. DEP, 1-103, 1983, and Hänsch, in Hrbek et al. (1984).
46. *The New Federalist*, 21 (1984) 9.
47. DEP, 1-288, 1982, p. 127.
48. See Cardozo, 'The Political Groups in the European Parliament and the Crocodile Initiative' (Ealing College: 1983, unpublished), p. 40.
49. Hume confirmed to the author that his abstention in one vote was a mistake with the voting machine.
50. DEP, 1-307, 1983, p. 61.
51. Two pro-integration MEPs were de-selected: Key and Enright.
52. See note 30 above.
53. After four years' consideration of a list of rights following the tabling of a motion (EP Working Document 1-476/80), it had failed to agree on a report to the House.
54. For example, 30 June 1982 in Luxembourg, and 31 May–2 June 1983 in Berlin.
55. IVth Congress in Paris (6–8 December 1982) adopted a resolution supporting the EP's initiative.
56. DEP, 1-303, 1983, pp. 131–46 (for explanation of vote).
57. Ibid., p. 48.
58. DEP, 1-309, 1984, p. 73.
59. The VIIIth ELD Congress in Venice in May 1982 adopted a detailed position on the reforms Parliament should seek with the DTEU.
60. DEP, 1-309, p. 42.
61. Tore Nedrebö ('Whence Europe? The Political Culture of European Unification'. Hovudfag Thesis, University, Bergen, 1986) also found that votes on the DTEU 'were fairly representative of attitudes at the European "grass roots"' and of national political public opinion over European integration' (p. 218).
62. Ibid., p. 94.

7. THE DRAFT TREATY

1. For a complete legal analysis article by article see the commentary published by the four lawyers who assisted the EP's Committee on Institutional Affairs: Capotorti et al. (1986). For a shorter overview, see D. Nickel and R. Corbett, in the *Yearbook of European Law* (1984) pp. 79–93, or D. Nickel in *Cahiers du Droit Européen* (1984).

   On the particular problems of Art. 82, see R. Corbett, 'Spaak II or Schuman II: The implications of Art. 82 of the Draft Treaty', in *The Federalist* (Pavia, 1985).

2. In 1976, the European Council had informally welcomed the proposal to involve the President-designate of the Commission at least in consultations with each national government on their nominations, though this had not been successfully implemented (see Bull. EC 4-1976, 83).

3. Rey Report. Minutes of the EP, OJ 1980 C 117, para. 7.

4. Modelled on the existing procedure and on the Federal German model; see R. Corbett, 'Reform of the Council: The Bundesrat Model', *The Federalist* (Pavia, 1984) 51.

5. A striking precursor of the Maastricht Treaty 'pillars'?

6. See also Spinelli letter to Thorn on draft Treaty, reprinted in *Crocodile* No. 11 (1983) 9.

7. Press conference EP, 14 September 1983.

8. See R. Corbett, 'Spaak II or Schuman II: the implications of Art. 82 of the Draft Treaty on European Union', in *The Federalist* (Pavia, 1985).

9. And its equivalents Art. 95 ECSC and Art. 203 EAEC.

10. See ECJ ruling in case 6/64 *Costa* v *ENEL* (1964) ECR 585.

11. See notably: Schwarze, 'Das allgemeine Völkerrecht in den innergemeinschaftlichen Rechtsbeziehungen', in *Europarecht* (1-1983) 1
    – Kapteyn VerLoren van Themaat (supra)
    – Schermers, *International Institutional Law*, 2nd edn (1982), ch. 8.
    See also Art. 40 Vienna Convention on the Law of Treaties.

12. e.g. Treaty on the Saar (1956), Convention on Certain Institutions Common to the European Communities (1958).

13. e.g. The 1970 and 1975 'budgetary' treaties.

14. Jacqué, 'The European Union Treaty and the Community Treaties', *Crocodile* No. 11 (1983) p. 7.

15. Art. 59, Vienna Convention.

16. Though quite what they would be able to do if the Union States unilaterally declared that they were leaving the EC is not apparent.

17. The committee on institutional affairs considered whether to put in the Treaty a reference to the need to negotiate with non-contracting Member States. It demurred, not wishing to indicate from the beginning that it expected that some Member States would not wish to go along.

8. FROM THE DRAFT TREATY TO THE 1985 INTERGOVERNMENTAL CONFERENCE

1. Term used for first elections in special issue of *European Journal of Political Science Research* (April 1980).

2. Even in countries where the press habitually neglects the EP e.g. *Le Monde* carried articles at least on 15, 16 February, 18 April, 26, 30 May, 5 June; *Financial Times* on 14 February, 29 May (plus a leading article), 4 June 1984.

3. The EUT was also the main theme of the debate on Belgian TV between the four list leaders in Flanders (Van Miert, Croux, De Gucht and Vandemeulebroucke), all of whom had been members of the Committee on Institutional Affairs.

4. Fifteen leaving aside Greenland, also won by an anti-marketeer.

5. Haagerup, a Liberal, was the only Danish MEP to have voted for the EUT.

6. Interview in *El Pais*, 4 June 1984 and EPP Congress, 5 April 1984.

7. Interview *Le Point*, No. 611/1984.

8. 29 March 1984, speech to Chamber of Deputies.

9. Ibid.

10. 29 May 1984.

11. 23 March 1984, Speech of President of Spanish Senate to Congress of European Movement in Brussels; Kohl, *Le Monde* 30 May 1984, and *La Stampa*.

12. *DEP*, 1-314, (1984), p. 266.

13. Debates of the European Parliament, 24 May 1984.

14. See, for example, open letter to Thorn, reprinted in *Crocodile*, No. 11.

15. Interview Spinelli, 25 May 1984.

16. e.g. Simone Veil, Statement quoted in 25/26 May 1984 editions of most French newspapers, and British Foreign Office officials quoted in *Financial Times*, 29 May 1984.

17. The UK government pursued a series of efforts to convince its partners of its good faith, starting with the Foreign Office publication 'Britain in the European Community: a positive approach' (HMSO Dd 8333507) in 1983, and continuing with the 'Thatcher Memorandum' to the Fontainebleau Summit and Sir Geoffrey Howe's speech in Bonn on 17 October 1984 in which he stated that Europe 'cannot be complete without Britain', thus indicating an awareness of the danger of others moving without the UK.

18. See, for instance, interview with Roland Dumas, published by *Le Matin* and referred to by the *Guardian*, 30 May 1984.

19. Interview Spinelli, 25 July 1984.

20. Letter No. 1642/CAB/JMR/LA, Ministère des Affaires Européennes. In English: 'enabling the convening of a conference of Member States *that have declared their determination to progress along the path of European integration*' (my emphasis).

21. The Members were: Herman (B), Moller (DK), Ruhfus (D), Varfis (G) (succeeded by Papantoniou after he became a member of the Commission), Faure (F), Dooge (Irl), Ferri (I), Dondelinger (L), Van Eekelen (NL), Rifkind (UK) and Andriessen (COM) (succeeded by Ripa di Meana for new Commission).

22. Including a meeting with the whole Italian government in January 1985.

23. Interim Report to the European Council, EC Official Publication Office ISBN 92-824-0186-3.

24. Dooge himself also expressed one reservation concerning security.

25. Report to the European Council SN/1187/85 (Spaak II), Council 1985.
26. Statement published in 'Europe Documents' No. 1344, Agence Europe.
27. Chairman of the Political Affairs Committee, replacing President Pflimlin who was fog-bound at Paris airport.
28. Conclusions of the European Council SN/1381/2/85.
29. Camera dei Deputati, Parliamentary Acts and Proceedings, 13 February 1984, pp. 13–45; 14 February 1984, pp. 5–64.
30. Senato, 112th public sitting, Verbatim Report, 10 May 1984, pp. 4–27.
31. Chambre des représentants, Annales Parlementaires, 24 May 1984, p. 2975.
32. Folketingstidene, Folketingsforhandlinger, second volume, 1983–4, pp. 7160–243.
33. Folketingstidene, Folketingsforhandlinger.
34. Interview Haagerup, 8 May 1985.
35. Drucksache 10/1247, Bundestag 1984.
36. Speech to the Congress of Europa-Union and UEF, Agence Europe, No. 3897 (10 December 1984) p. 3.
37. Assembly: Report No. 11/84 of the Delegation for the European Communities; Senate: report no. 120/84 of the Delegation for the European Communities.
38. Report No. 7/85 of the Delegation for the European Communities.
39. Report of the National Assembly Delegation for the EC, 30 September 1982 (annex to the minutes of Assembly 16 December 1982).
40. Report No. 14 'The European Parliament Draft Treaty Establishing the European Union' (PL 3063).
41. Agence Europe, no. 4079 (27 April 1985).
42. 7 May 1985.
43. 29 May 1985.
44. See, for example, David Coombes's chapter in Ryle and Walkland (1983).
45. Mr Nigel Spearing MP.
46. 21st Report from the Select Committee on European Legislation (15 May 1985).
47. Select Committee on the European Communities, 14th Report (23 July 1985) 'European Union', HM SO HL 226.
48. OJ (1985) C 12, pp. 47–8.
49. In some cases two 'scouts' from different parties were nominated. The scouts were B: Croux, DK: Toksvig, D: Zarges & Seeler, G: Mavros & Evregenis, F: Sutra, IRL: Clinton (later Ryan), I: Cassanmagnago Cerretti & Fanti, L: Estgen, NL: Nord, UK: Jackson.
50. The source material for the following considerations is drawn from the Explanatory Statement of the Seeler Reports (Docs. A2-16/85/B and A2-348/88) on the reactions of national parliaments, the individual country reports, discussions with MEPs and officials participating in the delegations, and press reports including Agence Europe Nos 4015, 4025, 4038, 4044, 4045, 4054, 4057, 4060 and 4097. The author also accompanied the delegations to Dublin, London and Copenhagen.
51. I am indebted to the late Klaus Toksvig MEP, former Danish TV current affairs correspondent for this point.

52. See Agence Europe, Nos 4014 (25 January 1985), 4036 (25 February 1985), 4048 (14 March 1985) and 4051 (19 March 1985).
53. Reproduced in PE 97.183/Ann.
54. See chapter 7.
55. Addressed, *inter alia*, by former Prime Minister Lynch, Foreign Minister Barry and Commissioner Sutherland, all of whom took a positive line on European Union.
56. A selection of headlines of leading articles alone gives a flavour of the debate and its evolution: 'Facing up to Union' (*Irish Times*, 21 March), 'European Ambitions' (*Irish Times*, 23 March), 'Success in Brussels' (*Irish Times*, 1 April), 'Catching the Euro-train' (*Sunday Independent*, 7 April), 'Neutrality' (*Irish Independent*, 10 April), 'Living up to Neutrality', (*Irish Times*, 11 April), 'Striking Attitudes in Strasbourg' (*Irish Times*, 17 April), 'The Price of Neutrality' (*Cork Examiner*, 13 April) 'Neutrality' (*Irish Press*, 15 April), 'No Danger' (*Irish Independent*, 15 April), 'European Union' (*Irish Independent*, 27 April), 'Not for Sale' (*Irish Press*, 27 April), 'Neither Hysteria nor Complacency' (*Irish Times*, 27 April), 'When Were We Ever Neutral?' (*Cork Examiner*, 2 May), 'Safely in Neutral Hands' (*Cork Examiner*, 13 May), 'The Real Europe' (*Irish Times*, 27 June), 'The EC's Future' (*Irish Independent*, 27 June), 'Staying Neutral' (*Cork Examiner*, 27 June).
57. The Centre for Policy Studies.
58. See following section.
59. Motion No. 630 in the Commons 'Notices of Questions and Motions': 22 April 1985, No. 7971.
60. ETUC Statement on European Union (1984). FS/AS/CL (Brussels: ETUC, 1984). The quote is from paras 9 & 10.
61. Agence Europe, No. 4109 (14 June 1985) p. 3. The 150 included the Mayors of Antwerp (Cools), Barcelona (Margall), Berlin (Diepgen), Bordeaux (Chaban Delmas), Frankfurt (Walmann), Florence (Conti), Hamburg (Von Dohnayi), Köln (Burger), Luxembourg (Würth-Polfer), Milan (Toggoli), Rouen (Lecanuet), Rome (Veltere), Rotterdam (Peper), Stuttgart (Rommel), Toulouse (Baudis).
62. Agence Europe, No. 4191 (25 October 1985) p. 5.
63. e.g. article in the *Guardian* 'Spinelli Ignites Europe's Federalists', 26 March 1984.
64. e.g. Andreotti, Jenkins, Heath, Thorn, Davignon, Albert, Debunne, Berlinguer.
65. Speech to Centre for European Policy Studies/Agence Europe, No. 3978 (28 November 1984) p. 1.
66. Agence Europe, No. 3984 (6 December 1984) p. 7.
67. Agence Europe, No. 3988 (12 December 1984) p. 4.
68. *The Times* (25 October 1984). Another leader along similar lines on 18 October 1984 provoked a letter from Spinelli printed on 31 October 1984 and which constitutes a concise summary of the case for institutional reform. This in turn engendered further correspondence including letters of support from Sir Henry Plumb, leader of the Conservatives in the EP (2 November 1984), Robert Jackson MP, ex MEP (5 December 1984), Hugh Dykes MP (8 November 1984) and others.

69. Agence Europe, No. 3998 (2 January 1985) p. 3.
70. Debates of the EP (16 January 1985) No. 2–321, pp. 105–6.
71. Kohl's speech to the Davos Symposium of the European Management Forum; Agence Europe, No. 4020 (2 February 1985) p. 3.
72. Agence Europe, No. 4026 (11 February 1985) p. 4.
73. Editorial by Emanuele Gazzo, Agence Europe, No. 4028 (14 February 1985), p. 1.
74. Dumas' talk with Spinelli (4 October 1984).
75. Agence Europe, No. 4038 (28 February 1985) pp. 3–4.
76. *Le Monde* (March 1985) and Agence Europe, No. 4038 (28 February 1985) p. 3.
77. Agence Europe No. 4040 (1 March 1985) p. 3.
78. *Le Monde*, March 1985.
79. Agence Europe, No. 4057 (27 March 1985) p. 3.
80. Agence Europe, No. 4080 (29 April 1985) p. 4.
81. The following quotes are from the *Financial Times* version (10 May 1985) p. 1.
82. The *Financial Times* headline was 'Mitterrand Rules out Talk on New EEC Treaty'.
83. Doc. A2-17/85.
84. Doc. A2-16/85.
85. OJ C 122 (20 May 1985) p. 82 and annex.
86. See debates of the EP OJ No. 2-325, pp. 107–27.
87. See debates of the EP OJ No. 2-325, p. 133.
88. Agence Europe, No. 4035 (23 February 1985) p. 3.
89. Agence Europe, No. 4069 (13 April 1985) p. 3.
90. Agence Europe No 4083 (4 April 1985) p. 3; Agence Europe, No. 4089 (13 & 14 May 1985) p. 3; Agence Europe, No. 4092 (20 & 21 May 1985) p. 3.
91. Agence Europe, No. 4061 (31 April 1985) p. 9.
92. Agence Europe, No. 4071 (17 April 1985) p. 1.
93. Question by Mr Edouard Klein (PRL) reported in Agence Europe, No. 4092 (20 & 21 May 1985) p. 3.
94. Agence Europe Nos 4088, 4089, 4092, 4103 (11 May 1985–6 June 1985).
95. See EP Bulletin, May 1985.
96. Agence Europe, No. 4083 (4 May 1985) p. 6.
97. Printed in EP working document, No. PE 98.890.
98. Agence Europe, No. 4097 (28 & 29 May 1985) p. 3.
99. Agence Europe, No. 4096 (25 May 1985) p. 3.
100. Draft European Council conclusions presented to the Stresa Council meeting by Sir Geoffrey Howe. Reprinted in PE 99.781, pp. 12–13.
101. Agence Europe, No. 4106 (10 & 11 June 1985) pp. 3–4.
102. See debates of the EP, OJ No. 2-327 p. 49 onwards.
103. OJ C 175 (12 June 1985) p. 109.
104. See debates of the EP, OJ No. 2-327, p. 93 onwards.
105. Article entitled 'Three Possible Roads to European Unity' in *Corriere della Sera* (25 June 1985). English translation by Marina Gazzo in 'Towards European Union', Agence Europe (Brussels/Luxembourg, 1985).
106. Agence Europe, No. 4110 (15 June 1985).

107. Agence Europe, No. 4111 (17 June 1985).
108. English language version printed in Gazzo (1985).
109. See J. Haywood, 'The French Socialists and European Institutional Reform', in *Revue d'Intégration Européenne* Nos 2–3 (1989).
110. English version printed in Gazzo (1985).

9. THE INTERGOVERNMENTAL CONFERENCE OF 1985

1. For a more detailed analysis of aspects that do not directly concern us here, see Corbett (1987).
2. Bull. EC 6-1985, points 1.2.5. and 1.2.6.
3. Taylor, in Lodge (1989).
4. OJ C 229 (9 September 1985), p. 29.
5. Bull. EC 7/8-1985, point 1.1.10.
6. Agence Europe, No. 4137 (22/23 July 1985), p. 3.
7. COM (85) 455 final. Reprinted in Bull. EC 7/8-1985, point 1.1.12.
8. The 1965 'Merger Treaty', the 1970 and 1975 'Budget Treaties' and the 1975 revision of the EIB structure.
9. The weekend 'conclave' was an Italian proposal. They had also suggested that a conclave or a summit of heads of governments lasting several days be held to thrash out the issues, if necessary between Christmas and New Year (Agence Europe, No. 4200, p. 3).
10. See 'Declaration of Principles Relating to Eureka' adopted by the Hannover Ministerial conference (5/6 November 1985); see *Europe Documents*, No. 1380 (20 November 1985).
11. Agence Europe, No. 4135 (19 July 1985), p. 4.
12. EP Doc. 1-575/83/B, p. 4.
13. Croux Report; resolution in EP Minutes (17 April 1985), OJ C 122 (20 May 1985), p. 88; other resolutions (12 June 1985) in OJ C 175 (15 July 1985), p. 109, and (9 July 1985) (see note 2 above).
14. EP Bulletin, No. 39 (special edition 26 September 1985), p. 6.
15. Press Release issued by Croux, acting chairman of the Committee (19 September 1985) EP INFO-MEMO Br. 110/85 UP.
16. Bull. EC 10-1985, point 1.1.3.
17. Speech by Spinelli to the German Bundestag on 25 October 1985, summary printed in M. Gazzo, *Towards European Union*, (Vol. II, p. 41; Brussels-Luxembourg, Agence Europe, 1986.
18. Debates EP (23 October 1985), OJ 2-331, p. 92.
19. Ibid., pp. 94–5.
20. The information used here on the proposals tabled and the reactions to them in the IGC derives from EP Bulletin No. 39 (26 September 1985) and its addendum 1 (7 October 1985), (10 October 1985), 3 (25 October 1985), 4 (5 December 1985), No. 57 (6 December 1985), Bull. EC 9-1985 (ch. 1), Bull. EC 10-1985 (ch. 1), Bull; EC11-1985 (ch. 1), the Dossier di Documentazione No. 13 (12 February 1986) of the camera di Deputati (Rel. Com. and Int.) and the press, notably Agence Europe.
21. Minutes EP (10 October 1985), OJ C 288 (11 November 1985) pp. 105–6.

22. EP debates, see note 15. Mr Goebbles attacked the EP for not holding ACP activities in Luxembourg.
23. Minutes EP (2 October 1985), OJ C 343 (31 December 1985), p. 59.
24. EP Bulletin No. 39/Add. 4 (5 December 1985).
25. See e.g. press release EP Info-Memo 117 (22 October 1985), and Bull. EC 10-1985 point 4.1.3. and Debates of the EP (23 October 1985), OJ 2-331.
26. Bull. EC 11-1985 point 1.1.3.
27. Minutes EP (11 December 1985), adopted by 249 votes to 47, with 8 abstentions.
28. See below.
29. Bundestag – 10 Wahlperiode–181 Sitzung (5 December 1985), Drucksache 10/4088.
30. Agence Europe, No. 4189 (21/22 October 1985).
31. Camera di Deputati (29 November 1985; unified text of resolutions 7-00240 and 7-00242.
32. Kohl, Lubbers, Martens, Santer, Fitzergald, Ardanza (Basque PM) and Forlani (Deputy PM).
33. As translated by Agence Europe, No. 4202 (12/13 November 1985) p. 4.
34. PS/CE/139/85.
35. Resolution: TB/arch (21 November 1985). Press Conference: Agence Europe, No. 4215 (30 November 1985), p. 5.
36. *ETUC statement on European Union* FS/AS/CL ETUC, Brussels.
37. Agence Europe, No. 4191 (25 October 1985), p. 5.
38. See note 17. In many cases the author has not seen English language versions of the texts.
39. Debates of the EP (23 October 1985), OJ 2-331.
40. 10 July 1985, p. 2.
41. See, for example, *Times* Leader, 4 July. The *Financial Times*, on the other hand, carried feature articles by their own journalists arguing for a more positive attitude by the UK (e.g. Davidson, 8 July 'The Case for Euro-froth'; Rutherford, 5 July, 'Britain out on a Limb Again').
42. Agence Europe, No. 4156 (6 September 1985), p. 3.
43. Agence Europe, No. 4159 (11 September 1985), pp. 3 and 4.
44. Speech to Foreign Policy Association, New York. Agence Europe, No. 4171 (27 September 1985), p. 4.
45. Agence Europe, No. 4208 (21 November 1985), p. 5.
46. Speech opening the academic year at the College of Europe, Agence Europe, No. 4194 (30 October 1985), p. 3.
47. Speech to CD 'Friendship Day', Rimini, Italy, Agence Europe, No. 4150 (29 August 1985), p. 2.
48. Debates of the EP (23 October 1985), OJ 2-331, pp. 146–51.
49. Information service of the UK Permanent Representation to the EEC No. 89 (5 October 1985).
50. See, for example, speech of Foreign Minister Elleman-Jensen to Liberal Party Congress in Agence Europe, No. 4163 (25 September 1985), p. 3 and article by Social Democrat spokesman Norgaard, in *Politieken* (22 September 1985).
51. Agence Europe, No. 4202 (12/13 November 1985).

52. VIIIth Jean Monnet Lecture (EUI, 1985).
53. For a more detailed analysis of the IGC, see Corbett (1987).
54. The three reports from 1970, 1973 and 1981 of the Foreign Ministers on which EPC practices were based.
55. At the end of the negotiations it was noted that one treaty amendment (the one on the Court) required amendment of the ECSC and EAEC treaties too. This required a new consultation of the EP in January 1986 which the latter could have used to delay the conclusions of the negotiations had it wished.
56. Art. 47 DTEU.
57. The date coincided with the end of the term of office of the next Commission, Delors considering that the lifetime of two Commissions would be an appropriate timetable.
58. For a detailed account see Corbett (1986).
59. Agence Europe, No. 4218 (5 December 1985) p. 3.
60. Advisory committees of national officials are consulted by the Commission but cannot block it. For an account of practice at that time, see Groeben, Boeckh, Thiesing and Ehlermann, *Kommentar zum EWG-Vertrag*, Vol. 2 (Nomos Verlag, 1983) pp. 187–90.
61. Attributed to British delegation by Agence Europe, No. 4194 (30 October 1985) p. 5.
62. Agence France Presse Telex HU 40 EUP 0322 (2 December 1985).
63. Reporting to Foreign Affairs Committee of Dutch Parliament on 28 October, Agence Europe.
64. DTEU, Art. 59.
65. AETR judgment, case 22/70.
66. See Marina Gazzo, *Pour l'Union Européenne*, Documentation Ed. Agence Europe, supplement, 10 July 1985.
67. Delors press conference, Brussels, 4 December 1985.
68. Arts 49, 51, 79 and 228 and those parts of Arts 99 and 100 that would continue to require unanimity.
69. Reserves were also expressed in German political circles, e.g. The European Movement, chaired by the President of the Bundestag Jenninger, rejected it as insufficient (Agence Europe, 1985, No. 4205, p. 1).
70. See Joint Declaration EP-Council of 4 March 1975, European Treaties (Official Publications Office) p. 900.
71. It would apply to Arts 7, 49, 51, 54.2, 56.2, 57, 63.2, 69, 99 and 100 and the new policy areas being negotiated.
72. Agence France Presse Telex UY 49 EUR 6338.
73. La Libre Belgique, 26 November 1985, Michel Theys.
74. Reuters Telex EUR 932 XDA 799, Paul Mylera quoting Belgian diplomatic sources.
75. In the 1986 budget the EP had voted a new budget chapter 102 for the creation of a first instance chamber for certain cases.
76. This was the last European Council before the French elections in which his Socialist Party lost their majority.
77. Bull. EC 11.1985 point 1.1.2.
78. Ibid.
79. Ibid.

80. Ibid.
81. Quote ibid. Criticism in 'Interpellation' in the Belgian parliament by Dierickx, Van Miert and others, and in TV debate on 22 December 1985 with members of EP Institutional Committee (see De Morgen, 24 December 1985).
82. Agence Europe, No. 4257 (10/11 February 1986).
83. Agence Europe, No. 4234 (9 January 1986) p. 3
84. Minutes EP, 16 January 1986. Approved by 209 to 61, with 42 abstentions.
85. See Minutes EP, 16 January 1986.
86. Senate debate 29 January 1986. Resolution 6.00007, which expressed 'dissatisfaction' with the 'limited and modest progress' and instructed the government, when signing, to declare its intention to seek a more complete reform, involving the EP in this process.
87. Spain and Portugal having joined the Community on 1 January.
88. A mistake which they were not to repeat in the 1992 Maastricht referendum.
89. This result contributed to complacency before the 1992 referendum on Maastricht when the same government and the Social Democrats too favoured ratification.
90. Evidence of this was found by Werner Feld and John Wildgen in their study 'National Administrative Elites and European Integration: saboteurs at work ?' (JCMS) pp. 244–64 in which they found that 'There is obvious resistance by a majority of our respondents to move beyond economic integration. The resistance is founded and bolstered by personal interests' (p. 264).
91. See e.g. Sutra: Debates of the EP 23 October 1985 (OJ No. 2-331 p. 99).
92. eg. P.M. Fabius's speech to Congress of the Parti Socialiste, Toulouse October 1985. Extracts quoted in *30 jours d'Europe* (October 1985), No. 327.

10. MAKING THE MOST OF THE SINGLE ACT

1. Council answer to Parliamentary Question 1121/86 by Mr Elles.
2. Council answer to Parliamentary Question 2470/87 by Mr Megahy.
3. See, for example, cases 184/87 (*Portugal* v. *Council*), 68/86 (*UK* v. *Council*), and 51/89 (*UK* v. *Council*).
4. See, for example, cases 45/86, 131/87, 165/87 and 242/87.
5. Article 40, draft Treaty.
6. Article 10 SEA.
7. Declaration No. 1, annexed to SEA.
8. COM (86) 35 final OJ C 70 (25 March 1986), p. 6.
9. As it would fall under the provisions of Article 149 (1) EEC.
10. Minutes EP, 23 October 1986, OJ C 297 (24 November 1986), p. 94 and Minutes, 9 July 1986, OJ C 227 (8 September 1986), p. 54.
11. 87/373/EEC OJ L 197 (18 July 1987), p. 33.
12. Statement entered in Council's minutes and referred to in Commission document SEC (89) 1591 final p. 3. Statement that it would not use the procedures made by Delors in Parliament (Debates of the EP, 7 July 1987). For an analysis of the decision, see C.D. Ehlermann, 'Compétences

d'Execution conferées à la Commission – la Nouvelle Décision-Cadre du Conseil', in *Revue du Marché Commun* (April 1988).

13. Roumeliotis Report A3-310/90.
14. See Commission Communication of 11 July 1989 on the Delegation of Executive Powers to the Commission by the Council. SEC (89) 1143 final Annex II.
15. Or, under the safeguard (b) procedure, by a minority.
16. e.g. Environment Committee challenging Commission on draft implementing measure regarding infant formula milk in 1991, eventually securing changes to the measures adopted.
17. Articles 4, 11 and 26 SEA.
18. Published as EP Doc. C2-225/87.
19. European Court Information Office press release, 13 June 1988.
20. Decision 93/350 – OJ L 144 (1993).
21. Report of the Legal Affairs Committee of the European Parliament, Doc. A2-107/88 Explanatory Statement, p. 15.
22. Article 2 (3) of the decision.
23. OJ L 319 of 25 November 1988, p. 1.
24. The SEA also extended the traditional consultation procedure (single reading) to Art. 99 (indirect taxation) and Art. 84 (sea and air transport) and used it for some of the new areas of competence (such as environment and some aspects of research).
25. Butler (1956, p. 157).
26. See Jacobs et al. (1992).
27. These figures, originally calculated for the first six months of the SEA by the author, have since then been calculated at regular intervals by Parliament's DG IV, in particular by Mr Wim Hoogsteder, in liaison with the Commission.
28. Protection of workers from exposure to benzene COM (85) 669. Rejection by EP on 12 October 1988.
29. EP Minutes, 9 April 1987, OJ C 125, p. 137 (Prout Report).
30. OJ C 280 (1991), p. 166.
31. OJ C 274 of 2 July 1987, p. 6.
32. Case 70/88.
33. e.g. case C-65/90 (Road cabotage).
34. e.g. Directive on titanium dioxide pollution (89/428 (EEC). Parliament's second first reading in May 1989 (Minutes OJ C 158 of 26 June 1989 / 37A Art. 149, para. 2b.
35. Code of conduct (see below, section on Annual Legislative Programme).
36. Art. 149, para. 2b.
37. See Bieber (1988, pp. 719–20).
38. Minutes EP, 18 November 1987, OJ C 345 of 21 December 1987, pp. 59 and 61.
39. EP Minutes, 28 October 1987, OJ C 318 of 30 November 1987, p. 41.
40. See Prag Report (EP Doc A2-348/88) EP Resolution of 16 February (OJ C 69 of 20 March 1989, p. 151) and undertaking of Member States in Solemn Declaration of Stuttgart, point 2.3.6.
41. e.g. Ken Collins MEP, chairman of the Environment Committee of the EP, had met the President of the Council before every Environment Council meeting since 1989 (interview with K. Collins, 6 July 1992).

42. Commission document SEC (86) 1928, p. 3.
43. Ibid., p. 4.
44. Ibid., p. 5.
45. Known as the Neunreither Group after the Director General of the Parliament who chaired these meetings at which representatives of the Commission, the Council and the Parliament participate.
46. The Secretary -General of the Commission, Williamson, stated on BBC Radio 4 that 40 per cent of his time was spent on matters related to the EP, compared to 5 per cent before direct elections (cited in Jacobs et al., p. 259).
47. Code of conduct of 4 April 1991, Reprinted in OJ C280 (1991), pp. 165–6.
48. Art. 30, para. 4.
49. The Commission's initial proposal had envisaged a limit of 1.4 per cent GDP, but including the EDF and UK rebate in the budget. The final agreement fixed a limit of 1.2 per cent GDP, but with the EDF remaining separate and additional to the general budget, and with the UK rebate settled as a deduction from revenue raised in the UK. These changes, and a technical one on refunding collection costs, meant that the new ceiling was in effect 0.01 per cent GDP *higher* than requested by the Commission.
50. OJ L 185 (1988), p. 33.
51. Sharp, in Lodge (1989, p. 215).

11. RELAUNCHING THE SHIP

1. Speech in European Parliamentary debate 16 January 1986 (Debate of the EP, January 1986, p. 204).
2. Strictly speaking, not decided on in the same context; but nevertheless with a bearing on the subject.
3. EP Minutes of 17 June 1988, OJ C 187 (18 July 1988), p. 229.
4. Debates of the EP, 6 July 1988.
5. It did, however, comprise the danger of giving ammunition to anti-integration politicians who would propose quite different remedies to the democratic deficit.
6. Senate Resolution 10 July 1986, House Resolution, 24 July 1986.
7. Ireland was holding its referendum on the ratification of the Single European Act at that time.
8. *Resolution on the procedures for consulting European citizens on European political union*, Official Journal of the EC No. C 187 of 18 July 1988, p. 231, adopted following the Bru Puron Report of its Committee on Institutional Affairs.
9. For the question and the results, see chapter 1.
10. See chapter 3.
11. *Report on the Institutional Consequences of the Costs of Non-Europe*, rapporteur: Sir Fred Catherwood, EP Session Documents A2-39/88.
12. Ibid., p. 21.
13. *Resolution on the Institutional Consequences of the Cost of non-Europe* of 17 June 1988, Official Journal of the EC No C187 of 18 July 1988, p. 244.

14. *White Paper on the Fundamental Rights and Freedoms of European Citizens*, Committee on Institutional Affairs, European Parliament, 1988, Doc. PE 115.274/fin.
15. *Resolution adopting the Declaration of fundamental rights and freedoms.* EP Minutes of 9 April 1989.
16. *Resolution on the results obtained from implementation of the Single Act.* EP Minutes of 27 October 1988, OJ C 309 (5 December 1988) p. 62.
17. *Resolution on the Strategy of the European Parliament for Achieving European Union*, EP Minutes, 17 June 1987 OJ C 190 (20 July 1987), p. 71.
18. Resolution on Parliament's strategy for achieving European Union (Herman Report); Minutes EP, 16 February 1989.
19. Ibid.
20. The Conservative Party Manifesto, on the other hand, in the drafting of which the MEPs had been more closely involved than in the running of the national campaign, was not so hostile in tone.
21. Minutes of the EP, 14 March 1990.
22. The Belgian Permanent Representative, De Schoutheete, met David Martin in the course of preparatory work for the memorandum.
23. Minutes of the EP, 11 July 1990.
24. Resolution on Economic and Monetary Union, Minutes of the EP, 10 October 1990 (Herman Report, doc. A3-223/90).
25. Largely through amendments tabled by David Martin. See EP Minutes, 21 November 1990, and Giscard Report (A3-267/90).
26. Martin II Report, Explanatory Statement.
27. The author was able to attend CIP meetings and the following is based on his own observations.
28. Duverger Report A3-87/90.
29. The author was able to attend the Assizes and the meetings of the drafting committee. The following is based on his own observations.
30. When an MEP he had been rapporteur of the Political Affairs Committee on relations with national Parliaments (see chapter 5).
31. 27th Report of the Select Committee on the EC.
32. Rome I European Council Conclusions; Bull. EC 10-1990.
33. Rome II European Council Conclusions; Bull. EC 12-1990.

12. THE IGCs ON ECONOMIC AND MONETARY UNION AND ON POLITICAL UNION

1. The text of many of the key proposals can be found in Corbett (1994, pp. 121–378).
2. EPP Dublin Congress Document: 'For a Federal Constitution for the European Union', 15–16 November 1990. ELDR Leader's Declaration, Berlin, 23 November 1990. CSP Leader's Declaration, Madrid, 10 December 1990.
3. Corbett (1992).
4. Paper delivered to the Institut d'Etudes Européennes of the Université Libre de Bruxelles on the occasion of their study day on 'European Union

after Maastricht' (Brussels, 21 February 1992). Published by them: D/ 1992/2672/27. My translation.
5. A view supported after the IGCs by the Belgian Permanent Representative, who was one of the most fervent supporters of the 'tree' approach. See De Schouthete, op. cit.
6. Martin II Resolution, para. 34.
7. This, in fact, puts Parliament in a similar position to the Council.
8. Martin II Resolution, para. 40.
9. Report of the debate in *The Independent*, 22 May 1992.
10. The US Constitution does not contain the word federal either.

13. MAKING THE MOST OF MAASTRICHT

1. For reasons of space, the process of ratification of the Maastricht Treaty, which gave rise to significant difficulties in three Member States, is not discussed in this chapter which is an additional chapter bringing the central arguments in this book up-to-date. For an overview of the ratification procedures, see Laursen and Vanhoonacker (1994).
2. O.J. L340.
3. Including the author.
4. (93/109/EEC).
5. De Gucht Report, EP Minutes, June 1992.

14. OVERALL CONCLUSIONS

1. And, in 1994, arguably France to a lesser degree with the De Villiers/ Goldsmith list.
2. Van Schendelen (1984, p. 58).

15. POSTSCRIPT

1. And, in particular, the adviser to Elizabeth Guigou (the author), who provided a key link and was the only Labour Party member to set foot in the IGC prior to the May UK election.

Bibliography

Argus, and Minos, *Le Parlement européen: cinq ans pour une revanche*, Brussels: Rossel, 1984.

Attina, Fulvio, 'The Voting Behaviour of the European Parliament Members and the Problem of Europarties', *European Journal of Political Research*, No. 5, September 1990.

Bieber, Roland, 'Democratic Control of European Foreign Policy', *European Journal of International Law*, No. 12, 1990.

Bieber, Roland, 'Legislative Procedure for the Establishment of the Single Market', *Common Market Law Review*, No. 4, Winter 1986.

Bieber, Roland, Pantalis, J. and Schoo, J., 'Implications of the Single Act for the European Parliament', *Common Market Law Review*, No. 4, Winter 1986.

Bond, Smith, and Wallace, *Eminent Europeans*, Greycoat Press, 1986.

Bogdanor, Vernon, 'Direct Elections, Representative Democracy and European Integration', *Electoral Studies*, No. 3, December 1989.

Bogdanor, Vernon, 'The June 1989 European Elections and the Institutions of the Community', *Government and Opposition*, No. 2, Spring 1989.

Bogdanor, Vernon, *Democratising the Community*, London: Federal Trust for Education and Research, 1990.

Bosco, Andrea, *The Federal Idea*, London: Lothian Foundation Press, 1992.

Boumans, Etienne and Norbart, Monica, 'The European Parliament and Human Rights', *Netherlands Quarterly of Human Rights*, No. 1, 1989.

Bourgignon, R., Wittke, E., Grabitz, O. and Schmuck, E.A., 'Five Years of the Directly Elected European Parliament: Performance and Prospects', *Journal of Common Market Studies*, No. 1, September 1985.

Bradley, K., 'Legal Developments in the European Parliament', *Yearbook of European Law*, Vol. 12, 1992. (The *Yearbook* has had a similar article every year since 1984.)

Bradley, K., 'Maintaining the Balance: The Role of the Court of Justice in Defining the Institutional Position of the European Parliament', *Common Market Law Review*, 1987.

Bradley, K., 'The Variable Evolution of the Standing of the European Parliament in Proceedings before the Court of Justice', in *Yearbook of European Law*, No. 8, 1988.

Bosco, Andrea, *The Federal Idea*, London: Lothian Foundation Press, 1992.

Brugmans, Hendrik, 'Europe: One Civilization, One Destiny', in *Europe: Dream, Adventure, Reality*, Rotterdam: Elsevier, 1989.

Burban, Jean-Louis, *Le Parlement européen*, 5th edition, Paris: Presses Universitaires de France, 1991.

Burgess, Michael, *Federalism and European Union*, London: Routledge, 1989.

Burgess, Michael and Gagnon, Alain (eds), *Comparative Federalism and Federation: Competing Traditions and Future Directions*, Hemel Hempstead: Harvester Wheatsheaf, 1993.

Busch, P. and Puchala, D., 'Interests, Influence and Integration', in *Comparative Political Studies*, Vol. 9, No. 3, 1976.

Butler, Michael, *Europe, More than a Continent*, London: Heinemann, 1986.

Capotorti, Francesco, Hilf, Meinhard, Jacobs, Francis and Jacque, Jean Paul, *Le Traité d'Union Européenne: commentaire*, Brussels, 1985; English language edition, Oxford: Clarendon Press, 1986.

Cardozo, Rita, 'The Project for a Political Community (1952–54)', in Roy Pryce (ed.), *The Dynamics of European Union*, London: Croom Helm, 1987.

Cardozo, Rita and Corbett, Richard, 'The Crocodile Initiative', in Juliet Lodge (ed.), *European Union: The Community in Search of a Future*, London: Macmillan, 1985.

Castle, Barbara, *Memoirs: Fighting all the Way*, London: Macmillan, 1993.

Coates, Ken, 'Towards a *European Socialist Party'*, *European Labour Forum*, No. 5, Autumn 1991.

Cocks, Barnett, *The European Parliament, Structure, Procedure and Practice*, London: HMSO, 1973.

Coombes, D., in M. Ryle and S. Walkland (eds), *The Commons Today*, revised edition, Glasgow, Fontana, 1983.

Colloquy, Papers for L'Institut d'Etudes Juridiques Européennes: *Le Parlement européen: pouvoir, élection, rôle, futur*, University of Liège, 1976.

Colloquy, Papers from *Le Parlement européen à la veille de la deuxième élection au suffrage universel direct: bilan et perspectives*. Colloquium organized by the Collège d'Europe and l'Institut für Europäische Politik, Bruges, 16–18 June 1983, Bruges: de Tempel, 1984.

Corbett, Richard, 'Reform of the Council: The Bundesrat Model', *The Federalist* (Pavia), Vol. XXVI, No. 1, July 1984.

Corbett, Richard. 'The 1985 Intergovernmental Conference and the Single European Act', in Roy Price (ed.), *An Ever Closer Union*, London: Croom Helm, 1986.

Corbett, Richard, *The Intergovernmental Conference*, European Community Research Unit, University of Hull, Hull, 1986.

Corbett, Richard, *Ein Dach für die Jugend Europas: Die Zusammenarbeit von Jugendorganisationen in Rahmen von EG und Europarat*, in Integration 3/88, Bonn: IEP, 1988.

Corbett, Richard, 'Testing the New Procedures: The European Parliament's First Experiences with its New Single Act Powers', *Journal of Common Market Studies*. No. 4, June 1989.

Corbett, Richard, 'Comitology: What it is, Why it matters', EP Socialist Group (document PE/GS/230/89), 1989.

Corbett, Richard, 'The Intergovernmental Conference on Political Union', *Journal of Common Market Studies*, September 1992.

Corbett, Richard, *The Treaty of Maastricht: From Conception to Ratification*, Harlow: Longman, 1994.

Corbett, Richard and Nickel, Dietmar, 'The Draft Treaty Establishing the European Union', in the *Yearbook of European Law 1984*. Oxford, Clarendon Press, 1985.

Cotta, M., 'Direct Elections of the European Parliament: A Supranational Political Elite in the Making?', in K. Reif (ed.), *European Elections 1979 and 1984: Conclusions and Perspectives from Empirical Research*, Berlin, 1984.

Critchley, Julian, 'The Great Betrayal – Tory Politics towards Europe', in Bond et al., *Eminent Europeans*, Greycoat Press, 1986.

Delors, Jacques, 'A New Frontier Takes Shape', *Europe Magazine*, December 1990.

Earnshaw, David, 'The European Parliament's Quest for a Single Seat', *Revue d'intégration européenne*, No. 1, Autumn 1984.

Ehlermann, C.D., 'Compétences d'Exécution conférées à la Commission – la Nouvelle Décision-Cadre du Conseil', *Revue du Marché Commun*, April 1988.

Elles, James, 'The Foreign Policy Role of the European Parliament', *The Washington Quarterly*, No. 4, Autumn 1990.

European Parliament, *Towards a Uniform Procedure for Direct Elections*, Florence: European University Institute, 1981.

European Parliament, *Forging Ahead, European Parliament 1952–1988*, 3rd edition, Directorate-General for Research, Luxembourg: Office of Official Publications, 1989.

Featherstone, K. 'What Has Happened to the EC? Evolving Patterns of Interinstitutional Relations within the Community', IPSA paper, 1983.

Featherstone, K., *Socialist Parties and European Integration, a Comparative History*, Manchester: Manchester University Press, 1988.

Fitzmaurice, John, *The Party Groups in the European Parliament*, London: Saxon House, 1975.

Fitzmaurice, John, 'An Analysis of the European Community's Co-operation Procedure', *Journal of Common Market Studies*, No. 4, June 1988.

Friedrich, C.J. and Bowie, R.R., *Studies in Federalism*, Boston, 1954.

Gazzo, Marina, *Towards European Union*, Luxembourg and Brussels: Agence Europe, 1985–6.

George, Stephen, *Politics and Policy in the European Community*, Oxford: Clarendon Press, 1985.

Gerbet, Pierre, 'The Origins: Early Attempts and the Emergence of the Six (1945–52)', in Roy Price (ed.), *The Dynamics of the European Union*, London: Croom Helm, 1987.

Goriely, George, see Colloquy of L'Institut d'Etudes Juridiques Européennes.

Gormley, L.W., Kapteyn, P.J.G. and Verloren van Themaat, P. (eds), *Introduction to the Law of the European Communities*, 2nd edition, Dordrecht, Kluwer Deventer, 1989.

Groeben, Boeckh, Thiesing, and Ehlermann, *Kommentar zum EWG-Vertrag*, Vol. 2, Nomos Verlag, 1983.

Haas, Ernst, *The Uniting of Europe*, London, 1958.

Haas, Ernst, 'The Uniting of Europe and the Uniting of Latin America', *Journal of Common Market Studies*, 1966.

Haas, Ernst, 'The Study of Regional Integration: Reflections on the Joys and Anguishes of (pre)-Theorising', in Leon Lindberg and Stuart Scheingold (eds), *Regional Integration: Theory and Research*, Oxford: Oxford University Press, 1971.

Hanson, 'Methods of Interpretation – A Critical Assessment of Results', ECJ Judicial and Academic Conference, Luxembourg, 1976.

Harris, Geoffrey, and Corbett, Richard, *A Socialist Policy for Europe*, 1985, London.

Hayward, J.E.J., *Crisis of Representation*, London: Cass, 1995.

Haywood, Elizabeth Z., 'The French Socialist and European Political Reform', *Revue d'Intégration Européenne*, Nos 2–3, 1989.

Herman, Valentine and Lodge, Juliet, *The European Parliament and the European Community*, London: Macmillan, 1978.

Heathcote, Nina, *The Crisis of European Supranationality, Canberra*, 1965.

Holland, Stuart, *The Uncommon Market*, London: Macmillan, 1980.

Hoffman, S., 'Obstinate or Obsolete? The Fate of the Nation-State and the Case of Western Europe', *Daedalus*, Vol. 95, 1986.

Hrbek, Rudolf (ed. with others), *The European Parliament on the Eve of the Second Direct Elections: Balance Sheet and Prospects*, De Tempel, 1984.

Hrbek, Rudolf, *The European Parliament, the Citizens and the Political Environment*, Strasbourg: TEPSA Symposium, 18/19 November 1988.

Jackson, Robert and Fitzmaurice, John, *The European Parliament – A Guide to Direct Elections*, London: Penguin Books, 1979.

Jacobs, Francis B., *Western European Political Parties: A Comprehensive Guide*, Harlow: Longman, 1989.

Jacobs, Francis, B., 'The European Parliament and Economic and Monetary Union', *Common Market Law Review*, No. 2, Summer 1991.

Jacobs, Francis B., Corbett, Richard and Shackleton, Michael, *The European Parliament*, 2nd edition, Harlow, Longman, 1992.

Jacque, Jean-Paul, Bieber, Roland, Constantinesco, Vlad and Nickel, Dietmar, *Le Parlement européen*, Paris: Economica, 1984.

Jenkins, Roy, *A Life at the Centre*, London: Pan, 1992.

Keohane, R. and Nye, J., *Power and Interdependence: World Politics in Transition*, Boston, 1977.

Kirchner, Emil Joseph, *The European Parliament: Performance and Prospects*, Aldershot; Gower, 1984.

Lake, Gordon, 'The STOA Experiment in the European Parliament: The Fusion Project', *Energy Policy*, No. 3, June 1989.

Laursen, Finn and Vanhoonacker, Sophie, *The Ratification of the Maastricht Treaty*, Dordrecht, Martinus Nijhoff, 1994.

Leonard, Dick, *The Single Act and the Parliament: Shifts in the Balance of Power*, The Economist Intelligence Unit, No. 4, London, 1988.

Levy, Paul, 'The Council of Europe', in *Europe, Dream, Adventure, Reality*, Rotterdam: Elsevier, 1989.

Lindberg, Leon and Scheingold, Stuart, *Europe's Would-be Polity: Patterns of Change in the EC*, Englewood Cliffs, NJ: Prentice-Hall, 1970.

Lindberg, Leon and Scheingold, Stuart (eds), *Regional Integration: Theory and Research*, Oxford: Oxford University Press, 1971.

Lipgens, Walter, *Documents on the History of European Integration*, Vols 1 and 2, Oxford: Clarendon Press, 1984 and 1986.

Lodge, Juliet, 'The European Parliament – From Assembly to Co-Legislature: Changing the Institutional Dynamics', in J. Lodge (ed.), *The European Community and the Challenge of the Future*, London, 1989.

Lodge, Juliet and Herman, Valentine, *Direct Elections to the European Parliament*, London: Macmillan, 1984.

Louis, Jean Victor, see Colloquy of l'Institut d'Etudes Juridiques Européennes.

Lowe, David, 'The French Socialist Party: The Congress of Metz and its Repercussions' (unpublished).

Marquand, David, *Parliament for Europe*, London: Jonathan Cape, 1979.

Martin, David, *Bringing Common Sense to the Common Market: A Left Agenda for Europe*, London: Fabian Society, 1988.

Martin, David, *Europe: An Ever Closer Union*, Nottingham: Russell Press, 1991.

Mayne, Richard and Pinder, John with de V., Robeto, Jan C., *Federal Union: The Pioneers*, London, 1990.

Millar, David, 'A Uniform Electoral Procedure for European Elections', *Electoral Studies*, No. 1, March 1990.

Minor, Jacqueline, 'Further Skirmishes on Election Spending. Case 221/86R Group of *European Right v. European Parliament*', *European Law Review*, 1987.

Mitrany, David, *A Working Peace System*, Chicago, 1943.

Montani, Guido, 'The Young and Federalism', *The Federalist*, Vol. XXVI, No. 2, Pavia, 1982.

Morand, Charles Albert, see Colloquy of l'Institut d'Etudes Juridiques Européennes.

Nickel, Dietmar, 'Le projet de traité instituant l'Union Européenne élaboré par le Parlement européen', *Cahiers de Droit Européen*, Nos 5–6, 1984.

Niedmayer, Oskar, 'Turnout in the European Elections', *Electoral Studies*, No. 1, January 1990.

Nord, Hans and Taylor, John, 'The European Parliament before and after Direct Elections', in *Government and Opposition*, special issue, 1979.

Northawl, Rod and Corbett, Richard, *Electing Europe's First Parliament*, London: Fabian Society, 1977.

Owen, Richard and Dynes, Michael, *The Times Guide to 1992. Britain in a Europe without Frontiers. A Comprehensive Handbook*, London: Times Books, 1992.

Palmer, Michael, *The European Parliment. What it is, What it does, How it works*, Oxford: Pergamon Press, 1981.

Partan, Daniel, 'Merger Control in the EC: Federalism with a European Flavour', in Cafuny and Rosenthal, *The State of the European Community*, Vol. 2, ECSA, Harlow: Longman, 1993.

Patijn, Schelto, see Colloquy of l'Institut d'Etudes Juridiques Européennes.

Penders, Jean J.M., 'The European Parliament and European Political Cooperation', *Irish Studies in International Affairs*, No. 4, 1988.

Pentland, Charles, *International Theory and European Integration*, London, 1973.

Pinder, John, 'European Community and Nation-state: A Case for Neo-federalism', *International Affairs*, 1986.

Pinder, John, 'The European Community, the Rule of Law and Representative Government: The Significance of the Intergovernmental Conference', *Government and Opposition*, 26/02, 1991, pp. 199–214.

Pinder, John, *European Community: The Building of a Union*, Oxford: Oxford University Press, 1992.

Pinder, John, 'The Future of the European Community: A Strategy for Enlargement', *Government and Opposition*, 27/04, 1992, pp. 414–32.

Pirlot, Jean, *Symphonie Europa*, Paris: Editions Laffont, 1984.

Plumb, Henry, 'Building a Democratic Community: The Rule of the European Parliament', *The World Today*, No. 7, July 1989.

Posselt, Martin, 'The European Parliamentary Union (1946–1952)', in Andrea Bosco, *The Federal Idea*, Vol. II, Lothian Foundation Press, 1992.

Pridham, Geoffrey, 'European Elections, Political Parties and Trends of Internationalization in Community Affairs', *Journal of Common Market Studies*, No. 4, June 1986.

Pryce, Roy (ed.), *The Dynamics of European Union*, London: Croom Helm, 1987.

Puchala, Donald, 'Of Blind Men, Elephants and International Integration', *Journal of Common Market Studies*, No. 3, 1972.

Puchala, Donald, *Trends in the Study of European Integration*, IPSA, 1983.

Rafuny, G. and Rosenthal, G., *The State of the European Community*, Vol. 2, Harlow: Longman, 1993.

Reif, Karlheinz, *Ten European Elections, Campaigns and Results of the 1979/81 First Direct Elections to the European Parliament*, Aldershot: Gower, 1985.

Rey, Jean, see Colloquy of l'Institut d'Etudes Juridiques Européennes.

Robinson, Mary, see Colloquy of l'Institut d'Etudes Juridiques Européennes.

Sasse, Christophe, see Colloquy of l'Institut d'Etudes Juridiques Européennes.

Sbragia, A., *Europolitics*, Washington: Brookings Insitution, 1992.

Schermers, *International Institutional Law*, 2nd edition, Rotterdam: Martinus Nijhoff, 1982.

Schmitter, Philippe, 'Three Neofunctional Hypotheses about International Integration', *International Organisation*, No. 23, 1969.

Schmitter, Philippe, 'A Revised Theory of Regional Integration', in Leon Lindberg and Stuart Scheingold (eds), *Regional Integration: Theory and Reseach*, Oxford: Oxford University Press, 1971.

Schwarze, Jürgen, 'Das allgemeine Völkerrecht in der innergemeinschaftlichen Rechtsbeziehungen', *Europarecht*, No. 1, 1983.

Schwed, J.J., 'La Commission des Communautés Européennes et le Parlement européen', *The European Parliament*, Athens, 1978.

Scott, Dermot, 'The European Parliament and European Security: Some Pointers for Ireland', *Administration*, No. 1, 1985.

Shackleton, Michael, *Financing the European Community*, London: Pinter for Royal Institute of International Affairs, 1990.

Sharp, Margaret, 'The Community and New Technologies', in Juliet Lodge (ed.), *The European Community and the Challenge of the Future*, London, 1989.

Short, Anthony, 'European Federalism and the Attlee Government', in Preston King and Andrea Bosco (eds), *A Constitution for Europe*, London: Lothian Foundation Press, 1991.

Spinelli, A., 'Pourquoi je suis européen', *Preuves*, No. 81, November 1951.

Spinelli, A., 'Une Constituante Européenne', *Pensée Française*, Fédération, Nos 9–10, 1957.

Spinelli, A., *The Growth of the European Movement since World War II*, Baltimore: Johns Hopkins University Press, 1957.

Spinelli, A., *L'Europa non cade dal Cielo*, Bologna: Il Mulino, 1960.

Spinelli, A., *The Eurocrats: Conflicts and Crisis in the EC*, Baltimore: Johns Hopkins University Press, 1966.

Spinelli, A., *L'Avventura Europea*, Bologna: Il Mulino, 1972.

Spinelli, A., 'Reflections on the Institutional Crisis in the European Community', *West European Politics*, No. 1, 1978.

Steed, M., 'The European Parliament: The Significance of Direct Election', *Government and Opposition*, Vol. 6, 1971, pp. 462–76.

Sweeney, Jane P., *The First European Elections: Neo-functionalism and the European Parliament*, Ann Arbor, Westview Press, 1984.

Sweeney, Jane P., 'The Left in Europe's Parliament: The Problematic Effects of Integration Theory', *Comparative Politics*, No. 1, 1984.

Taylor, Paul, 'The Gradualist Process of Integration', in *The Limits of European Integration*, London: Croom Helm, 1983.

Taylor, Paul, 'New Dynamics of EC Integration', in Juliet Lodge (ed.), *The European Community and the Challenge of the Future*, London: Pinter, 1989.

Teitgen, Pierre-Henri, 'Le Parlement européen au lendemain de son élection directe', *The European Parliament*, Athens, 1978.

TEPSA Symposium, *Beyond Traditional Parliamentarianism: The European Parliament in the Community System*, Luxembourg: TEPSA, 1988.

Tindale, Stephen, 'How Labour Went European', *Tribune*, 13 September 1991.

Tönnies, F., *Fundamental Concepts of Sociology*, New York, 1940.

van den Berghe, Guido, *Political Rights for European Citizens*, Aldershot: Gower, 1982

van Hamme, Alain, *The European Parliament and the Cooperation Procedure*, Brussels, 1988.

van Schendelen, M.P.C.M., *Het Europees Parlement*, Utrecht: Het Spectrum, 1984.

Vedel, Georges. 'Report of the Working Party Examining the Problem of the Enlargement of the Powers of the European Parliament ("Vedel Report")', *Bulletin of the European Communities*, Supplement 4/72, 1972.

Vedel, Georges, 'The Role of the Parliamentary Institution in European Integration', Symposium on European Integration and the Future of Parliaments in Europe, Luxembourg, 1975.

Wallace, Helen, 'Direct Elections and the Political Dynamics of the EC', *Journal of Common Market Studies*, Vol. XVII, June 1979.

Wallace, Helen, 'The European Parliament: The Challenge of Political Responsibility', *Government and Opposition*, special edition 1979.

Wallace, Helen, Wallace, William and Webb, Carol, *Policy Making in the European Community*, 2nd edition, Chichester: John Wiley, 1983.

Webb, Carol, 'Theoretical Perspectives and Problems', in Wallace et al., *Policy Making in the European Community*, 2nd edition, Chichester, John Wiley, 1983.

Weiler, Joseph, 'The Community System: The Dual Character of Supranationalism', *Yearbook of European Law*, 1981.

Weiler, Joseph, 'Supranationalism Revisited – a Retrospective: The EC after 30 Years', in *Noi si Mura*, Florence: European University Institute, 1982.

Weiler, Joseph, 'Institutional and Jurisdictional Questions: European Pride and Prejudice – Parliament v. Council', *European Law Review*, No. 5, October 1989.

Weiler, Joseph et al., 'European Democracy and its Critique', in J.E.J. Hayward, *Crisis of Representation in Europe*, London: Cass, 1995.

Westlake, Martin, *Britain's Emerging Euro-élite? The British in the Directly Elected European Parliament 1979–1992*, Aldershot: Dartmouth, 1994.

Westlake, Martin, *The Commission and the Parliament*, London: Butterworth, 1984.

Wheare, Kenneth, *Federal Government*, Oxford: Oxford University Press, 1963.

Wood, Alan, (ed.), *Times Guide to the European Parliament 1989*, London: Times Books, 1989.

Wyldavsky, Aaron, *Budgeting: A Comparative Theory of Budgetary Processes*, Boston and Toronto, 1975. (Also cited in Teato and Graff, *Das Europaische Parlament under der Haushalt der Europaischen Gemeinschaft*, Nomos Verlag, 1994.)

Index